MW01672717

Kirsten!

Thank you so much

I Hope you enjoy it!

[signature]

P.S.: I loved your Christmas/
Halloween picture!

ISBN: 978-1-4507-6044-7
Proudly Produced In the United States of America

Hand Written Productions assumes no liability for the resurgence
of pride in being a citizen born in the Bronx.

A Memoir

"YOU CAN'T TAKE THE **Bronx** OUT OF ~~THE BOY~~ MY DAD"

Cameron James Richard Philip Hand
Kelsie Lyn Gardner Collins Hand
Kenneth Michael Hand

This book is dedicated to my daughter
Kelsie Lyn Gardner Collins and son Cameron James Richard Philip,
the two most precious people in my life
who have listened patiently, attentively, and with interest
to the stories of my life.
I will be forever grateful to you for allowing me
to relive my childhood by telling you my stories.

Foreword

As the oldest child of six growing up in the Bronx in a two bedroom apartment, I had a great incentive to make my way in the world at an early age. As I read my Brother Kenny's book, I began to realize I missed out on a great opportunity to have been a better brother. The stories really made an impact on me but the book is more than just a family tale.

In this book Kenny tells the life tales of a teenager growing up in the Bronx in a funny, clever, and always touching way. Listening to stories has always been a time honored tradition as a way to pass down advice to the next generation, and he continues that tradition in "You Can't Take the Bronx Out of ~~The Boy~~ My Dad". He incorporates his two wonderful children, Kelsie and Cameron, in a way that adds to the reader's amusement and to drive home the important advice children need to understand to be successful in life.

The stories are true, and to put it in perspective, the High School Kenny and I went to, John F. Kennedy was recently shut down for dismal results, gang related activity, a murder, and for not recycling. I don't know if the rest of America grew up the way we did, but many of the lessons in life are universal whether you live in the Bronx or Loversville, Kansas. I know the people that grew up in the Bronx will love the stories but I will bet that anyone courageous enough to read the book will be able to relate with the stories in one way or the other.

When I say I grew up in the Bronx, I often get a surprised look followed by, "you don't sound like you're from the Bronx." I never ask the person what they mean because I know exactly what they mean; I don't end all of my sentences with an "A". Betta, Gotta, Neva, hada, and I don't pronounce my "a" or "o" as "aw" or "u". Dawter (daughter), bruta (brother), muta (mother), and Fatha (father), and so on. The Bronx paints certain pictures in the minds of people that have not lived there, and have been perpetuated by movies like "Fort Apache the Bronx." The stereotype of a Bronx character always has a certain "flair", and in this book the reader will be treated to why this stereotype actually has a lot of truth behind it.

Kenny left a number of stories on the cutting room floor at my suggestion. I was concerned that people who didn't know him might get the wrong impression from the book. It is a testament that we need guidance when we are young, and as parents we must stay as close to our kids as we can. It also proves that our teenage years do not necessarily have to be the final chapter in our lives. Kenny's success as an individual is the truly incredible story not told in the book. He overcame the insecurities of a teenager, the stigma of a High School dropout, and never gave up.

Kenny went back to school, graduated college and is a successful Financial Analyst for a fortune 500 company. He is a fantastic husband and father. He is a successful member of his Church and community, and he is a wonderful brother to his siblings with special care and attention going to Philip and Gena, our handicapped sister and brother. That is the real story; never giving up on life. I wish everyone had the drive that Kenny has lived since his days growing up in the Bronx.

Growing up in the Bronx was an easy place to take the wrong track in life. At every turn there was a distraction, choice, or detour that could have ended in a much different outcome. I am convinced he had a very strong Guardian Angel that worked overtime to keep Kenny safe for most of his teenage years. To that Guardian Angel I say, Thank You!

I hope the people that read this book get to know my brother the way I have over these last thirty years. He has taken lousy odds and played them to perfection. He can now add the title of Author to his list of accomplishments in life. He has truly captured the essence of the Bronx in this book, and success in his life. I commend him for both and I couldn't be prouder to be his brother.

Rich Hand

Introduction

"Daddy, tell me another story," is something my sister Kelsie and I have said to my father millions of times since we were young. Like most kids, when we were young, we believed our dad was the greatest dad in the world because he was smart, cool, and fun – all at the same time. But most of all, he was interesting; what made him so interesting were the stories he told us about his childhood. As early as I can remember, his stories were a regular part of our lives; they sometimes made us laugh, they sometimes made us cry, they always made us think and imagine. Usually, he told us a story in response to a question we asked him, but sometimes he initiated a story when we were feeling down or going through a tough time. At these times his story always related to what we were going through, and it was intended to let us know, 'I know what you're feeling, and it's hard but don't worry you'll make it through.' Or sometimes it was intended to show us how he handled the situation, and by implication – how we should handle it. We liked that he told 'what to do' without telling us 'what to do' but there were times when we said to him, "Dad, we know what you're doing. You're trying to tell us what to do without telling us what to do." He always responded, "Hey, I'm just telling you a story about my childhood. You have to figure out what to do on your own. It's your responsibility to stand on your own two feet – not mine." Then he gave us a tiny little smile and a wink as if to say, "You're right but I'm not going to admit it to you."

Looking back, his stories were always about friends, family, sports, fighting, dating, working, playing, drinking, smoking, loving, hating – in short they were about life. Like I said, he rarely gave us the typical fatherly advice of, "Kelsie, you should do this…" or "Cameron, you shouldn't do that…" His hidden advice always came in the form of one of his stories; these stories actually made it easier to listen to his advice because it wasn't about us – it was about one of his friends his family or himself. We liked being taught about life in this way; it never felt like he was preaching to us – we felt like we made our own decisions.

We never really knew, and we still don't know if his stories were true, exaggerated, or just plain made up, but we usually sat quietly and listened to them (with an occasional question) because they fascinated us. This book, "You Can't Take the Bronx Out of ~~the Boy~~ My Dad", is a gift to our dad, from his "favorite daughter" and his "favorite son" two people who will be eternally grateful for having Kenny Hand as their dad.

This book is more than a compilation of my father's stories; it's about the time we spent with him and the special relationship we developed over the years by listening to his stories. We begin the book with an overview of New York, The Bronx, Kingsbridge, and the people in my father's life from his perspective. We then move into the stories he told us while we were experiencing challenging situations in our own lives. This book is not intended to teach anyone how to raise their children or how to prepare them for the life ahead of them – but if anyone is to learn anything from this book we hope it is this – parents need to talk to their children. Parents have experienced many of the trials and tribulations their children will undoubtedly be faced with in their own lives. Parents should use their experiences to help their children, and this can only happen by talking and listening to their children, just like our dad did.

Although our father has told us hundreds of stories it's not possible to share all of them; for the sake of brevity we focused on his stories which we hope will have universal appeal and which will make clear the difference between his world and ours.

The world my father grew up in was much different from the world my sister and I live in. What's funny is most people would naturally assume our world is better than his was. What I mean is, we have everything kids could want. In fact, I can't remember having a need go unfilled. We live in a large house with a big back yard; we have computers, the internet, iPods, cell phones, U-Verse, a PSII, and all the other gadgets our hearts desire. Our parents drive us everywhere we need or want to go, like baseball, basketball, soccer, piano lessons, band, school, and the mall. We drive our large SUV, with its air bags and seat belts when we go out to dinner or when we drive through the "drive thru" at one of our twenty or so favorite fast food restaurants. Most days our schedules are so busy –

staying home and eating at the dinner table is an unusual treat. We go on vacations several times a year to exciting places like Florida, California, Colorado, and Hawaii. In our world we are protected by the government with product warnings on everything from food to driver seat air bags. My dad had little or none of these: as a child he lived in small apartments or small homes with little or no backyards; computers and technology were still in their infancy, he walked to games, malls barely existed, vehicles were unreliable, and going out to dinner happened once or twice each year; vacations were few and far between and they weren't to exotic places; and the government didn't try to protect people – people protected themselves.

Given a choice between my dad's world and ours, many people would choose today's world because of the physical comforts, material possessions, and promise of safety from harm – but not us! If you gave us a choice we'd choose my dad's world every time and without hesitation. In our world, people, places, and things are so similar – if you were placed on a plane in New York and flew somewhere, anywhere, in the country, would you know where you were when you landed? Probably not. In the attempt to improve our world by making everyone, richer, healthier, and safer there was the unintended consequence of making people and their experiences less unique, less interesting, and less exciting. My dad taught us through his stories that life is intended to be lived and lived to the fullest – with all its surprises, excitement, and yes – occasionally danger. One of my father's favorite quotes is:

"Do something you're afraid to do every day of your life!"

He's not sure where he read or heard this quote but he told us this is how we should live our lives. He didn't mean we should do something dangerous – just something we're uncomfortable doing. He said if we're not doing something we're afraid to do, we're probably living a life that is too safe and too boring – and life is a contact sport – it should be lived to its fullest!

As we stated earlier, we were never sure if our dad's stories were true, exaggerated, or just plain made up, and therefore this book should NOT be considered a reliable source for any information other than that which can be found in my father's memory and imagination. To be fair to the people in our dad's stories I have changed their names, because I realize not everyone shares their youthful experiences and indiscretions with their children – some consider it "airing their dirty laundry". This is a term our father uses, and he tells us it has to do with the fact many families like to keep things they're not proud of to themselves.

One final point before we move on – my father is NOT proud of the way he conducted himself in all of his stories. In fact, he is ashamed of some of the things he did as a youth. He told us on more than one occasion, "If I whitewashed my life and only told you stories about how perfect I was – would you learn anything from my stories? I don't think so. That's why I tell you everything – or almost everything – because I want you to learn from my mistakes so you can avoid them."

SECTION I
On the 8th Day God Created...

♪ There are places I remember all my life
Though some have changed ♪
♪ Some forever, not for better
Some have gone and some remain. ♪

♪ All these places have their moments
Of lovers and friends I still can recall ♪
♪ Some are dead and some are living
In my life I've loved them all...♪

♪ And I'll never lose affection
For people and things that went before ♪
♪ I know I'll often stop and think about them
In my life, I love you more...♪ [1]

...New York

By the time we were born our father was living in the Midwest, far away from the city where he was born – New York. The first time I remember visiting his birthplace was in September 2002 to attend a family get-together, the annual Hand Family Open. A family event, on my father's side of the family, where we get together on Labor Day weekend for a BBQ and golf tournament. We drove 16 hours from St. Louis to New York in our 1996 Chevy Venture van; my sister and I argued with each other from the time we left until we reached Indianapolis, Indiana.

It was at this point my father got tired of yelling at us to "quiet down" and he decided to take a different approach.

He asked us, "Do you know where we're going?"

"Yes, we're going to Grandma and Grandpa Hand's house to play golf."

"Well, that's true but we're going to my home; the place where I was born, where I grew up, and where I lived until Mommy and I got married – we're going to New York City. Do you guys know anything about New York City?"

"Not really, I just know it's a big city where the Statue of Liberty is and where a lot of TV shows and movies are filmed."

"Well do you want me to tell you about the place I was born?"

I said, "Yeah Dad – I want to hear about it."

Kelsie said, "Yeah, sure."

As far as I know this was the beginning of my dad's stories; he might have told us a story or two before, but I couldn't recall any – yeah, I think this is when they began.

"Okay, Kelsie and Cameron are you ready to hear all about New York City?"

"Yeah, Daddy, tell us, tell us!"

"Well, it all started in the year 1524 when a European explorer, Giovanni de Verrazano, sailed through the narrow passage between the areas which would later be called Brooklyn on the northeast and Staten Island on the southwest. Verrazano was a great sea captain and also a great bridge builder and somewhat of an egocentric guy."

"What's egocentric?"

"Let's just say he thought he was really cool. As soon as he 'discovered' this area he built a bridge connecting Brooklyn and Staten Island and he named it after himself – he called it the Verrazano Narrows Bridge. Also, since he was an Italian, he set up his own crime family and required the Native Americans to pay him $24 in beads for protection. When I say he discovered it, that doesn't mean it didn't exist before he found it – actually there were a lot of Native Americans, who used to be called Indians when I was your age, before political correctness was invented. They lived in the New York area and all over North America for that matter long before the Europeans acquired it."

"Dad, what are Europeans?"

"They're a bunch of white guys who look like you and me from England, France, Spain, and a few other smaller, less important countries.

By the time the Europeans discovered North America there were about 5,000 Native Americans in this area. If you asked a politically correct historian, they would probably tell you there were 1,000,000 Native Americans living on Manhattan Island at the time, they built the Empire State Building, there was no crime, and everyone lived in harmony until the Europeans settled there and screwed it all up, but their history is even less reliable than mine – so accept my number of 5,000 Native Americans. Now let's fast forward to 1625."

"Why Dad?"

"Because that's what Wikipedia did last time I read the history of New York, and so I don't know what happened between 1524 and 1625 – probably just a lot of raping and pillaging by the Europeans against the Native Americans – your typical European exploitation stuff – you'll hear all about it once you start public school.

In 1625, the Island of Manhattan, where all the tall buildings like the Empire State Building are located, was supposedly purchased by a Dutchman by the name of Peter Minuet for about $24 worth of glass beads. Yeah, beads were really popular back in those days. Now, I know you're wondering what happened to the Italians, like our friend Verrazano, if they discovered this area why didn't THEY buy Manhattan Island. I'm not sure, remember Wikipedia skips over about 100 years of history, but my guess is Verrazano was in prison for racketeering, and so he didn't have a chance to bid on the island. Anyhow, the Dutch were now living on the lower east side and vacationing in the Hamptons during the summer.

At the time the Dutch named New York, New Amsterdam, after old Amsterdam – a big city in the Netherlands. By the way, have you ever wondered why people from the Netherlands are called Dutch?

"No, I didn't know people from the Netherlands are called Dutch."

"Well they are. We call people from America – Americans. We call people from Canada – Canadians. We call people from Mexico – Mexicans. Why do we call people from the Netherlands – Dutch?"

"We give up Dad – tell us."

"I don't know –that's why I'm asking you. Wouldn't it be easier to call them Netherlanders, or Netherlandites, or even Nethers – something other than Dutch – it's very confusing – but I digress. When the Dutch were trying to come up with a name for their new colony they thought of 'New and Improved Amsterdam', 'Amsterdamerland', and 'Amsterdamopolis', but they couldn't agree so they decided to put it to a vote of the people. The voting was very controversial due to problems with hanging chads – but in the end New Amsterdam won, the day after the Colonial Magistrates voted to certify the vote without another recount.

Later on – around 1664, the English came across the ocean and said to Peter Stuyvesant, 'Hey, we like what you've done with the place. Especially the wall – we'd like to build a stock exchange there. Can we buy it from you?' When Peter told them, 'No, but thank you for asking', the English decided to take a play out of the Italian play book, and they made the Amsterdamerlandites an offer they couldn't refuse."

"What's an offer they couldn't refuse?"

"It's a 'God Father' reference Cam. You'll understand when you're older. Okay, where was I? Oh yeah, unfortunately, the Dutch didn't accept the offer and so they went to war. It couldn't have been a very long or brutal war because it only took one line in Wikipedia to explain it, 'In 1664, the English conquered the city and renamed it 'New York' after the English Duke of York and Albany.'

By the way, remember those 5,000 Native Americans? They were down to 200 by the time the English moved in. I'm not sure if they were killed by the Europeans, or if they died from the English; who had chicken pox, had not washed their hands before serving the Native Americans food at the local diner, or maybe the Native American's saw the English moving in and thought, 'Well, there goes the neighborhood – I'm going to move out before all the property values go down. You know I heard that the Manahattoes down the street from us only got $24 for their place.' Whatever the reason for the Native American population drain – all I know is there were a lot fewer of them by 1700.

By 1754, New York was the place to be in the New World for several reasons – Kings College was founded, Studio 1754 opened to raving reviews, Sardis was the place to go for theater district crowds, and Sabrett hot dogs stands were popping up on every street corner. A short time later the American Revolution began between the English and the Colonists. The details of the American Revolution are long and boring, so I'll give you the Reader's Digest version."

Kelsie asked, "What's the Reader's Digest version, Dad?"

"It's short and to the point – we won – they lost. End of story.

After the American Colonists whooped the English, they established the first capital of the new United States of America. Actually there was some form of government related to the Articles of Confederation, but no one remembers that time in our country, so I'll leave it out. Do you know where the first capital of our country was?"

"Let us guess, New York City?"

"You guys are so smart – that's right – this was because the first delegates to the First or was it the Second or Third Continental Congress met in New York City and they all loved the Sicilian pizzas and the fact you could purchase hot Rolexes on every street corner for just a few shillings! The capital didn't stay in New York for long, only until 1790, because a few of the founding fathers had some unfortunate incidents which involved stage coaches, interns, and stains on petty coats. I'll go into more detail when you two are older but one of the most famous quotes from this era came from our first president who, putting his long forefinger in the air, said with confidence, 'I didn't have sexual relations with...that woman...Mrs. Betsy Ross'

After it was decided not to make New York the permanent capital of the new United States, the city planners were bummed out and they decided to come up with a plan to organize the city and make it more appealing next time a capital was being selected. They figured if it didn't help them win the next Capitalship at least it might help them win the next Summer Olympics or at the very least the 1964 Worlds Fair. So in 1811, a plan was put together by the city planners to develop New York City in an orderly way.

By the way, isn't it annoying in St. Louis how the same road has five different names depending on which city you're in?"

"Uh, no Dad. We never even noticed that. We don't drive."

"Well believe me it is! It drives me crazy when the streets go in circles, they're called different names, and there are dead ends all over the place.

Unlike St. Louis, in New York they decided to build the streets in a way that made sense. They developed a plan which called for the development of sixteen 'avenues' running north and south, parallel with the Hudson and Harlem River coast lines; they were planned to be 100 feet wide. The streets were set up to run east and west and they were to be 60 feet wide. Certain streets were set aside for particular purposes; 42nd through 54th streets were set aside for the Theater District, every street was required to have at least one Irish Pub whose name began with Mc or Mac, and of course 34th and 42nd Streets were set aside for peep shows and ladies of the evening."

"What's a lady of the evening?"

"Ask your mother. Okay, so this plan worked out so well they decided to use it in the Bronx, but somehow they didn't line up the east and west sides of the streets very well but hey – at least they tried.

By 1835, New York was the largest city in the United States – leaving Philadelphia in the dust. It probably passed Philadelphia as the biggest city because local politics were taken over by Tammany Hall and the Irish. The Irish kept inviting their friends and families in Ireland to New York for a few bottles of beer, and they never left. The influx of Irish increased dramatically in the late 1800's when

Ireland began running out of potatoes. The American Irish told their family and relatives, 'Hey, lads and lassies come across the Atlantic to New York! We have potatoes galore but they're called French fries, and you have to buy them from a clown named McDonald – but at least he's Irish.'

By 1857, the city was so big many people in the city decided they needed a large city playground – so they decided to build a central park. They came up with a creative name for this central park – they named it Central Park.

Well, throughout the 1800's immigrants came through New York City in search of a better life in the United States; this included opportunities for jobs, land, freedom, and Red Lobster's All You Can Eat Shrimp Meal Deals. When they entered New York Harbor on October 28, 1886 they were greeted for the first time by the Statue of Liberty – a gift from the people of France who helped the United States win their independence from England during the Revolutionary War."

"Dad, the French helped us gain independence from England? I thought you said the French were a bunch of wimps and their flag should be white to make it easier for them to surrender to the Germans."

"Well, yes. I did say something like that, but let me get back to my story. Unfortunately, the ships which came into the harbor couldn't dock on Liberty Island due to the excessive amounts of school children on field trips, and so they docked on Ellis Island, which was actually a blessing because the snack bar and gift shop lines were shorter. During this time, there were several near tragic accidents when the Staten Island Ferry and the Circle Line narrowly avoided collisions with the ships carrying massive amounts of immigrants, but that's a whole other story.

Due to the high levels of immigration during the 1800's, the city became extremely overcrowded, and therefore in 1898 the city planners decided they had to expand. Most people don't realize the original New York City only included Manhattan – it didn't include any of the other four boroughs."

"Borough, what's a borough?"

"Cam, the Bronx is a borough, Manhattan is a borough. It's what New York City calls the five areas which make up all of New York City. Do you understand?"

"No, but you can continue."

"Okay, so to determine where they would expand to – they put an advertisement in the New York Post – it read, 'Wanted – Land for burgeoning population – will pay top dollar!' They received various offers from New Jersey to sell some of their 'most help needed' cities like Hoboken, Weehawken, Jersey City, and Bayonne, but the New York City planners said, 'Thanks, but no thanks. There's a reason New Jersey is known as the arm pit of the country, and your cities haven't seen deodorant since the Revolutionary War.'

By 1898, the city planners worked out a deal with the surrounding New York areas. They annexed Staten Island, Brooklyn, Queens, and THE BRONX – each with a specific purpose in mind.

They annexed Brooklyn because they needed beachfront property to put a boardwalk and a prototype amusement park, which had been in the works for several years.

They annexed Queens because they needed a place for a couple of airports to be built (they received an inside tip from a couple of Wright Brothers who claimed they were about to make a breakthrough discovery), they needed a place to host the world for some kind of big fair, and they needed a place for the New York Metropolitans to play the new exciting game of baseball.

They annexed Staten Island because they needed a residential area for their yuppies and to give the Staten Island Ferry more business.

FINALLY, they annexed THE BRONX because they wanted the most beautiful piece of land, with the most interesting people in the world, to be a part of the GREATEST CITY in the WORLD! And that's the story of New York City!"

"That's it Dad? That's all? What about The Bronx? I thought that's where you were born. Dad, why didn't you tell us about The Bronx?"

"Do you want to hear about it?"

Kelsie and I said, "Yes! Of course! But can I ask you a question?"

"Sure."

"Did you make up some of the story about New York?"

"Make it up? Absolutely not!"

"Really?"

"Would your daddy ever lie to you?"

"♪ Start spreading the news
I'm leaving today ♪
♪ I want to be a part of it – New York, New York
These vagabond shoes, are longing to stray ♪
♪ Right through the very heart of it – New York, New York [2]

...The Bronx

"So Dad, can you tell us about THE Bronx?"

"Of course. The Bronx was named for a Swedish guy named Jonas Bronck; he settled in the area around the year 1639. The Bronx is located at the northernmost tip of New York City and is the only borough not located on an island."

"Can you tell me what a borough is again?"

"Well, let me try to explain it this way; New York is divided into five boroughs; Manhattan, Staten Island, Brooklyn, Queens, and the Bronx. Each borough is run by a Borough President who is kind of like a mini-mayor who reports to the main Mayor of New York City. Do you understand now Cam?"

"Yeah, that makes sense."

"Now when I was growing up, the Bronx wasn't known as the greatest place to live. In fact, when I told someone, who wasn't from New York, that I was from the Bronx, they usually said, 'You're from the Bronx? Have you ever been mugged?' I'm sure the Bronx didn't always have a reputation for being a dangerous place to live, but in the 1970's, when I was young, the Bronx was considered to be the most dangerous place to live in the United States!

"Why did people think it was dangerous?"

"Well Kels, the 1970's were bad times for New York City. Democrats were running the city, crime was out of control, drugs were everywhere, prostitution and peep shows were everywhere – open minded liberalism had taken over government."

"What's open minded liberalism?"

"It's when liberals are so open minded their brains fall out."

"Funny."

"Things were bad enough because of liberal policies but something happened in July of 1977 causing things to get worse. During a brutally hot summer, a couple of power stations were hit by lightning which led to a city wide blackout. All the electricity went off in the city and in some poor neighborhoods the people went wild and acted like animals."

"Like animals?"

"Yes Kels – animals! People smashed store windows, lit stores on fire, stole TV's, air conditioners and anything else they could get their hands on."

"Why?"

"I don't know, but it's amazing what grown people do when they don't think they'll get caught. In my neighborhood things were fine, but in other parts of the city it seemed like the world was falling apart.

In addition to the blackout, there were also other problems. It was around this time; I think it was in 1976 and 1977 the 'Son of Sam' was running loose."

"Who's the 'Son of Sam'?"

"He was a deranged killer whose actual name was David Berkowitz. He killed several people, mostly girls, at night while they were parked in their cars. All the girls in my neighborhood were terrified to be alone at night because they were afraid of being killed by the 'Son of Sam'.

As a result of these real problems, several movies based on life in New York City were released around this time. Many of these movies were not flattering to the city and they focused on the most dangerous, deranged, psychotic aspects of New York City life. Movies like *Death Wish*, *Taxi Driver*, *Serpico*, *The Seven-ups*, *The Taking of Pelham 1-2-3*, *The French Connection*, and *Rocky* all depicted the city as a dark, cold, dangerous place where only the seediest people lived."

"*Rocky* took place in New York?

"Hmmm, actually I think it took place in Philadelphia, but you get my point. So as I was saying, The Bronx legitimately earned part of its reputation for being a rough place to live, but Hollywood made it appear a lot worse than it was. The combination of all this caused good, decent people to move out of The Bronx to 'greener pastures'; New Jersey and the New York suburbs.

A part of me liked living in a place which had a reputation for being tough – I guess it made me feel tough too – but it was exaggerated and not the Bronx I knew. The Bronx I knew was like a small town where everyone knew each other and looked out for each other."

"Why did you look out for each other?"

"Because if we didn't we'd get mugged."

My dad smiled and said, "Have I ever told you about the 'The Shea Stadium Mugging Affair'?"

"No! YOU WERE MUGGED?"

"Of course, I'm from The Bronx! As you both know, my mother raised me to believe it's wrong to discriminate against anyone. When anyone criticized the 'blacks', 'Hispanics', 'Jews', or any other race or religion my mother taught me not to listen to them because they were 'wrong'. She taught me there are good and some bad people in every group and that it's wrong to stereotype people."

"What does stereotype mean?"

"Well, this is my definition of it. It's when you believe all the people in one group are the same – usually in a bad way – without getting to know them. When I was growing up, there was a lot of stereotyping; 'the Irish are drunks', 'Black people don't like the cold', 'Polish people are dumb', but I'm putting stereotyping nicely. Usually, stereotyping is much worse and a lot meaner; some people will say this group is lazy or that group is a bunch of criminals. Stereotyping is not a good thing and that's why you never hear me say anything bad about groups of people."

"Dad, can a person stereotype about men and woman?"

"Yes Cam. They can do that too."

"Well, if it's wrong why do you always say women are bad drivers?"

"Well, that's different Cam. Stereotyping is wrong; saying women are bad drivers is a proven fact."

My dad smiled and got on with his story. "To this day I believe my mother raised me the right way, but it's important to remember that although no one group has a monopoly on bad people – every group has some bad people. This is something I didn't understand when I went on a trip to the Shea Stadium with Kingsbridge Little League and all the other Little League leagues in the city.

I was dressed in my Art Steele uniform when my friend Billy asked me to go to the concession stand to get a hot dog. I was only 10 years old, but Billy and I decided to walk all the way around the stadium instead of just going to the nearest concession stand. In 1977, the Mets were terrible so the stadium was always empty – that's why they gave thousands of free tickets to Little Leaguers from around the City.

Billy and I decided to wander to the farthest part of the stadium to the upper deck and all around – there was absolutely no one around, other than Billy and me and five punks – who happened to be black kids. These kids started yelling at us, 'Hey, come here! Hey, wait for us!' Billy said to me, 'Come on let's run and get out of here.' Being an open minded young man I said, 'Why should we run? Let's find out what they want.' Billy said, 'They're going to kill us, come on. If you don't run, I'm leaving you here.' I thought he was stereotyping, you know, making decisions about people based on their race, and so I made the conscious decision not to run just to make a point to Billy.

These boys looked to be around 14 years old. They caught up to me on the escalator while I was riding down, and they surrounded me. One of these punks said, 'Hey kid, you got any f%$#ing money?' As they asked me this, they pushed me and stuck their hands in my back pocket and took all the money I had – about $3.95. I was really scared! I thought to myself, 'Oh no, I'm being mugged! Like I said, I was raised not to discriminate against people based on race, but this had nothing to do with race; it had everything to do with a bunch of young punks picking on a young kid. You know there's a saying, 'a conservative is a liberal who has been mugged.' Another saying is, 'If you are 20 years old and you're not a liberal – you don't have a heart. But if you are 40 years old and you're not a conservative, you don't have a brain.'"

"Are you a conservative?"

He smiled, "Yup, I've been mugged. So remember – even though God made us equal there are still some bad people in every group and if they are chasing you – RUN!"

"Okay, although the Bronx had graffiti and a lot of trash floating around as a result of Democrats and Liberals running the city for years it was still a beautiful borough underneath all the litter. It took a Republican to clean up all the trash and graffiti and restore the city to its current magnificence. In the 1970's, underneath all the trash, were the most beautiful places in the country like Van Cortland Park, Pelham Bay Park, the New York Botanical Gardens, the Bronx Zoo, Orchard Beach, City Island, Yankee Stadium, Arthur Avenue, Wave Hill, and dozens of other places.

Of course, The Bronx isn't faultless; it does have places which aren't perfect. If you divide it into four sections; the South Bronx, Southeast Bronx, Northeast Bronx, and the Northwest Bronx there were certain sections you'd want to stay away from. The South Bronx was particularly bad, and it gave the rest of the Bronx a bad name."

"But I thought you grew up in Kingsbridge. Where did you grow up? New York, The Bronx, or Kingsbridge?"

"Good question Cam. You see New York is so huge it's not only divided into boroughs, it's also divided into neighborhoods which have names. I don't know all of them but I think the South Bronx consists of the neighborhoods of SoBro, Melrose, Hunts Point, Highbridge, Morris Heights, Tremont, and East Tremont.
The Southeast Bronx consists of West Farms..."

Kelsie interrupted my dad, "You're not going to tell us EVERY neighborhood in New York, are you?"

My dad sneered at Kelsie and continued, "The Southeast Bronx consists of West Farms and Soundview. The Northeast Bronx includes the neighborhoods of Wakefield, Williamsbridge, Allerton, Olinville, Edenwald, Eastchester, Baychester, Co-op City, Pelham Manor, Pelham Parkway, Bronxdale, Pelham Gardens, Morris Park, Van Nest, Indian Village, Westchester Square, Castle Hill, Zerega, Parkchester, Pelham Bay, Country Club, Spencer Estates, Throggs Neck, Schuylerville, Edgewater Park, Locust Point Beach, Silver Beach, and City Island. The Northwest Bronx includes the neighborhoods of University Heights, Fordham, Bedford Park, Bainbridge, Woodlawn, Riverdale, and finally...what do you think I left out?"

"Dad, we know. It's Kingsbridge."

...Kingsbridge – 10463

"That's right. Kingsbridge is where I lived, and it's without a doubt the greatest neighborhood in the world. Do you know why it's called Kingsbridge?"

"No. Why?"

"Well, according to historians – you know, people who make things up, the neighborhood received its name from 'The King's Bridge', which was built in 1693 by Frederick Philipse.

Many people, maybe just me, believed the King's bridge crossed the Harlem River at the current location of the 225th Street Bridge but they were wrong. Yes, believe it or not your dad isn't always right. The real King's bridge actually crossed the Spuyten Duyvil Creek. Now, I'm sure you're wondering, 'What's the Spuyten Duyvil Creek?'"

"No, but you can tell us."

"Okay. If you're in the Bronx heading south on Broadway near 225th Street, going into Inwood, you cross over a bridge we called the 225th Street Bridge. I'm not sure if it has a real name but that's what we called it.

If you stopped on the bridge and looked around you'd see a river to your left, below you, and to your right – some people call it the Harlem River or maybe Spuyten Duyvil, well anyhow, this area of the river didn't always exist. This part of the river is actually manmade and is technically called, 'The Harlem River Ship Canal'. You see? It's like a mini Panama Canal.

The Harlem River Ship Canal was built around 1895 to allow the larger boats, ships, and really big fish to go from the Harlem River to the Hudson River. I bet you're wondering why they couldn't just use the Spuyten Duyvil Creek. They couldn't use it because it was a creek! Creeks aren't deep enough for boats, ships, and big fish! I bet you're wondering where the Spuyten Duyvil Creek was."

"Sure Dad."

"Well Kelsie, first of all, the creek flowed from the Harlem River near the 225th Street projects, through the ground the projects were built on, down 230th Street, past the project park, it made a left past the U-Haul building down toward John F. Kennedy High School, along the train tracks, where it met up with the Hudson River near Columbia Rock. In other words, the creek flowed around Marble Hill."

"Where is it now Dad?

"It was filled in with dirt. Here's more interesting information for you; Marble Hill is NOT part of The Bronx it's part of Manhattan – I'm sure you understand why."

"Not really. It's hard to understand since we've never been there."

"Well, it's because Marble Hill was surrounded by the creek and therefore it was physically a part of Manhattan until the Harlem River Ship Canal was built which permanently separated it from Manhattan. After they built the ship canal, they filled the Spuyten Duyvil Creek in with the dirt which was dug up to create the canal.

Here's another interesting tidbit of information that ticks me off. The people of Marble Hill voted, at least once – maybe more, to stay a part of Manhattan. In other words, they didn't want to be considered part of The Bronx! I guess Manhattan looks better on their resumes than The Bronx – those snobs.

Okay, let me get back to the King's Bridge. The King's Bridge crossed over the creek somewhere near 230th Street and Kingsbridge Avenue – that's why they named Kingsbridge Avenue – Kingsbridge Avenue."

"Dad, do you think this is interesting?"

"Yeah Cam – I do. I guess you don't, but I think it is."

"Okay Dad, continue."

"Now I'll explain what it looked like when I was a kid. To help you understand and to be able to picture it, I'm going to take you on a stroll through the neighborhood. We'll start our walk on Broadway in Inwood and we'll cross over the 225th Street Bridge and enter THE Bronx. We're going to start on Broadway because it's the backbone of Kingsbridge, it literally runs through the middle of the neighborhood, and it will make it easier for me to explain Kingsbridge to you – just trust me – let's start walking."

"Start walking Dad?"

"Figuratively speaking, Cam. You don't have to walk – just stay in your seat, and we'll walk down Broadway in our minds. As we walk north on Broadway, you'll notice above you the EL."

"Dad, what's the EL?"

"The EL is short for the ELevated train tracks which run from the tip of Manhattan to 242nd Street near Van Cortland Park. In Kingsbridge the tracks are elevated above Broadway by metal pillars which are positioned about 30 feet apart on both sides of the street. While we're walking under the EL we need to be careful the pigeons don't drop a bomb on us, especially near the train stations because they're the home to millions of pigeons."

"Did that ever happen to you?"

"Yes, many, many times. Like the day I was walking back from a day of playing basketball in Van Cortlandt Park. I had my shirt off and was dripping sweat when I was bombarded by a load of pigeon poop. After it hit me on the shoulder it oozed down my shoulder on down my back…"

"Dad, that's gross."

"Kels, I know it is, but Cameron asked. Okay, back to the walk. If we look to our left, we'll see store fronts; bars, bodegas, grocery stores, bars, and clothing stores. All around us are cars, buses, taxis, and pedestrians impatiently rushing to their destinations. At street level the wind blows newspapers and miscellaneous trash around on the sidewalks and in the gutters. The buildings are covered with murals of graffiti down low while up high they're covered with gray city soot and pollution."

"What's a bodegas Dad?"

"Bodegas are Spanish delicatessens. They sell cold cuts, beer, rolling paper, cigarettes, nasty looking bananas, and Spanish food.

On top of these stores, and on the streets behind Broadway, are apartment buildings filled with the snobs from Marble Hill. When we walk a little farther down Broadway, there are 'The Projects' on both the left and right of the street; they occupy land roughly between 225th and 230th Streets. Projects are government apartment buildings intended to provide low cost housing for low income families. I never walked through the projects after dark because there was a lot of crime and drugs there.

After the projects, we come to 230th Street and Broadway. When we look to our left, we can see the streets which run parallel to Broadway on the west side of Kingsbridge; Godwin Terrace, Kingsbridge Avenue, Corlear Avenue, Tibbett Avenue, Irwin Avenue, and finally Riverdale Avenue. These streets are mostly filled with apartment buildings and houses. If we look to our right from 230th Street we can see all the roads which run parallel to Broadway on the east side of Kingsbridge; the Major Deegan Expressway, Bailey Avenue, Heath Avenue/Fort Independence, Kingsbridge Terrace, and Sedgwick Avenue. Again, these streets were mostly filled with apartment buildings and residential areas along with a few parks and stores smattered around.

Continuing our stroll down Broadway, we pass by Burger Chef or Burger King on the right, Bensons (where St. John's school uniforms were purchased), Donaghy's Steakhouse, Land & Sea, Woolworth's, St. John's Grade School, OTB, and A&P's along with dozens of other stores."

"Dad, what's OTB?"

"Cam, OTB stands for Off Track Betting. It's a place where people who want to bet on horse racing go to lose their money. Betting was illegal when I was growing up except at the race track and OTB.

The epicenter of Kingsbridge is 231st Street and Broadway. It's at this point where we'll see the real Kingsbridge. There are stores, people, cars, trains, cabs, buses, pigeons, and noise everywhere – the exciting hustle and bustle of city life! To the east is P&K's (the Best Burgers in Town), Johnny Mac's After Hour Joint, Furman's (the neighborhood's Department Store where my grandmother worked), the Dale Movie Theater, and North Side Savings Bank. To the west is Sam's Pizza Shop, Riviera Pizza Shop, Cold Cut City, The Army

Navy Store, Bill's Friendly Shop (where we can get the best Egg Creams), Ehring's (the best German food in the neighborhood), Hebrew National (where they have the best knishes in the world), several Asian Produce Stands, Bippen's Convenience Store, the Donut Shop, Pat Mitchell's, Washington Heights Savings Bank, and in the distance Ewen Park.

With all the city life raging around us it's difficult to notice where Kingsbridge is situated. Before all these man made items were built; the buildings, houses, train tracks, etc – we could see Kingsbridge is actually a valley nestled in between the high hills of Riverdale on the west (left) and the hills leading up to the Jerome Avenue Reservoirs on the east (right).

As we continue walking down Broadway toward 233rd Street we pass by Williams Funeral Home on the right and the International House of Pancakes on the left. I lived up the hill on 233rd Street on the left, there's Bailey Field (also know as Cooney Grauer Field) and the Bailey Avenue Projects across the Major Deegan on the right. There are the two competing supermarkets on the right – Waldbaums (where I worked) and Finest (where my friend John worked). On our way to 238th Street we pass by the 50th Precinct, Kelton's Ice Skating Rink, McDonalds, Off Broadway (which was just OFF Broadway one street over), the Car Wash, Stella Dora Bakery, and the Riverdale Diner.

Once we passed 238th Street, there's Gaelic Park, the Pool Hall, and some Manhattan College buildings on our left and Van Cortland Football Stadium on our right. Past the stadium is the Van Cortland pool which is at the end of the line for the '1' train. Across from the pool were the college bars where Manhattan students drank and sang 'Build Me Up Buttercup'. There were also a couple of pizza places, Burger King, and Side Kicks in case the students got the munchies. Just slightly past the pool are the Vanny Flats – an enormous open park where everything from soccer, football, baseball, softball, jogging, sexual deviance, and muggings took place.

If we keep walking up Broadway, we'll eventually fall off the end of the earth into another world – Yonkers. However, there was a final Bronx Oasis before you entered Yonkers; Doubledays' – a popular restaurant/bar located near the city line."

SECTION II
The Origin of Species

♪ Memories, like the corners of your mind
Misty water colored memories – Of the way we were ♪
♪ Scattered pictures of the smiles we left behind
Smiles we gave to one another – For the way we were...♪
♪ So it's the laughter – We will remember... [3]

Uncle Richie (left), Grandpa Hand, Evil Aunt Chris,
Aunt Gena (right), My Dad (in rocker).
Missing: Grandma Hand, Uncle Philip, and Aunt Tricia

Richard Allen

One of the first people my dad told us about was his father. This story was a typical story of my dad's; it was interesting, but like most stories it had some poop in it and ended up with my father's feelings being hurt.

We asked him, "Can you tell us about your family now?"

"Alright, let's start out with my father. Do you know Grandpa's name?"

"No."

"His name is Richard Allen Hand; he was born on September 27th, 1933 during the height of the Great Depression. He grew up in the Bronx on Review Place – right off of 238th Street. His father's name was Frank Howard Hand – we called him Pa. My father's mother's name was Margaret Jane Harford-Hand – we called her Nanny. He has an older brother, Raymond Sloan Vincent, my Uncle Ray. And he has a younger sister, Dorothy Ann, my Aunt Dot.

I don't know a whole lot about my dad's childhood but I do know he loved sports, he was a great bowler, and when he was a teenager he found his lifelong love…"

I interrupted my dad and said, "Grandma?"

He smiled and said, "No – gambling."

"Grandpa fell in love with gambling?"

"Well, maybe it's not love, but it's a deep, deep, like." He smiled and continued, "I'm sort of kidding but, again, I don't know a lot about his childhood, however, I do know he was known in the neighborhood as a great bowler. He wasn't the only great bowler in the neighborhood, there was a punk named Duke Shea. Duke was my dad's nemesis."

"Dad, what's a nemesis?"

"Cam, it's a rival. Someone a person competes with, who is tough to beat. Someone you fight with. For example, you could say the Boston Red Sox are the Yankee's nemisisisisisisi. Wait, I got it Cam – your teacher, Mrs. Burrows is your nemesis."

"Oh, I got it. It means someone you don't like."

"I guess that's right. Let's get back to my dad. Duke Shea and my dad played against each other at the bowling alley on 233rd Street. It was such a heated rivalry all the guys and girls in the neighborhood came to watch them play each other. What made it even more interesting is there was always a lot of money riding on the game. This put a lot more pressure on my father, but it also made it more interesting. My dad didn't win all the time, but I'm told he won more games than he lost.

This is about all I know about Grandpa Hand's childhood. Oh wait. I know he went to Cardinal Hayes High School, and later he worked for Ford. When he was young, after he saved up some money, he bought a 1956 Ford Fairlane Convertible. It was the nicest car in the neighborhood and he was very proud of it – I'm sure he picked up a lot of chicks in that car."

"Chicks, Dad?"

"Yes Kels – CHICKS! They had chicks back in the 1950's"

"Yeah, but Grandpa didn't pickup chicks – that's gross! Can you tell us something else? Like what was he like when you were a kid?"

"Are you sure you want to hear about my dad when I was growing up?"

"Yeah, we want to know what he was like?"

"Alright, you've asked for it. Whatever you do, don't tell Grandma Hand I told you this story! Do you both promise you won't tell Grandma – no matter what?"

"We promise."

"Okay. I'll start out with the good stuff first. Grandpa Hand was a big sports fan when I was a kid; he followed the Giants, Yankees, Knicks, and the Rangers. Whenever he was home, he sat in front of the TV in his boxers and watched Jeopardy with Art Fleming or sports. He had season tickets for the Giants, and every year for my birthday present he gave me his ticket to the game. I remember him managing Richie's Little League team – the Orioles. He was also a big fisherman. He took Richie and me on several one day fishing trips in the area and we went on several family vacations to the Thousand Islands."

"Where are the Thousand Islands?"

"Kels, they're in northern New York, on the Canadian border. What I remember most about my dad was his sense of humor but I also remember his love of gambling. He loved handicapping the horses."

"Your dad handicapped horses? That's mean!"

"No Kels, handicapping horses means betting on horse races. It's when you look at all the horses in a race and you research their past history to determine who you believe will win, place, or show. He gambled money on the horses he thought would win the race. He taught me how to handicap them too, but I usually stuck with the 'MO' method. You know – 'eanie, meanie, minie, mo' – I always bet on mo. My dad also loved to play poker with his friends, and he loved going to places like Atlantic City.

One of my other favorite memories of my father is him taking me and Chris to a Pancake House on route 59 when we were young. I'm really not sure how often we went there; maybe only a few times, but in my memory we went there all the time. The trips to the Pancake House with my dad are one of the reasons I take both you and Kelsie to McDonalds every Saturday."

"But Dad, there was nothing bad about these stories. I thought you were going to tell us bad things about Grandpa Hand."

"So you want to hear the really bad stories about Grandpa Hand? Okay, I'll tell you one story about him you won't believe. You probably think your Grandpa is a nice man, but I'm going to tell you a story which will BLOW YOUR MINDS! It's a dark, ugly tale of pain, heartache, and betrayal. Are you sure you both want to hear it?"

"YES!"

"You better be sure because this horrid story is likely to leave emotional scars on your life like it has on mine. Are you sure you want to hear it?"

"YES, DADDY, TELL US!"

"Alright but when you're 45 years old and you wake up in the middle of the night in a cold sweat because of this story – don't blame me! I warned you!

He bit hit right pointer knuckle and pretended to cry, "Well, the poo story is a story about how grandpa traumatized me and made me a neurotic, schizophrenic young man. It's a story of my loss of innocence!"

"Dad, did you say poo story?' Oh, my gosh! This is going to be a disgusting story; isn't it?"

He turned to us and smiled, "Yes. It started one day when Aunt Chris and I were building a fort in the woods behind our house. Keep in mind this was before I moved to the Bronx. It's when I lived in Suffern."

"You didn't always live in the Bronx?"

"No, Kels but that's a story for another day. Okay, Aunt Chris and I were building a fort in the woods behind our house, but we needed more wood to complete it. In our backyard there was a large wooden board and Chris and I wanted to use it for the roof of our fort, but there were a couple of problems with it. The piece of wood wasn't ours, and when we asked our mother if we could use it she said, 'Ask your dad when he gets home.' Another problem was, Tipper, our dog at the time, dropped a big old load on the board. In other words, there was poo on it."

"That's gross Dad!"

"Yes it was. It was nasty, but we needed this board to finish our fort. Since we weren't sure if we could use it until we talked to our father, we continued to work on other parts of the fort. An hour or so later my mother stepped out on the back porch and called, 'Chris, Kenny, it's time for dinner!' We knew this meant my father was home, and so we dropped what we were doing and ran into the house. We got ready for dinner as fast as we could so we could ask my dad about the board. We ran upstairs into the bathroom, washed our hands, and we ran back down the stairs excited to tell my father about the fort we were building."

"What was this fort like?"

"Well, the fort wasn't big and fancy. It might have been about half as big as our van on the inside. It was made of a lot of old 2 by 4's. It wasn't real fancy, but for a couple of young kids it was pretty nice. But remember, it didn't have a roof and that was the problem.

Now this night was a special night, not only because of the fort, but also because our dad was going to eat dinner with us. He rarely got home early enough to eat dinner with us; most nights we ate dinner in the kitchen, but when my dad was home we ate in the dining room and we used our best china. This means we didn't use paper plates.

For the kids my mother made one of my favorite meals, spaghetti and meatballs, but she made liver, onions, and bacon for Grandpa and herself."

"Liver – that's nasty."

"Tell me about it. The whole house smelled when my mother made liver, but for some reason they liked it. Well, as soon as my dad sat down at the dinner table Chris and I told him about our great fort, 'Dad, our fort is great! You have to come and see it! You'll be so proud of us! We found a lot of wood and nails in the woods behind our house, we used them to build it, and we're already almost done with it!' My dad said, 'That's good Christine, that's good Kenny.' I continued to talk, 'Dad, we can finish it tomorrow, but we need a roof. There's a big piece of wood in the backyard, but before we use it, we thought we should ask you first.' I was so proud of me and Chris for being responsible; we didn't just take the board, we asked for it first. We were such well mannered kids! I continued, 'So can we use it, Dad, can we use it? The only thing that's wrong with it is it has some poo on it.' I looked at him with my little puppy dog eyes hoping he'd say yes.

But his response surprised me. Apparently I said something wrong!

As I looked at Grandpa he threw his fork down, pushed his chair away from the table and screamed, 'I CAN'T BELIEVE IT! I CAN'T BELIEVE YOU ARE TALKING ABOUT POO AT THE DINNER TABLE! HOW CAN I EAT MY DINNER WITH YOU TALKING ABOUT POO?' He got up and stormed out of the dining room leaving his half eaten stinky liver, onions, and bacon on his plate

I sat there dumbstruck with my eyes wide open, my chin quivering, and my stomach in a knot. I thought to myself, 'I didn't know I wasn't allowed to talk about poo, I talk about it all the time. 'Mom, I have to go poo.', 'Mom, my stomach hurts; I just went loose poo.' 'Mom, Patricia went poo, she needs her diaper changed.' 'Mom, I wiped my bottom but my finger went through the toilet paper, and I have poo on my finger'. I talked about poo more than I talked about food. I didn't know poo was bad. How could something with such a nice name be so bad? The name was so nice we sometimes said it twice; we sometimes referred to it as poo poo. Why couldn't I use this word at the dinner table?

After this experience I became extremely self conscious and second guessed everything I said. I mean, I didn't know which subjects were okay and which weren't? To be 100% sure I didn't upset my father again, I immediately took all other bodily functions out of my vocabulary. I no longer talked about pee, snots, boogers, puking, farting, ear wax, or hocking loogies. I considered taking other words out of my vocabulary like, underwear, bras, panty liners, and toilet paper, but I wasn't sure. OH THE CONFUSION! OH THE PAIN!

To make matters worse, I was reminded of this horrible experience everyday during my trip to the bathroom. In the morning after the paperwork was done, I turned around, flushed, and watched my poo twirl down the toilet bowl with my tears following close behind."

"Are you sure you're not making up some of this?"

"Absolutely not! In fact, the insecurity this experience created in me carried over into other aspects of my life, and it's all Grandpa's fault, sniff, sniff! It took me years to get over the poo story and I'm not even sure I'm 100% over it yet. OH, THE PAIN!"

"You're weird Dad!"

Anne P

After hearing the story about Grandpa Hand we asked my dad to tell us about his mom.

"Okay, but again, I don't know much about it, and so this won't take long. By the way, do either one of you know what Grandma Hand's name is?"

"Yeah, Grandma."

"Funny, Cam. Grandma's name is Anne – her maiden name is Anne Patricia Doyle."

"Give Cameron a second, Dad, you know he's going to ask you what a maiden name is."

"Before you ask Cam, when a woman gets married she usually stops using her last name and starts using her husband's last name. For example, let's say Kelsie marries Clyde Schmelsi when she's 45 years old. Kelsie would change her last name and her new name would be Kelsie Schmelsi."

"Very funny."

"Okay, Grandma was born on March 17th, which is Saint Patrick's Day, in 1938. She grew up in Kingsbridge with her family; her father, William Anthony Doyle, her mother, Anne Agatha Dolen-Doyle, and her six brothers.

My mom, your Grandma Hand had six brothers. Yes Kelsie – six brothers! Can you imagine having six Cameron's in our house? Wouldn't you love that?"

"I'd sue you and Mom if you two ever did that to me!"

"Well, my mother was very smart – she was a straight A student – I inherited my brilliant mind from her."

"Brilliant, Dad?"

"YES KELSIE – BRILLIANT! YOU GOT A PROBLEM WITH THAT?"

"Not if you don't. You can continue."

"Alright, where was I? I was telling you how smart my mother is. Alright, another thing about Grandma is she was a great athlete. Her favorite sport was basketball; she played in grade school for St. Johns and in high school for St. Barnabas. She loved basketball so much, she never missed any of my games, and after every game she critiqued my play and told me everything I did right and everything I did wrong.

As you probably know, she grew up in THE BRONX. From 1939 until 1953 she lived in a three room apartment in 3410 Kingsbridge Avenue near 234th Street. When she turned 15 her family moved into the house her grandfather designed and built; a beautiful two story house located on 3249 Corlear Avenue."

"Do you have any stories, like the poo story, about Grandma Hand?"

"No, I don't have any poo stories which involve my mother – she never traumatized me. My mother is a very nice person – she's reserved but friendly. Everyone who knows her considers her to be very smart and easy to talk to. If I heard it once, I heard it a million times; 'your mother is a saint!'"

"Why'd they say she's a saint?"

"I'm not sure, but maybe it was because she was raising a family of six children, maybe it was because she had to take care of two handicapped children, or maybe because she had an evil child – who knows?"

"Evil child?"

"I'll get to that later. Although she's reserved, she's still a very passionate person with strongly held beliefs of right and wrong. She instilled her beliefs in us kids by both her words and her actions.

I have vivid memories of my mom doing all the things moms do with little or no recognition from their children. I can remember her bringing us to Shopper's Paradise in Nyack for school clothes, shopping at Grand Union on East Park Place for groceries, making lunch for me before school, making dinner every night, giving us desert if we finished our dinner, putting Band-Aids on my 'boo boos', and rubbing my back when I was sick.

I can remember many examples of the type of person my mother was when I was growing up. She was always caring, compassionate, and unselfish; she didn't have a mean bone in her body, and she was a perfect example of what a mother should be. She worked hard inside the house and outside. She had the very challenging, but rewarding job of raising six kids. There was the washing, the cooking, the cleaning, the homework, the haircuts, the doctor visits, the shopping, the sports, and of course the disciplining. This is not an easy thing to do especially when one of the six kids is evil."

"Why do you keep saying one of her kids was evil? Are you talking about yourself?"

"No, I'm talking about your Evil Aunt Chris! She was my archenemy when I was growing up. Aunt Chris was a strong willed child before the term 'strong willed child' was invented. When I was growing up my mom and Chris fought like cats and dogs.

They say mothers and daughters have a lot of conflicts, but with my mother and Chris their conflicts were like World War I and II combined – they CONFLICTED all the time! They fought about everything; they fought about clothes, bedtime, food, baths, TV shows, and homework – just to name a few of the more controversial subjects. There was one particular week when the fighting was particularly vigorous and Chris said to me, 'I can't take it anymore! I'm moving someplace where I'll be appreciated and won't have to live by mommy's rules!'

Chris was so upset she wrote out all her complaints on a piece of paper for my mom. Just like Martin Luther posting his Ninety-Five Theses on the front door of the Castle Church in Wittenberg – Aunt Chris posted her grievances on the dining room table for my mother to look at."

"Who's Martin Luther?"

"He's a guy who lived a long time ago who thought the Catholic Church had become corrupt, and so he demanded they change some things. Like him, Chris was demanding my mother change some things."

"I bet Aunt Chris got into big trouble. I can't imagine what mommy would do to us if we 'demanded' she do something."

"That's right Cam. It didn't go over well. She wanted my mother to change about 10 things in the house. She wrote her demand on a piece of paper with a red crayon and left it for my mother to read. As I recall her demands went something like this:

'I, Christine Lyn Hand, henceforth referred to as party of the first part, being of sound mind and body, do hereby make the following demands of Anne Patricia Hand, henceforth referred to as party of the second part. Whereas the party of the second part has heretofore engaged in and has been desirous of engaging in the torture of the party of the first part, the party of the first part does hereby present the following demands to be met in full, forthwith, and without hesitation by the party of the second part. In the absence of full agreement to the terms of these demands, the party of the first part, reserves the right to implement, in part or in full, action intended to mitigate the party of the second parts impact on the party of the first party up to and including the Nuclear Options which will be detailed in full or in part at the appropriate time.

Below are the demands, which if not met in full will oblige the party of the first part to implement the Nuclear Option to be imposed in full or in part on the party of the second part:

> No more Spam, No more Meatloaf, No more Peas, No more Instant Mashed Potatoes, No more Creamed Corn, No more Green Beans, No more Rice Krispi's, Wheaties, or Cheerios, No more Baths with Kenny, No more 9:00 Bedtime, and No more Homework!

Aunt Chris was good. Even at such a young age she had a sharp legal mind – she was the Johnnie Cochran of 7 year olds."

"Who?"

"Oh it doesn't matter…

♪ Oh yes, I am wise – But it's wisdom born of pain
Yes, I've paid the price – But look how much I gained ♪
♪ If I have to – I can do anything
I am strong (strong) – I am invincible (invincible) ♪
♪ I am woman…" [4]

We stopped my dad in the middle of his song, "Well, what happened?"

"Aunt Chris and grandma met on Thursday to discuss her grievances in a neutral territory, the living room. Aunt Christine made her case, 'Mommy, I have been your daughter for the past seven years, and as you know I am dissatisfied with the way you are running things around here. First of all, the food you serve leaves a lot to be desired. I mean, really Mom, you feed us Spam – what is that mystery meat? What part of a pig, cow, horse, or dog, does Spam come from? No! Don't answer that – I don't think I want to know! Second of all, you don't buy good cereal – you make us eat Rice Krispies, Wheaties, and Cheerios – this is considered child abuse in about 25 states in the union. And you make me take a bath with Kenny! Mom, do you know where those bubbles come from? Here's a hint – we don't have a whirl pool! This is totally unacceptable – we're not living in the 50's anymore, Mom, things are, or at least should be, different nowadays. If you don't agree to my demands, I promise I will run away to a place where things are different and where people appreciate me!"

"Did Aunt Chris actually say this?"

"She said something like this, but unfortunately for her, my mom rejected all of her demands, 'Sorry, Christine, if you don't like it here, I'd recommend you run away because things are NOT going to change.'

Chris seemed surprised, 'Hmmm, I'll tell you what, Mom, I'm feeling a little charitable today. I'll tell you what, how about we take this to arbitration?'

'Um, no, sorry, Christine.'

Chris seemed even more surprised, 'Alright, I'll tell you what, Mom, I'll retract my demand to change my bed time. What concessions will you make?'

'None.'

'Oh, I see how it's going to be, you're playing hardball. Good move. Okay, I'll also take the cereal demand off the table – your move Mom.'

'No move Chris.'

'Alright Mom, I didn't want to do this but you've forced me to break out the nuclear option! Is this what you want? Do you really want me to break out the NUCLEAR OPTION?'

'You need to do what you need to do.'

'Okay, you asked for it! I'll be leaving on Saturday morning at 10:00 a.m.! Saturday! This Saturday! At 10:00! This is your last chance to reconsider, Mom – do you want me to leave on SATURDAY AT 10:00?'

'Do you need help packing your suitcase?'

My sister said, 'NO!', and she walked away.

Her pending departure was the talk of the neighborhood.

"How did the neighborhood find out she was running away?"

"She told everyone! She told the Laverchio's, Greeley's, Trigger's, Van Tassel's, Gianelli's, Schobble's, Hegman's, the mailman, the milkman, and the cashier at Vertusso's.

When Saturday rolled around, she hopped out of bed and dressed herself, and prepared to run away. In her bedroom she packed her suitcase with all her prized possessions and proceeded to walk down the stairs to the kitchen for her last meal. She went to the pantry and looked for a box of cereal and said to me, 'You see why I'm leaving – the only cereal we have is Rice Krispies. I HATE

Rice Krispies! It tastes like snap, crackle, and poop.' Since she was hungry she grabbed the cereal, a plastic bowl, a spoon, the sugar bowl, and she sat down at the kitchen table to eat.

Once she finished it and placed her bowl in the kitchen sink, she picked up her suitcase and walked to the front door. She screamed at the top of her lungs, 'Mom, I'm leaving now! I'm running away from home and I'm not coming back!'

My mom said, 'Good bye, good luck, and keep in touch.'

Aunt Chris walked out the front door with her suitcase with a look of stern determination; I followed her to say goodbye. She turned again and said, 'I'm leaving! I'm walking out the door!'

'Ok, I'll see you.'

Aunt Chris, walked down the steps, she turned around and said, 'I'm really leaving! I'm walking down the steps! Look I'm in the front yard! I'm not joking this time!'

'Good, be sure to visit during the holidays.'

Chris walked down the driveway, stopped and turned back to Grandma and said, 'I'm walking down the driveway! I'm really, really leaving! I'm not coming back!'

'Ok, I'll miss you. Don't be a stranger.' After my mom said this she quietly shut and locked the front door of the house.

Chris finally figured out her plan wasn't working as planned, so she began reconsidering her decision to runaway. With her back facing the house she dropped her suitcase, and it popped opened. Her pair of socks, shirt, toothbrush, and Crissy doll fell out of the suitcase to the ground. She slowly tuned around, her chin was visibly quivering, and I could see tears flowing down her cheeks. She ran back toward the house and tried to open the front door, but it was locked, so she pounded on the front door and yelled, 'Mommy, please let me in! I want to come home! I want to come home!'

I was in the living room looking out the window with my mother, and I said, 'Mommy, should I let her in – she's crying?'

She said, 'Chris made a decision to runaway from home; when you make decisions you have to live with their consequences. I'll let her in the house in a moment, but I want her to think harder about her decisions in the future. I also want her to realize she has a good life here, and she needs to appreciate it a little bit more.'

When I looked out the window again Chris was still crying, but now she was clicking her heels together and whispering, 'There's no place like home, there's no place like home…'

My mom let Chris suffer for a couple more minutes. Then she told me, 'Kenny, you can let your sister in now.'

I opened the door and said, 'Hi Chris, long time, no see. Welcome back. I really missed you.'

She walked by me and said, 'Shut-up Kenny!'

I think she learned her lesson that day because from that point on she never, ever complained about life in the Hand House – until later on the same night when my mother made meatloaf, instant mashed potatoes, and peas for dinner."

He continued, "Okay, that's a story about Aunt Chris and what a challenge she was."

"Dad, you told me I remind you of Aunt Chris. Does that mean that I'm a challenge too?"

My dad smiled, cleared his throat, and said, 'Oooooh noooo Kelsie – not you! You're an angel!"

We then reminded him to tell us more about Grandma Hand.

"Oh yeah, I almost forgot. Where was I?"

"You were telling us about your mother taking care of you and your brothers and sisters. You said something about cooking and cleaning."

"Oh, that's right. I said she took good care of us but she also worked at Camp Venture and Club Venture."

"What are Camp and Club Venture?"

"I'll tell you about them later, but did you know my mother was also an excellent auto mechanic? You see our Volkswagen had a problem with 'racing'…"

"She raced Volkswagens?"

"No, 'racing' doesn't mean she drove the car fast – it means the car's engine revved very high and would have driven fast if she didn't know how to fix it. Whenever the car raced she jumped out of the car, lifted up the hood, worked her magic, and it was fixed.

For relaxation she enjoyed talking on the phone, reading Harlequin Romance books, and watching soap operas. To this day I still can't get the opening of 'The Days of Our Lives' out of my head, 'Like sands through the hour glass, so are the days of our lives…da, da, da, daaaa…'

Grandma Hand is one of those people who is very easy to talk to, and so a lot of people called her on the phone for a little 'chit-chat', so when I was young she spent quite a bit of time talking on the phone. For some reason this occasionally caused some consternation between my mother and father. I remember one evening, while all of us kids were supposedly sleeping, my mom and dad had a lively discussion over the virtues of phone conversations. When I woke up the next day and walked downstairs I noticed a bowl of spaghetti stuck to the ceiling and the phone pulled off the kitchen wall. It was neatly placed on the living room floor next to my mom's favorite chair. It wasn't connected to the phone jack and it still had all the wires hanging out of it. At the time this seemed like a great idea because it made it more convenient for my mom to watch soap operas, read romance books, and talk on the phone at the same time."

"Funny, Dad. Can you tell us when were they married?"

"Hmmm, that's a little vague too. I'm not sure they were ever married. Yeah, I've seen wedding pictures and wedding rings, but what does that prove? Nothing! They've probably been living a life of sin for years and years and years! Oh, the pain! Oh, how embarrassing!"

Kelsie said, "Dad, can you stop fooling around and tell us?"

"Okay, maybe I got a little carried away. My mother and father were married on October 11, 1958 at St. John's Church in Kingsbridge. My dad was 25 years old and my mother was 20. That's all I know. Oh wait. I do know where they went for their honeymoon. Based on what I've told you about my father, where do you think they went for their honeymoon?"

Kelsie said, "I bet they went to Hawaii."

"Close Kelsie. What do you think Cameron?"

"I bet they went to the beach somewhere."

"Close Cameron. They went to Atlantic City. See, you should have guessed it after I told you about my dad's first love – gambling. Their honeymoon was full of long romantic moonlight walks from slot machines to Roulette Wheels, from Poker games to Craps tables. My father had a reputation for being very charming man who knew how to turn a romantic phrase. My favorite one came while he was throwing dice during a game of craps, 'Anne, without your love, my life would be full of the blues, now Annie blow on these dice – CAUSE MOMMY NEEDS A NEW PAIR OF SHOES!'

"Cam, don't believe him. He's being weird again."

"Okay, what else should I tell you? Oh yeah, let me tell you where they lived. After they got married, they moved into a 2 ½ room apartment on the corner of Bailey Avenue and Albany Crescent. Back in those days men and woman didn't shack up together; they waited until after they were married to shack up. My brother, your Uncle Richie, was born while they lived there. A few years later they moved to another much, much larger 3 room apartment on 238th Street near Bailey Avenue. While my parents lived on 238th Street, Gena was born, Christine was born, and then – DA, DA, DA, DAAAA – I was born! Actually, I wasn't born – I descended from heaven down onto their fire escape.

When I was born, Grandpa Hand worked for the New York City Bus Company – Manhattan and Bronx Surface Transit Operating Authority; they called it by its' abbreviation MABSTOA."

"MAB WHAT A?"

"I know – it's a crazy name, but that's who he worked for. He began as a bus driver. He drove a bus on the #20 line which ran from 262nd Street and Broadway to West Farms Square in the East Bronx and, according to everyone I've talked to, the people who rode his bus everyday loved him."

"He was loved by his customers? Are you exaggerating again, Dad?"

"No I'm not exaggerating, I'm really not. Everybody loves him – they really do! Some people just have a way about them that make people like them. My father has the 'people like me' gene. Unfortunately for me the 'people like me gene' skipped one generation."

Then we asked my dad if he had anything else to tell us about his parents.

"Nothing I can think of right now, but I'm sure I'll remember some other stories later."

"What about your brothers and sisters?"

"Yeah, I have a few stories about them. You both know I have two brothers and three sisters; just like the Brady Bunch. My brother Richie is the oldest, Gena is second, then Christine, me, Philip, and finally Patricia. Who do you want to hear about first?"

"Why don't you tell us about Uncle Richie, then Gena, and then everyone?"

"Good idea Kels. Give me a minute to think of a few things to tell you about Richie."

Big Brother

"Okay. My earliest memories of my brother Richie are from when we lived in Suffern. I considered Richie to be my best buddy even though Richie didn't realize it. Richie is five years older than me, and like most big brothers, he didn't pay much attention to me, but I paid a lot of attention to him. Richie was smart, athletic, and the most popular guy in the neighborhood. Because of this, I spent a lot of time tagging along behind him and his friends. I loved to play catcher, while him and his friends played Whiffle ball in the Gianelli's backyard. It was great playing with the older guys, and the best part of it was Richie and his friends liked me catching for them.

I remember going to Cuckolow Field, on the other side of the MTA train tracks on summer nights to watch him play baseball. I think I mentioned earlier that Richie played for the Orioles. He was the best pitcher, third baseman, and catcher on the Orioles. He was also the best player in Suffern Little League. Richie hit more home runs than anyone else in the league, but what made me the proudest of him was how humble he was about it. He didn't brag or boast about himself, and he was very encouraging to the other players on the team especially the ones with the least skill. He was a natural born leader and very popular with all the kids in the neighborhood. I always felt a lot of pride when I told people, 'I'm Richie Hand's brother.

Richie and his friends didn't only play sports; they did many other things to make being a kid in Suffern fun. I still remember their annual inner tube rides down the Mahwah River and them making 'go-carts' from old wood and broken down baby carriages. I told you about the fort Chris and I built, but the forts my brother and his friends built were much more impressive. They built elaborate forts in the 'woods' with multiple rooms, high up in the trees, with locks, and windows, and doors.

They turned their ordinary Schwinn bicycles into fabulous 'choppers' by cutting the front forks off of old bicycles and connecting them to the front forks on their newer bicycles.

They played hockey at the Salvation Army man-made lake, they raced motor 'go carts' and mini-bikes down Riverside Drive; and they did millions of other things I thought were awesome when I was a little kid. I bet my brother doesn't know how much I looked up to him when I was a kid. I know I've never told him."

"Did you two fight like me and Kelsie?"

"No, we didn't fight, he was my big brother and I looked up to him. Plus – he didn't want a piece of this – just like you don't want a piece of this!"

"You're right Dad, I don't want a piece of you – I want the whole thing! Bring it!"

"Yeah, yeah, yeah, you two. Dad, can you tell me some other stories about Uncle Richie?"

"Yeah, I think I have a few more stories to tell you. Let me see. Okay, when we lived in Suffern, Richie, Philip, and I slept in the same room. Philip and I slept on the bunk beds and Richie slept on a single bed on the other side of the room. Well, the mattresses on the bunk beds were so out of shape it felt like I was sleeping in a hammock. I'm not joking. When I got into bed it was hard to get out because it was like I was in a deep hole. My parents thought they bought cheap beds but actually the beds sagged because my brother and I played 'Flying Bunk Beds'.

"What's Flying Bunk Beds?"

"I'm getting there. You see after Grandma told us kids, 'It's bedtime', we went upstairs as we listened to Chris argue with my mother about being forced to go to bed too early. After we got upstairs Richie put on his favorite 45's like 'Chicaboom', 'Judy in Disguise (with Glasses)', 'Jeremiah was a Bullfrog', 'Smoking in the Boys Room', 'The Streak', 'Sister Mary Elephant', and 'American Pie' on his record player."

"Dad, what's a 45?"

"It's a record kind of like a CD. Well, not only did we listen to his music; we also played 'Flying Bunk Beds' or 'Sit on My Younger

Brother's Face and Fart on It'. I didn't like playing 'Sit on My Brother's Face and Fart on It' – I thought it stunk."

We all laughed at that joke. I think this was the first joke of the day we understood. Then I asked, "I understand how to play 'Sit on My Brother's Face' but what is 'Flying Bunk Beds?'"

"To play 'Flying Bunk Beds', Richie lay on his back on the bottom bed, and I lay on the top bed. Richie lifted his legs up and pressed his feet against the bottom of the top bed's mattress. Then he kicked the bottom of the top bed, or maybe I should say he pushed it will his legs. The bottom line is, it made me fly in the air – sometimes I flew so high I almost fell off the top bunk. We used to play 'Flying Bunk Beds' for hours or until we heard, 'Richie, Kenny, what are you two doing? It's time to go to bed. Now I told you to go to bed – if I come up there and the lights are not out you'll get the belt!'

I have a lot more stories about Richie like, 'I'm in Love with my Van' and 'Brawling with the Lady of the Sea'. I'll tell you about them some other time. For now let me tell you about THE EVIL ONE!"

The Evil Aunt Chris

"Dad, Aunt Chris isn't evil. She's nice."

"Aunt Chris, nice? Aunt Chris, nice? Are you crazy, Kelsie? Well, I have to admit she's a great sister now, but she wasn't always nice. When she was older than me..."

"What do you mean 'when she was older than me'? Isn't she still older than you?"

"No, when we were growing up she was about a year older than me, but now she tells people I'm ten years older. I'm not sure how it happened, but she looks so young people believe her. Okay, now let me get back to the Evil Aunt Chris. When I was a kid she was like Beelzebub and Jezebel rolled into one! She could even spin her head around and spew green puke from her mouth!

I'll tell you a few more stories about her, and you tell me if I'm exaggerating about her evilness. And by the way, whatever you do don't tell Aunt Chris I told you these stories!"

"Why not?"

"Because she'll put an Evil Hex on me – SHE'S EVIL!

Okay, when Chris and I were young we fought like cats and dogs over anything and everything you can imagine. We fought over who got to read the cereal box in the morning we fought over..."

"Wait! What do you mean you fought over who would read the cereal box? Why would you fight over that?"

"I'm not really sure; there wasn't anything to read on the side of our cereal boxes. Our cereal, like Wheaties, had a picture of some athlete on it but that's all. It wasn't like Fruit Loops or Lucky Charms which had tons of things to read! They had jokes, games, mazes, riddles and tons of other things but not Wheaties! Do you know what Chris and I fought over?"

"No what?"

"We fought over having a box of cereal in front of us to read about Riboflavin!"

"What?"

"My point is there was nothing to read on a box of Wheaties other than the side of the box. If you guys ever get on 'Who Wants to be a Millionaire' and you're asked a question about the nutritional information, the serving side, or the ingredients of Wheaties, you need to call me – I know everything about it! Go ahead and try me – go ahead!"

"What are you talking about?"

"Serving size is 33 grams or 1.2 ounces. Bam! It contains 25% of the recommended daily allowance of Riboflavin, Niacin, and Thiamin. Bam! It's made of Wheat! Double Bam! I can't believe I still remember this!"

"Dad, you are so weird!"

"The worst part about Wheaties is it wasn't sugar frosted, and so we had to sprinkle the sugar on by ourselves. This was another thing Chris and I fought over – who got to put the sugar bowl next to us. When the sugar bowl was next to me I had a great system; a scoop of sugar, sprinkled on top of the Wheaties, a scoop of some Wheaties, shoveled in my mouth. Scoop, sprinkle, scoop, shovel, scoop, sprinkle, scoop, shovel, scoop, sprinkle, scoop…well you get my point. After I ate all the cereal I had a sugar milk shake sitting in the bottom of my bowl, and with it came an awesome sugar rush – my body shook all the way to school!

So let's get back to Beelzebub – I mean Aunt Chris. We fought over everything! We fought over cereal boxes and bowls of sugar, we fought over who changed the channel on the TV, we fought over which radio station we listened to, and we fought over which car seat we sat in, we fought over everything – AND IT WAS ALL HER FAULT!

Kelsie sat up and said, "Would you stop, Dad! Aunt Chris is

really nice, and I can't imagine her being mean to you."

"Kelsie, Kelsie, naïve little Kelsie. Aunt Chris was, is, and always will be – EVIL!

Okay, I didn't want to do this, but it looks like I'm going to have to tell you a few more stories about the Evil One. I already told you about the time she ran away from home, but there are a lot more examples of her evilness.

♪ I am [evil] woman, hear me roar – In numbers too big to ignore
And I know too much to go back to pretend ♪
♪ Because I've heard it all before

And I've been down there on the floor ♪
♪ No one's ever gonna keep me down again" [4]

"Didn't you sing this song before?"

"Maybe, you got a problem with that?"

"Yeah, Dad, a little."

"Okay. Let me get back to Evil Aunt Chris or as I like to refer to her – EAC. The Helen Reddy song 'I Am Women' has always reminded me of your Aunt Chris. Opps, I meant to say EAC.

Alright, as a reminder when we were growing up we fought like cats and dogs; it didn't matter where or when – we were always yelling, screaming, pinching, scratching, punching, and throwing knives at each other – AND IT WAS ALL HER FAULT! Did I mention that before?"

"Yeeeeeeessss!"

"Okay, there was this one night after a long day of swimming at Camp Venture…"

I interrupted my dad and said, "You haven't told us about Camp Venture yet."

"Let me finish this story first, and then I'll tell you about Camp Venture later. When we were driving home from Camp Venture my mother said we had to pickup some food on the way home because the pantry and refrigerator were both empty. They were empty because Grandma had a busy week working at camp, and she didn't have a chance to go shopping at the A&P; because of this, she decided to buy Kentucky Fried Chicken for dinner – we all loved KFC, it was a HUGE treat.

Remember, back in those days there wasn't a fast food restaurant on every street corner like there is nowadays and so anytime we ate KFC, Burger Chef, Burger King, or McDonalds it was a day of celebration…"

"Wait, Dad! You didn't have fast food every night? You mean you went to nice restaurants EVERY night?"

"No, when I was growing up my mom made 'supper' every night and we ate it in the kitchen – AND WE LIKED IT!"

"Really?"

"Well we did eat dinner at home but, no, we didn't always like it. Like I think I told you before, we sat down at the kitchen table every night and my mother served us supper. My mom's specialties were spaghetti, meatloaf, Spam, fish sticks, some nasty vegetables, and instant mashed potatoes. We weren't allowed to leave the kitchen table until we cleaned our plate because there were 'starving boys and girls in Africa'."

"What do 'starving kids in Africa' have to do with your dinner?"

"Cam, I have NO idea, but my mother said this to us all the time. I think she believed it helped us to eat our dinner."

"Did it work?"

"No."

"Did you eat your dinner?"

"Well I always cleaned my plate – sometimes with the help of Tipper."

"What? Why?"

"We cleaned our plates because my mother blackmailed us kids every night of our lives, a cruel and unusual thing for her to do to her children! If we didn't finish our dinner, we didn't get dessert. And as you know, a night without a Twinkie, Yodel, Cruller, or a Suzie Q is like a night without sunshine."

"Weird, Dad!"

"Okay, let me get back to my story. When my mom stopped in KFC she bought the family pack which included chicken for eight. The chicken came in a flimsy little red and white box with a picture of the Colonel on the side; it also came with a large container of mashed potatoes, a container of coleslaw, and eight butter milk biscuits – Mmmm Mmmm good! The food was placed in a large white bag with a big picture of the Colonel on the side; the girl behind the counter handed it to my mom, and we got back into the car and drove home.

On the way home I carried the bag of food on my lap, and it smelled SOOO good I could hardly wait to sink my teeth into a big juicy piece of chicken. When my mother pulled the Volkswagen into the driveway Aunt Christine and I began to argue over who would carry the bag of food into the house.

Aunt Christine yelled at me, 'You got to hold it in the car. It's my turn to carry it.'

I yelled back, 'I only got to hold it for a little while, I should still be able to carry it in.'

Grandma said, 'You can both carry it in. So I held one side of the bag and Aunt Chris held the other side and we walked up the gravel driveway to the front yard.

The front yard was 100% dirt because my father just dug up the front yard to plant new grass seed. As we both walked side by side to the front yard, we began to argue again, but this time she pulled her side of the bag away from me and, in what appeared to be slow motion, the bag tore apart, the box of chicken flew in the air, the container of mashed potatoes, coleslaw, and biscuits were sent flying, and at precisely the same time they all fell to the ground.

The box of chicken dropped to the ground and burst open leaving all the chicken lying in the freshly turned up top soil, the container of mashed potatoes was fine for a second until I accidentally stepped on it and squeezed the potatoes out. It seemed like the coleslaw would be safe but then Aunt Chris slipped on the mashed potatoes, and her bottom landed on the container of coleslaw forcing it out – all over the dirt. The biscuits were the only survivors of the disaster."

"Oh, no! I bet your mom whooped you two!"

"Well, Cam, when the episode was over, I think it only lasted a few seconds, I was lying in the dirt with mashed potatoes in my shoes, coleslaw on my backside, and chicken all over the front yard. When I turned and looked at Chris, I saw her sitting in the dirt with a small piece of the large white paper bag still in her left hand. Her jaw dropped down to her chest, her eyes were popped out of her sockets – we both knew what was about to happen.

Grandma was so upset with her two beautiful little angels, she wanted to strangle us! She cursed at us in her typical mommy way, 'Jesus, St. Mary, and Joseph!' She was so mad she didn't seem to be concerned about our physical well being. She had a few more choice words for the two of us like, 'Oh CHRISTMAS!' as she dragged us by our ears into the house and up the stairs into our rooms. She whacked us on our bottoms with a belt and told us, 'There WILL NOT be any dinner for either of you tonight!'

I thought to myself, 'What? What did my mom say? Did she say what I think she said? No dinner? No food? What? This can't be! She wouldn't! She couldn't! This would be child abuse and my mother would never do this to me – I don't blame her for doing it to Chris – she deserved it – but not me – I'm her favorite son! How could my mother even think of doing this to me? I haven't eaten since 2:00 p.m., I'll starve to death!' I screamed and cried, 'Mom, I'm starving! Mom, I'm going to starve to death! Oh, the pain! Oh, the misery!' I kept this mantra going and then Chris stuck her head out of her room and joined in – we whined in stereo!!!

Finally, after about an hour, my mom gave in and allowed us to come downstairs to the kitchen table to eat cereal for dinner. We were so thankful for my mother being so kind and generous, 'Thank you Mom! We're sorry! We didn't mean to drop the chicken! We'll never fight again! We'll be good, we promise! We love you! Thank you, thank you, thank you!' About ten minutes later, my mother heard me and Chris in the kitchen, 'You always get the box in front of you when we eat cereal – it's my turn! No, it's my turn…!'"

"Dad, this story doesn't prove Aunt Chris was evil. Actually it sounds like it was your fault. You held the chicken in the car – she should have been able to carry it into the house!"

"What? What did my little girl just say? Did you just say what I think you said? Did you say it was my fault? My fault?"

"Uh, yes Dad!"

"Oh, Noooooooo! It was Jezebel's fault! You see Cam – all evil women stick together!"

"Don't I know it, Dad!"

My Favorite Nudges

"Well now that you know about the evil one, it's time for you to learn about the Nudges."

"What's a Nudge?"

"A nudge is someone who pesters you and annoys you. Of course Aunt Gena and Uncle Philip weren't really pests, and they didn't really annoy me; this was a family joke, and it was a way we teased them to show how much we loved them. I remember times when Philip motioned to my father he wanted to go to P&K's for lunch. My dad would look at Philip and say, 'Would you stop nudging me? We'll go once you stop nudging me!'

They were nudges, but they are also the two people who had the biggest impact on my life. Aunt Gena is four years older than me, and Uncle Philip is two years younger; they are both mentally handicapped – which means they learn things a little bit slower than most people, but it also means they love people more than most people. Growing up with Gena and Philip shaped my life in so many ways; they laughed so hard, they were fun to be around, they helped create a loving atmosphere in the house, and along with my mom; they are the main reason our family has become very close over the years."

It was obvious my dad loved them, because as he told us about them, he had a glow on his face. He said, "I'll never forget how outgoing Gena was when I was growing up. At Camp Venture and Club Venture she was so happy, and she had such a great personality; everyone loved her. I remember how she used to drag her camp counselors to meet me, Tricia, Chris, or Richie when she saw one of us. And at weddings and parties she was and still is the life of the party; she'll dance with anyone willing to get out on the dance floor with her.

At home she loved to watch Soap Operas, American Bandstand, and Soul Train. If my mother ever missed one of her Soap Operas,

Gena could recite the whole show back to her verbatim. Gena was like having a living Soap Opera Digest in our home.

Her home routine called for a big cup of Coke on her TV tray while she watched her favorite TV shows. The only time Gena became a nudge was if I asked her if I could change the channel to watch a different show.

But without a doubt my favorite memory of Gena is her love for Michael Jackson. In Gena's room she had dozens of pictures of Michael Jackson hanging on the wall, and when one of his songs came on the radio she screamed with excitement! Christmas presents for Gena always included something related to Michael Jackson; Michael Jackson records, tapes, CD's, shirts, posters, or videos always made perfect gifts for Gena.

Uncle Philip was a character too! At Camp Venture he was also extremely happy, but unlike Gena – when Philip saw Tricia, Richie, Chris, or me he totally ignored us like he was embarrassed of us. Just like Aunt Gena he is the life of any party he goes to. If there is music playing and a dance floor, he spends the whole night dancing. By the time the night is over he's drenched with sweat.

But although they were great and I love them very much – I'm ashamed to say it was sometimes hard for me having a handicapped brother and sister when I was growing up.

When I was young I was very sensitive to what other people thought and said. I'm still sensitive, but I've learned to cover up my sensitivity a little."

"You don't cover it up, Dad. When I make fun of your toes, you always cry."

My dad's chin started quivering, and he yelled, "Kelsie, leave me feet alone! What have they ever done to you! And, and, and you've never seen my feet – no one has!"

Kelsie smiled and said, "Very weird, Dad! Very weird!"

He smiled and got back to his story, "Having a handicapped sister and brother was emotionally difficult for me, not because of Aunt Gena and Uncle Philip, but because of how some people reacted to them. Before people got to know them, they weren't sure what to think about the boy with the loud, infectious laugh, or the girl with the giggle and the silly skip in her step. Too often I noticed people's furrowed brow trying to figure out, 'Are they handicapped or just kids who love life?' While they were trying to figure this out they usually stared – especially young kids who didn't know any better. Once my friends, or anyone, realized Gena and Philip were handicapped it was fine, because almost everyone was very kind and understanding toward them. Plus, once anyone got to know them – they came to like them. Everyone enjoyed their company and loved to joke around with them. It was just the initial reaction I wish I could have learned to deal with better."

"♪The road is long – With many a winding turn♪
That leads us to who knows where – Who knows where♪
♪But I'm strong – Strong enough to carry him [and her]♪
He [and she] aint heavy – [they're] my brother [and sister]♪" [5]

"Hey Dad, are you going to start singing after every story you tell us?"

"I might, Cam. I might. Is that a problem?"

"Maybe."

"Too bad, bud – you'll get over it. Okay, let me tell you a little more about Uncle Philip and how he impacted my life. You know what Philip helped me to do?"

"What?"

"He helped me to see the heart and character of people. I could tell what kind of person a friend or a girlfriend was by how they treated Philip. I usually told them about my brother to prepare them for the 'Philip Welcome' – a great big 'Hi', along with a handshake for a boy or a hug and kiss for a girl! He has shaken more hands than Bill Clinton, kissed more woman than Richard Dawson, and danced with more woman than Fred Astaire."

It was obvious my dad loved and was proud of Uncle Philip. He didn't turn his head toward us and smile like he did when he told us a funny story. When he told us about Philip and Aunt Gena he stared out the window with a little smile on his face and his eyes were a little glassy.

He continued, "You know I love Philip and so did everyone else, but that doesn't mean he was perfect. Like most men, Philip is a big baby when he's sick. But when most men are sick they lie down in bed and ask to be waited on hand and foot. But remember, Uncle Philip can't tell people, 'I'm sick' or 'I have a headache', instead he communicates his sickness and discomfort by moaning and groaning and moaning and groaning.

I can remember a time my family was on vacation at the New Jersey shore in Belmar. Belmar was a quiet little shore town which, except for Mary's Husband's Brother's Place, shut down by 9:00 p.m. Bungalows were lined up and down the narrow streets and when the town closed down, it was so quiet you could hear the crickets chirp and the TV in the bungalow next door.

One afternoon while we were on vacation, Philip polished off a box of Nilla Wafers and a quart of Coca Cola while sitting in front of the TV watching sports. As you can imagine this healthy diet didn't sit well with his stomach and by 9:00 p.m. his stomach was doing flips, and he was about to 'toss his cookies' – literally speaking. Unfortunately, instead of tossing them he decided to fight it and he moaned and groaned all night long! Did you hear me? ALL NIGHT LONG!"

"He sounds like he's a lot like you. When he throws up, does he make those loud strange noises like you?"

"I don't know – probably. Anyway, his moaning wouldn't have been much of a problem in the Bronx, because the trains and city noises would have drowned it out. But bungalows didn't have air conditioning, and so everyone left their windows open and the fact they were so close together made it easy for the whole neighborhood to hear Philip's moans! As I sat on the front porch trying to get away from his endless, monotonous, moans and groans I noticed our neighbors were walking by our bungalow looking to see if we were performing some kind of weird, satanic ritual. I can look back on it now and laugh, but at the time it was painfully embarrassing."

"Why didn't you just drive him to the beach where nobody would have heard him?"

"We tried to, but when we picked him up he stopped moaning and he began screaming like we were torturing him! I don't know what people would have thought if they heard his screams while we were forcing him in the car. I'm sure they would have called the police."

"Do you have any other stories about Aunt Gena and Uncle Philip?"

"Hmmm. I think I can come up with another one but you have to have a strong stomach because it's pretty nasty. Do you have a strong stomach?"

"Of course."

"Okay, but don't say I didn't warn you."

"We won't."

"IT" Happens

"Alright, but this story happened when I was older. I was in my early twenties; mom and I lived in St. Louis in a two room apartment in Raintree Apartments. The complex was beautiful; it had tennis courts and swimming pools.

Well, my parents, Aunt Gena, and Uncle Philip came to visit us a year after we moved there. They came during the summer, and since Gena and Philip loved to swim I asked my parents if I could take them swimming. It was early July which, in St. Louis, means the temperature is typically around 90 degrees. Since it was early in the summer it was the first time Gena and Philip went swimming that year. When they went to Camp Venture they loved pools, and when they went swimming they didn't just wallow around in the pool – no, they had fun! They jumped in, swam on top of the water, dove under the water, they splashed, kicked, yelled, and screamed – in other words they had a great, active time in the pool! Whenever it was time to leave they had to be dragged out of the pool, not only because they didn't want to stop swimming, but also because they were exhausted.

But not only did they have a love of swimming, they also had a love for cookies and soda. If they were left alone for an extended period of time with the box of Nilla Wafers cookies and quart of Coke – they could easily devour a box of cookies and a bottle of soda in one sitting.

This one particular day it was 92 degree and sunny outside – a perfect day for swimming. Earlier in the day I went out with mom, Grandma and Grandpa to the store; we left Gena and Philip at my apartment for about an hour with a box of cookies and some soda. Oh and by the way, did I mention Uncle Philip had just gotten over a bad cold? Swimming, cookies, soda, and Uncle Philip's congested nose was creating a perfect storm.

When we got back from shopping everything seemed to be perfect – no one could have anticipated the events which were about to unfold. Grandma Hand helped Gena and Philip put their bathing suits on while Aunt Gena complained, 'Come on, Mom, hurry up! I want to go swimming!'

Uncle Philip tapped me on my shoulder and shook his hands which meant, 'I can't wait to go swimming!' When we all got our bathing suits on, I grabbed three towels from the bathroom and we hurried down the apartment building steps leading to the pool area.

There were about thirty people already at the pool; half of them were swimming and the other half were sitting or lying on lounge chairs relaxing by the side of the pool. The pool was encircled by a chain link fence with green metal slats.

To enter the pool I lifted up the gate latch, opened the gate, and we quickly walked in. When we got inside we threw our towels on the nearest chairs and jumped in the pool; splashing several of the older woman who were wading around in the pool. These snobby women gave us disapproving looks, but I did my best to ignore them – Gena and Philip didn't notice at all.

As soon as they were in the pool, they jumped up and down, they splashed, swam, and dove all over the place – we were having a great time together! But then – almost without warning – IT happened!"

"What happened, Dad?"

My dad said, "Cameron! IT happened!! The most incredibly embarrassing experience of my life HAPPENED!"

"But what was IT?"

"I'm getting to IT, I'm getting to IT. I have to compose myself – it's hard for me to tell this story. Remember, I have a weak stomach myself, and this story is NOT for people with weak stomachs!

Remember what I said earlier about the perfect storm? Well, keep in mind, Philip recently got over a cold, and he was still a little bit congested. And as everyone knows – when you go under water the pressure can cause your body to clear out some bodily orifices, and so it was with Philip. He was showing me how he could hold his breath; he put his head under the water for about 10 seconds and then he'd pop back out of the water. He popped up and down, up and down, up and down; the last time he popped up something popped out of his nose – IT WAS THE BIGGEST, GREENEST, WETTEST SNOT YOU EVER SAW IN YOUR LIFE!!

But it wasn't your typical snot – NO, it was different! It was strong like a piece of rubber and it seemed to have a life of its own. It almost seemed like it was peaking out of Uncle Philip's nose – it wanted to look out but it didn't want to leave his nose – because when Uncle Philip turned his head the portion that was laying below his nose, over his lips would release and swing from it's current position over to the other side of his face – all the while the other end was clinging on for dear life to the inside of his nose. Philip didn't realize this was happening and so when I said something to him he looked to his left and right and behind him – and with every turn of his head this monstrosity of a snot swung from one side of his face to the other – leaving snot remnants all over his face! It was at the same time one of the funniest things I had ever seen but also one of the most disgusting.

When Gena came up from her underwater diving activities she said, 'What Kenny? What's so funny? What are you saying to Philip?' I made the biggest mistakes of my life when I said, 'Gena, take a look at Philip's face!" Aunt Gena looked at his face, saw the snot from the black lagoon on his face – and immediately she made a sound that can only be compared to a sound made by an elephant seal during mating season. Immediately, almost in unison, every head turned toward Gena to see what the awful noise was. But almost as soon as Gena finished her elephant seal mating call – 2 liters of Diet Coke and chewed up Nilla Waffers came spewing from Gena's mouth like Old Faithful at Yellowstone Park – only this time the noise was more familiar to the surrounding people – BBBBBBAAAAARRRRRRRFFFFFFFFF!!!!!!

As you guys know – in my family throwing up is not a quiet event – you can hear anyone in my family throw up from miles away – and so when this happened not only did everyone in the pool know about it, but everyone in the complex heard it. It was like the star when Jesus was born – people came from miles away to see what everyone heard – AND SEE THEY DID! They had the rare opportunity to see, the biggest snot of their life on the side of Philip's face, they saw a Diet Coke oil slick, with little chucks of Nilla Wafers floating on top of the water…getting bigger by the second, they saw old ladies, old men, young boys, young girls racing out of the pool – it was like a scene from Jaws! And they saw me beet red with embarrassment – not knowing what to do while being engulfed in the floating barf. I have NO idea how I survived that day, but I do know one thing for sure – I never showed my face at the Raintree apartment pool EVER again!"

"That's funny, Dad. Is it really true?"

"Of course it is, Kelsie! Do I look like the type of guy who would make up a story like that? But Kelsie, the story isn't over yet!

You two might think this very traumatic experience would have hampered Philip and Gena's love for swimming – at least for a day or two – but NO!! Like I said, I could never show my face again at the Raintree apartment's pool but there were many other pools in the St. Louis area my brother and sister felt the need to christen. When my family visited me in St. Louis, they stayed at The Mary K Motel, a quaint little motel located near I-270 and Lindberg Boulevard. The next day it was again above 90 degrees, so Grandma Hand allowed them to swim at the motel's pool. This sounded safe enough to me, so I agreed to come over to go swimming. I drove to the motel from my apartment, and I brought one of my new beach towels. When I arrived at the motel my dad, Philip, and Gena were already in the pool swimming around so I laid my towel down and prepared to hop in the pool – and then IT happened – AGAIN!"

"IT happened again?"

"Yes, Kels, IT happened AGAIN! I couldn't believe IT! Uncle Philip dunked his head under the water and when he popped up – there IT was again – as green, and as slimy as ever! Only this time IT appeared from my brother's other nostril. IT was like *The Wizard of Oz* when Dorothy was told the Wicked Witch was dead only to find out there was another witch who was even more wicked than the first one. This snot was bigger, greener – it was kind of a translucent green – and this one even appeared to have several little wild hairs in IT – IT was the mother of all snots!

I screamed, 'Oh no, not again! Gena, turn your head – don't look! Get out of the pool! Run, run, and don't look back!' I turned to Philip – and saw him standing there with this fluorescent green, hairy snot – which seemed to be alive – hanging from his right nostril, down across his mouth, dangling from his chin! Philip was well aware of the situation and knew what to do. As he stood in the 3 foot section of the pool – he raised his right arm, pointed his finger in the air as if to say, 'Don't worry – I've got the situation under control.'

With the confidence of General George Custer marching into battle – Uncle Philip marched out of the pool, walked around the side of the pool, over to where I was sitting. He reached across my body for a towel hanging on the fence behind me. As he reached across me the snot dangled above my body like the Sword of Domiciles, Uncle Philip grabbed my new towel and proceeded to wipe the green, slimy, hairy monster from his face – WITH MY BRAND NEW TOWEL!"

Both Kelsie and I said, "Dad, that's gross! Please don't tell us any more stories like that again – I'm going to be sick!"

My dad smiled and said, "I warned you…"

Then I asked him, "What about Aunt Tricia? What was she like?"

Baby Sister

"Aunt Tricia, Aunt Tricia…let me think…let me think. Aunt Tricia was five years younger than me. I can remember when Tricia was born; we were living in Suffern. When she was born my mother was in the hospital for several days."

"Why? What happened?"

"I don't think anything bad happened. Back in those days women stayed in the hospital for several days after they had their baby, but now it seems like they're barely in there for a day."

Kelsie said, "It's terrible women only stay in the hospital for a day or two now! They should be allowed to stay in the hospital for a week like your mother."

"Well Kelsie, Grandpa Hand doesn't agree with you. I can remember him telling me, 'I can't believe women stay in the hospital for a week after they have a baby. If men had babies it would be like passing a fart. Men would lift up one cheek, they'd feel a little burning, the baby would pop out, and there'd be a lingering smelly odor, but he'd be back to work the next day!'

"Dad, that's terrible! Grandpa Hand didn't really say that, did he?"

"He said something like that. Anyway, it was great when my mother was in the hospital, because my father took several days off of work and took care of us kids. My dad cooked us dinner every night. My favorite meal was his hamburgers. Instead of broiling our hamburgers, like my mom, he fried them in a frying pan. For a side dish he served us Wise Potato Chips, and he gave us Schafer Beer to drink."

"Don't believe him, Cam! Grandpa did not give daddy beer when he was five years old!"

"Well, maybe he gave us soda instead of Hawaiian Punch; all I know for sure is the food and drink was great! While my mom was away he also made us his world famous Omelet's, Pancakes, and French toast – they were delicious. When my mom got back from the hospital with Tricia I asked her, 'Can you have another baby – I love daddy's cooking!'

Anyway, when Tricia came home from the hospital she slept for hours and hours, which drove me crazy, because I wanted to play with my new little sister. To wake her up I blew on her face. Of course, when I did this she woke up crying. And of course my mother yelled at me, 'Kenny, leave your little sister alone.' When Tricia was older I remember she had an outgoing personality, she was very athletic, and she was very popular, but I don't have a lot of stories about her. Wait, actually I do have a few stories about her, but I'd rather tell you them later along with some other stories. Okay?"

"Okay but I thought you would have a lot of stories about Aunt Tricia – you guys seem to have really good relationship."

"We do, but that really happened when we were older. I'm really impressed with the woman Tricia has become. Maybe the fact I didn't spend much time with her when we were younger is the reason I don't have many stories about her, and maybe that's one of the reasons she's turned out to be such a great mother, wife, and person."

"Well, I guess that's good, but I'm disappointed because I wanted to hear some good Aunt Tricia stories.

"Cam, I'm sure she has a lot of them. You'll have to ask her."

"Okay. Dad, do you have any stories about growing up in New York?"

The Greatest Show ~~on Earth~~ in New York

"Let me think. Oh yeah, I have one I think you'll like. Do you want to hear about the first time I went to the circus?"

Both Kelsie and I said, "Yeah."

"Okay. When I was growing up we usually had two cars; a station wagon for my mom and us kids and a smaller car for my father's commute to and from work in New York City. The vehicles in the 1960's and early 1970's weren't the most reliable, and so occasionally they broke down without any notice. I can remember the night my dad came home and told the whole family he bought tickets for 'Ringling Brothers and Barnum and Bailey Circus' for the following Saturday Night. I had never been to a circus, and so I was really excited about going. Since it wasn't until the following Saturday, the week at school seemed to drag by so slowly but, of course, eventually Saturday arrived and it was CIRCUS TIME!

The circus was being held in the city at the world famous Madison Square Garden, which made it even more exciting because we got to go downtown! The show was scheduled to begin at 7:00 p.m. and end by 9:00, and so we had to be ready to leave by 5:00 for the hour long drive to the city. All us kids, except for 2 year old Patricia, loaded into the station wagon at 5:00 and waited patiently for my parents to get in. When our parents got into the car, my dad turned the ignition key and instead of the vroom of the car starting up we all heard the click, click, click of a dead battery or a bad alternator. 'Oh, no', we all shouted, 'We're going to miss the circus!' Grandpa got out of the car, looked under the hood of the station wagon, pulled and pushed on a few wires, analyzed the situation, cussed a few times, and said, 'Yeah, it's dead – let's take the Volkswagen?'

Our Volkswagen was an extremely small car with just enough room for two small adults in the two front seats, two small adults in the tight back seat, and maybe a few odds and end in the small storage area behind the back seats. Yes, Cam and Kelsie, you have the picture – my family of eight! Yes, eight! My family of eight was considering packing the whole family into a Volkswagen which could barely fit four small people comfortably.

My mom said, 'Richie, do you think it's safe to put the whole family into such a small vehicle for over an hour trip?' My dad said, 'Anne, no it's not safe. In fact, it's very, very dangerous! Then he turned to us and said, 'Come on kids – everyone in the Volkswagen!'

EAC and I were the first in – we climbed into the very back of the car – the storage area behind the back seat. We had to sit facing each other with our knees up to our chests, while our backs and necks were bent over in order to fit – I felt like a contortionist! Wait, Cameron…let me say that again – I felt like a pretzel!

My mom said, 'Richie, Gena, and Philip – it's your turn now. Get in and sit in the back seat. Also, Richie – Tricia will sit on your lap.' Finally, my mom and dad got in and shut their doors and off we went. We drove down Riverside Drive, made a right on Route 6, and in time we got on I-87 going south; once we were on the Thruway we drove over the Tappan Zee Bridge, through Westchester County, past Yonkers Raceway, through the Bronx, and into Manhattan.

When we got into Manhattan we drove along the West Side Drive until 42nd Street. When our car came to a stop light on 42nd Street, a nice gentleman with a big coat, winter gloves, a winter hat, and a shopping cart came over to our car and washed our windshield. My father rolled down his window and gave him a dollar bill and said, 'thanks, buddy.' Although it was nice of him to wash our window I asked my dad, 'Why did he wash it with a dirty newspaper? It's dirtier now than it was before?' My dad said something, but it was hard to hear him over the rev of the Volkswagen engine. He made the turn on 42nd Street going towards 7th Avenue. I said, 'Mom, we must be getting close. Look at those ladies over there with the big hair, big shoes, and the little skirts. They have two big round things coming out of their shirts and they're all wearing really colorful clothes. Are they clowns?' 'Don't look at them, Kenny – look straight ahead.

My dad made a few more turns until we made it to the corner of 33rd Street and 7th Avenue. At this point we pulled into a parking garage down the street from the Garden. Once in the garage my family and I had to be pulled out of the Volkswagen by the parking attendant; it was like popping the cork out of a bottle of Champaign. After being popped out and shot across the garage floor, I tried to stand up but couldn't; I felt and looked like a seven year old Quasimodo."

"Who?"

"The Hunchback of Notre Dame."

"Oh. Why were you hunched over?"

"Because after being curled up in a little ball, in the back of the Volkswagen, for an hour and a half my muscles cramped, and I couldn't stretch out. I wish my father put me in the glove compartment instead; I would have had a lot more room."

"Oh my gosh! I'd be claustrophobic if I had to be in such a small space for that long!"

"I was claustrophobic, but we didn't care as long as we got to the circus. Let's see, where was I? Oh yeah. When we were all out of the car my father gave his keys to the parking attendant, and he was given a ticket in return. And off we went to the circus.

We walked across the street, past several Sabrett Hot Dog vendors, past a few guys sleeping on the sidewalk, up the Garden's steps, and into the Felt Forum. Our seats were in the mezzanine level across from the center ring and so when we walked through the turnstiles we had to take the escalators up to our seats.

The circus was really exiting for all of us, especially me; the horses, clowns, elephants, and trapeze artists performed some of the most amazing tricks I had ever seen, but the part of the show I was the most excited about seeing was the man being shot out of the cannon! Since the cannon man was the highlight of the night it was strategically positioned at the end of the show, but I just couldn't keep my eyes open. Toward the end of the show, no matter how hard I tried, I just couldn't keep them open – and finally I dozed off for a few minutes. When I awoke I asked my mother, 'When will the man be shot out of the cannon?'

My mom said, 'Oh, Kenny, you just missed it.' I was SO disappointed that I began to cry, but before I could make much of a fuss the show was over and so we started our trip back to the Volkswagen. We walked down the escalators, down the steps, outside the Felt Forum, down the street, past the homeless people, across the road, to the parking garage.

When we finally arrived at the parking garage, it was packed with all the families who just left the circus. The parking garages had pretty cool set-ups. The parking attendants took the ticket from the father, he ran up the ramp or the steps to where the car was parked, then you heard the screeching of car tires, and within seconds you saw the car whip around the corner and down the ramp to where the families were waiting. The attendant hopped out of the cars and walked over to the father – at which time the father handed the guy one or two dollars, and then the family loaded into the car and off they went.

Now this is the key – most of the families consisted of a mother, father, and one or two kids AND their car was either a station wagon or another large vehicle like a Buick or a Chevy something. Now keep in mind I was very sensitive to embarrassing situations, and this was a potentially embarrassing situation! Remember, these SMALL families were getting into very LARGE cars while my family was a very LARGE family getting into an extremely SMALL car. And think about it. We just came from the circus where one of the funniest parts of the show was when about 30 clowns piled into a small car which looked amazingly like my family's Volkswagen!

I looked around and every time the parking attendant drove a car around the corner it was a BIG car, and every family to get into a BIG car was a SMALL family! I think this was the first time I learned to pray. I prayed my family's little Volkswagen would be the last car the attendant drove around the corner! 'Please God don't bring my car. Please, please, please!'

Then to make matters worse – this little boy who was about my age came over to me and started talking to me – he said, 'Did you go to the circus? Where are you from? My name is Johnny – what's yours?'

I thought to myself, 'Hey kid, get away, you bother me…' I didn't want to talk to him because once he saw our little Volkswagen pull up – his next questions would be, 'Are all you going to fit into that LITTLE car? Is there really enough room for all of you in there? Is your family part of the circus?'

I got back to my praying, 'Please don't bring my car down now, please, please, please.' Now I know God answers prayer, but for some reason he didn't answer mine that night. I heard the familiar sound of our Volkswagen and when I turned and looked up the ramp, I saw it coming. I know all the people still standing their waiting for their cars expected a SMALL family of two or three to get into the car, but NO – my family of EIGHT walked to the curb and stood waiting to get into the car. I could hear gasps and murmuring from the crowd, 'They're not going to try to fit in that car – are they?' 'It's impossible, it just can't be done!' 'There's no way!'

I was dying! I felt like the final act of the circus. Christine and I got into the back cubby hole first. I put my head between my legs; I didn't want to see the people staring at us, but I could hear the crowd outside screaming, 'Wow, they're really going to try!' Then Richie, Gena, Philip, and Tricia got in. I could hear the crowd yelling, 'Holy Cow – they're doing it!' Finally my mom and dad squeezed in, and the parking attendant pushed the overflowing arms, legs, and stomachs that were oozing out of the car doors and windows back in. He turned his body around and leaned against the doors and pushed and pushed until he heard the sound of the door locking. I heard the crowd screaming, "I don't believe it! They fit! They all fit in that little car! That's incredible! Incredible, they did it!" Then I heard the crowd clapping and cheering for us – the final show of the night!"

I said to my dad, "Why would that bother you? I think it's cool to be able to fit all those people into a small car. All these things you say made you, what did you say, sensitive and self conscious, I don't think are bad at all."

"Not bad, not bad! You get embarrassed when I sing in public!"

"Yeah, Dad, but that's different – that really is embarrassing!"

"Well, sometime I'm going to tell you the story about my dad going through a toll booth and paying with all pennies – we'll see if you think that's embarrassing like I did."

"Really? Your dad paid with all pennies?"

"Yes, but that's a story for another day."

"Okay, what about your aunts, uncles, and cousins? Are you going to tell us about them?"

"You mean the perfect families – who didn't have any problems?"

"Yeah, I guess. If your aunts, uncles, and cousins are perfect, then I guess so."

Team Doyle

"Alright, I'll start with my mother's side of the family."

"How did you get to know the history of your mom's family? Did your mom tell you stories like you tell us?"

"Are you kidding, Cam? No! My mother is an Irish mother even though she might not think she is."

"What does that mean?"

"What I mean is, my mother doesn't talk much about the family. She doesn't brag about her kids and more importantly she never airs the family's dirty laundry. Dirty laundry are the things you don't want anyone outside the family to know about; for example, Kelsie probably doesn't want anyone to know she can fart the 'Star Spangled Banner.'"

"Daaaaad!"

"Well, even though I think we're a close family now, communication has never been something my mom's side of the family did well. Most of the things I know about my parent's and my aunts and uncles, I learned in recent years. There have been times when I've felt like I've been interrogating my mother; I've asked her a million questions about her life and her family. I really wish my mother and my father would have told me about their lives when I was younger – I'm sure I could have benefited from their experiences. That's one of the reasons I tell you my stories. Of course, I hope you find my stories funny and interesting, but I also hope you can learn things from my stories."

"Yeah Dad, I'm sure stories about poo, snots, and farting will help mold us into a fine, productive members of society someday."

"Funny, Kels. Let me get back to my mom's family. As I stated before, my mother's maiden name is Doyle, and her family is Irish, Catholic. They emigrated from Ireland back in the late 1800's. Your great, great grandfather..."

"Why was he so great Dad?"

"Oh, no, not again! Cam, he was great, I'm sure he was, but saying someone is your great, great grandfather just means he was your father's, mother's, father's, father."

"Oh, why didn't you say so? ...continue."

"His name was Eugene Doyle, and he emigrated from Bally Bunion, I think this is who I inherited my ugly feet from. Get it? Bally BUNION – ugly feet? Get it?"

"No."

"I can't believe my best material gets wasted on two kids with no sense of humor. Alright, so Eugene Doyle emigrated from Bally Bunion in the County Cork around 1895. He lived in Harlem for several years after he moved to the United States, but eventually he was married and moved to the Bronx. His future wife, Anna Beglin, was also from Ireland but she was from West Meath in the County Devlin.

I'm not sure when or where they met or when they were married, but on November 17, 1906 they had a son, and they named him William – William Anthony Doyle. After William was born, Eugene Doyle designed and constructed the family house; it was built near the corner of 234th Street and Corlear Avenue – the address was 3249 Corlear Avenue – and of course it was in the Bronx."

"Is that the house you lived in when you lived in the Bronx?"

"Yup – I lived there for a couple of years. William was my mother's father and, as you can probably figure out he was my grandfather.

My grandmother's maiden name was Dolan. Her father's name was Thomas Dolan, and her mother's name was Anna Clark. I'm not sure when they emigrated from Ireland; this history isn't clear but they must have moved to New Jersey before 1909, because in 1909 my grandmother, Anna Dolan was born in Hoboken.

So, my grandfather grew up in the Kingsbridge section of the Bronx, living part of his childhood in 3249 Corlear Avenue, while my grandmother grew up in Hoboken, New Jersey. Sometime before 1937 they met, because they were married in 1937 – in my grandmother's home town of Hoboken. After they were married they moved into a small apartment located on Naples Terrace in Kingsbridge where they lived when my mother, Anne Patricia, was born. My mother was born on St. Patrick's day in 1938 – My grandfather was mad because he wasn't able to march in the St. Patrick's Day Parade because my grandmother was in labor."

"Really?"

"No, not really. But I bet he was sorry she was born on St. Patrick's Day because that meant he couldn't drink, wait a second, that's not right, I'm stereotyping Irish people, you better scratch that. When my grandparents were expecting their second child, my Uncle Larry, they moved to a bigger, more luxurious apartment located in 3410 Kingsbridge Avenue. While they lived in 3410 they had five more children – ALL BOYS – my mom's brothers – my uncles. My grandfather was a very successful, hardworking man; he was actually the highest ranking official in the City of New York without being a political appointee – his job title was 'Chief Inspector for the City of New York Department of Water Supply, Gas, and Electricity.' He got writers cramp after signing his name and title."

"Really?"

"No, not really, Cam. My grandmother, on the other hand, was a stay at home mom for most of her life. As you can imagine, she had to stay home to keep an eye on her SEVEN children. When the kids were older she went to work, but my grandfather wasn't too happy about it!"

"Why?"

"Well, years ago many husbands considered it to be a sign he was a poor provider if his wife worked. So, he felt his friends would think he didn't make enough money to take care of his family. But actually she didn't work because the family needed the money; she worked because she was an independent woman. She was a woman's libber, before being a woman's libber was cool. She was like Aunt Chris. My grandmother mainly performed clerical work from home for a local company, Stella Dora, while she was raising her young children, but when they got older she began working at Fuhrman's.

"Will we ever meet your grandparents?"

"Not until we go to heaven. Your great grandfather died in 1964 – the year I was born – and your great grandmother died in 1984. I'll show you pictures of them someday."

"What about your uncles?"

"Okay, I'll tell you a little bit about them, but I can't go into a lot of detail because, well, because I don't know a lot of details. I'm sure there are A LOT of stories about them, but I've never heard anything but good things. I think it's because my mother and father were afraid if they told me the bad stories, I might try to imitate them and get into trouble. Looking back on this strategy, it didn't work out so well. I can tell you a little bit about them, but it won't be too interesting because I don't know the fun stuff."

"That's okay."

"Alright, so let's talk about my mother's six brothers."

"Wow, Dad! I can't believe Grandma has six brothers?"

"That's right! Grandma Hand grew up in a typical Irish, Catholic family."

"What's a typical Irish, Catholic family, Dad?"

"Well, I don't know the official definition, but every Catholic family I knew had a lot of kids, mostly boys; they all went to Catholic school; they went to the bars on Friday night – got into a fight or two; they played sports on Saturday – got into a fight or two; they went to bars on Saturday night – got into a fight or two, and they went to church on Sunday to sleep it off. They went to confession every few months and asked to be resolved of their sins, 'Bless me father for I have sinned, it's been three months since I've been to confession. I drink too much; I swear too much; I fight too much; I chase too many woman – and worst of all I don't feel a bit of remorse.' 'Well my son, go say three Our Fathers and four Hail Mary's and keep the part of not feeling any remorse to yourself.'"

"Dad, are you saying your uncles were heavy drinkers, they fought and cursed a lot, and they chased woman?"

"I can't say for sure because my mother never told me any stories about them, but since they're Irish Catholic, I think I'm pretty safe in saying, YES!" My dad laughed at this – I guess he thought it was funny.

"Okay, where was I, oh yeah, I was telling you about my uncles. I don't think I ever mentioned this to you, but all my uncles were very athletic. When I was your age and I visited my grandmother; she had one room where she kept all her kid's trophies – there must have been several hundred track, basketball, baseball, and football trophies, ribbons, and medals.

My oldest uncle is my Uncle Larry. He's the typical oldest brother; he was the level headed and very responsible one. He attended PS 7, which is a Public School located on 232nd Street between Kingsbridge Avenue and Corlear Avenue. He went to PS 7 for his first few years of school before his Catholic education began; from fourth grade to eighth grade he attended St. John's. During high school he attended Fordham Prep, and he went to Fordham College, Oklahoma University, and Cornell during his college years.

When he graduated from college he got a job with Union Carbide, and he had a very successful career with this company. While he was still attending college, he married a girl named Christine Virtullo – my Aunt Christine. One of the finest Christian women I've ever known. She passed away several years ago – I miss her. They had three girls; Barbara, Denise, and Shannon.

The second oldest brother is my Uncle Billy; he also went to PS 7, then St. John, then Fordham Prep, and for one or two semesters he went to Fordham University because my grandfather encouraged him too."

"Dad, why did he encourage him to go to college?"

"Kelsie, my mother says my Uncle Billy was an excellent student, but for some reason he had no desire to go to college. Even though college was not as much of a requirement to get a good job back in those days, my grandfather still thought my uncle was making a mistake by not utilizing his natural intelligence to do great things. After going to a semester or two of college to satisfy his father, he decided to become an electrician, and he had a very successful career in the electrician trade. Later on in life he married a girl name Liz – she, like my Aunt Chris, was a wonderful woman who loved to travel. She was taken away way before her time too. They had three children; Sheila, Nancy, and Billy.

Then there is my Uncle Gene, his story is very interesting. He also went to PS 7 and St. John's, but for high school, instead of going to Fordham Prep, he went to Berrytown to become a Brother in the Catholic Church."

"A brother, what's a brother, Dad?"

"I'm not really sure, but I always thought they were like amateur priests or in baseball terms – they are minor leagues priests who haven't made it to the major leagues of priests. Clear as mud, Cam?"

"Clear as mud. Continue."

"Thanks, Cam. After about three years at Berrytown, my uncle Gene decided being a Brother or a Priest wasn't for him, and so he decided to switch high schools. His fourth year of high school, he went to Bishop Dubois in Manhattan. After high school he graduated from Manhattan College, which by the way is located in the Bronx."

"Dad, why do they call it Manhattan, if it's in the Bronx?"

"I don't know Cam. Why do they call it a driveway when you park on it? Why do they call it a parkway when you drive on it? Why do they call it a building when it's already built? It's one of those unsolved mysteries of life."

"I thought daddies know everything!"

"Well, there are a few things...very unimportant things...that daddies don't know...but we know everything that's important. Don't ever forget that!"

"Okay, if you say so."

"Okay, let's get back to my mother's brothers. Gene graduated from Manhattan College, and he originally planned on becoming a teacher, but one thing led to another, and he became an electrician like his brother Billy. Later on he married his first, a girl named Rose, a very interesting, independent woman. While they were married they had two boys; Billy and Michael. Rose was actually the sister of Christine – my Uncle Larry's wife."

"Who's next Dad?"

"Next is my Uncle Tommy. He went to PS 7, St. Johns, and then he went to Bishop Dubois for high school. He was an excellent athlete, and he had a basketball scholarship to college, but he blew out his knee playing football, and his scholarship was cancelled. His father knew basketball was his sport, and so he told Tommy not to play football because it might jeopardize his basketball scholarship; he was specifically told by his father – you can't play football. You see Cameron and Kelsie – you should always listen to your daddy – daddies always know best. After Tommy blew out his knee, he decided to follow the lead of his two older brothers, and he became an electrician. Later in his life he married a girl named Cathy, my Aunt Cathy, who has such a great, outgoing, personality which she passed onto her three children; Kelly, Christopher, and Tara."

The next brother is Kenny; yes, Kenny – just like your daddy. He's not as good looking as me, but he does have the same name."

"Oh nice, Dad, and you tell me to be humble and not to brag."

"Yeah, yeah, yeah – do as I say not as I do."

My dad continued, "Okay, Cam, back to Uncle Kenny. Uncle Kenny also went to PS 7, St. Johns, and Fordham Prep, but after high school he attended the Coast Guard Academy, Stoney Brook College, and he spent some time in the Army. I think he graduated from college with an accounting degree because he had a long career in the FBI, and I believe having a degree in accounting helped him to get in. When I was growing up he used to send me the FBI Most Wanted Posters – the Evil Aunt Chris was always in the top 10. He was also the uncle who taught me how to greet someone. He said, 'Look them straight in the eyes, put out your hand, and give them a firm handshake. He married a girl named Elaine; my Aunt Elaine, who like my Aunt Cathy has a great personality and is a lot of fun to be around at family get-togethers. They had three children; Karen, Kenny, and Kathleen. Elaine is actually the sister of Liz' – my Uncle Billy's wife."

"So, two brothers married two sisters twice in your mother's family?"

"Yes Kelsie – that's right. It's kind of unusual, but it worked for them.

See, I don't know a lot of interesting details about their lives. From what little my mother has told me they all lived squeaky clean lives – but I know that can't be true because I couldn't have gotten all my bad habits from my father – it's just not possible."

"You only named five brothers. I thought you said there were six. Did you miss one?"

"Oh yeah, there's one more. My Uncle Richie."

"Dad, how many Richie's are there in your family?"

"A lot! My Uncle Richie is the uncle I know best and who I'm closest to. I lived with him for a short time in my grandmother's house, and I worked for him for several years – which helped me to turn my life around. My Uncle Richie also went to PS 7, St. John's, and Fordham Prep – surprise, surprise. He also attended several years of college; I believe he attended Fordham College, but I know for sure he attended Lehman College because that's the college he was attending while we lived with him at my grandmother's house.

I can still remember him coming home from college at night. I specifically remember him coming home after a Critical Thinking class he took – at least that's what I think it was. His professor asked the class brain teasers to get them to think. There was one particularly interesting one I've always remembered – we were up for hours trying to figure out the answer. I don't think we ever figured it out but eventually my uncle told us the answer."

"What was it?"

"Let me think. Okay, it went something like this. There was a man driving to Albuquerque, and he came to a fork in the road. He didn't know which way to go and so he had to ask for directions. In the middle of the fork was a house. Inside the house were two brothers who were identical twins. One of the twins ALWAYS told the truth and the other twin ALWAYS lied. The man driving to Albuquerque could only ask one question to find out which way to go. What one question could he ask to figure out how to get to Albuquerque?"

"I don't know, Dad. What?"

"I'm not telling you – you have to figure it out. Trying to figure out the answer is what makes it fun. I'll tell you the answer later. Let me get back to my Uncle Richie. My Uncle Richie is a jack of all trades; he has been in the restaurant business for most of his adult life, but he also spent several years in the Corporate World. He married a girl named Marion, my Aunt Marion who is a fun and interesting woman. When they were married they had two children; Brian and Jean.

That's all my Uncles on my mother's side of the family. I know it wasn't all that interesting, but, wait, I do have a quick story about one of my uncles, but I can't tell you which one."

"Why not?"

"Well, if you ever write a book and you include this story it will create a family scandal."

"Really?"

"No, not really but I'll still leave out his name. Anyway, when this uncle was a teenager, his friends and him would walk places, like the George Washington Bridge, and for fun they'd stop off at every bar on the way for a drink. By the time they made it to their destination they could barely walk straight."

Kelsie asked, "Why'd they do that?"

My dad smiled and said, "Because they're Irish and they thought it was fun. So guys, that's all of my uncles on my mother's side of the family. I know I didn't have many stories about them, but you can blame it on your grandmother."

I asked, "Dad, can you tell us about your cousins too?"

"What? It would take me hours to tell you all about them. You know I have about 30 cousins; my family is singularly responsible for world overpopulation – Al Gore hates my family."

"Really?"

"No, not really. I'll tell you about my cousins some other time."

"Okay but aren't you going to tell us about your father's side of the family?"

Team Hand

"Sure. Let me see. Okay, my father was also born into an Irish, Catholic family just like my mother. He might have some German in him too. My dad used to tell me we were Irish, German but based on what I've learned over the past few years, I don't think we have any German blood – which makes sense – I've never had an uncontrollable urge to invade a country. Plus when I took a semester of German in college, I only passed with a C – so I'm pretty sure I'm not German at all."

"You got a C in college?! You told us you were a straight A student?! Huh? What happened to 'Hand's always get A's'?"

"Did I say C? Opps, sorry, I meant to say a low A! Let's move on. So I was about to tell you about my father's side of the family."

"Dad, you're not going to get away with it that easy. We'll talk about this later."

"Alright, Kels. We'll get back to that subject later. Now where was I? Oh yeah, I was about to tell you about my father's side of the family. We called my Grandpa Hand – Pa – when I was growing up; his real name was Francis Howard Hand. He was the son of John Raymond Hand and Ida Mae Schnebbe or maybe it was Billingsly – I'm really not sure. I'm not sure when his parents immigrated to the United States – I only know they lived in Manhattan – in Hell's Kitchen."

"Oooooo Mommy…Daddy just said the H word!"

"Cam, it's okay to say hell as long as you don't say it in anger."

"Oh really – I didn't know that? This is one hell of a story Dad. When the hell are you going to tell us the rest of it? Hell you've been…"

"Cam, wait a second! I think you're missing my point. It's best for you to only use the word hell when you're referring to the place the devil lives or stories about my grandparents neighborhood – okay?"

"That's a hell of a way to confuse me…"

"Cam! Alright, let me get back to Hell's Kitchen. You know I don't really know much about it either – I just always thought it sounded cool. Recently I looked it up on Wikipedia – and it said Hell's Kitchen was a neighborhood in Manhattan between 34th and 59th Street, which goes from 8th Avenue to the Hudson River. A lot of criminals lived there – it was known as the center of Irish-American organized crime. That's about all I know about it.

So that's where Pa grew up. He was one of eleven or twelve children; I don't know much about his childhood but apparently he was an excellent athlete. As a teenager he played minor league baseball for one of the New York Yankee farm teams. My dad has a picture of him wearing a Yankee uniform when he played for a team in Chattanooga, Tennessee. Maybe that's why I was good at baseball and why you were swinging a bat by the time you learned to walk. It must be in our blood.

Since Pa didn't make a career of professional baseball, he focused his attention on getting a good paying job, getting married, and starting a family. 1929 was an important year in the life of this country, but it was also a busy year for Pa; he became a stock broker on Wall Street in March and married the love of his life, Margaret Harford, in June. Do you know what else happened in 1929?"

"No, what?"

"1929 was the year the stock market crashed which was the beginning of the Great Depression."

"Oh, really. Uh Dad, what's the stock market crash and what's the Great Depression?"

"Cam, it's too complicated to go into a lot of details, but it was a time when a lot of people in this country lost their jobs."

"Why did so many people lose their jobs?"

"Well, there are many reasons for it, but the main reason for it was because the government tried to help the economy. As you get older you'll realize the more the government tries to help – the worse things get for all the regular people."

"Oh, really? Can you talk about Grandpa again?"

"Oh, sorry, okay, back to the story. Unfortunately for the country, Pa came down with a terrible case of the flu on October 29, 1929. He called work and told them he was too sick to make it to work. This was one of the worst days in the history of the United States known as Black Tuesday – the Dow Jones Industrial Average lost 38 points which was more than a 12% drop."

"Dad, who is Down Jones?"

"Kels, it's not a person it's kind of a measure of how well the economy is doing. It's pretty complicated to explain, and so let's just leave it at that. The point is – Pa missed one day of work at the stock market – the stock market crashes – a coincidence – I think not! Most historians and economists agree Pa was the only man in America who had the knowledge and technical expertise to prevent this disaster, and if he made it to work that day the stock market crash and the subsequent Great Depression could have been averted."

"Is that true, Dad?"

"Would your daddy ever lie to you?"

"What about you're grandmother? Is she the one you call Nanny? Didn't she take care of me while you were golfing once?"

"Yes, Kelsie. You met Nanny at the Hand Family Open. Nanny's real name was Margaret Jane Hartford. Her father's name was Thomas Hartford, and he emigrated from Dublin, Ireland in August 1894 along with his half sister, Mammie Donor. When he arrived in America he worked in the slaughter houses in downtown New York. He fell in love with a woman named Anna Scully, and they were married just after the turn of the century. Thomas and Anna Hartford had six children; Margaret born in 1907, Mary born in 1909, Anne born in 1911, Thomas born in 1913, James born in 1921, and Robert born in 1929. I only knew one of my Nanny's relatives; her brother Robert who I called Uncle Bob. He was actually my father's uncle, but since he was so close in age to my father they were like brothers or cousins – and so to my family he was called Uncle Bob.

I don't know the story of how Nanny and Pa met, but I do know they were married in 1929. They lived the first few years of their married life in a small apartment near Bainbridge Avenue in the Bronx. They then moved to Review Place in Kingsbridge between 238th and 239th Street. It was while they lived on Review Place they had their three children; Ray, Richie – my dad, and Dorothy.

My dad's older brother Ray was born in 1931 and, like my Uncle Larry, is a typical older brother – level headed and responsible. He attended Visitation Grade School from kindergarten through eighth grade. During high school he attended DeWitt Clinton for his first two years of high school and Xavier High School for his final two years. After high school he joined the Air Force where he met his future wife Barbara, my Aunt Barbara, a really nice, interesting woman from Minnesota. They have five children; Ray Jr., Kevin, Karen, Kelly, and Gerry.

My dad's younger sister Dorothy – we call her Aunt Dot – was born in 1940. She also attended Visitation like her two brothers for grade school. She attended a Catholic High School, Tolentine, and after high school she attended Grace Secretarial School. During her early adult life she married Jack Benentendi, and they had three children; Toni, their only daughter, Jack, and Dean.

"Dad, I'm glad you told us about your aunts and uncles but do you have any funny stories about them? Do you have any stories about them with poo, boogers or flying beds?"

"No Cam, my aunts, uncles, and cousins are perfect! My family was the only family with problems. They all lived in New Jersey, the New York Suburbs, Massachusetts, or Connecticut – they didn't have any problems – none at all! When Chris and I were growing up, we threw knives at each other; we hit each other with baseball bats; we cut each other's hair while the other was sleeping – it wasn't pretty. My cousins, on the other hand, were perfect. They never fought with each other; they got straight A's in school; they were all presidents of the student council; they were great athletes; they had perfect hair, shiny teeth – it was like being related to the Brady Bunch!"

"Is that true, Dad?"

"Well it seemed that way when I was growing up, but it's probably not 100% true. I'm sure they had problems like every family does, but I never heard about their problems, and so when I was growing up I thought they were perfect."

"Did you spend a lot of time with them when you were growing up?"

"I wouldn't say we spent a lot of time with them, but we did get together on holidays and other special occasions."

"Can you tell us about them?"

Family Ties...

"Of course. Let me think about it a little first."

My dad paused for a moment and said, "Okay. Well, as you already know there are two sides of my family; the Doyle's and the Hand's. Every year between Christmas and New Years we had a family get-together with the Doyle side of the family. When I young we used to get together with the Doyle's over at my mother's Uncle Gene and Aunt Eddy's apartment in Marble Hill. My Uncle Gene and Aunt Eddy were actually my mother's aunt and uncle. By the way, I take back what I said about the snobs who lived in Marble Hill – I forgot they lived there. We went there for the Doyle get-togethers until the family got so large we needed a bigger place to meet. Eventually, we moved from their apartment to my Uncle Larry and Aunt Chris' house in New Jersey and later to their house in Connecticut.

I loved the get together at my Aunt Chris and Uncle Larry's house. They had a large beautiful house, and they were great hosts. Early on my aunt and uncle provided the main course and everyone else brought appetizers, side dishes and desserts. When we arrived at their house, we put our food down in the kitchen or the dining room. Then the men went into the family room to watch football games, eat appetizers, and drink beer. The women went into the kitchen or living room and stood around talking and drinking coffee. After the football games were over we ate dinner, and afterward we had a gift exchange for all the kids. Later on in life my aunt and uncle had the get-togethers catered and we just sat back, watched TV, argued, and pigged out.

The kids always had a couple of gifts to open; one from the aunt and uncle who drew their name and one from my grandmother. My grandmother always bought us nice clothes from Fuhrman's, where she worked. After the football games, dinner, and the gift exchange the adults spent time together in the living room arguing about sports and politics. I never really understood what they were arguing about when the subject was politics, but it was interesting.

Even though they argued I never noticed anybody getting angry. It seemed like they enjoyed arguing, because in between the yelling there were a lot of smiling and laughing.

When I was young we spent most Thanksgivings with my father's side of the family. Usually, we had Thanksgiving over at my Nanny and Aunt Dot's house. Most years the whole family showed up; my family, my Aunt Dot's family, and my Uncle Ray and Aunt Barbara's family. Nanny and Aunt Dot lived in Ridgefield Park, New Jersey with my cousins Tony, Jackie, and Dean. The house was a two family house; the upstairs is where my Nanny lived while Aunt Dot and my cousins lived downstairs.

I loved visiting the Benintendi's…"

"Who were the Benintendi's?"

"Oh, I guess I didn't, wait, I think I mentioned my Aunt was married to Jack Benentendi and so that was my cousins' last name. I loved going over to their house because Jackie was my age, and Dean was just a year younger. When we got to their house we played basketball, or we'd throw around a baseball or football. They loved sports just like me; they were diehard Yankee, Giant, Knick, and Ranger fans. Another thing was when we weren't playing sports they had a million toys and games to play like 'Rock'em Sock'em Robots', 'Stretch Armstrong', 'Toss-a-Cross', 'Concentration', and 'Operation'.

When we lived in Suffern it seemed like we spent a lot of Sundays at 'Nanny's and Aunt Dot's' house visiting. After a busy day of playing with my cousins, I remember lying down in front of the TV at night watching Mutual of Omaha's Wild Kingdom with Marlon Perkins and The Wonderful World of Disney. When Disney ended and the 'Sunday Mystery Movie' came on I knew it was almost time to go. I didn't mind leaving when 'Columbo' or 'McCloud' was on but when 'McMillan and Wife' was on I wanted to watch the whole show because I thought Susan St. James was a babe."

"You're getting weird again Dad."

"Sorry, Kelsie, but when 'McMillan and Wife' was on I always asked my mom, 'Can't we wait to leave after 'McMillan and Wife' is over – Susan St. James is a babe.' The response was usually, 'No, you have school tomorrow, and you have to get up early.' But typically my parents took an hour to say goodbye, and so I was normally able to catch most of it.

But let me get back to Thanksgiving. I had the best times over at Nanny's and Aunt Dot's on Thanksgiving, but on the other hand, preparing our family to go to their house was always an adventure – especially for my mother."

"Why?"

"You try getting six procrastinators ready at 12:00 p.m. for a 1:30 get-together while living in an apartment with one small bathroom. Grandma had all the pressure on her to get everything done. She had to get the food ready; she also had to get Gena, Philip, and my dad ready."

"She had to get your dad ready too?"

"No, but she had to yell at him, 'For Pete's sake Rich would you get out of your boxer shorts and get ready!' She had to yell at Chris, 'Christine, what the blazes are you doing? Why aren't you ready yet?' She had to yell at me, 'Jesus, Mary, and Joseph, Kenny, you need to get ready right away!' And she had to yell at Tricia, 'Oh Christmas, Patricia, why aren't you ready yet?'"

"What about your brother Richie?"

"He was the responsible one – he got ready before all of us."

He got back to his story, "Of course after everyone was ready and got into the car we had to fit in a visit to the local bookie for a bet on the two Thanksgiving football games. Oh yeah, and there were the Swedish meatballs which needed to be cooked, there was the beer and wine which needed to be purchased, there was gas which needed to be pumped into the car, and of course there was the drive to Ridgefield Park.

Once we were on the road, my dad drove South on Broadway to Dykman Street where he entered the West Side Drive to get to the George Washington Bridge. He always went across the lower level and once he went across the bridge he drove on Route 46 which crossed the Pasaic River on our way to Ridgefield Park.

It's amazing how my family was able to do all these things in an hour and a half and how we were never ever late for a family get-together! Even more amazing was the fact we were able to accomplish all of this without any yelling, screaming, or arguing!"

"Really, Dad?"

My dad smiled and said, "No, not really! Getting ready for a family get-together was like a Chinese fire drill (whatever that means) and we were always late. It drove me crazy to be late, and that's one of the reasons we're always on time when we visit our family now."

"We're always late too, Dad."

"No, we're not."

"Yes, we are. We're always late for church every Sunday."

"Are you crazy Kelsie? Two or three minutes late doesn't count. My family was 2 or 3 hours late to family get-togethers. One year we made it to Thanksgiving when my Aunt Dot was serving dessert.

Okay, where was I before I was rudely interrupted by my little girl? Oh yeah. When we finally made it to Nanny's and Aunt Dot's, we walked into the house put down the drinks and the food we brought and said hello to everyone. This meant kisses and hugs for everyone – which I would have preferred to avoid. Similar to get-togethers with the Doyle's, the men plopped themselves down in front of the TV on the main floor while the woman worked in the kitchen preparing the turkey, stuffing, mashed potatoes, sweet potatoes, corn, carrots, peas, cranberry sauce, and everything else you can think of.

Dinner was usually served between the first and second games – if it was served before the end of the first game the 'blessing' was frequently interrupted, 'Thank you Lord for...GO, GO, GO...all the food...THAT WASN'T HOLDING, WHAT A LOUSY CALL...and for our family...STOP HIM, BREAK HIS LEGS...and this time we have together...YES! TOUCHDOWN...Amen..."

After we ate, the men went back to their positions; the couch in front of the TV, but this time we let out our pants and took a short nap. After the naps and games were over, the adult conversations began which included more talk about sports and politics. The conversations between the more liberal side of the family and the more conservative side were sometimes combative but always interesting. After arguing we normally broke out a game like Trivial Pursuit which allowed everyone to show off their cerebral alacrity."

"What's cerebral alacrity, Dad?"

"I mean it gave everyone a chance to show off how smart they were. I didn't have much cerebral alacrity, and so I couldn't show off too much. Although at that time in my life, I was a walking sports statistician – I could tell you anyone's batting average, ERA, rushing yards, goals, points per game – I could tell you any statistic you ever wanted to know. So if a question came up about sports, I could answer it with the best of them. When I was older, as you know, we started a new tradition on the Hand side of the family – The Hand Family Open."

"Yeah, when did that start?"

"I think it started about twenty years ago and as you know it's when we get together in Massachusetts with all my aunts, uncles, and cousins on the Hand side of the family for a weekend of BBQ, games, and golf. It's a great time of fun, conversation, and golf.

We are really blessed to have the family we have. We not only have us three and mommy but also the rest of our family, my aunts, uncles, and cousins. There are so many of them and I honestly mean it when I say, they are all incredibly nice people. I don't know how else to say it – they are all good people, and I'm proud to have all of you and them as part of our family."

"Okay, Dad, you told us about New York and your family – what about your friends? Tell us about them."

"You know I didn't have any friends when I was growing up. Nobody liked me."

"Come on Dad – we know you had to have at least one friend."

"I'll tell you about my friends later. Let me tell you about my life from the beginning."

SECTION III
Genesis

♪ When I was young
It seemed that life was so wonderful ♪
♪ Oh it was beautiful, magical
And all the birds in the trees ♪
♪ Well they'd be singing so happily
Joyfully, playfully, watching me…♪ [6]

Uncle Richie (left), Grandpa Hand (back)
Evil Aunt Chris (In Grandpa's arm),
Aunt Gena (right), My Dad (front)
Missing: Uncle Philip, and Aunt Tricia

In the Beginning

Alright, I'm going to start from the beginning – from the time I was born. First of all, my birthday was a long, long time ago on October 26, 1964. I was born in St. Jewish Memorial Hospital, which was located in Manhattan on the corner of Broadway and 196th Street. St. Jewish Memorial Hospital was named in honor of the Jewish soldiers who died in World War I. The hospital was a ten story red brick building which had about 175 beds and was state of the art for its time."

"Wait, what happened to descending down from heaven to the fire escape? And one more thing – how can a hospital be named St. Jewish Memorial?"

My dad looked confused for a second and said, "You're right, Kels. It's not St. Jewish Memorial – it's just plain Jewish Memorial. I said this once before when I was a kid and I had to tell my baseball coach where I was born. But anyway, where was I? Oh yeah. Jewish Memorial closed down in 1983 because it went bankrupt.

After I was born I was brought home to 183 West 238th Street; a 5 story apartment building in the Bronx which overlooked the Major Deegan Expressway. I moved out of the intensive care unit in Jewish Memorial into a three room, one bedroom apartment with my parents..."

Kelsie said, "Oh, my gosh! You were in intensive care? Why? What happened?"

"Ohhhhh – sure now you care about your daddy! Finally! It's about time someone in this family cared about me! But seriously, to answer your question, yup, I was born with a heart murmur – it was touch and go there for a while. The doctor gave me two weeks to live, but I made it through. He said I was a throw back to a time when babies were babies – tough as nails!"

"Really, Dad?"

"Well, the part about me having a heart murmur and being in intensive care is true – the rest of it is probably true too but I can neither confirm nor deny it. Okay, where was I? Yeah, I was about to tell you about moving into a one bedroom apartment with my parents, my brother Richie and two sisters Gena and Chris. I only lived there for one year because when my brother Philip was born we had seven people living in a one bedroom apartment which probably broke several New York City fire codes. Because of this my parents decided to move the family to greener pastures.

We moved from 238th Street to a house off of Route 9W in Haverstraw, NY. Haverstraw is located about 20 miles north of the city up the New York Thruway across the Tappan Zee Bridge. It was a comfortable house on a secluded mountain side with 3 bedrooms, a large living room, and kitchen. The rent was only $100 per month which was a bargain even in 1965. At the time we only had one car and so when my father went to work my mother was stuck in a house with 5 children. After several months of being cooped up in a house with 5 children for 24 hours a day my mother told my father, 'Rich, we need to move closer to civilization – my evil daughter and the other kids are driving me crazy!' A short time later Grandpa found a house for us in Suffern, NY. Suffern was a perfect place to raise children, and the best part about it was there were already family and friends living there.

♪ When I was young it seemed that life was so wonderful
A miracle, oh it was beautiful, magical ♪
♪ And all the birds in the trees, well they'd be singing so happily
Joyfully, playfully watching me ♪ [6]

Suffern is a village located near the base of the Ramapo Mountain Range in the southeastern edge of New York State. When I grew up there it was a fairy tale town like Mayberry on the Andy Griffith Show. It's about 40 minutes north of New York City up the New York Thruway. To get there from the New York Thruway you take exit 14B, near Suffern Park, and make a right on Route 59. You know you're in Suffern when Route 59 turns into Lafayette Avenue and you see Good Samaritan Hospital on the left and the Tagaste Monastery on the right. Good Samaritan Hospital is where your Aunt Tricia was born and the Monastery is the first place I played baseball. I whooped those Monks at baseball – they couldn't run in those long robes."

"Really, Dad?"

"No, just kidding. Okay, a short distance further down the road is an office building where Dr. Frankaviller's office was; this is where I received a tetanus shot after I stepped on a rusty nail. I screamed bloody murder when he shoved that huge needle in my left buttock!

If you make a left turn after his building you can get to my grade school, Cypress Road. A little further down Lafayette Avenue, on the left, is the Salvation Army. There was a manmade lake there; this is where my brother Richie played hockey and where I ice skated during the winter. As you passed by the Salvation Army you go down a steep hill. At the bottom of this hill is a street named Riverside Drive – the street where I lived. It's called Riverside Drive because a river, I think it's the Mahwah River, flows parallel to the road, behind the houses. I lived about halfway down the street in 24 Riverside Drive.

A short distance past Riverside Drive on the right is Avon's Research and Development facility where Rocco Laverchio's mother worked. Across the road, near Avon, are Sacred Heart Catholic Church and school where Richie went to grade school.

Just past Sacred Heart is Washington Avenue which is also where town square is. Near the center of town square is a very impressive statue of some military hero from the Korean War; I think there's also a cannon there. If you make a right on Washington Avenue the fire house is on the right and if you continue past it, you eventually run into the Suffern Pool. If, instead, you made a left on Washington Avenue you pass by Washington Avenue Middle School, the library, city hall, the police station, Harry Hunt's house, and if you continued for a half mile past Harry's house you enter Mahwah, New Jersey.

Going straight ahead on Lafayette Avenue you enter the shopping area; kind of Suffern's main street. This is where the Lafayette movie theater, Woolworths, the Bright Spot, a bank, a hardware store, and dozens of other stores are or were. Lafayette Avenue ended at the train tracks and just over the train tracks are Cucolo field where my brother Richie played Little League baseball.

I did a little bit of research, and I learned Suffern was founded in 1796 and was named after John Suffern; a judge who was originally from Ireland. I guess Suffern was important during the Revolutionary War even though it wasn't Suffern at the time; it was a place where George Washington and his men camped during the Revolutionary War. I don't know if this really makes it important but Wikipedia mentioned it."

"Hmmm. Interesting, Dad."

"Yes, it is, Cam. This is where I lived from 1967 until 1973. My mother said we actually moved there on July 4th 1967. Like I mentioned before, we lived in 24 Riverside Drive; a duplex located between Bridge Street and Route 59. Our house wasn't big, but it was nice. We had a living room, dining room, and kitchen on the main floor, three bedrooms and a bathroom upstairs; there was a dark, dirty basement and an eerie, mysterious attic where the Boogeyman lived!"

"What's the Boogeyman, Dad?"

"The Boogeyman is a creature who's half man, half vicious animal who stalks little boys like you, Cameron. He lived in the attic, and every night he walked down my creaky attic steps and snuck into my room after the lights were turned off. Late at night while I was hiding underneath my covers, I could hear his heavy breathing, and I felt his hairy body touch me as he came into my room and hid under my bed..."

Kelsie interrupted my dad and said, "Did you ever think it might have been Uncle Philip or Uncle Richie breathing and maybe the hair you felt came from your pink fuzzy slippers?"

My dad ignored Kelsie and continued, "The Boogieman waited all night for me to step out of bed so he could drag me under the bed, rip off my skin, gouge out my heart, and eat me piece by piece! My brother warned me every night – 'Kenny, don't let your arms or legs hang over the bed because if you do – THE BOOGIEMAN WILL GET YOU!"

"Nice Dad."

"Nice? It wasn't nice! It was horrible! It was horrible living in a house with the Boogieman!"

"Can't be much worse than living in our house with Kelsie."

"Nice, Cam. So what was I about to tell you? Oh, yeah, I was telling you about my house. Our house had a small front yard without any grass. We planted grass seed millions of times, but it never grew. I'm not sure why, but come to think of it, some of the fattest birds in the neighborhood lived near our house. There were three or four rotten steps leading up to the front porch. Richie, Chris, and I sometimes slept on the front porch on hot summer nights. The only time Chris and I were allowed to leave the porch was to buy an ice cream cone from the Good Humor man. The back yard was also small but behind our yard were the woods. This is where Richie and his friends built their forts and where we played 'Hide and Seek'.

Our house was nice, but it was different; it had a strange way of keeping us warm. It had a large metal grating on the floor between the living room and dining room. Below the grating was the heater which shot out hot flames when it was cold outside. It was like having a large BBQ grill built into our living room and dining room floor. On cold days my brothers, sisters, and I stood around the metal grating to warm our bodies. We had to be very careful.

If we accidentally stepped on the grating, our feet or shoes would have looked like waffles because the metal was so hot it could melt rubber. The house didn't have any metal ductwork to bring the heat from the lower floor to the rooms upstairs; instead, it relied on the hot air rising to heat the upper floors. Every room upstairs had a small metal grating in the floor where the hot air from downstairs was supposed to heat the room. This was a great theory but it didn't work well in practice – the rooms upstairs were freezing during the winter time. They didn't help heat our bedrooms, but they were great to listen to our parent's conversations downstairs late at night."

"Did you have air conditioning?"

"Cam, I didn't have most of the things you have. We didn't have air conditioning, cell phones weren't invented yet, and neither were cordless phones. We only had one telephone which was located in the kitchen and we couldn't send text messages. If we were outside the only way to call someone was from a pay phone on one of the street corners. Computers didn't exist, and Al Gore hadn't invented the Internet yet..."

"Al Gore invented the internet?"

"He thinks he did, but I'm getting off message here. Keep in mind since we didn't have the internet it means we didn't have e-mail, Facebook, Google, Wikipedia..."

"No way Dad. Without all this – what did you do?"

"We called people on the phone, or we wrote letters. When we had to look something up we went to the library, or we asked our parents.

We didn't have iPods, CD's, or DVD's. We listened to music on the radio or we bought 45's from the local record store..."

I stopped him again, "What are 45's?"

"It's a little piece of plastic, a little bigger than a CD, which played music when it was placed on a record player. The record player spun the record around 45 times per minutes, hence the name 45's, and a needle was placed on the record which made the music play.

Another thing that was different is we only had a handful of TV stations – we didn't have the hundreds of stations you guys have now; we only had ABC, NBC, CBS, PBS, and a couple local stations. Oh wait, another thing that was different were TV's. We didn't have big screen or color TV's, and we didn't have U-Verse – if we missed a show, we have to wait for it to go into reruns or until next year.

Every year I couldn't wait to watch Rudolf the Red Nosed Reindeer, Frosty, The Little Drummer Boy, The March of the Wooden Soldiers, A Charlie Brown Christmas, The Grinch Who Stole Christmas, and many other shows. It was a big deal the night they were on TV because if we missed it – we missed it until next year!

The TV we had was a little 12 inch TV; the screen was about the same size as our laptop screen. The reception was never perfectly clear because we didn't have cable. Some families had an antenna on top of their roof, others had rabbit ears; my family usually used a wire hanger to get a clear picture. Sometimes the only way to get a clear picture was for someone to touch the TV with their hand. I can remember many nights standing next to the TV so everyone could watch a clear picture, 'Mommy, I'm tired of standing next to the TV – can you tell Chris it's her turn?' Don't ask me why it worked, but it did.

We didn't have remote controls; we changed the channels the old fashioned way – with pliers..."

"Why did you change the channels with pliers?"

"TV's had knobs on them to change the channel. I should say they had knobs when they were new, but they always broke off. When my brothers, sisters, and I changed channels with the knob, we twisted our wrist and turned as quickly as possible – it sounded like a machine gun! This machine gun technique was an everyday experience, so the knobs never lasted long. After the knob broke off we went to the tool box and pulled out the pliers or vice grips. You and Kelsie don't know how good you have it. The biggest problem you have with the TV is when you can't find the remote because it fell between the couch cushions.

Okay, what else do I need to tell you? Oh, yeah. Sacred Heart was the local Catholic School which went from Kindergarten through 8th grade. This is where Richie went to grade school while we lived there. Chris and I went to Cypress Road Public School from 1st through 4th grade. Cypress Road was about 1 mile away. To get there we took the school bus which went down Riverside Drive, took a left on Boulevard Avenue, and then a right up Hillside Avenue until it reached Cypress Road school about a half mile up the hill. Washington Avenue School was the public school for 5th through 8th grade; the Evil Aunt Chris went here for a month or two before we moved from Suffern."

"Dad! She's not evil!"

"So you say Kelsie. So you say. Okay, where was I? Oh yeah. The high school in the area was Suffern High School which was located across the New York Thruway. My brother Richie went there for a month or two before we moved to the Bronx.

Gena and Philip went to a special school which was associated with the BOCES Special Education Division. BOCES stands for, I think it stood for, Board of Cooperative Educations Services. Gena and Philip also went to Camp Venture during the summers and Club Venture on Saturdays the rest of the year. Camp and Club Venture were about 30 minutes away north on the Palisades Parkway.

Okay, what else. Alright, let me tell you about our neighbors. In my neighborhood there were the Triggers who lived on the other side of our duplex, across the street were the Van Tassle's and Greeley's, down the street there were the Gianelli's, Schobble's, Hegmans, and several other families I can't remember. Further down the road were the Laverchio's and the Piggie's."

"Piggie's? Dad, no way!"

"Yes, way. I know it's a strange name but so is Hand. Oh by the way, like I told you before, when we lived in Suffern Aunt Tricia was just born and so she never attended school while we were there. She only sat in her crib and cried when I blew in her face."

"That's real grown up, Dad?"

My dad turned to Kelsie and blew air in her face and said, "I still haven't grown up yet, Kels. So where was I? Okay, like I said, our house was on a small piece of land, but there was a lot of land all around it. Or at least it seemed like it when I was a little boy. There were 'woods' behind the house, an empty lot on the side of the house, and a river behind the houses across the street.

During the summer, on weekends, and after 3:00 p.m. on school days the streets, backyards, woods, and rivers were filled with kids doing kid things. Suffern was the type of place where parents felt comfortable letting their young children play outside from morning until 'supper- time' without having to worry. When my mom wanted us kids to come home, all she had to do was stand on the front porch and call us. A few seconds later we appeared with our dirty hands and faces with sweat dripping down our faces. It was a perfect place to grow up, and I still visit Suffern every time I go to New York."

"What did you do to have so much fun?"

"Oh, I don't know – it was just a lot of fun. My friends, Rocco and..."

"I heard you say that name earlier. You didn't really know someone named Rocco. No, way!"

"Yes, I did little girl. My friend was, I should say is because I'm sure he's not dead, his name is – Rocco Laverchio."

Kelsie shook her head and said, "Don't believe it, Cam – nobody would name their kid Rocco Laverchio."

"I know it's a different name but it's true – look it up. Rocco had a sister named Chicky – Chicky Laverchio. It kind of makes Kelsie Lyn Gardner Collins Hand sound boring doesn't it?

"Yeah – kind of."

"Like I was starting to say, Rocco, Johnny Greely, Joe Gianelli, Bobby Trigger, and a bunch of other kids whose names I can't remember now used to play Army, Tag, Red Light/Green Light, and other games. In the fall we rode go-carts down Bridge Street hill. During the winter we went sleigh riding down the phone company hill. The summer was when we went swimming at the Suffern Pool, rode our choppers around town, caught lightning bugs at night, and caught crayfish on the banks of the Mahwah River.

Do you want to hear a quick story about my brother riding his chopper?"

I said, "Sure," and Kelsie nodded her head.

Easy Rider – Pull Down Your Pants

"Well, there was this one evening when my mom and dad went out to dinner with friends, and they left my brother Richie and me over at my Aunt Joan's house. I can't remember where Gena, Chris, Philip, and Tricia were – maybe they were locked in a closet somewhere..."

"Dad!"

"Take it easy Kels – I'm just kidding. Since Richie was 12 years old, my Aunt Joan let him and my cousin, Robert, ride their bicycles for a while after dinner. At the time Suffern was putting in a new sewer system and so there were lots of large, concrete sewer pipes lying along the streets and on the sidewalks.

Richie and Robert had to be careful not to accidentally ride their bicycles into them; but you know what happened?"

"They rode into them?"

"That's right, Cam. It was kind of dark out and Richie was riding his bike too fast. He accidentally ran into one of the pipes, his bike came crashing to a halt, he flew over his handlebars; and his hands, legs, and head slammed into the concrete pipe. The bike was mangled and my brother was hurt badly, but luckily it happened close to my Aunt Joan's house. Robert picked him up and carried Richie up to the front door. When they arrived at the door, Robert was screaming to his mother, 'Mom, help! Help! Help! Richie's hurt! He's bleeding, and he's hurt! Help!'

My Aunt ran out of the kitchen to the front door and helped Richie in the house. As soon as they walked in I knew there must have been a bad accident because Uncle Richie's pants were soaked with blood down the inside of his left leg. My Aunt Joan was calm as she helped him. She said, 'Richie, what happened?' My brother was crying as he said, 'I was riding my bike, and I hit something hard. I flew in the air and I came down on something hard and sharp – it hurts really bad!' She asked him where it hurt, and he said, 'Right here?' pointing at the inside of his leg, near his zipper. I was sitting there watching with my eyes scrunched and my heart pounding. I was worried about my brother. My Aunt Joan said very calmly, 'You're going to be alright Richie. Don't worry. I need you to pull off your pants so I can see what's bleeding.'

I couldn't believe my ears! I thought to myself, 'Did my Aunt say what I thought she said? Did she say, 'I need you to pull down your pants?' Pull down his pant? Pull down his pants? She can't do that! Pull down your pants in front of a woman – never! If he does that she'll see his underwear! I don't care how badly I'm hurt – I would never pull my pants down – especially in front of my Aunt or any girl.'"

Kelsie said, "Dad, he was hurt. She had to see what was wrong with him."

"You're right, Kels. All I'm saying is that when I was 7 years old the last thing I would do is let a girl see me in my underwear! How about you, Cam? Would you pull your pants down in front of a girl?"

"No way, Dad!"

"See, Kelsie. Cam knows. Well when Richie pulled down his pants there was blood flowing down his leg. He either ripped his skin apart by doing a split or maybe he landed on something sharp. I'm not sure how it happened but my Aunt took him to Good Samaritan Hospital, which was just down the road. After he got to the emergency room one of the doctors gave him about 10 stitches to sew him up, and then he was sent home. But I can still remember thinking 'This better not happen to me, because I would never pull down my pants in front of anyone – I'd rather bleed to death!'"

"Cute, Dad. What else did you do in Suffern?"

"I became an award winning artist."

"Really?"

"Yes, really! When I was lived in Suffern I watched *The Flintstones* and one day I picked up a pencil and a piece of paper and I drew a picture of Fred Flintstone. I got good at drawing him and soon I realized I had a talent for drawing. So I started drawing all the other characters on *The Flintstones* along with anything else that interested me – like naked women – but that's a whole other story."

"Dad!!"

"Okay, scratch the naked stuff. My mother noticed my pictures and she told me several times, 'Kenny, you're a very good artist.' So, when my father brought the newspaper home one day, my mother noticed an advertisement for a drawing contest, and she said I should submit a picture. It was near Christmas time, and the ad said to draw a Christmas picture and submit it to the newspaper. I decided to draw a picture of Fred Flintstone and Pebbles along side a Christmas tree with a couple of presents underneath it. A few weeks later my dad came home and handed me the newspaper. He told me to flip to page 25 and right there in black and white was my picture with the words, 'Kenny Hand is the 8 year old winner of the…'"

"What did you win?"

My dad had a smirk on his face when he said, "It was either $10,000, a trip to Hawaii, or maybe it was $1 – I'm not sure.

But wait, I have a story I think you'll like. It's the story about my first day of school. This is a story about me becoming a wild, untamed animal. This is when your dad became a rebel without a cause!"

The Great Escape...

Kelsie looked at my dad and said, "You were a 'rebel without a cause'; oh boy, this one I have to hear."

My dad squinted his eyes at Kelsie and said, "It happened on the first day of kindergarten..."

Kelsie sat up in her chair and laughed, "Kindergarten, Dad! Kindergarten! You became a rebel without a cause while you were in kindergarten! That's hilarious. How can a person become wild and untamed in kindergarten? I guess I should listen to this story because I'm interested to find out how a five year old becomes a 'rebel without a cause.'"

My dad smiled and said, "Well, missy, pay attention and you'll find out. After my story is over, you tell me if I became untamed in kindergarten. Now, will you let me finish the story?"

"Yes, go ahead Mr. Rebel."

"Alright, where was I? Oh Yeah. Wait; let me backup a little bit to the time before I attended kindergarten. When I was four or five years old I was so nice and innocent; I'd go along to get along. My mother said I was an independent, self sufficient child – and just as sweet as could be – until the day I CHANGED! I have to be honest, as a pre-school young man I was naïve; I saw the world through rose colored glasses. I thought life consisted of cereal, Sesame Street, cartoons, soap operas, and peanut butter and jelly sandwiches. My privileged, patrician upbringing insulated me from the cold hard reality of the world, but as every four or five year old knows, this pampered life style has to come to an end sometime. For me I knew it was about to come to a crashing halt when my mother said the big FOUR LETTER word to me – SCHOOL!"

"Dad, 'school' has six letters."

"Well, 'Miss I Like to Interrupt My Daddy', I couldn't spell at the time and school sure sounded like a four letter word to me! Where was I? Oh, Yeah. Although my mother tried to convince me school was a great opportunity for me and I would love it – I was sure I didn't want my life of leisure to come to an end.

The night before the dreaded day, my mom put my clothes out on the foot of my bed: a yellow turtle neck, green pants, fruit of the looms, tube socks, and hush puppies. All my clothes, except for the tube socks, were brand new. The next day when I woke up for school I put on my new, stiff, itchy, clothes; it felt like millions of little ants were crawling all over my body! After I got dressed I went downstairs to eat my Cheerios and to watch my last episode of Sesame Street. After one of the finest performances of 'One of These Things Is Not Like the Other' my mom said, 'Kenny, it's time to go outside to wait for the bus.' Solemnly I stood up, I scratched myself all over my body (the ants were still crawling on me), walked over to Tipper and gave him a hug goodbye. I then walked the long green mile to my bus stop – just outside my front door."

"What's the long green mile?"

"When a person, who's in prison, is about to be executed they call the walk from the prison cell to the electric chair – green mile. Do you get the symbolism here?"

I said, "I don't know what symbolism is, but I get it now – you can continue."

"Okay. So outside my front door, while we waited for the bus to come, my mom tried to lighten the mood; she laughed and joked about how much fun school was going to be, but she also mentioned how much she was going to miss me. Then BAM! The realization of how my life was about to change hit me like a ton of bricks! But it was more than that; not only was my life about to change – my mother's life was going to change too! I started thinking; this is the end of our quality mother/son time – no more Sesame Street, no more Electric Company, no more cartoons, no more 'sands through the hour glass', NO MORE 'THESE ARE THE DAYS OF OUR LIVES!' I couldn't do this to my mother. What would she do during the day without her favorite son to keep her company? No! I couldn't and wouldn't do this to my mother!

But before I could do anything – I saw it! A huge yellow school bus was barreling down Riverside Drive toward me – it came to a complete stop right outside the front of my house. The door opened and inside I saw a scary old man with bad teeth who was preparing to take me away from my mother. My mother gave me a kiss and said, 'Have a great time at school, Kenny,' and she stepped back. I turned to her and screamed, 'No! I won't do this to you Mom – YOU NEED ME!' I ran back to save her; she was shocked by her little boy's response. She might have thought I was scared of school, but nothing could be further from the truth – I wasn't doing this for me – I WAS DOING THIS FOR HER!

When I got back to her I wrapped my arms around her legs and said, 'Mom, sniff, I, sniff, can't, sniff, do, sniff, this, sniff, to, sniff, you, sniff!' She said, 'Kenny, you're a big boy now and you need to go to school so you can grow up to be the greatest Finance Manager in the world! You'll only be gone for a few hours – I'll be fine – trust me. Now, I need you to get back on the bus so you can become the man I want you to be!'

For a second – I was weak – I let my mother talk me into getting on the bus – even though I knew in my heart that's not what she really wanted. Once I sat down in my seat I thought to myself, 'What have I done?' I realized I was wrong to get on the bus – but it was too late! The driver slammed the door shut and pulled away from my house! Through the bus window I saw my mother waving goodbye to me. My face was plastered up against the window, tears trickling down my face, and then I let out a scream at the top of my lungs, 'Mommy I don't want to leave you!' I cried the whole way to school!"

Kelsie said, with a smile on her face, "Dad, I thought this was when you became an untamed man! Sounds like this is when you became a girly man!"

"Kelsie, did I say I was finished? Be patient! Sometimes it takes a crisis to really change a person – and this was a crisis! You'll see the rebel come out in me before this story's over.

When we finally arrived at the school, which was actually a Methodist Church on Sundays, we were led off the bus like convicts going to prison – the only things missing were the orange jump suits, shackles, and the chains. We were led to our classroom where we would be confined for four hours a day, five days a week, to be indoctrinated. My teacher, Mrs. Vorhees assigned us to our cell blocks, which she called tables. At my 'table' were four kids including me, Lisa Vertusso, John Signerelli, and Julie Puncherelli.

"Cam, don't listen to Dad – these aren't real names!"

"Is too, Cam – don't listen to Kelsie."

"Is not!"

"Is too, is too, is too, is too – infinity!" My dad smiled and got back to his story, "I didn't talk much to my new cell mates because I was preoccupied developing the most foolproof escape plan known to man. It was a perfect, flawless plan which if implemented properly would allow me to break free from this nightmare called school! I noticed when we pulled up to the school it was surrounded by woods and those woods, if my calculations were correct, would lead to my Aunt Robbie's house just off of Hillside Avenue. The key was waiting for the right time.

After all the kids got settled in their seats, Mrs. Vorhees told us she would read us a story after she went over some of her Neo-Nazi school rules. Her rules were actually a bunch of fascist commands which included raising our hands before talking, sitting quietly, single file lines, plus many other rules intended to brainwash us into conformity and to take away our freedom! After she finished going over the rules she said, 'Alright everyone please stand up quietly, push in your chair, line up in single file at the door; we're going to the library for our story. As all these five year old SHEEPLE stood up, pushed in their chairs, and gave the Fuer, I mean teacher, a 'Heil Hitler' I saw my way out! As my class lined up I made sure I was at the end of the line; when we walked out of our classroom all the other kids made a right turn – I quietly made a left turn. Once out of the sight of the teacher I ran straight for the front door of the school – to my freedom!

When I made it outside I was standing in a deep puddle I looked straight up into the sky, the rain poured down my face and I threw my hands in the air and let out a scream..."

Kelsie spoke up, "Dad that sounds like the movie we watched on TV a few weeks ago, 'The Shawshank Redemption'."

"Kelsie, will you let me finish my story without interrupting!? Where was I? Oh, yeah, when I got outside I looked over the landscape trying to decide where to make my get away. I decided my best hope for freedom was through the woods behind the school. I looked back and saw my teacher through the glass doors AND SHE SAW ME! I turned and started running as fast as my legs could carry me. I ran through bushes, I crawled under dead trees, I ran across streams – I ran and ran without looking back. My heart was pounding, I was huffing and puffing, my body was covered wit sweat – now my body was really itching! I couldn't run anymore – I dropped to the ground exhausted and crawled behind a wide oak tree, trying to catch my breath. In the distance I heard some commotion; I heard some adult voices say, 'There he is – let's get him!'

The thought of going back to ALCATRAZ scared me and my adrenaline started flowing – I got my second wind! I took off again into the deepest, darkest parts of the woods. I ran as fast as my kindergarten legs would take me, and for a little while I lost them again. But then I heard my teacher yelling, 'Kenny, where are you! Kenny, come back to school! Kenny!' Then I heard the blood hounds! They set free three or four blood hounds to track me down; they were hot on my trail, but they couldn't catch me..."

I had to speak up this time. I said, "Dad, there is NO WAY they sent out blood hounds after you! No way in the world! You don't expect us to believe that do you?"

"See, Kelsie, do you see what you've done? You've turned your little brother against me – he's starting not to believe my stories just like you! I hope you're happy with yourself. Okay Cam. I'm not saying I actually saw the blood hounds, but I know I heard a dog bark so I assumed they sent them after me. But if you choose not to believe your daddy you can scratch the blood hounds from the story – but the rest of the story is...cough, cough...true!

A short while later I heard my teacher coming after me, unfortunately for me, she was much faster than I was – she caught me a short distance away from school, she carried me back, and placed me in solitary confinement which was actually the table next to her desk. Over the next several weeks Mrs. Vorhees worked with me every day trying to reprogram me – kind of like the communists did to ex-capitalists in the Soviet Union and Communist China. She tried to break my spirit and break it she did; after she 'Water Boarded' me for the 112th time I couldn't take it any longer – I finally gave in and accepted the fact my life of freedom – my life of Sesame Street, the Electric Company, cartoons, and soap operas had come to an end, and I must conform or lose my mind!

So Cameron and Kelsie – that's the story of my first day of school. I didn't get off to such a good start, and actually this was the highlight of my school years – it was all downhill after this day."

My dad was smiling as he told us this. He then continued, "Kelsie how's that for a rebel without a cause? Now you know exactly what a wild man your dad really is!"

Kelsie said, "Yeah, Dad. You're a real rebel."

The Fingerling Affair

I have to tell you my dad's favorite story about growing up; it happened with he lived in Suffern. He liked this story so much he told it to us a million times, especially near Christmas. He always started it the same way.

"Cam, I had a very emotional childhood...sniff...sniff...sniff."

"Okay, Dad, you can stop crying now. Tell us about your emotional childhood."

He smiled, sat-up, and said, "Okay, my worst memory happened when I was 7 years old while I was attending Cypress Road Elementary School. It all began in November when my second grade teacher, Mrs. Ross, told us we were having a 'Kris Kringle' exchange. I had never heard of this before, but she explained it to my class, 'Everyone will put their name in a hat, and then you'll pull a name out of the same hat – as long as it's not your own. When you pull a name out', she continued, 'it's very important you keep the person's name a secret. Then you'll buy a gift for that person and bring it into school for that person on Kris Kringle day! Then on Kris Kringle day, each of you will be allowed to open the present that has your name on it; it's at that time you'll be able to tell everyone who you bought a present for!'

This, of course, sounded like a lot of fun and so each of us wrote our names on a piece of paper, and we placed it in the hat the teacher was passing around the class. When it came around to me, I put my hand in and I pulled out Anthony Mostacholli's name."

I said to my dad, "Anthony who? Anthony Mostacholli? That isn't a name. No one is named after pasta!"

"Well, Cam, I guess you're wrong because his name was and is Anthony Mostacholli! Now let me get back to my story. It was perfect that I picked ANTHONY MASTACHOLLI'S name. Anthony was my best friend in the second grade. Everyday, after lunch Anthony and I hung out together; when I broke my collarbone he was the one who brought my homework to my house. He was also the one who told everyone 'Kenny was bleeding all over the place…' when I broke my collarbone. He pointed to my shoes, which had red paint on them, as proof that I was bleeding all over the place. The bottom line is that I was very happy to have pulled my best friend's name out of the hat for Kris Kringle!

When I got home that day I rushed to my mother and told her about Kris Kringle because I thought Kris Kringle was something new. I told her, 'I picked Anthony's name.'

She said, 'Oh, the nice boy who's named after spaghetti.'

I said, 'Yeah, that's the guy. Mom, can we go to Woolworth's to buy Anthony's present? And Mom, Anthony is my best friend – I want it to be the best present ever!'

Several days later my mother took me, my brothers and sisters to Woolworths to shop for Christmas presents. I spent A LOT of time trying to pick out the perfect present! I looked at balls, bats, books but I couldn't find the perfect present. Then I saw it – the perfect present! It was an action figure similar to GI Joe! By the way, GI Joe was an extremely popular action figure in 1971. It was a rough and tough action figure that every boy would love and would be proud to have – but it was even better! It was better because you could put your fingers, your pointer and middle finger, in the back of the action figure's legs and walk him around by moving your two fingers – because of this feature it was called a Fingerling Action Figure. Cool guys would kill for a present like this, and so I bought it for my best friend!

I can still remember the excitement I felt when I walked into class the day of the Kris Kringle exchange. I couldn't wait for Anthony to open the present I bought for him. I carefully placed his present next to the other student's presents on the table next to the teacher's desk. Ms. Ross said, 'We'll exchange the gifts after lunch time', which was almost unbearable for all of us. That morning was the longest day of my school career; it seemed to drag on – even lunch seemed to take longer than usual – but then it came! It was time for the Kris Kringle exchange!

Ms. Ross stood up and walked over to the reading area, and she sat down; she asked all of the students to sit on the floor around her. She continued on, 'I'll hand out the presents, and we'll open them one at a time.' All the kids ran over to the reading area and sat of the floor around Ms. Ross. I sat on the floor towards the back of the crowd of kids. I couldn't wait to see the expression on Anthony's face when he opened the coolest present in the world. Ms. Ross handed presents to several other students first. They opened their present, they acted excited, and then the person who bought the present raised his or her hand and said something like, 'That was from me!'

Finally, after what seemed to be hours, Ms. Ross called Anthony's name – my heart was pounding with excitement! She handed him the present – I couldn't wait – I knew he would love his present! He ripped open the wrapping paper – he turned the box over – I was about to burst wide open with excitement – he looked at the present – and he screamed – in the loudest voice I have ever heard, 'SOMEBODY BOUGHT ME A DOLL!'

I thought to myself, in a nervous dread I can never verbally express, 'Did he just say what I thought he said?' My heart dropped to my stomach. I thought to myself, 'Did my best friend just say what I thought he said? Does he think this GREAT action figure I bought for him is a doll? How could he not love this ACTION FIGURE?' Anthony turned around and asked each and every one of his classmates, 'Did you buy me this doll? Hey, did you buy me this doll?' When he walked over to me and asked, 'Did you buy me this doll?' I replied, 'Are you kidding? Do you think I'm the type of guy who'd buy a guy a doll?'

To this day Anthony doesn't know it was me who bought him the cool action figure, action figure, action figure – yes I did say action figure because it WAS an ACTION FIGURE! This fingerling episode left such a deep scar on my life – I stopped buying gifts for people for years and years."

"Okay, Dad. So the worst thing about Suffern was giving Anthony Spaghetti a doll?"

"IT WASN'T A DOLL – IT WAS AN ACTION FIGURE CAM!!!!"

"SOOORRRRYYYYY Dad…action figure!"

So Anthony Spaghetti was your best friend. Who were your other friends in Suffern?"

"Well instead of my other friends let me tell you about my archenemy – Wes – Wes McCulley."

Breaking Out the Can...

"When Wes was 8 years old there was a picture of him in the dictionary next to the word 'Bully'."

"Dad! That's not nice!"

"You're right, that wasn't nice, but it's nicer than WHITE TRASH!"

My dad smiled and continued, "So where was I? Oh yeah, Wes McCulley's immediate family, figuratively speaking, lived on the other side of the tracks, while his cousins literally lived on the other side of the tracks. Wes was the type of boy mothers tell their kids, 'Stay away from Wes – he's bad news.' Most people in his family were addicted to drinking and smoking – about the only thing they weren't addicted to was work. To give you a better idea of the type of family they were, let me tell you what they did to my family's pumpkin one year, a few days before Halloween."

"Okay, we're listening."

"Okay, my father stopped at a nearby vegetable stand and bought a nice big, orange pumpkin for my family. When he got home Richie, Chris, and I drew a picture of a face on the pumpkin but since it was late we had to wait until the next day to cut out the eyes, nose, and mouth. Although the pumpkin wasn't finished yet we decided to leave it on the front porch.

The next day I woke up and got ready for school, but when I walked out on the front porch – the pumpkin was gone! I ran in the house screaming, 'The pumpkin's gone! Mom! Richie! Chris! The pumpkin's gone?!!' No one in the family had moved the pumpkin; the last time it was seen was when it was left on the porch the night before. It was the great pumpkin mystery, but the mystery didn't last very long.

The same day, when the sun went down, the mystery was solved. When it got dark and the street lights came on, low and behold, what did we see when we walked by Wes's house? You guessed it – they had a new Jack-O-Lantern which looked exactly like the face we drew on our pumpkin the night before. I was mad, and so I went to their front door and knocked – the oldest brother, who was about fifteen years old, answered the door. I said, 'Someone took our pumpkin last night and it looks exactly like the pumpkin in your window – did you take our pumpkin?'

I received a typical Bully response – 'No! Are you accusing me of stealing your f$%^*&g pumpkin, if you are I'll punch you in your f#$%^&g mouth?' He then slammed the door in my face.

This was the type of family they were – they could steal, cheat, and lie and not feel the least bit of remorse about it. They liked to bully people and they stuck together like glue. Wes, who was the same age as me, used to tell people, 'If you don't do what I tell you to do, I'll punch you in the face.' This is basically what he said to me one day – and I'm sure he regretted he did."

I asked, "Why did he regret it?"

"You'll see, Cam. Be patient. It happened at Cypress Road School after gym when I was waiting in line to get a drink of water. Wes liked to cut in line in front of the other kids, but this day he decided to cut in front of me. One of the things I don't like are bullies and so when Wes did a 'Frontsy Backsy' with a boy in front of me I told him, 'No 'Frontsy Backsies' – get in the back of the line.' When Mrs. Ross, my 2nd grade teacher, heard me say this she said, 'Wes, get to the back of the line there is no cutting in line – you must wait your turn.' Wes turned to me and said, 'Your ass is grass, Kenny! Meet me after school!'"

"Did he really curse at you?"

"Yes, he was a punk, Cam. Okay, so I knew everyone else was afraid of him and although I was confident I could defend myself, I was still nervous the whole afternoon and especially on the ride home on the bus. It seemed like every minute of the day one of the kids in my class came up to me and said, 'I heard Wes is going to beat you up after school – are you afraid?' I was so afraid I felt like I was going to throw up but I didn't let anyone know.

"♪ War, huh, yeah – What is it good for?
Absolutely nothing, Uh-huh ♪
♪ War, huh, yeah – What is it good for?
Absolutely nothing – Say it again, y'all ♪ [7]

Kelsie said, "Dad, do you have to do that every time you tell a story?"

My dad said, "Yup!" and he continued, "On the bus ride home Wes kept looking and pointing at me saying, 'I'm going to kill you!' When we reached my bus stop most of the kids got off, but they didn't walk with me – they walked behind me. It's funny how even in school fights the good people don't stick together. While I was walking Wes ran up behind me and said, 'So Kenny where do you want me to beat you up?' Before I answered he said, 'I want to fight you next to the Van Tassel house'.

The yard next to the Van Tassel house was filled with pine trees which were in a circular formation which served as a perfect boxing ring, and it would conceal the fight from the parents in the neighborhood. The whole crowd walked down Riverside Drive to the Van Tassel house which was the longest walk of my life. I was getting really nervous because I started believing Wes was going to beat me up. I was so nervous I could barely hear the kids screaming, 'Fight, fight, fight, there's going to be a fight!'

As soon as Wes, me, and the other kids reached the yard next to the Van Tassel's house – the fight was ready to begin. The kids wrapped around us so that no one could run away and Wes said, 'Get ready, you faggot!' I was like Adam Sandler in the Water Boy – it got me mad and all of a sudden I forgot about my nervousness, and my anger took over my emotions! I threw the first punch – an upper cut to Wes's stomach, next came a right cross to Wes's face, and then another upper cut to his stomach.

I was still running on adrenaline, I yelled, 'You want more, you want more! I got five more cans to crack open; I got five more cans, Wes!'"

"Cans of what Dad?"

"Don't tell mom I told you this but I was saying I have 5 more cans of whoop ass."

"Dad!"

"I know, I know but sometimes you get so angry you say things you shouldn't. And after all Wes was a punk – he deserved what he got. After I yelled at him, it was clear by the look on his face he didn't want no more! He didn't want another piece of this!"

My dad was smiling as he told us the rest of the story. He continued, "Wes, yelled at me, 'Hold it, hold it!' and so I stopped. Then he turned and ran outside the circle of kids and pine trees. A few of the other kids ran behind him to find out what he was doing. When they came back they said, 'His mouth is bleeding, he thinks he is going to throw-up, and he doesn't want to fight anymore.

Wes never, ever bothered me or any of the other kids in the neighborhood again. In fact when he tried to bully some of the younger kids in the neighborhood they told Wes, 'I'm going to tell Kenny if you don't stop.'

"Interesting Dad, do you have any other stories about growing up in Suffern?"

"I have a lot more but would you rather hear about my move from Suffern to The Bronx?"

"Yeah, of course!"

SECTION IV
Exodus

♪ If I leave here tomorrow
Would you still remember me ♪
♪ For I must be traveling on now
Because there's too many places I need to see ♪
♪ But if I stayed here with you
Things just couldn't be the same ♪
♪ Because I'm as free as a bird now
And this bird you cannot change ♪ [8]

A New Beginning...

Okay, I'll tell you about my move from Suffern to The Bronx, but first let me tell you why we moved.

I don't know or remember all the details, but as I recall the owner of the house didn't renew our lease because his daughter was about to be married, and she needed a place to live. So he decided to give us the boot and give the house to his daughter. I think we might have been able to find another house to live in nearby, at the time I wish we did, but my father was tired of the long commute to work, so he decided to move us back to the Bronx.

It was in the summer of 1973 when my mother told me we were moving back to the city. It took me totally by surprise. I didn't want to move away from my home and friends. I didn't want to move away from Cypress Road School, away from the Suffern Pool, away from Rocco Laverchio, Joe Gianelli, Johnny Grealy, Harry Hunt, or Franz Heinze but there wasn't anything I could do about it. I asked my mother, 'Where in the city are we moving to?' She told me, 'Kenny, we're moving into your grandmother's house on Corlear Avenue.'

This didn't make me feel any better, because I remembered the Bronx from a field trip I went on to the Bronx Zoo when I was in 3rd grade. Like I told you earlier, during the 1970's the Bronx was falling apart – crime was at an all time high, and it was a dirty, filthy borough. When we went on the field trip to the Bronx Zoo, I saw trash and newspapers being blown all over the streets, and there were stripped down cars scattered along the roads everywhere. When I told my friends at Cypress Road I was moving to the Bronx; they asked me, 'Why would you want to move there?' Of course you have to remember my friends and I lived in a place which had trees, grass, houses, front yards, back yards, rivers, and open space – on the other hand – the Bronx was all about concrete, buildings, noise, and lots and lots of people. Moving from Suffern to the Bronx was scary at first – it wasn't easy for me.

We moved to the Bronx in October 1973 – just a month after I started 4th grade at Cypress Road. We moved into the house my Great Grandfather Doyle built in 1930. It was a two story home with a basement which was fixed up for the kids in my family as a play room, the main floor had a kitchen, dining room, living room, and the sun parlor which is where my grandmother slept. The upstairs had my room, which I shared with Richie and Philip; Gena, Christine, and Patricia shared a room, and my parents had their own room, and of course there was a bathroom.

There was also an attic which you went through my room to get to. The attic door was covered by the bunk beds Uncle Philip and I slept in. I can still remember how scared I was sleeping next to the attic stairs because I wondered if the Boogieman moved to the Bronx along with me.

The house was built on about a quarter acre of land which in New York is a pretty big piece of property. There was a huge brick wall facing the side of our house which was actually the side of one of the row houses which ran up and down Corlear Avenue between 232nd and 234th Streets. I loved this brick wall; I used it to practice my pitching by throwing a rubber Spalding ball, pronounced spall-dean, against it. It was also great for playing Whiffle ball or stick ball. I'll tell you more about stick ball later. There was a two car garage which my grandmother rented out to two families who lived in an apartment building around the corner.

The best part of the yard was the basketball court; I LOVED it!! I loved it even though the concrete had cracks all over. Actually, the cracks helped me to become a pretty good ball handler because the ball bounced in every direction when it hit one of the cracks. The hoop wasn't very reliable; it fell off all the time, especially when I took an outside shot. It was screwed into a rickety old wooden pole which was so weak I spent half the time nailing and re-nailing the hoop into it.

The Bronx was so much different from the Suffern. In Suffern some of the stores were close by, but in the Bronx everything was within walking distance. There were two grocery stores three blocks away, Finest and Waldbaums, and on 231st Street and Broadway there were restaurants, bars, fruit stands, pizza shops, and clothing stores. There were schools, baseball fields, football fields, a golf course, a movie theater, and bookies just a few minutes away. Anything which wasn't within walking distance was only a subway or a city bus ride away.

Keep in mind moving to the Bronx meant I needed to meet new friends, go to a new school, join sports teams, and go to a new church. My parents had to decide where Chris and I would go to school. They already decided Richie would go to John F. Kennedy High School, a new school built down the road from 230th Street. They decided Gena and Philip would go to the Special School District, and since Patricia wasn't 5 years old yet she stayed at home with my mother. Kingsbridge had two Catholic parishes in the neighborhood; St. John's and Visitation."

"What's a parish?"

"A parish is the neighborhood around a Catholic church. Catholic people are expected to go to the church in their parish or their neighborhood. It's kind of like you choosing your school. Since we live near Russell Elementary, you are expected to go to Russell."

"Thanks."

"Alright, where was I? Oh yeah, I was telling you about the school we were going to. Both St. John's and Visitation had a church and an elementary school which went from kindergarten all the way to eighth grade. At this time Catholic schools were transforming from schools which were almost exclusively run by strict nuns, brothers, and priests to schools which were taught primarily by lay teachers."

"What are lay teachers?"

"Cam, lay teachers are teachers who aren't nuns or brothers. When my mother went to school, I think she only had nuns and brothers as teachers. Before you ask Cam – Nuns are woman who devote their lives to God and something else – like teaching. The nuns I knew devoted their lives to God, teaching, and beating children to a pulp."

My dad smiled and said, "I'm just kidding about the beating part, but I did know some really mean nuns! I remember when Sister Margaret Mary Elephant threw a math book at Julia Malvey when she thought Julia had her book opened to the wrong page."

"Are you kidding?"

"I'm kidding about the name Sister Margaret Mary Elephant but not about her throwing the book. If it hit Julia she would have broke her nose! Where was I? Oh yeah. One of the reasons it was hard to decide which school I would attend is because my father went to Visitation and my mother went to St. John's when they were kids. They finally agreed to St. John's because my grandmother's house was just a little closer to St. John's than Visitation and because my Grandmother attended St. John's church."

"How was it living with your grandmother?"

"I liked it, but I'm not sure my grandmother ever got used to it. Even though my mother had dinner sitting on the table when she got home from work every evening and all the dishes were washed afterwards, I don't think my grandmother ever got used to having the eight of us living at her house. My father had a joke he used to tell people. He said, 'Anne's mother loves coming home to a warm dinner on the table – it's just the coming home part she doesn't like."

"Did he really say that?"

"Yes, but I'm pretty sure he was half joking. Anyway, I think we all drove her a little bit crazy by the things we did. My grandmother used to tell me not to throw my spaldeen against the wall, not to play basketball outside at 8:00 a.m. on weekends, and it annoyed her when I read 'her newspaper' before her on Sunday mornings. But of course she fought all the time with you know who."

"Aunt Chris?"

"Bingo, Cam. The Evil Aunt Chris strikes again! You know people who are similar sometimes drive each other crazy; especially when those two people are opinionated and stubborn. This was the case with my grandmother and my sister Chris. From the first day we moved into my grandmother's house, I knew my grandma was a strict disciplinarian and she saw the world in black and white. We were expected to go to church every Sunday without exception, and we had to present the church bulletin to her as proof we attended. Dinner was served every night at 6:00 and after dinner all the dishes were cleaned, and us kids were expected to finish our homework and go downstairs to the playroom. Bedtime was at 8:00 every night which meant lights out at 8:30. If the lights weren't out my grandmother opened up the bedroom door, reached her hand into the room, and turned them off.

I didn't like turning off the lights at 8:30, but I didn't complain very much and I certainly didn't complain to my grandmother – I was afraid of her! If I wanted the light in my room on, I quietly walked over to the light switch, near the door, after she walked downstairs, and I'd turn it back on. If I heard her coming back up the steps again, I quietly walked over to the door and turned the light back off. This was the smart thing to do, maybe it wasn't the most honest thing to do, but it was smart. Your Aunt Chris, on the other hand, didn't handle it the same way. Nooooo! She couldn't just let grandma turn off the lights. Nooooo! Instead she started World War III every night when grandma turned off her lights. She'd say, 'You can't turn off my light! You're NOT my mother! When you leave I'm going to turn the lights back on!' I'd listen in my room with Philip and think to myself, 'Chris, please be quiet and wait until she goes back downstairs!' But nooooo! Chris couldn't let grandma think she could tell her what to do."

I asked my dad if this happened every night.

"Yes, EVERY NIGHT, at 8:30 p.m. sharp! I set my wrist watch by their arguments. I heard the squeaking of the steps as my grandmother came upstairs, my door opened a crack, I saw her right hand, it turned off the light, the door closed, and I heard my grandmother walk over to the girl's room. Again, I heard the door open, I heard the click of the light switch, and then I heard, 'You can't turn off my light! You're not my mother! When you leave I'm going to turn the lights back on!'

Your Aunt Chris has said to me on several occasions, when we were older, she thinks she would get along great with Grandma now. I think that's probably true. They had so much in common; they were both strong willed woman who were opinionated, they viewed the world in the same way, and they both hid their cookies from their children."

"What do you mean?"

"Both my Grandmother and my sister Chris hid their cookies... oh never mind, you'd have to know both of them to understand. Okay, do you want to hear about St. John's Grade school."

"Yes, of course!"

St. John's School, Church, & Day Camp

"When I moved from Suffern to the Bronx my life changed in many ways; the biggest change was school. When I left Suffern I left behind Cypress Road Public School, a school I was familiar with, comfortable with, and a school I liked. My new school was a Roman Catholic School; a large brick building which was cold and intimating. St. Johns had two schools; the grade school which was located on Godwin Terrace between 230th and 231st Streets and the middle school which was located on Kingsbridge Avenue between 231st and 232nd Streets.

Unlike Cypress Road, where we could wear our play clothes to school, St. Johns had a strict dress code. Students had to wear a uniform; the girls wore brown plaid skirts, a yellow blouse, a brown vest, brown knee sox, and shoes. The boys wore brown pants, a yellow shirt, and a brown tie. There were three types of ties; a clip on, a tie which wrapped around your neck and was hooked on, and a traditional tie. I usually wore the clip on because I didn't know how to tie a real tie.

St. John's grammar school was a large three story fortress with a basement. The gym was located in the basement where it was built about 6 feet below street level. I was told the gym was originally supposed to be a pool but they ran out of money and decided to make it a gym. I'm not sure if this is true; I doubt it. The gym was used for the 1st through 6th grade students and also by the 7th and 8th grade basketball teams and all the older CYO teams.

The first floor was for the kindergarten, 1st grade, and 2nd grade; the second floor was for the 3rd and 4th grades; and the third floor was for the 5th and 6th grades. There was a large auditorium which was utilized for assembly, school lunch, and after school and on weekends it was used for Bingo, and other adult events. There was a school yard which was used for the younger students, but it wasn't big enough for everyone, so Kimberly Place, a street located on the south side of the school, was blocked off with police barricades during school hours for the 4th, 5th, and 6th graders for use before school and after lunch. We used this street to play bottle caps, fly's-up, curb ball, tag, and to line up before we went back into school.

The kids who went to St. John's grammar school were good kids; they didn't get into much mischief until they reached 7th and 8th grade. The students were about 85% Irish-Americans, 5% Italian-Americans, 5% German-Americans, 3% Hispanic-Americans, and 2% were African Americans. Many of the students had parents who were 1st or 2nd generation immigrants, so quite a few of the parents still spoke with a foreign accent."

"Why did you mention where the kids were from?"

"Well, in the Bronx everyone knew what nationality everyone else was. You knew if they were 'Irish American', 'German American', 'Jewish American', 'Polish American', 'African American', or whatever they were. When you met someone new the first question you asked them was, 'Hey, what are you?' They'd respond, 'I'm Irish American, what are you?' I have no idea why it was so important to people – it just was.

Alright, I started attending St. John's one month after the beginning of school because my family didn't move from Suffern until one month into the school year. My mother walked me to

St. John's on my first day of school. We walked south on Corlear Avenue for two blocks, then we made a left on 231st Street for two blocks, and then we made a right on Godwin Terrace for less than one block. We opened the heavy wooden doors of the school and walked through the foyer to the principal's office. The principal at this time was Sister Margaret Mary Elephant, a petite nun with grey hair and a mean disposition."

"Dad, were all the nuns named Sister Margaret Mary Elephant?"

"Actually, I can't remember her name; I got that one from a Cheech and Chong skit, but I'm sure she wore a habit and was old and mean. I remember walking into her office with my mother. When we entered the office we filled out all the standard paperwork. After all the paperwork was completed my mother left, and Sister Margaret Mary Elephant pulled me by my ear and walked me to my new classroom. She walked me down the hallway with the tall ceilings; I glanced at all the pictures of the previous graduating classes which lined the walls. The hallways were like echo chambers; you could hear our footsteps as we walked by the 'fallout shelter' signs. We walked up the steps to the second floor of the school to Sister Margaret Mary Quinn's class. I later found out Sister Margaret Mary was actually a classmate of my mothers when they attended St. John's in the 1950's.

When the principal knocked on the wooden door with the window Sister Margaret Mary Quinn opened the door and let us in. When I walked through the door it all hit me at once; I was never going back to Suffern, this was my new home, and I wouldn't see my friends again. As I stood there in the front of the class Sister Mary…"

"Dad, was her name Sister Mary or Sister Margaret?"

"I'm not sure; she had so many names I couldn't keep them straight in my head. I'll call her Sister Mary from now on. So there I was standing in front of the class with all the students staring at every move I made. It was very uncomfortable for me, and I wanted to cry, but I was able to control myself when Sister Mary said, 'Attention children, we have a new student in our class. His name is Kenny Hand, and he's from Suffern.'

My new classroom had two long tables running down the middle of the room which were created by pushing all the small desks together. Sister Mary walked me over to my new desk in between Salvator Nemo and John McGowan; both of these boys helped me to become comfortable with my new class and school.

After walking to school with my mother the first day, I began walking to school with my Evil Sister Chris…"

"Dad! She's not evil!"

"Yes she was. Do you know she called me names all the time?"

"Like what?"

"Well, sniff, she, sniff, called me, sniff, Kenny Penny!"

"I bet you called her names too!"

"I might have but they weren't as bad as Kenny Penny."

"What did you call her?"

"Um, I think one of the names I called her was, um, Crissy Pissy."

"WHAT? That's much worse than Kenny Penny."

"Okay, anyway Kelsie, I'll stop referring to Aunt Chris as Evil for a little while. So where was I? Oh, yeah. I started walking to school with Chris, but later when I met a few other kids, I walked with them. Most kids ate their lunch at school, but I walked home for lunch, and my mother usually made me either a peanut butter and jelly or a baloney sandwich along with either milk or Hawaiian Punch. After eating lunch I had a few minutes to play basketball in my backyard before I walked back to school.

There were times when I asked my mother if I could eat lunch at Sam's Pizza Shop on the corner of 231st and Godwin Terrace. If I wasn't very hungry I ate a $.45 'slice' of pizza, and I drank a $.50 cup of soda. If I was really hungry I bought a slice for $.45 and a Sicilian slice for $.55. One of the reasons I liked to eat lunch at Sam's is because it gave me more time to play Bottle Caps or Fly's-up with my classmates on Kimberly Terrace after they ate lunch.

Let me tell you a little about church because this was a big change in my life too. My grandmother was a strong Catholic woman and so she encouraged, also known as forced, me to go to church every Sunday.

When I lived in Suffern, we didn't attend church on a regular basis. I can vaguely remember going to church on holidays like Christmas and Easter. And I can clearly remember going to Sacred Heart Church when Tricia was baptized. All my aunts, uncles, and grandmothers were there when the Priest poured water on Tricia's head, and she began screaming bloody murder. She screamed a lot louder than when I blew on her face. Even though we didn't attend church on a regular basis, my parents still wanted me to be brought up in the Catholic Faith. When I lived in Suffern every Wednesday afternoon the Catholics at Cypress Road loaded onto a school bus and were driven to Sacred Heart for religious instruction.

My life as a part-time Catholic came to an end when I moved to the Bronx because, like I said, my grandmother was a devout Catholic. She attended church every Sunday and went to church on all the special days like Ash Wednesday, Good Friday, Yom Kippur, and Ramadan…"

"Are you sure they're all Catholic holidays?"

"Hmm, maybe not, but you get my point. She was very active in the Catholic Church, and she wanted the same for her family. My grandmother expected all of us to attend St. John's church on Sunday, and she never accepted any of my excuses to stay home. Attending church every Sunday was not an easy thing for me to do, especially during football season, because I didn't want to miss the Sunday NFL football games or the pregame shows on TV. Even though church only lasted for about an hour it felt like it lasted forever when I was a 9 year old boy, but like a good obedient Catholic boy, I went every week. I started to get pretty good at all the rituals; I stood, sat, and kneeled at all the right times, and I picked up on the part when you cross your forehead, mouth, and heart. I even got comfortable saying, 'Peace be with you…and also with you', 'We lift up our heart…we lift it up…' I followed almost all the ceremonies and traditions of the church, although I didn't always understand why.

One part of being a Catholic I never fully bought into was the sacrament of confession. I knew I did things wrong, but I didn't feel the need to share my problems with anyone else, and I certainly didn't want to tell a guy with a black and white collar. I asked my friend John Sullivan, 'What do YOU say in confession?' He told me, 'I start out with the basics, like bless me father for I have sinned; it's been three months since I've been to confession. Then I say stuff like: I fight with my brother, talk back to my mother, and I occasionally throw in something about reading the National Geographic and having impure thoughts just to make it more interesting.'

I thought about using some of John's material, but it just didn't seem right to me. What if the priest stood up and said, 'Hey, wait a minute young man! Those are the same exact sins the last boy who came in here had – WHAT KIND OF SIN SCAM ARE YOU RUNNING HERE! You do know plagiarizing sins is illegal, don't you? You'll end up in purgatory if you keep it up?' I also considered using some of my own material like, 'I fight with my EVIL SISTER CHRIS and it's all her fault', but I decided I didn't like that either..."

"Dad! The fights were YOUR fault!"

"Yeah right, Kelsie. You EVIL girls always stick together, don't you? So where was I? Oh yeah. I was telling you about confession. Another thing I didn't like about confession was the priest telling kids to say 'Ten Hail Mary's' or 'Five Our Fathers' which seemed to be capricious and arbitrary to me. And what about those rosary beads – come on now! All in all, confessing to a priest just didn't appeal to me, so whenever my school went on a field trip to church to say confession, I confess – I never confessed."

"Dad, what do you mean you confess you never confessed?"

"Cam, I mean I never went to confession. When we were in line waiting to get into the confessional, I waited for my teacher to turn her head, and I sat down with the kids who had already gone to confession. I snuck back to the pew, kneeled down, and pretended to say a few 'Hail Fathers' and 'Our Mary's.'

Hail Mary Who Art in Heaven
Blessed are thy Fruit of thy Whom
Holy Mary, How Led be Thy Name
Thy Kingdom Come
Thy Will Be Come
Pray for Our Sinner
Now and at the hour of our Death
But Deliver Us from Evil Chris
Amen

If my Grandmother knew I snuck out of going to confession, she would have been upset with me. But she would have been even more upset if she knew I found a way to get out of sitting through church on Sundays. Now keep in mind, when I first moved to the Bronx I went to church religiously every Sunday morning, but then my friend John Sullivan told me, 'Everyone goes to church on Sunday night at 5:00. We sit outside the side door and wait for church to end; we always bring home a bulletin to prove we went to church.' At first I was too afraid and I didn't want to lie about going to church, but eventually peer pressure got the best of me and I started hanging out with the guys outside."

"That's terrible Dad! You always tell us not to lie to you."

"That's right Kelsie. Do as I say. Not as I do. Let's see. I need to tell you about St. John's Day Camp now.

Like I mentioned to you earlier, in Suffern I spent the summer days and nights either at Camp Venture or running around the neighborhood. But when I moved to the Bronx, my mother wanted my Evil Sister Chris and me to have something to do during the day so she signed us up for St. John's Day Camp. St. John's Day Camp was a great experience for me, even though I didn't realize it at the time. I made some of my best friends during day camp like: Timmy, Joey, Mike, Tommy, Billy, Pat and Kenny, Mike, and a ton of other guys."

"You were friends with Uncle Kenny when you were a kid?"

"Yeah, he was a good guy and very good at sports, but don't tell him I said it. Anyway, St. John's Day Camp was run by my Uncle Richie's friend – Mark Sweeney. He was a quiet guy, but he did a fantastic job. Day camp lasted for about 9 weeks during the summer; it went from Monday through Friday, and it began at 9:00 a.m. and ended at 4:00 p.m. There were 8 groups of campers; 1st and 2nd graders were the Midgets; 3rd and 4th graders were the Intermediates; 5th and 6th graders were the Juniors; and 7th and 8th graders were the Seniors."

"That's only 4 Dad."

"There were boys and girls groups in each group. Okay, the counselors were neighborhood teenagers; most of them were responsible, but not all of them."

"What did they do?"

"Oh, I don't know, let's put it this way; I learned everything I know about sex, drugs, and Rock n' Roll, from them but that's another story."

"Don't believe him Cam."

"You're right Kels, I'm teasing. Anyway, everyday we met in the St. John's School Yard on Godwin Terrace and played box ball, punch ball, or Whiffle ball while we were waiting for camp to start. Just before 9:00 we lined up, and then we loaded up onto a Liberty Lines bus for an excursion to some of the finest locations in the New York suburbs.

We went to pools, lakes, beaches, and parks outside the city for a day of swimming and excitement. We went to places like Mohansic State Park, Rockland County Pool, Reis Park, and, and, and, and I can't remember anymore, but there were a lot more. The only exception to this was the one day per week we stayed at the school – we called it 'Home Day'. When it was my group's turn to stay at school, there were many activities to keep us occupied; like basketball, football, soccer, Whiffle ball, punch ball, etc, etc, etc. Regardless of whether we went outside the city to go swimming, or if we had a home day – I had a great time.

There were rules at day camp which we followed very closely; like we couldn't go off the diving boards or swim in the deep end unless we passed a swimming test. Anyone who wanted to go off the diving boards had to swim across the width of the pool and back, which was not a small feat, because most of the pools we went to were wider than Olympic swimming pools. Passing the swimming test wasn't important for the young campers because they were too afraid to go off the diving board, but when an older kid passed – it was big news. When someone passed the test it spread like a wildfire, 'Hey everyone, did you hear? Timmy passed the swimming test! He can go off the diving board now!' Occasionally you'd hear rumors of a scandal, 'Did you hear? Timmy didn't pass the test; he paid the counselor off with a peanut butter and jelly sandwich!' There were other rules like not going off by yourself; you couldn't smoke, you couldn't drink – you know, all the typical camp rules."

"Yeah right, Dad. Like they had to have a rule to tell little kids they couldn't drink or smoke."

My dad smiled and said, "Yeah, Kels, you wouldn't think rules like this were necessary, but they were.

We didn't only go to pools in Day Camp; sometimes we went on special field trips to places like Coney Island, Lake Hopatcong, the Museum of Natural History, and other cool places. We also had an annual overnight camping trip which was the highlight of the camp year. We camped deep in the beautiful Catskill Mountains; I think it was the Catskills, in a relatively secluded area.

When we got to the camp site, we laid out our sleeping bags and set-up camp. There wasn't much to set-up because we slept right under the big sky not in a cabin or tent. After we set-up camp we went to the main campground for a cookout and prayer service with Father Stroud. The cookout was great! We had hamburgers, hot dogs, chips, and soda; while we ate, Father Stroud gave an inspirational sermon.

After the food and devotional, we walked back to our own campsite while it was getting dark, so we needed our flashlights to find it. When we got back to our sites our sleeping bags were always wet because of the evening dew."

"Dad, why didn't you unroll your sleeping bag after you ate? Wouldn't this keep your sleeping bag from getting wet?"

"Cam, you're a thinker. You're right, that's what we should have done. I'm not sure why we didn't, but we didn't. So where was I? Oh yeah. After we got back to our sleeping bags it was time to plan out our panty raid."

"You're what? You went on panty raids when you were a kid?"

"Of course! Everyone knows that's what you do on an overnight! So Timmy, Joey, Michael, and the rest of us planned our panty raid of the girl's camp. We always raided the camp of the girls who were our age. The Intermediate Boys raided the Intermediate Girls camp, and the Senior Boys raided the Senior Girls camp. When we raided the girl's camp we pulled out their clothes, food, and whatever else we could find, and we threw them all over their camp site.

After the panty raid the highlight of the overnight was the ghost story. The ghost story served a couple of different purposes; it was a great form of entertainment, but it also kept the kids in their camp site because afterwards everyone was afraid to leave. The story always had the same theme; a man with a hook for an arm, who just recently escaped a mental institution, which just happened to be located right down the road from the camp site – and he always swore revenge on little boys who wandered off into the darkness.

After a long night worrying about the man with the hook, we usually woke up to a beautiful day and the smell of bacon. The breakfast was delicious; it included eggs, bacon, cereal, rolls, and orange juice. After breakfast we packed up our stuff and hopped on the bus for a short trip to a nearby lake for a day of swimming.

I remember the overnight trip when I was 11 years old; that was the year I decided to take up smoking..."

"What? You smoked when you were 11?"

"Yes, Kelsie. Now you see why the rule about not smoking was important? This one particular day a few of the cool kids and I brought cigarettes on the overnight, and we decided to smoke behind the barn at the lake. At first I didn't inhale, but after some of the older experienced smokers pressured me to inhale – I tried it. At first when I tried it I thought I was going to choke to death. I began coughing and coughing, and I didn't think I would stop, but after trying again and again I finally got the hang of it. I was smoking like a grownup in the hot afternoon sun. I was feeling pretty cool smoking cigarette after cigarette, but then I started to feel sick, I got dizzy, and I fainted. When I woke up I turned over, and I proceeded to puke my brains out! This helped me to kick my smoking habit almost immediately."

"Serves you right for smoking!"

"You're right, Kels. I was sick as a dog, and I deserved to get sick because smoking is one of the dumbest things I ever did. So where was I? Oh yeah. I was going to tell you about the last day of camp.

The last day of day camp was the best and the worst day of camp. It was the best day because of the Camp Show and the worst day because it meant the swimming, games, and fun were coming to an end, and school was about to begin. The last day of camp was the Camp Show, the slide show, and the awards. The Camp Show was about a 2 hour show where all the groups put on a 30 minute skit – which we had to develop, practice, and perform. My group, along with the girls, put on Cinderella one year – I played Prince Charming..."

"No way! You're making that up Dad!"

"Kelsie, I'm serious. Look at this face, I was perfect for the job! All I had to do was dance; I didn't have to say anything. Another year we put on a Hula Show; all us boys put on bikini tops with balloons in them and we had grass skirts wrapped around our waist. I can't remember what we sang but I do know we were the hit of the show. When the Camp Show was almost over they put on a slide show with pictures which were taken during the camp year, and they played the song 'The Way We Were' by Barbra Streisand and 'There Are Places I Remember All My Life' by the Beatles. When I saw the pictures of me and my friends playing Whiffle ball, punch ball, swimming, smiling, laughing, and having fun I realized how much I loved St. John's Day Camp and my friends there. While these songs played I had to hold back the tears.

♪ Memories, like the corners of your mind
Misty water colored memories – Of the way we were ♪
♪ Scattered pictures of the smiles we left behind
Smiles we gave to one another – For the way we were...♪
♪ So it's the laughter – We will remember... [9]

After the slide show and the songs, there wasn't a dry eye in the house. When everyone finished wiping away the tears, they announced the awards for 'Camper of the Year'. Each group had a camper of the year, and usually the cool campers didn't want to win the award because it meant you were a 'brown noser' but one year my name was called, and I have to admit, it gave me a warm fuzzy feeling on the inside. I was secretly very proud of myself because it meant people liked me."

My favorite sport is baseball and so I asked my dad, "Did you play baseball when you were growing up?"

He said, "Of course. I was the best baseball player Kingsbridge has ever seen! But it didn't start out too well for me. Do you want to hear about it?"

Kelsie and I said, "Yes, of course Dad!"

Are You My ~~Mother~~ Coach?

"Okay, this story took place when I was about 9 years old. It was April, there was a chill in the air, and baseball season was right around the corner. As you know I was a sports fanatic, and one of my three favorite sports was baseball, so I begged my mother to sign me up for little league.

Kingsbridge Little League was a baseball league for kids from 9 to 12 years old who lived around my area. The league had minor and major league teams; the younger players and the less skilled older players played in the minors, while the older, more skilled players played in the majors. The minors had four teams; there were Timmy's, Teddy's (both neighborhood bars), Exxon, and another team whose name I can't remember. The majors had six teams; Art Steele, VFW, Stella Dora, Washington Heights, Northside Savings Bank, and Williams Funeral Home – all the kids were dying to play for Williams Funeral Home. You get it? They were dying to play for Williams Funeral Home..."

My dad thought his 'joke' was funny, but Kelsie and I didn't laugh because we heard a version of this joke every time we drove past a cemetery or a funeral home.

My dad looked a little disappointed we didn't laugh, but he quickly got over it and got back to his story, "So where was I? Oh yeah, I was telling you about Little League. Okay, in order to determine which team you played on there was a draft for all new players and players who were in the minors the previous year. The draft took place early in April inside the PS 7 gym; all the coaches from the major league teams watched the boys throw a ball back and forth for a minute or two, and based on this they decided which players they'd draft. Of course being drafted didn't mean you made the team – it only meant you had a try out. By the way, the pressure of making the majors was incredible; every boy knew if he didn't make the majors he would be considered a scrub by all his friends in school.

A week or two after draft day I received a letter in the mail which said I was drafted by VFW – the best team in the league. I was told to report to the Van Cortlandt Flats on Saturday, May 7th for tryouts. The Van Cortlandt Flats were part of the larger Van Cortland Park. Vanny, which is what everyone called it, was great. It had a football stadium, baseball fields, basketball courts, tennis courts, racquetball courts, a golf course, and lots of swings, slides, and sprinklers for the kids. It was always filled with people especially in the spring, summer, and fall. In addition to all of this – Vanny also had a huge open field which we called the Flats. The Flats had several softball fields, a few Irish football and hurling fields, but mostly it was just a huge open field.

On a nice Saturday afternoon the flats were packed with thousands of people. Most people used the flats for jogging, playing softball, baseball, football, soccer, and Irish football. Some used it for laying out and picnicking. Others used it for less pure and wholesome reasons; homeless men used the trees as bathrooms and the benches as beds; muggers used shadowy areas to stalk their victims, and perverted men cruised the streets outside the park looking for innocent young boys to violate – but that's a whole other story.

The night before my first tryout I went to bed at 9:00 p.m. to be sure I'd be rested for the big day, but no matter how I tried – I couldn't sleep. I lay down in bed, on my back, and tossed a ball in the air a million times; I pictured myself catching deep fly balls like Elliot Maddox. Every once in a while I got out of bed and practiced my swing and my pitching; I pictured myself hitting homeruns like Bobby Mercer and striking out batters like Doc Medich. Tryouts were scheduled for 10:00 a.m. so that meant I had to leave my house at 9:15 to be there on time. I woke up at 7:00 and went downstairs to eat my Wheaties. After I ate I took a shower and got dressed; by this time it was 8:00 – I couldn't believe I still had to wait another hour and fifteen minutes before I could leave! I decided to go outside to throw a spaldeen against the wall to practice my pitching but mostly to pass the time which was crawling by.

When 9:15 finally came I grabbed my Yankee cap, my CPO jacket, and I screamed, 'Mom, I'm leaving for baseball tryouts – bye!' She yelled back, 'Bye, good luck!' Looking back on it I can't believe I was allowed to walk to Vanny by myself, but it was a different time; when I was growing up parents didn't worry when their kids left the house – kids could leave in the morning, run all around Kingsbridge during the day, and as long as they returned before dinner – parents didn't worry about them.

When I left my house all I knew was VFW's tryouts were at the 'Van Cortlandt Flats' – this sounded simple enough to me. A few days earlier my dad told me, 'Kenny, the Flats are right up Broadway – past the pool. After you pass the pool on your right, you'll come to a road that leads into the park. Once you get to that road you can't miss it – it's a huge grassy flat area.' I didn't think I needed anymore information, I mean, how hard could it be to find a huge, grassy, flat area? And how hard could it be to find a baseball team playing baseball on this huge, grassy, flat area? So I assumed it would be easy finding my future VFW teammates – but you know what happens when we assume."

"No, Dad. What happens when we assume?"

My dad had a smirk on his face and said, "I'll tell you what it means when you're older." Then he got back to his story, "To get to the Flats I walked up Corlear Avenue until I reached Gaelic Park on 240th Street, and I made a right and a quick left on Broadway. I walked north on Broadway, under the El, past the pool hall, and past a few Manhattan College buildings. When I reached 242nd Street I crossed over Broadway heading toward the pool. Once I got across the street it was a relatively short walk to the road my father had mentioned, but when I reached it I was surprised by what I saw.

Unfortunately for me, I didn't see a huge, wide open, grassy area – I saw a sea of people! There were thousands of people everywhere; there were kids playing baseball, men playing softball (some of them wearing their jock strap on the outside of their pants), there were high school boys and girls running track, there were soccer games, Irish football games – there were people EVERYWHERE –

and none of them had VFW written on their chest! I stood there with my mouth wide open – I didn't expect this at all. I thought to myself, 'Where do I go? Who do I talk to? WHAT DO I DO?' I felt like that little bird that fell out of the tree in the Dr. Seuss book. And like the bird I decided to walk around and ask people if they were my ~~mother~~ coach.

The first person I walked up to was a man with a baseball glove, a baseball hat, and a jock strap over his pants. I asked him, 'Excuse me sir, are you the coach of my baseball team – VFW?' He looked at me and said, 'No halbo English.' This kind of scared me because I never talked to someone who didn't speak English, so I turned and quickly walked away.

The next person I came to was a teenager sitting on the ground putting on a pair of sneakers. He was wearing gym shorts and his shirt had a big number on the back. I asked him, 'Excuse me sir, are you the coach of my baseball team – VFW?' He looked at me and said, 'Do I look like a baseball coach? I'm a runner kid. Why don't you ask that guy over there?'

When I reached him I stopped and asked, 'Excuse me sir, are you the coach of my baseball team – VFW? He looked at me as he kicked a big round ball up in the air and he said, 'Do I look like a baseball coach? I'm playing soccer kid. Why don't you try that guy over there?' I was starting to get upset. I was trying to figure it out by myself. I was trying to find my team on my own. I was trying to do my best – but it wasn't working. I didn't know what else to do so I took a deep breath and I tried to be tough – but my chin started quivering.

I walked over to the man he pointed to; he was wearing a big green army coat, he was dirty, and he was smoking a cigarette. When I spoke I didn't want it to sound like I was about to cry, but my voice cracked when I said for the last time, 'Excuse me sir are you the coach of my baseball team?' He looked at me. He took a long drag of his cigarette. He squinted his eyes. Then he stepped closer, and he reached for me and said, 'Ah yeah man, I am. Come with me. Come on.' I started following him at first, but when he walked toward the wooded area of the park I knew something was wrong – I turned around and ran. I was so scared; I didn't stop running until I reached the entrance to the park – leaving the strange man far behind.

When I finally looked back for him – he was nowhere in sight. By now I was tired, scared, and so upset I had to sit down. I walked over to a park bench near the entrance, and I asked the man sleeping there if I could sit down. He grunted, bent his knees to make room for me, and accidently knocked over his can of beer. I sat down on the edge of the bench near his dirty, untied, smelly boots, and I put my head between my legs, and I sobbed like a little baby. There was nothing more important to me than playing baseball that day, but I felt lost and alone, and I didn't know what to do!"

"What did you do?"

"After sobbing for a while I accidentally woke up the man who was sleeping on the bench; he stretched out his arms, yawned, and sat up on the bench. Then he proceeded to lean over, and he passed gas in my face. I got up from the bench and ran all the way home – with tears streaming down my face and the aroma of beer farts permeating the fabric of my CPO jacket."

I said, "Funny Dad. Do you have any other baseball stories?"

My dad nodded his head, "I do but let me tell you about football."

"Okay."

St. John's Football

"When I moved to the Bronx, I think I was the only kid in the neighborhood who was a New York Giant fan. The Giants during the 1970's were awful; they only won 50 games, while they lost 93. My family had been Giants fans for generations, dating back to the time they played at the Polo Grounds. My father and most of my uncles had season tickets to their games and because of this, I frequently went to games. My birthday took place during football season, October 26th, and so I could always count on a ticket to see the Giants around this time. I was a huge football fan; I dreamed of being the next Ron Johnson, Bob Tucker, John Mendenhall, or Brad Van Pelt. So when I found out St. John's had a football team, I couldn't wait to try out.

St. John's actually had two football teams; the Hawks and the Eagles. The Hawks were for kids from 9 years old to 12, and the Eagles were for 13 year olds. Both teams practiced on Cooney Grauer Field and played their games at the Van Cortlandt football stadium.

Joe Bubbalow, as some people called him, was the coach of both teams when I played. He was a short, stout, single Italian guy who was loud, abrasive, and resembled Fred Flintstone. He liked to lay around in his king sized bed wearing only his boxer shorts, like Jabba the Hut, when the players picked up their equipment from his house. Although he was loud and sat around at home in his boxers, he was probably the best football coach in the area. Players on the Hawks feared this 5'6" tall mailman who wore black, ankle high, steel toed boots. If you missed a practice, a meeting, or a block Joe screamed, 'I'm going to stick my size 9 steel toed boot up your ass if you don't…'"

"If you didn't do what?"

"If we didn't do whatever he told us to. I guess it worked because the St. John's Hawks were the perennial Pop Warner champs in the Bronx for many years. The Eagles were good, but never as good as the Hawks. The reason for their success was Joe's system. He had a great football system for young kids; it was logical and easy to learn."

"What was the system?"

"Cam, it was really easy. The offensive system we utilized was a very simple numbering system. We had three running backs and one quarterback. The quarterback was called the '1 back', the running back to his left was the '2 back', the running back in the middle was the '3 back', and the running back to the right was the '4 back'. On the line there was the left end, the five linemen, and a right end. Beginning to the left of the left end was the '1 hole', to his right was the '2 hole' and this sequence continued all the way to the 8 hole which was to the right of the right end. All the running plays were numbers. A '28' was the '2 back' running through the '8 hole'. A '45' was the '4 back' running through the '5 hole'.

Joe called all the plays. After each play a new player came into the game with the play Joe called. The new player told the quarterback what the play was, and the quarterback announced it in the huddle, '28 sweep on 3, ready, BREAK!' After they broke the huddle all the players jogged to their positions and stood up. The quarterback yelled, 'down', the players got into the two point stance and yelled, 'go', the quarterback yelled, 'set', the players got into the three point stance and yelled, 'go', then the quarterback yelled 'go, go, go' if the play was 'on 3', and the ball was snapped and the play began.

This very simple system was the main difference between winning and losing. It's not easy teaching 9 to 12 year old boys to work together in a coordinated way, but Joe's system worked like a charm. In comparison to the other teams in the league, the Hawks were professionals. This organized approach to the game allowed the Hawks to be virtually unbeatable even against teams who were bigger and faster.

In the Bronx Pop Warner league the Hawks played in a league with several other teams; the Jaguars, Crusaders, Terriers, and a couple other teams I can't remember. Like I mentioned before, the Hawks were from St. Johns, and so they were mostly Irish Catholic kids. The Lions and Terriers were from the East Bronx and were mostly Italian Catholics, and the Jaguars were from the South Bronx near Yankee Stadium, and they were mostly African American and Hispanic kids.

The Jaguars were the most talented teams, and they usually competed with the Hawks for the championship. They were bigger and faster than the Hawks but they had poor coaching and terrible equipment. I can remember a game I played when we almost lost to the Jaguars on the last play. The Jaguars were losing to us 7 to 6, and they were on their own 10 yard line with only 10 seconds to go. On the last play of the game they handed the ball off to their best player, Jimmy Norris, and he broke through the line. He was so fast nobody could catch him, and so he had free sailing to the end zone, but then something happened. When he crossed the fifty yard line his pants started falling down. By the forty yard line they were down to his thighs, and he slowed down while he tried to pull them up. By the thirty yard line they were around his knees, and his underwear was showing. By the twenty yard line his pants finally wrapped around his ankles, and he tripped and fell down on the ten yard line – the game ended with us winning 7 to 6."

"Dad, did that really happen?"

"Yes, I'm serious Cam. I felt bad for Norris but it was hilarious watching him trying to hold up his pants.

Let me get back to Joe. He said what he wanted – how he wanted. You name the racial or ethnic slur; I learned it from Joe.

On Friday nights, before each game, we had a 'Skull Session' which was a football strategy session. A time to make sure every player knew their roles and what they needed to do the following day in order to win. During these meetings we talked about the other team's best players and who was going to key on the 'whop', break the 'jigaboo's' legs, or kill the 'mick'. I didn't think anything of these comments at the time; it was just part of football.

I can remember one meeting we had before we played the Jaguars. We had one African American boy on the team – Tony Miller. Tony was an excellent wide receiver and a really nice guy. Well, during the meeting Joe was telling us how cold it was going to be the next day. He talked about a lot of things, but then he said, 'Remember, Jigaboos hate the cold! Ain't that right, Tony? Your people hate the cold – don't they? Come on, Tony, you can be honest – you hate the cold too – don't you?'

I still remember Tony looking very uncomfortable while he shrugged his shoulder as if to say, 'I have no idea.' I remember sitting in the back thinking to myself, 'Doesn't everyone hate the cold. I know I hate the cold. I don't want to play in the freezing cold.'

Joe was brutal, especially to the quiet kids and the kids who weren't tough. I was one of the quiet kids; especially the first year I played on the Hawks. My main role was going in as a wide receiver after a touchdown to catch the extra point. I caught a few extra points, but I missed most of them, and Joe told me many times – 'you stink Hand' or 'you can't catch Hand, I don't know why I put you in.' It killed me when he said things like this, and it was the reason I didn't play the following year.

He said awful things to the kids on the team, but nothing was as brutal as what he said to a kid named Andrew. He was a really nice kid, but he wasn't tough, as a matter of fact, it wasn't unusual for Andrew to cry if he was hit hard, yelled at, or teased. His father was one of the assistant coaches on the team, and he wanted to make his son tough. He not only allowed Joe to be tough on his son – he encouraged it. I remember Joe picking on Andrew many times. Do you know what Joe called Andrew?"

"No. What Dad?"

"His nickname for Andrew was Puke – yes, I said Puke! He would tell Andrew, 'Puke, I need you to play center' or 'Hey Puke, if you miss that block again, I'm going to stick my size 9 steel toed shoe up your ass.' But nothing was worse than when Joe said, 'Hey Puke! Do you know why I call you Puke? It's because you make me sick!'

He not only said terrible things about the kids on the team he also had choice words to use about Mrs. Ryan. Mrs. Ryan was the coach of the St. John's Cheerleaders and the Hawks and Eagles Team Mom. One of her jobs was to make sure the players turned in their raffle tickets and money for their uniforms. She was very detail oriented and persistent when kids didn't turn in their money or raffle tickets. She followed up with Joe on a regular basis, and this drove him crazy. In the Skull Sessions he told us, 'Hey O'Neal, the QB told me you still owe $20' or 'Hey Quigley, the QB told me you haven't sold your raffle tickets yet'. I didn't realize what QB stood for until he didn't spell it out one time, 'Hey Mahoney, the Queen Bitch told me you still owe $20…'

"He doesn't sound like a very nice man."

"Well, I wouldn't let you play for him but when I was a kid it's just the way it was. Okay, let me see. Do you want to hear about my move from my grandmother's house to 222 West 233rd Street?"

We both said, "Sure."

Moving on Up

"My family knew our grandmother's house was only a temporary living arrangement until we found a house or apartment of our own. I think we moved out in 1976, when I was 11 years old. When we moved out, we lived on the streets for several months. Luckily we had a station wagon..."

Kelsie sat up and said, "No way! You didn't live in your station wagon!"

"You're right Kels – I'm kidding about living on the street, but we did move out of my grandmother's house.

When I found out we were moving out I had mixed emotions; I loved to play basketball, football, and stick ball in my Grandmother's backyard but on the other hand, most of my friends lived in apartments, and it seemed like it might be pretty cool. As a young kid I loved watching Fat Albert..."

"Who's Fat Albert?"

"Fat Albert was a TV cartoon which took place in a city where the kids played in empty lots, on roof tops, and fire escapes. It all looked like a lot of fun, so I thought it could be cool to live in an apartment. Before we moved my father, my Uncle Richie, and my brother Richie painted the apartment – apartment 1D. It was a big four room apartment. When you walked in the front door you were in the hallway of the apartment, down the hallway five feet on the left was the kitchen, a short distance further on the left was the living room, if you continued walking straight down the hallway you walked into the first bedroom, if you took a left before the first bedroom you walked down the back hallway and fifteen feet down the hallway on the right was the second bedroom and to the left was the bathroom.

The first bedroom had the fire escape and is where Richie, Philip, and I slept. The second bedroom had one single bed and a high riser which was pulled out at night. The living room was a duel purpose room; during the day it was the living room, but at night the couch was pulled out and the room became my parent's bedroom. The kitchen is where we ate our breakfast and my mother made our lunches and dinners; it's also where the laundry was hung out the window on the clothes line."

"Your parents slept in the living room? Really? That's not a lot of room."

"It's funny you say that. When I moved into the apartment I felt uncomfortable with the fact our family, all eight of us, were moving into a two bedroom apartment. Richie was adamantly opposed to moving to 233rd Street, and he told my mother, 'I'm not moving into an apartment! We have eight people moving into a two bedroom apartment – that's crazy!' I never told my parents how I felt about the move because I thought it might hurt their feelings, but I was prepared to tell my friends I lived in a three bedroom apartment if they asked – technically I was right; because like I said at night the living room became a bedroom.

It wasn't until I was older I realized our living arrangement wasn't unusual. In fact, my mother grew up in a one bedroom apartment in 3410 Kingsbridge Avenue – with her mother, father AND HER SIX BROTHERS! All six boys slept in the one bedroom on army surplus bunk beds, she slept on the couch in the living room, and her parent slept on a bed in the same living room. Luckily they had a lot of privacy; they had French doors in the living room and when they needed privacy they opened one of the doors to block their daughter's view."

"View of what?"

"Uh, nothing. My point is there were a lot of other families who had creative ways to fit their whole family into their apartment – without using the fire escape. A good friend of mine, who had six people in his family, lived in a one bedroom apartment; his parent's slept in the living room, three of the kids slept in the bedroom, and his oldest brother had his own room – a bed in the hallway with a curtain surrounding it.

"No, Dad. You're joking. Aren't you?"

"No, this is true. I promise you. Another family in the neighborhood had ten kids – yes, I said ten kids – I have no idea what their living arrangements were, but they had a giant shoe horn standing up outside their apartment door.

The most interesting living arrangement was a friend of mine who went to St. John's with me. She was from a nice Catholic family; her father was the custodian at the local Synagogue. Her family actually lived in an apartment in the Synagogue. She was the only Irish Catholic girl in the neighborhood who ate Kosher Corned Beef and Cabbage on St. Patrick's Day every year. Hey, wait! You guys keep getting me off track! Where was I?"

"Dad, it's okay if you get off track. We like hearing your off track stories!"

"Thanks Cam. Alright, I was telling you about my apartment and what it was like. Oh yeah. I can remember the radiators – also known as heaters, Cam. These radiators usually pumped out so much heat you could barely breathe. In the winter time we had to open all the windows to cool down the apartment. In the summer time it was brutal. Unlike you guys – I didn't grow up with air conditioning. I didn't have air conditioning until I was about 17 years old. It was so stinking hot in the summer; it was almost unbearable. I can't believe I didn't die from suffocation."

"Why was it so unbearable?"

"Cam, you guys will never, ever understand how hot it was before we had air conditioning. I can remember not being able to sleep at night. I remember my bed being soaking wet because of my sweat!"

"Dad, that's gross."

"Kelsie you think it's gross hearing about it – try sleeping in it. To try to keep cool most people had fans running 24 hours a day, but this barely helped. Sleeping with a cold wash cloth on your head was typical; sleeping in the bath tub helped. The best relief from the heat came from being outside on the front stoop. It was the nightly meeting place for many of the parents and older people in the neighborhood. A lawn chair, radio, a cooler full of beer, and your friends and neighbors were helpful remedies to the stifling heat of a city apartment. Because adults where outside, I could hangout in front of the building with my friends all night long during the summer; we played box ball, king-queen, or roundup in the streets, courtyards and alleyways. Playing in the streets, in and around the cars was always a very dangerous thing to do, not because of cars, but instead, because of poop minefields."

"Please Dad, not another poop story!"

"No, it's not another poop story, Kels! Anyhow, I can still remember the first day I moved into my apartment; I decided to go exploring. I thought for sure the roof could be used to play football, baseball, or dribbling a basketball or just running around in general – just like they did on Fat Albert. I took the elevator to the sixth floor, and pushed the door open. By the way, in New York, apartment buildings with more than five floors are required to have an elevator. When I got to the sixth floor I walked up the last flight of steps to the roof. The roof had a wall about three feet high to keep people from falling off, the roof was covered with roofing and a lot of tar – during the hot days of summer the tar would stick to your shoes and so you had to avoid it. On top of the roof there were heat stacks, clothes lines, and antenna's growing throughout the roof.

I walked over to the east side of the roof and could see the El, IHOP, Williams Funeral Home, the Bailey Avenue Projects, and all the buildings on the hill leading up to the Jerome Avenue Reservoir. Looking north I could see Manhattan College, Kelton's Ice Skating Rink, when I looked west and south my view was obstructed by the other buildings on my street, but I could see down into the alleyways and the clothes line jungle. If I fell off the roof I don't think I would have made it to the ground because there were so many clothes lines.

After I checked out the neighborhood, I was ready to use the roof for its intended purpose; basketball, baseball, football, and running. I began dribbling my basketball like I was on a breakaway; I practiced my spin moves and dribbling between my legs. Then I decided to just run all around the roof. It was at this point I heard yelling from over the wall of the roof, I think someone yelled, "Hey, stop all the racket!" I walked over to the roof door and opened it a crack and it sounded like a bunch of woman complaining about something, so I thought maybe it had something to do with me. I walked down the steps and there were several older women in their house coats, and they asked, 'Was that you making all that racket on the roof?' I said, 'Umm, yes, I guess so. I'm sorry I didn't realize I made that much noise.' That was the last time I played basketball on the roof."

"Well, Dad, at least you got to meet your neighbors!"

"That's true but I got to know all my neighbors a lot better after I lived there."

"Why?"

"Because when you live in an apartment building, it's almost impossible to have any privacy."

"Why?"

"Why? Why? How can you have privacy when all your friends can look at your underwear hanging on the clothes line? If you lived there, Kelsie, everyone in the neighborhood would know you wear Power Puff underwear."

"Dad!!"

"Well, it's true, Kelsie. And not only did everyone know what kind of underwear you wore – they could also see you walking around the house in your underwear. People could look into your apartment from across the alleyway or from across the street. But one of the worst parts about apartment life was people knew your business. If my parents had an argument my friends knew all about it, because they heard it clear as day in the alley way or in the hallway. With some families the yelling and screaming got so bad people called the 50th Precinct to break up the argument. Not because they were afraid someone would get hurt – it was because they wanted to sleep. You could hear yelling and screaming so clearly it could keep you from getting to sleep. But sometimes instead of calling the police people opened up their window, stuck their head out, and screamed, 'Hey Buddy, you didn't get home until three in the morning last night and you were smashed, just apologize, you know you're wrong – and I gotta get some shut eye!' In response you'd hear, 'Hey *#$% y&^ Buddy, why don't you mind your own &*^&$%^ business or I'll come down there and kick you're @*&!' – but this usually ended the yelling."

"Are you being serious, Dad?"

"Would your daddy lie to you? The yelling and screaming was bad, but that wasn't the loudest part of living in 222 West 233rd Street."

"What was?"

"It was having the El about 100 feet away from my window.

The trains ran about every 15 minutes during the day and maybe once an hour at night. You know what was really strange? When I first moved to the apartment the trains were so loud I couldn't hear the TV and they woke me up several times at night when I was in bed, but after I lived there for a while I didn't even notice when a train went by. It's strange how your mind can selectively filter out unpleasant noises."

'What do you mean selectively filter out unpleasant noises?'

My dad pretended not to hear Kelsie; I could see his little smirk, he thought he was funny. I asked him, 'Did you like living in the apartment? It sounds like you didn't.'

He said, "Oh no, no, no – I loved it! It was great! For example, alleyways weren't only good for listening to everyone else's problems, they were also useful for 'calling for' my friends. My friends and I rarely called each other on the phone, and we rarely knocked on each other's door or rang the apartment buzzer or doorbell. Calling for my friends meant I went into the alleyway or stood in the street and yelled at the top of my lungs, 'John! Pat! Tony!' I'd yell until someone came to the window. In the apartment my friends were told, 'Hey John, Kenny Hand is calling for you.' When you were 'called for' you went to the window, lifted it open, stuck your head out the window, and yelled, 'I'll be right down!' or 'I can't come down I'm still eating supper.' or 'I'll be out after I do my homework'.

But when I think back to it, one of the strangest things about apartment life was knocking on a friend's apartment door. I say this because I was rarely invited in; there were exceptions to this but not many of them. When I knocked on a friend's door, I heard a person walking to the door, I saw the peep hole open, and then I heard from behind the door, 'John, it's Kenny!' or 'Hold on Kenny, I'll get John!' When the friend who was being called for came to the door, they cracked it open just enough to talk or to walk out the door, and that was it. I was rarely invited in to wait or invited in for coffee cake and tea. Instead, I sat down on the steps near the door and waited for my friend to come out. It was like the wizard in *The Wizard of Oz* – you weren't allowed to look behind the curtain to see what was behind it. Maybe they didn't want me to see their beds in the hallway."

I don't remember when he told us this other story, it was probably also at one of our weekend breakfasts, but I kind of found it interesting. It wasn't one of his best stories but it was pretty good.

He was talking about apartment life when he said, "Let me tell you one of the most frustrating parts of apartment life. You might not be able to appreciate this yet, but I'm going to tell you anyway. It doesn't actually have anything to do with life inside the apartment – it had to do with parking your car on the street. You see you two won't understand this because we park our car in a garage. And when we go somewhere it's usually to a place with a giant parking lot. You guys are so soft – you take parking a car for granted."

"Huh? We take parking for granted? What does that mean? We don't even drive."

"What I'm trying to say is when I lived in the Bronx, it was almost impossible to find a parking space. Even though there were buses and subways many people still owned cars, but there weren't a lot of places to park. To make matters worse every few days you couldn't park on one side of the street because of 'alternate side of the street parking'.

"What's alternate side of the street parking, Dad?"

"It's something that was developed by the DEVIL to incite otherwise regular, non-violent people to murder and maim meter maids for 'Just doing their job.' Alternate Side of the street parking takes place Monday through Friday, and here's how it works. On Monday, between 9:00 a.m. through 11:00 a.m., no cars are allowed to park on one side of the street so the Sanitation Street Sweeper can clean the garbage from that side of the street. The street sweeper looks like a great big Zamboni, but instead of cleaning ice, it cleans poop, pee, paper, cigarette butts, and other trash off the city streets."

"More poop Dad?"

"Just listen, Kels. The side of the street which was cleaned alternated each day and therefore the side of the street you could park on between 9:00 and 11:00 alternated each day – that's why it's called alternate side of the street parking. I know it sounds pretty easy and it makes a lot of sense for a big city to keep the streets clean, BUT in reality it was a pain in the – Alternate Side of the Street! What makes this process such a mess is the fact that even without it there weren't enough spaces for all the cars in the Bronx."

"What did people do when they had to move their car?"

"They double parked them."

"What's double parked mean?"

"It's when you park your car next to another one which is parked legally next to the curb."

"Where do people go after they double park their car?"

"Sometimes they go back to their apartment to eat, take a shower, or to go back to sleep."

"Dad, how can the car near the curb get out?"

"Kelsie, you ask good questions. They can't get out until the double parked car moves."

"How do you know if they want to move their car?"

"The driver that's blocked in honks their car horn."

"What if they don't hear the horn?"

"They honk louder."

"What if they're in the shower or went back to sleep?"

"They honk louder and longer."

"What if they still don't hear them?"

"What is this? 1,000 questions. Who's telling this story anyway? Kelsie, they sit on their horn and wake everyone in the neighborhood up!"

"Can't they do anything else?"

"Sometimes they can. It depends on where they're parked. They can try to maneuver their car onto the sidewalk and drive down the sidewalk to the corner to get out."

"What else can they do?"

"They can call work and tell their boss they'll be late."

"Dad, that was another bad thing about living in an apartment. What about the good things?"

"Okay, let me think. Alright, here's one. Have you ever wondered why I call a plumber whenever we have a leak? Or why I call an electrician whenever we have an electric problem? Well, there's a good reason for it. I never, ever had to do anything handy when I lived in our apartment, and so to this day – I am the most unhandy, that should be a word, I am the most unhandy man in the world. I didn't have to do anything handy because I had a 'Super'."

"What's a Super?"

"It's short for superintendent. Supers are the hardworking men and woman responsible for keeping the apartment building clean and in good repair. Whenever anything went wrong in our apartment all we had to do was pickup the phone and call the super. If a light switch went bad – what did I do? Call the Super. If a water pipe broke – what did I do? Call the Super. If a light bulb burnt out – what did I do? Call the Super. Well actually I could do that – but not much more.

In addition to fixing anything that broke in the apartments the Super was responsible for the day-to-day cleanliness of the building. He mopped all the steps, hallways, and the lobby on a weekly basis. On Mondays and Thursdays he took all the bags of garbage that collected in the apartment basement out to the curb for the Sanitation workers to collect. And on a regular basis he was seen hosing down the sidewalk outside the building so all the poop and garbage was moved to street where it was collected by the street cleaners.

We loved the Super most of the time; the only time people hated him was when the boiler wasn't working!! The screams and gnashing of teeth could be heard for miles when the dreaded sign on the elevator was posted, 'Boiler Down for Repairs'! It always seemed to be posted at the worst times; like on cold days when you had a hot date. On the days when the boiler was down you had a few choices; you could take a shower in the frigid shower water, you could wash your hair in the sink and shower the rest of your body in cologne or perfume, or you could boil water and take a bath. Being a Super was generally a thankless job, but the tenants usually took care of the Super financially around Christmas with a $20 bill or more for all their hard work throughout the year."

"Dad, was $20 a lot when you were going up?"

"It probably wasn't a whole lot to the super but if all the tenants gave him $20 it would add up to a lot of money. It's like when I was a paperboy; most people gave me a $1 tip each week and this added up to be a lot of money."

"You were a paperboy?"

"Yes. Do you want to hear about it?"

"Sure."

The Pendulums Swing...

"Like I said before, I was about 11 years old when I moved from my grandmother's house to 222 West 233rd Street. It was around this time I started my first job. There was this guy, Joey Hoyt, who lived around the corner from me in 333 Kingsbridge Ave with his parents and two other brothers; his older brother Tony and his younger brother John. Joey was a few years older than me, he was 14 and, like I said, I was 11. Even though he was older, we became friends when I moved to 233rd Street. Joey had a paper route in the neighborhood, and since I was his friend, he asked me if I wanted to cover his route for him while he went on vacation.

I jumped at the opportunity to have my first real job so I could earn some extra money. To prepare to cover for Joey I had to learn the paper route business. This required I work a few mornings with him learning how to deliver papers and a few evenings to learn how to 'collect' payments from the customers. Joey delivered the New York Daily News, a tabloid newspaper read by all the 'regular people' in New York – it was my favorite paper because I loved the comic strips and Bill Gallo's cartoons in the Sports section.

Being a newspaper boy was a great job for a kid my age living in the city; I made good money, and it didn't interfere with school or sports, but it wasn't easy. The hardest parts about it were the early hours and working seven days a week – I never got a day off.

♪ [He] works hard for the money [10]

Kelsie said, "Dad, I thought the words were, 'SHE works hard for the money.'"

My dad gave Kelsie the evil eye and continued his story, "When Joey trained me I had to wake up at 5:30 a.m. to meet him at 5:45

in the lobby of his building. Everyday a bundle of newspapers was left under the steps of Joey's apartment building by a man in a New York Daily News van.

The first thing we did was count the newspapers to make sure there were enough papers for the customers. He had anywhere from 45 to 55 customers located in 5 apartment buildings on 233rd Street and around the corner on Kingsbridge Avenue. After we verified we had enough papers we began 'delivering' them. Most of the buildings in the area had locks on their front doors for safety, so we either had to be buzzed in by a tenant, or we needed a key to get in. The first building we delivered to was Joey's; he only had 3 customers in his building. We took the elevator up to the fifth floor to deliver a newspaper to apartment 5G then we walked down the steps delivering newspapers to 4C and 2B as we went down.

When we finished in Joey's building, we moved onto Aimen Ireland's building on 233rd Street; his building had an A side and a B side, and it was locked so Joey rang Mrs. O'Malley's apartment every morning and she let him in. The building didn't have an elevator so we walked up the A side of the building and delivered to several apartments on the way up. To deliver to the B side we walked up to the roof and crossed over to side B and we delivered to several apartments on the way down. The next stop was Mike Flanagan's building which only had one entrance but had three separate sections with their own stair cases. The building didn't have a lock on it, so we walked right in. It was only a five story building, so it didn't have an elevator; later on this became my least favorite building to deliver to because I had to walk up the stairs and down the stairs, up the stairs and down the stairs, and up the stairs and down the stairs. We delivered to about twelve customers in this building and moved on to our last building.

The final building was mine – it had an elevator and two sets of stairs cases – a paperboy's dream. We delivered the final fifteen newspapers in my building, and we were done for the morning. To make sure I remembered what I needed to do I brought a small note pad with me, and I wrote down the apartment buildings, apartment numbers, and names of the customers on it. It took about 45 minutes to complete the entire route – which wasn't bad. If I needed to rush, I could get it done in about 30 minutes.

The other part of the job I needed to learn was 'collecting' payments for the newspapers we delivered. 'Collection day' began on Thursday and sometimes lasted until Saturday or later. To collect, we walked around to the customer's apartment doors, knocked, and said, 'Paperboy.' The person looked through the 'peep hole' to make sure it was the 'paperboy' and then asked, 'How much is it?' The customer paid the weekly amount along with a 'tip'.

After Joey taught me the route, I covered for him a few times, but it wasn't long before he decided he was too old for a paper route. He asked me if I wanted to take over for him; again, I jumped at the chance. I was paid $20 each week by the New York Daily News which wasn't much, but I could count on $1.00 tip from each customer so I earned a whopping $65 to $75 per week – not bad for an 11 year old.

When I took over the reigns of the paperboy empire I wasn't alone. Have you ever heard the saying, 'Behind every successful man there is a woman'?"

"Nope – never heard that one."

"Well, it's a saying, but it's not important. Behind me there was my mother pushing, pulling, and encouraging me to get the job done. Grandma Hand woke me up every morning, she helped put together the Sunday Newspapers, and when I went away on vacation without her – she delivered the newspapers for me (maybe not every time, but several times). I loved my paper route and the lavish lifestyle it supported; I always had money for pinball, for pizza, soda, candy, and whatever my heart desired.

There were also some other perks of the job like the Ferrah sisters; Janet and Joanne, the older sisters of Eddie Ferrah – a teammate on my baseball team. When Janet answered her door on collection night she always said, 'Can I help you?' My immediate response was, 'Why, yes you can my little cream puff...'"

"You did not, Dad!"

"Well, maybe I just thought about doing it. So where was I? Oh yes, the perks. There were also anti-perks. On collection night several elderly ladies came to the door with their hair in curlers wearing their house dress – without a bra! Not a pretty picture seeing their boobie woobies swinging around, like grandfather clock pendulums, knocking into their knees.

Some people thought it was dangerous for me to walk around the streets alone at 6:00 a.m. or carrying around a couple hundred dollars in my pocket on collection night, but I never had any problems with these kinds of things. But I did have several frightening experiences; like the time I thought I was going to be mauled to death.

"You were almost mauled to death?"

"Yes! Remember what I mentioned earlier, I walked from the A side of the building to the B side by walking across the roof. I did this for months without any problems until, until, until the day I was almost eaten alive – sniff, sniff, sniff – it was horrible, horrible I tell you, horrible…"

Kelsie looked at my dad as he pretended to cry and said, "Get yourself together, Dad. Be a man, rub some dirt in it."

He pretended to calm down, "Okay, I'm okay – thanks Kelsie. Alright, this horrible experience happened to me one morning while I was delivering newspapers in Aimen's apartment building. After I walked halfway across the roof I heard someone or something on the roof breathing very heavily. As you can imagine, this scared me; I stopped and tried to figure out where it was coming from. I couldn't tell so I didn't know if I should go back or keep going across the roof. A few seconds later the heavy breathing got louder and louder as if it was getting closer and closer to me – I turned around, and I saw a 70 pound German Sheppard racing toward me ready to pounce on me!"

"Why would a German Sheppard be on the roof?"

"I guess because the owner wanted to give his dog some exercise. Most dogs in the Bronx got their exercise when they were walked or taken to the park by their owners, but I guess this guy wanted to treat the roof like it was his own back yard…"

I interrupted my dad and said, "I didn't think there were any dogs in New York, because there aren't any yards for them to play in."

Pepper – A Bronx Tail

"Yeah Cam – I know what you're saying. It doesn't seem to make sense for large families living in small apartments to own a dog, but surprisingly many families do. Even though there's not a lot of room in apartments, I guess people liked having them for protection, companionship, or both.

It was easy to tell who owned dogs, because the owners walked their dog two or three times a day. It was even easier to tell which streets had the most dogs living in the apartment buildings based on the number of loads of poop which filled the streets."

"Here we go again, Cam! More poop stories."

"Anyway, the poop was everywhere. When I was Cam's age dog owners didn't have to clean up after their dogs; their dog just dropped a load in the street and the owner left it. Some streets in the neighborhood were disgusting; you literally couldn't walk in the street without stepping in poop. The worst, poop infested, street I remember was Naples Terrace; it was so bad we gave it a nickname – Poop Street USA."

"You called it Poop Street USA?"

"Well, not exactly. The name was a little different but the idea was the same.

"I think I understand. Continue."

"Stepping off the sidewalk and into the street was very dangerous when I was your age. Remember when we watched that nature show where Zebras crossed a river filled with crocodiles? Remember how the crocodiles snuck up on the zebras and ate them?"

"Yeah that was cool."

"Well that's how it was when we stepped off the sidewalk. I was attacked by many rogue piles of poop when I wasn't paying attention to where I was walking. Avoiding hot steaming land mines and flowing urine rivers was an accepted part of my life growing up.

During the cold winter months these mines and rivers posed little threat; freshly laid mines became hardened turds within minutes, and yellow rivers froze before they ran their full course. The only danger from a large winter turd was accidentally stepping on it and twisting an ankle. On the other hand, during the hot, humid summer months the dangers from a steaming turd were real. One misstep or lapse in concentration and the results could be devastating; many Converse and Pro Ked sneakers fell victim to piles of poop sneaking up on unsuspecting pedestrians. When an attack took place and casualties were sustained, the curb was the triage center. A regular sight in the Bronx was people scraping their shoes on the corner of a curb attempting to de-poopify their shoes."

"Dad, you're really obsessed with poop; aren't you?"

"Yeah, Kels, you got a problem with that?"

"No, not really, I just wanted to point it out to you."

My dad got back to his story, "This poop nightmare didn't last for too long. By the time I was Kelsie's age things changed. This is when New York City passed the 'Pooper Scooper' law..."

"Cam, don't believe Dad. There is no way a law was called the 'Pooper Scooper Law' – no way!"

My dad said, "Cam, ignore your sister. She doesn't believe anything I say. So where was I? Oh yeah. After the pooper scooper law was passed, all dog owners were required to pickup their dog's poop and place it in a bag instead of leaving it on the ground. When the law was first passed it was interesting to watch dog owners outside in the street in a squat position, like a catcher in baseball, waiting for their dog to squeeze out a turd. It was kind of like waiting for a huge piece of Play Dough to be squeezed out in the shape of a star or like a doctor delivering a baby. I remember listening to dog owners encouraging their dogs, 'Come on Spot...

push, push…it's almost there…come on you can do it…come on… right into the bag…you're doing great…yes…yes…ALRIGHT… good dog!'"

"Again, Dad, you don't expect us to believe this do you?"

"You believe what you want little girl. I'm just telling you what I saw.

Okay, so where was I before I was so rudely interrupted again by Miss Smarty Pants over there? Oh yeah. I was beginning to tell you not everyone caught the poop before it hit the ground. In fact, most people didn't, instead they waited for the turd to hit the ground before they picked it up and put it in their little baggies. The pooper scooper law really cleaned up the streets in the Bronx but there were some unintended consequences.

To understand some of the unintended consequences you need to realize dogs liked being walked for exercise and to relieve themselves, but they also liked it because it was a time for socializing with the other dogs in the neighborhood. In other words, being walked was the dog's time to talk to other dogs in the typical dog way – by sniffing and licking each other's rear ends."

I said, "Now, Dad, that really is gross!"

"I know. I'm glad we don't talk like this, but that's how dogs do it. Sniffing another dog's bottom is their way of saying, 'Hi, Spot, how's it going?' Then the other dog sniffs and that's his way of saying, 'Oh, pretty good – how about you?' On the days I walked Pepper, when there weren't any dogs on the street, he pulled me from poop pile to poop pile and he'd say, 'Oh jeez, I missed Lady, sniff, sniff. She must have been fed left over pot roast and vegetables – I can still see the corn. Come on Kenny, let's go over to that load; it's big; it must be Spike. Sniff, sniff – yup, that was Spike, there's no mistaking that aroma.'

You see what I mean guys? The unintended consequence of the pooper scooper law was it made it more difficult for dogs to keep track of their dog friends."

"Here we go again Cam. You know he's making this up."

My dad just ignored Kelsie and he continued his story, "Before the pooper scooper law Pepper knew where his friends dropped their loads, but after the pooper scooper law there was no more loads to sniff. Immediately after the law was passed I remember Pepper yanking and pulling me all over the street looking for piles of poop. He was acting strange as he yanked, pulled, and sniffed. He finally screamed from the top of his lungs, 'What have you done to Lady, Fluffy, and Spike? What have you done to them? I know you humans have done something horrible to them! What have you done?' I tried to calm Pepper down by explaining to him nothing happened to his friends. I told him they were still around but now their owners picked up their poop and put it in a baggie. I said to him, 'You can't keep track of them by sniffing their poop anymore but they still pee all over the street – why don't you just keep track of them by sniffing their pee?' Pepper stopped, looked up into my eyes, tilted his head, and said, 'Sniff their pee – oh, you're sick!!'"

"Funny, Dad, but seriously what was Pepper like? I mean, other than him having the ability to talk. What kind of dog was he?"

"Pepper was a great dog. He was a mixed breed with jet black hair and..."

"What's a mixed breed?"

"It means he was a mutt. He wasn't a Poodle or a German Sheppard – he was a mix of a lot of different types of dogs. Clear as mud?"

"Clear as mud. Continue."

My dad went on, "Now, of course when my mother brought Pepper home we didn't have a name for him yet. We discussed and debated many names, but in the end we decided on Pepper – the WHOLE family agreed on this name except for...except for...you guessed it...Aunt Chris. Yes, the Evil Aunt Chris strikes again!

She didn't like the fact we decided to name him Pepper – she thought it was a dictatorial decision made by my mother. She felt a more appropriate name for a dog with Jet black hair was Jet. I didn't think Jet was a bad name for a dog, but it wasn't the name we agreed to. Chris said, 'I didn't agree to it – his name is Jet, and that's what I'm going to call him!' I said to her, 'You can't do that – Jet is not his name – Pepper is his name!' 'No, it's not!' 'Yes, it is!' 'No, it's not!' You get the picture. Sounds a lot like you two having an argument.

No matter what he was called – Pepper was a great dog, and we loved him. Like most dogs in the city, he provided some protection, but mostly he kept us company."

"How did he protect you?"

"Well, I don't think we really needed protection but whenever a person buzzed 1D, or knocked on the front door of our apartment, Pepper went into a barking fit, and he sounded like a mean, vicious dog. Because of Pepper's bark, if there ever was a burglar in our building, there's no doubt he would have avoided our apartment. But if a burglar happened to enter our apartment, he would have found out Pepper wouldn't hurt a fly – unless, of course, a burglar could be licked or humped to death.

In fact, Pepper was such a wimp, he walked around the house shaking like a leaf with his tail between his legs during thunder storms. When he got really scared, I picked him up and laid him on my lap to comfort him. I'd say, 'It's okay Pepper, don't worry, it's just thunder.' Pepper responded, 'Just thunder! Just thunder! What? Are you crazy?! The world is coming to an end – don't you get it?? We're all going to die!!! Hold me tighter, Kenny…' When there wasn't anyone around to comfort him he found refuge in the front coat closet, far in the back, underneath a bunch of coats which had fallen down.

Pepper was a wimp when it stormed outside, but he was brave when it came to stealing food. When he was a puppy we fed him Alpo, but as he got older we usually fed him table scraps. He liked people food so much he occasionally jumped up on the kitchen table to steal our food right off our plate. This maneuver usually earned him a swift whack on the rear with a rolled up newspaper, but I'm sure he felt a whack on the rear was a fair exchange for a hamburger or spaghetti.

My brothers, sisters, and I got tired of walking him after we had him for a few years, even though we loved him. When he was a puppy all of us kids fought over who would walk him, but after the honeymoon period wore off we stopped fighting over who would walk him, and we started fighting over who would walk him…"

"Dad, you just said the same thing."

My dad said, "Yeah, I know, but you get the point. Eventually the only person in the family who walked him was my mother. Even though none of us kids walked Pepper he still let us know when he had to go poop."

Kelsie rolled her eyes and said, "Here we go again – more stories about poop!!"

My dad smiled and said, "Yes, I'm going to talk about poop one more time. Okay, where was I? Oh yeah. When he had to go poop he stood by the door and spun around and around, barking and barking. He also yelled at the top of his lungs, 'I gotta go…I gotta go…I gotta go…please someone take me out…I gotta go…I gotta go…please someone…anyone…I gotta go…I gotta go…Hey guys, I just drank a whole bowl of toilet water – I just polished off three plates of spaghetti – I gotta go…gotta go!!!'

Most of us ignored Pepper's warnings except to scream, 'Mom, I think Pepper needs to go out!' When we ignored Pepper he yelled even louder, 'If you don't take me out soon, you're going to have a mess near the front door! Come on…I gotta go…I gotta go…I can't hold it – I don't have hands! If you don't take me out right now, I'm dropping a bomb right here…here it comes…don't say I didn't warn you!' Of course when it was time for one of us to leave for the night, and we walked to our front door we yelled, 'Mom, look what Pepper did near the front door! Pepper!!! Bad, Bad, Dog! Bad, Dog!'

When Pepper was told he was a 'bad dog' he yelled back at us in disbelief, 'What? I'm a bad dog? Are you freaking crazy? I don't think so!! I warned you!! If I had fingers and could speak, I'd dial the Humane Society's phone number and tell them you kids don't take me for walks anymore – I'd show them my bladder to prove it. My bladder is the size of a volley ball because I have to hold my pee in for days at a time – I feel like a freaking camel!! If you don't start taking me out more often it's going to happen again, and again, and again! Next time I'm not going to be so nice and drop it near the front door – I'm going to leave my present for you on your dinner plate!! Would you like that??!! I didn't think so – just like I don't like not being taken out when I have to poop! I hope you step in a load tonight with your new Converse sneakers, and it gets into those little nooks and crannies – and I hope it never comes out!"

Kelsie said, "Are you done telling us about poop? I'm starting to get sick."

"Yeah, I'm done talking about poop for now, but I still have to tell you about the time I almost killed Pepper."

Kelsie sat up and said, "You almost killed your dog. You are so bad. You're the one who didn't take him out – he should have killed you!"

My dad said, "This doesn't have anything to do with taking Pepper out for a walk. It has to do with him and my food.

It happened one night at 4:00 a.m. when I got home from a night of hanging out with my friends at *Off Broadway*. I had gone out early that night, before my mother made supper, and since I only had enough money for a few drinks I was starving by the time I got home – I had a vicious case of the 'MUNCHIES'! Because I was starving, the walk home that night seemed a lot longer than normal – all I thought about on the way home was, 'I hope my mom made something good for dinner and I hope there are leftovers!'

When I reached my building, I stumbled up the steps on my way to my apartment. I tried to quietly open the apartment door, but when Pepper heard the door being opened he started barking his head off! I quietly said, 'Pepper, Pepper, shhhh, shhhh, it's me, quiet down buddy…quiet down.' When I got inside I looked in the refrigerator and I saw a big pot of my mom's famous spaghetti! I thought to myself, 'Mmmm, mmmm good, this is perfect!'

"Your mom had famous spaghetti?"

"It was famous to me that night – I was starving!"

Now keep in mind when I was a teenager nobody owned microwave ovens, and so I had to warm up my spaghetti in the oven. I pulled the pot of spaghetti out of the refrigerator and put it on top of the washing machine. Then I shoveled mounds of spaghetti out of the pot onto a ceramic plate, and I placed it in the oven.

Back in those days we didn't have the fancy schmancy ovens we have now – NO – we had to light the oven with a match. This meant I had to turn on the gas, light a match, and put it in a little hole in the bottom of the oven to light the pilot light. This night I found a book of matches on the stove, and I turned on the gas. I could hear the sound of the gas coming out of the oven – Sssssssss. When I opened up the book of matches I found there was only one match left. I struck the match against the striker but it was worn out so the match didn't light. I could still hear the gas coming out of the oven – Sssssssss. I looked around the kitchen for another book of matches, but couldn't find any so I walked out to the living room – Sssssssss – and I found a book of matches next to my mother's pack of Parliaments. I walked back into the kitchen – Sssssssss – bent down, lit the match, began to reach into the oven, and before I knew what happened – BOOM!!! A fireball shot out from the oven towards my face! I quickly jumped back with my cat like reflexes and landed on my back in the hallway. From the floor I looked around and I didn't notice anything burning, and when I looked in the mirror my eyebrows were still there – I was very lucky! A second later, from the back bedroom I heard, 'Kenny, what happened? Be careful if you're heating up the spaghetti. Remember, 'Don't turn on the gas until you light the match.' I said, 'Thanks Mom. I'm fine – you can go back to sleep!'

With the oven now lit I waited and waited for my food to warm up. Waiting for food to warm up when you have the munchies is like an eight year old waiting for Christmas morning to come. I checked on my food a million times to see if it was hot enough, 'Come on, come on, would you heat up, I'm starving! Come on! I'm not asking for much, I don't need it HOT, I just need it lukewarm, come on, I'm starving, come on baby, heat the food, I'm starving, come on baby!!!' Eventually the food was warm enough to eat and so I grabbed the plate with one of the pot holders hanging on the wall and I carried my plate into the living room and placed it on the coffee table.

When I put down my food Pepper walked into the room. He said, 'Hey Kenny, can I have some? There's an awful lot of spaghetti there, and I'm sure you can share some – how about it dude?' Pepper walked over to the table sniffing, sniffing, and sniffing. I said, 'Pepper, don't even think about it! You will regret the day you were born if you touch my food!'

I walked over to the TV and turned on WPIX, Channel 11, to watch a rerun of *Welcome Back Kotter*. While I walked to the TV I watched Pepper carefully and I said, 'Don't you dare. Don't you dare!' I sat back down on the couch and began shoveling spaghetti into my mouth. As I was chewing Pepper inched closer and closer to me and with my mouth full of food I said, 'Stay away…don't you dare!' Little pieces of spaghetti spewed out of my mouth as I warned Pepper.

He sat down two feet away from my food, and he looked at me with the most sympathetic puppy dog eyes he could muster. He said to me, 'Kenny, look at me. I'm sitting here being such a good dog. Can you find it in your heart to share some of your food with me – please?! Look – I'm not begging – I'm being a good dog.' I looked at Pepper and said, 'No way! Get your own food!'

Then it happened. As Pepper sat two feet away from my food he began turning his snout to the left and the right. He said, 'What's that? I feel a tickle in my nose. Wow, something is really tickling my nose. It's really tickling my nose and I can't stop it. I, ahhh, I, ahhh, ahhh, I, AAAAHHHHHH CCCCHHHHOOOO!!!' With little warning Pepper let out the biggest sneeze I had ever seen. It seemed to happen in slow motion – I saw his head tilt backward then forward and like an explosion I saw a load of snot and mucus shoot out of Pepper's nose and fly through the air toward my food! I tried to dive in front of the snot and mucus, like a Secret Service Agent dives in front of an assassin's bullet to save the president – but it was too late. Before I knew it the damage was done – my spaghetti was covered with a translucent green, oozing blob of snot!

Pepper knew he was in trouble as soon as it happened! He raised his eyebrows, his eyes popped out of their sockets, and he ran into the front closet. I ran after him to the hallway closet, and I dove in after him. I yelled, 'Get out here Pepper! Get out here now! I know you did that on purpose!!!' He yelled back, 'No I didn't! It was an accident! I promise! I'm sorry!' I said, 'Don't lie to me! You did it on purpose – I know you did – you're mad because I don't walk you anymore!!!' Pepper said, 'Yeah, well that's true, but I didn't mean to sneeze on your food – come on – like you've never sneezed before! It could have happened to anyone!' I said, 'Yeah right! Pepper, come out here and take you're beating like a man!!' Pepper said, 'I'm not a man – I'm a dog! I'm calling the ASPCA if don't leave me alone!!!' Luckily for Pepper there were so many coats in the closet I was never able to get my hands on him."

"Pepper, the talking dog. Yeah, that could happen. Cam, don't believe him. I think Dad has lost it.

Uh, Dad, just a little innocent observation here. Do you realize you have more stories about poop, snots, and Pepper than you do about Aunt Tricia."

"So what's your point, Kelsie?"

"I'm not sure, but I'll come up with one."

"Okay, while you're figuring out your point let me get back to my original story. I was telling you about the German Sheppard racing toward me and how he was about to pounce on me. Yeah, that's right. So when I saw the dog racing toward me I started to run but it jumped on me and was about to bite me, but then I stopped and covered my face. When I stopped moving, the dog stopped barking – so I didn't move a muscle. I was near the edge of the roof, and so I decided to scream for help over the ledge into the courtyard – but the German stinking Sheppard didn't like that either; when I yelled the dog moved closer, showed his teeth, and growled. It was like that dog in Cugo..."

"Who is Cugo?"

"It's a Steven King story about a mean dog. Anyway, about 45 minutes later the stinking dog's owner showed up? I wanted to kill this guy – he didn't even say sorry. He just looked at me and whistled to his dog and said, 'Come on Joe.'

I was so mad; I ran up behind the dog, picked him up over my head and I flung that lousy, stinking dog off the roof and his blood and guts splattered all over the courtyard!"

Kelsie jumped up and said, "DAD! You didn't!"

"No, I'm just kidding – I love dogs but I should have thrown the dog's owner off the roof!

So that was my life as a paperboy. I think I did it for about 2 years, but when I turned 13 I decided to quit because I thought I was too old to be a paperboy – it just wasn't a sophisticated enough job for me."

"Hmmm, interesting Dad. What else can you tell us about? Can you tell us about your best friends?"

Butch Cassidy and the Sundance Kid

"Alright, when I moved to 233rd Street I started hanging out with Pat. The fact that Pat was as much of a sports fanatic as me was probably the reason we became friends, but it was his sense of humor and his positive attitude which made us best friends. Early on, when we weren't playing organized sports, we spent most of our days in a four block area near our apartment buildings playing city sports. We could usually be found playing basketball behind St. John's middle school, stick ball behind PS 7, or playing football in front of St. John's middle school.

Pat lived in apartment 2B around the block from me on the corner of 232nd street and Godwin Terrace. It was a four room apartment with a small kitchen, living room, a 'master' bedroom, and a bedroom for Pat and his sister Mary. Pat's father immigrated to the United States from the County Cork in 1963 and he spoke with an Irish brogue. Early on when I met him I learned not to imitate his brogue in front of him because Pat's father believed anyone imitating a brogue was actually belittling his Irish ancestry. Nothing could be further from the truth; I actually thought his brogue sounded cool, and I had a lot of respected for Mr O'.

Mr O' was different than most of the other fathers in the neighborhood. Unlike most fathers who stopped off at the local tavern after work he not only didn't stop off at the local tavern – he didn't drink alcohol at all. Furthermore, he enjoyed spending time with his family, and it showed. He drove Pat and other kids in the neighborhood, to baseball, football, and basketball games in his 1975 Volkswagen station wagon. He loved going to Pat's games and practices, and in fact he was very athletic himself. When he was growing up in Ireland he was known as one of the toughest Hurley players in the County. Later in life, when I knew him, he was an avid long distance runner; after work he could be found running several laps around the Vanny Flats.

Pat's mother was a second generation Irish immigrant and one of the nicest mothers in the neighborhood. She was a stay at home mom for many years until a few years before Pat attended college. It was at this time she began working at Manhattan College because Pat would be able to attend the college at a discounted rate. Pat's sister Mary was the nicest sister you could ever imagine. Unlike Chris and me, Pat and Mary had a close relationship. They never threw knives at each other, and they never chopped off each other's hair when the other was sleeping.

Pat also had an awesome apartment for an 11 year old boy – his foyer was wide which made it perfect for a puff basketball court. He also had the latest technology, like Pong, Super Pong, and Calico Pro Football, but most importantly he received *Sports Illustrated* on a weekly basis from a friend of his fathers. *Sports Illustrated* was the greatest printed material on earth for two sports fanatics but it also peeked our interest for another reason. My first exposure to naked women came from Sport Illustrated..."

Kelsie sat up and screamed, "WHAT? YOU LOOKED AT NAKED WOMEN IN *SPORTS ILLUSTRATED*?!!"

My dad smiled and said, "Kelsie, the human body is beautiful! And oh my gosh – Cheryl Teague in a see-through bathing suit – is really beautiful! I'm kidding, Kels,...kind of...sort of.

As we got older, sports weren't the only things we did to stay busy – during the winter months we spent a lot of time sleigh riding down Ewen Park Hill. Pat and his sister Mary each had flexible flyers and so when Pat and I went sleigh riding...wait, that's a whole other story for another day. Let me tell you something else; one of the coolest things we did when we were kids.

Pat was the first guy I knew who had a skateboard, so I learned how to skateboard by riding Pat's. It wasn't long before I began pestering my mom for a skateboard of my own. The pestering turned into nagging, the nagging turned into badgering, and the badgering eventually turned into torture until my mom finally gave in..."

Kelsie said, "Now I know where I got it from. I do the same thing to mommy when I need new clothes."

My dad nodded his head and said, "I know, that's right. So where was I? Oh yeah, I was telling you about skateboarding. After my mom bought a skateboard for me, Pat and I spent every second of every waking hour on our skateboards. We began slowly and safely, mostly skateboarding down the IHOP parking lot hill, maneuvering in and out of the parking bumpers on our way down the hill. During the early days of skateboarding we wiped out often, and we got a lot of bumps, bruises, scrapes, and cuts, but like most 11 year old boys we just picked ourselves up, brushed off the dirt, wiped the blood on our shirts and did it all over again. As we became more and more comfortable and confident in our skateboarding ability we increased the level of difficulty of the hills and obstacles we maneuvered down and around. We began skateboarding down the steeper hills in the neighborhood like Kingsbridge Avenue, 234th Street, 233rd Street – the steeper the hill, the better!

The only exception to 'the steeper the hill, the better' was skateboarding inside of Manhattan College. Pat's dad worked as a Security Guard in the Manhattan College Engineering building on Corlear Avenue on Saturday mornings. After skateboarding on Saturday morning we stopped off at McDonald's near Off Broadway for lunch. Pat always ordered his 'plain hamburger' and I always said, 'Pat, this isn't Burger King. Special orders DO upset them!'"

"Dad, what do you mean 'Special Orders' upset them?"

"Cam, Burger King used to have a motto or TV commercial that said, 'Special Orders don't upset us' and McDonalds didn't…oh never mind. Where was I? Oh yeah. After Pat ordered his special order that upset McDonalds, I ordered a Big Mac, fries, and a coke. After lunch we skateboarded down the street to see Pat's dad and to skateboard on the smooth floors of Manhattan College. We usually spent about an hour or so visiting with his father on Saturday, and then we left to continue skateboarding down the hills of Kingsbridge.

As I said before, Kingsbridge is essentially a valley between the high, steep hills leading up to Riverdale on the West and the high, steep hills leading up to the Sedgwick Avenue Reservoir on the East. One Saturday afternoon after visiting Pat's dad we were trying to decide which hill to conquer next. I can't remember if it was Pat or me who came up with the idea, but since it was a really, really stupid idea the chances are it was mine. The incredibly stupid idea was to skateboard down Riverdale Avenue! Riverdale Avenue is a long, steep, winding, four lane road with a lot of bumps and cracks AND it's a busy road; at any given time of the day there were dozens of cars flying down the road. It was a totally insane idea and an even more insane thing to actually do! It was stupid, insane, and an extremely dangerous thing to do, but this never seemed to stop us from doing anything and so...up the hill we went."

"What was it like skateboarding down the hill?"

My dad said, "Cam, it was GREAT! It was stupid – but GREAT! We started at the top of the hill near a bar called Doc Fiddlers. At first we started off slowly because Riverdale Avenue was relatively flat near Doc Fiddlers but once we crossed the street the hill got steeper, and so we started to pickup speed very quickly. We rode down the right side of the hill close to the wall. The wind was blowing in our faces and our coats were flapping behind us – it was GREAT! But just as we were enjoying the wind blowing in our faces the cars started driving past us going 30, 40, and sometimes 50 miles per hour. This made it difficult to skateboard down the hill because we couldn't swerve back and forth; this caused us to go faster and faster and faster! When we were about half way down the hill we reached the point of no return! We were going too fast to jump off and we had nowhere to slowdown – there was nothing we could do – we had to stay on the skateboards! We were flying down the hill next to each other with cars honking their horns at us and yelling out their car windows, 'Hey! What are you schmucks doing? Get off the $%^&% road!'

We were going so fast it was hard to hear each other; Pat screamed, 'If we try to jump off now, we'll crack our skulls open!' I screamed, 'I know! Whose stupid idea was this? I think we're going to die!' At this point we stayed on our skateboards, our eyes were watering, our noses were running, we bent our knees to use them as shock absorbers when we hit the many rocks, cracks, and small pot holes in and on the road. All we could do is look straight ahead and pray. I yelled my prayer, 'Please God let the light at the bottom of the hill be green! PLEASE!' Pat yelled at me, 'But first God – Please help us to make it down the hill!'

If the light was red when we got to the bottom of the hill it meant the cross traffic would cut us off which meant certain disaster and possible death. Skateboarding down this hill was the most exciting thing we ever did, but at the same time, the most terrifying, because if we hit a big pot hole or hit a big rock we would have literally flew off the skateboard into the air, and without a doubt we would have broken some bones! If we fell off we certainly would have broken some bones but if cars ran over us we would have died! When we approached 231st Street we had already broken the sound barrier, and we were flying towards a RED light! There were several cars stopped in front of us and a city bus was turning left from 231st onto Johnson Avenue. Pat and I had to split up; Pat yelled, 'I'll go in between the cars – you go around them near the wall!' I listened to Pat and we both maneuvered past the stopped cars then we made a sharp right turn toward Ewen hill – we narrowly missed the bus!

Once we made the turn toward Ewen hill and the parked cars, our skateboards started slowing down. When we finally came to a stop we hopped off and staggered over to one of the benches at the bottom of the hill, and we plopped down. Our hearts were pounding, our knees were shaking, and we were out of breath. We leaned back, looked up in the air, said a prayer of thanks, and then I turned to Pat, smiled, and asked, 'Do you want to try skateboarding down Snake Hill tomorrow?'

Not only did my friend, Pat spend a lot of time running around the neighborhood with me playing sports and almost getting killed – he also taught me an important life lesson. It happened a few years after Pat and I began hanging out with each other. We started hanging around with a cool group of guys, Tommy, John, Tony, and Timmy, along with a few others. This one particular day we were playing football in PS 7, and after playing for several hours straight all the boys sat down on the concrete for a rest before calling it quits for the day and going home for dinner. When Pat came over to the rest of us he said, 'I feel like s#$t.' I was trying to be funny and I said, 'Pat, you are s$%t.' and everyone laughed. I didn't say it because it was Pat – I would have said it in response to anyone making this comment – and I certainly didn't really mean it because Pat was my best friend. Since I didn't mean it, I didn't think anymore about it.

Shortly after I got home for dinner the phone rang and it was Pat. When I got on the phone, Pat told me in no uncertain terms he didn't appreciate what I said to him and not to do it ever again. Pat didn't yell; he didn't lose his composure; he dealt with the situation like a man. I told Pat I didn't mean what I said, but I also knew whether I meant it or not was not the point – the point was I said it. I was embarrassed by what I said to Pat. Also, I realized it wasn't easy for Pat to call me, but the call had to be made in order for him to keep his self respect.

My dad told me many times that there will be times when people will do things or say things that are hurtful or just plain wrong. We have a choice we can either address them directly, or we can put our heads in the sand and ignore these things and hope they will get better. I remember him saying, "The best way to handle these situations is to confront the person in a mature, matter of fact way – no matter how difficult it might be. In the long run you and everyone else will be better off. You need to handle the situation like a man – just like Pat did."

My dad always considered Pat to be the best friend he ever had, even though they grew apart when they got older and attended different high schools. Although they grew apart, Pat was still the best man at my father's wedding. My father told me he can still remember telling Pat he was getting married to my mom and Pat looked at him and said, 'I'm going to be your best man...right?' My dad told him, 'Of course!' and they just went on talking and making plans, but he said, Pat will never really know how much it meant to him – to have his best friend after all those years still want to be his best man. At the time my father wasn't sure if Pat even remembered the agreement they made many years before when they were 12. The agreement they made was that Pat would be the best man at my father's wedding and my father would be the best man at his."

"What about your other friends?"

SECTION V

Only the Good Die Young

♪ You might have heard I run with a dangerous crowd
We aint too pretty ♪
♪ We aint too proud
We might be laughing a bit too loud ♪
♪ Awe but that never hurt no one

They say there's a heaven for those who wait ♪
♪ Some say it's better but I say it aint
I'd rather laugh with the sinners than cry with the saints ♪
♪ The sinners are much more fun
You know that only the good die young ♪" [11]

The Godwin Gang

"Okay, I'll tell you a little about them, but what I tell you in McDonalds stays in McDonalds."

"Why?"

"Because the statute of limitations hasn't expired on all the things my friends and I did when we were younger. I'll tell you a few things but not everything – I have to leave out some of the dirty little details until I'm on my deathbed or when you're 45 – whichever comes first."

"Oh, come on Dad. Can you tell us some of the bad stories?"

"NO! Absolutely NOT! Never, ever! Not in a million years!"

"Pretty please!"

"Okay – maybe just a few.

But first of all, you need to know I grew up with a lot of friends. Like I mentioned earlier, there were a lot of apartment buildings in Kingsbridge, and this means there were a lot of people who lived in a relatively small area. Okay, follow me on this one. In my building there were about 11 apartments on each floor and there were 6 floors which means in my building alone there were 66 families. On each block there were about 4 apartment buildings which means there were about 264 families living on each block. When I grew up families usually had at least 4 kids which means there were about 1,056 kids to play with on my block alone."

"Really?"

"No, I'm exaggerating a little, but my point is there were a lot of kids in the neighborhood to hang out with. Of course, I knew most of them because they almost all went to St. John's school; they attended St. John's church; they played football and basketball for St. John's, and played baseball for Kingsbridge Little League. I got to know the kids who didn't go to St. John's by playing pickup games all over Kingsbridge."

"What's a pickup game?"

"Well, when I say 'pickup game' I'm talking about a bunch of guys getting together to play baseball, basketball, football, soccer, or hockey in one of the school yards or parks in Kingsbridge. For example, during football season we played touch football in the front of PS 7 or behind St. John's Grammar School. During basketball season we played basketball behind St. John's Middle School, or behind PS 7, or the 230th Street Park, or the courts in Ewen Park. When we played a pickup game a bunch of us guys picked two captains and they picked their teams. We played for hours and hours after school and on the weekends. We played until it got dark out or until dinner time; by the time we were finished we were exhausted and our feet were covered with bloody blisters.

My best friends were Pat, John, Tommy, Shawn, Timmy, Mark, Tony, Bobby, Billy, Scott, Joey, John, and there were dozens of other friends we'd play sports and other games with like, Johnnie, Johnnie, Billy, Chris, Kenny, Danny, Eddie, Raymond, Mike, Dan, Jimmy, John, Tommy, Rickie, Rick, and I could go on and on and on."

"Okay, so what other games did you play with your friends?"

"Well other than sports we also played games like stick ball, curb ball, king-queen, box ball, round-up, and some other games I can't remember right now. Sometime I'll tell you all about these games. All my friends were athletic and fun to be around but most of all, like I think I said before, they were all good guys. My mother refers to people she likes as 'regular guys'. I think this means they're not phony or pretentious; they don't act like they're something special; they're easy to talk to, but mostly it means they're nice guys. My mother would consider all my friends to be regular guys. They all came from big families who loved them. They didn't necessarily have a lot of money; but they had enough. But let me point out that although they were regular guys it doesn't mean they were perfect – they all got into their share of trouble." My dad paused, nodded his head and said, "Just like me."

He continued, "When we got a little older my friends and I started hanging out with girls. Most of the girls were from the neighborhood and also went to St. John's. Like the guys I grew up with, the girls were also nice – they were regular people too."

"I thought city girls were wild, Dad."

"Well Kels, I'm not saying they were always perfect, but they were very nice and a lot of fun to be around. They were sometimes wild, but not in a bad way – they were wild in a good way. Some of them were very athletic like the guys I hung out with. Some of the girls played basketball, softball, soccer, and they all played the city games together with the guys."

"What kind of games did you and the girls play?"

"We played basketball, soccer, and other games like Punchball..."

"Wait, what's Punchball?"

"It's like baseball except it's played with a spaldeen. The pitcher bounced the ball once to the batter and the batter punched the ball. Once the ball was punched into the field the game was exactly like baseball. We used to play Punch in the back of St. John's Grammar school with the girls. We played some pretty competitive game of Punch, but one of the reasons I liked it was it was a great way for a shy guy like me to pickup chicks."

"Nice, Dad."

"But seriously, all the girls were very nice and came from good families. My best friends, who were girls, were Jordan, Robin, Denise, Susan, Kathy, Cathy, Cathy…"

"Dad, why do you keep saying Cathy?"

"Because Kelsie, a lot of the girls were named Kathy and Cathy – I guess it was a popular Irish Catholic name when I was growing up. Some of my other best friends were Lori, Michelle, Maureen, Joanne, Eileen, Mary, Kelly, Caroline, Caroline, Marie, Pam, Lorinda, Mary, Bernadette, Bridget, Jackie, Diane, Jennifer, Beth, Teresa, Frannie, and, and, and I could go on and on and on.

Most of the guys and girls I hung out with were similar in a lot of ways; we all came from a working class background; we were mostly Irish Catholics; we went to the same school; we went to the same church; we played on the same teams; we had big families; we lived in small apartments; we liked the same music; we liked the same movies; none of us were rich; we were all nice, but we got into our share of harmless trouble, and, and, and, well you get the picture.

All of us began hanging out together when we were young, but we became better and better friends as the years went by. As we got older our group expanded when our friends met new friends and brought them into our group. Going to a neighborhood reunion with my friends is like going to a family reunion – the friendships we developed as kids were very unique – at least I think they were.

When we were in grade school, we met after school on the O'Grady's stoop on Godwin Terrace, right across from St. John's Grammar School. Because we hung out on Godwin Terrace, just up the block from 231st Street, sometimes people referred to us as the Godwin Gang."

"You were part of a gang?"

"Uh – no, we weren't a gang. If we were a gang we would have made up a tougher name than the Godwin Gang. We would have come up with a name like the Bloods, Crips, Sharks, or at least the Jets. No, we were just a bunch of friends who hung out on Godwin Terrace. There were many different groups of kids, who hung out in different areas, all over the neighborhood. When we talked about these other groups we usually referred to them by the area they hung out; there were the 'groups' in PS 7, Pat Mitchell's, Bailey Avenue, Corlear Avenue, Marble Hill, The Park, 238th Street, Naples Terrace, Johnson Avenue, and dozens more."

"What do you mean when you say hang out?"

"That's what we did – we hung out. Hanging out meant standing or sitting around talking with the other people in your group, but it also meant more. It meant you played sports or went to parties with these people."

"Did you fight with the other groups?"

"No, most of the other groups were good people too but they were either older, younger, or they just had different interests. Actually, when it came to organized sports people from all the groups played for the same teams. For example, when I played on the Bronx Steelers, and we won the Bronx Championship we had guys from all the groups on the team. Sometimes we played softball, football, hockey or basketball against the other groups for fun. Most of the time we played against other groups it was for a keg of beer to make it interesting.

I remember one time when I was low on money I organized a game of softball with the guys from Bailey Avenue for a keg of beer. The only reason I organized it was because I thought for sure we'd beat them and I'd have free beer for the night. But that's not how it worked out. When we started losing to them I was ticked! When one of my friends asked me why I was taking it so seriously I said, 'Because if we lose I don't have any money to pay for the keg!'"

"Dad!"

"Okay Kelsie. Anyway, back to my group. We were always together and we spent most of our time laughing, talking, sometimes fighting, playing, but mostly we just enjoyed each other's company. The laughing, talking, and singing usually took place on the O'Grady's stoop and so we were frequently kicked off because the tenants complained about the noise we made.

It was during these hours and hours of playing sports and hanging out together I made my best friends. One of my favorite quotes is from the movie, *Stand by Me*. At the end of the movie the main character, who is an adult writing about his childhood friends, said, 'I never had any friends later on like the ones I had when I was twelve…does anyone?' That's exactly how I feel about my childhood friends – I'll never have friends like them again.

"Cool, Dad. What did you say about the O'Grady's stoop? What's a stoop?"

"A stoop is in the front of an apartment building and it consists of the steps leading up to the front door of the building. The O'Grady stoop was a perfect place for us to meet because there were three or four flights of concrete steps, all with a short rock wall that came up to your knees which gave everyone a place to sit while we were hanging out. It was also a great place to listen to Scott's boom box which was about the size of a microwave oven; its speakers were so loud the music could be heard throughout the neighborhood if the volume was turned up to the max.

Scott's radio played a major role in determining the popular songs and types of music we liked. The cool music to listen to was hard rock like Led Zeppelin's 'Stairway to Heaven', Lynyrd Skynyrd's 'Free Bird', Jethro Tull's 'Aqualung'. Although I was a fan of hard rock I was a bigger fan of pop music like Billy Joel, Meat Loaf, Hall and Oats, and yes, I even liked Disco. I liked Donna Summer, the Bee Gees, and other Disco Groups even though most people said, 'Disco sucked'. There were a couple of groups, or singers, I have to admit I never admitted to liking but I did. I was a closet Abba and Barry Manilow fan. I used to listen to them late at night under my covers with a flashlight on so no one else knew I was listening to them."

♪ You are the dancing queen, young and sweet, only seventeen
Dancing queen; feel the beat from the tambourine ♪ [12]

"You listened to them under your covers?"

"No, not really, but it really wasn't cool to listen to Abba and Barry Manilow."

He continued, "When we started to hang out with the girls most of our days were spent in the back of St. John's school yard playing soccer, punch ball, or stick ball, or on the street playing stick ball, king-queen, or curb ball. At night most of our time was spent in the very back of St. John's drinking beer and listening to music. One of our favorite songs was 'Only the Good Die Young' by Billy Joel. It kind of captured the attitude of our group pretty well.

♪ You might have heard I run with a dangerous crowd
We aint too pretty ♪
♪ We aint too proud
We might be laughing a bit too loud ♪
♪ Awe but that never hurt no one

They say there's a heaven for those who wait ♪
♪ Some say it's better but I say it aint
I'd rather laugh with the sinners than cry with the saints ♪
♪ The sinners are much more fun
You know that only the good die young ♪" [11]

"Nice, Dad! You said you hung out at night and drank beer. How old were you when you started drinking?"

"I was about 13 years old?"

"YOU DRANK BEER AT 13?!"

"Yes Kels, I drank from the time I was 13 and all throughout my teenage years. In fact, after I graduated from middle school, I don't think a day went by when I didn't drink and most days I was drunk."

"That's horrible! Were you an alcoholic?"

"I don't know, I don't think so, at least not physically but maybe mentally. You see, when I was young and I found myself in uncomfortable situations I turned to beer to help me deal with my discomfort. I was like Underdog with his energy pill. If I wasn't drinking I was shy and quiet, but once I had a few beers in me I was a different person. I was much more outgoing, and I thought I was more fun to be around but it came with a price."

"But you weren't an alcoholic?"

"I guess I'm saying I didn't get the shakes, and I never drank rubbing alcohol, like Kitty Dukakis, to get my alcohol fix but I didn't feel relaxed around people unless I was drinking. I probably drank more often than most of my friends, but in the neighborhood, my drinking wasn't unique because there were many kids who drank on a regular basis. In my neighborhood drinking was as much a part of the fabric of everyday life as eating and sleeping. It was such an important part of our lives there were at least 20 bars within a short walking distance of my apartment building."

"No way, Dad! Don't listen Cam, he's making this up!"

"Little girl, I'm not making this up. Let me see. There was P&K's, Teddy's, Timmy's, Ehring's, Kennan's, Off Broadway, the Terminal, the Punch Bowl, the Liffy, the Green Alligator, Brandon's, Jesse James, Pauline's, and, and, and, and I can picture the other ones in my head but I can't remember their names."

"With all those bars there must have been a lot of alcoholics in the neighborhood."

"Well, Cam, you're probably right but I never considered people who drank everyday to be alcoholics. The only type of person I considered to be an alcoholic was a guy sleeping on a park bench with his pants wide open, pee all over his pants, snots coming down his nose, and a pint of whiskey in a brown paper bag – that was an alcoholic to me.

♪ Sitting on a park bench
Eyeing little girls with bad intent ♪
♪ Snot is running down his nose
Greasy fingers smearing shabby clothes ♪ [13]

"You might think I'm exaggerating but this is how I remember it."

"Did you and your friends do anything else – like drugs?"

"Well, we did a lot of things we shouldn't have. Most of the guys drank beer, and I think most of the girls smoked cigarettes."

"What about drugs?"

"We mostly just drank beer, but when we were older one or two of us experimented with marijuana occasionally but very rarely. So I'd have to say very few of my friends tried drugs."

"What about you?"

"I'm not proud of it Cam but, yes, I did. I tried it all; glue, magic markers, pot, crack, ludes, mesc, peyote, and, of course, I dabbled in frog licking for a short period of time. I'm very thankful I didn't like any of these things, except for the frog licking; I liked how it put a hop, skip, and jump into my step. No, I'm just kidding. I didn't like any drugs, they made my body feel very strange and uncomfortable – they made me want to sleep or so paranoid I never wanted to try them again.

I actually didn't like beer at first, but we drank so much I eventually acquired a taste for it. I didn't even like hard liquor like whiskey or rum, because it made me barf my brains out. So I guess I should be thankful my body couldn't handle anything but beer because the people I knew who liked these other drugs sometimes had serious problems. Some kids in the neighborhood, none of my close friends, liked drugs so much they got addicted. It's very sad because a few of them died from drugs, some are in jail, and some just wasted many years of their lives.

♪ And I said no, no, no, no I don't smoke it no more
I'm tired of waking up on the floor ♪
♪ No thank you… [14]

"Dad! Stop and get back to your story."

"…please it only makes me sneeze…oh okay Cam…again, my friends and I were all nice people who enjoyed doing some things we probably shouldn't have, but mostly we just liked hanging out – we didn't cause too many problems."

"What else, Dad? Don't you have any stories about them?"

My dad had a smirk on his face as he nodded his head and said, "Oh, yeah. I have a million stories about my friends."

Skitching, City Steps, and Car Hoods...

It wasn't long before he told us a few stories about his friends. One of the coolest stories he told us was about the things him and his friends did during the winter time. He told us several stories one day when Kelsie and I were off from school because of a heavy snow.

My dad took off from work that day to stay home with us. He helped us to build a fort in the front of our house; we had snowball fights with him, and we went sledding down the hill behind our house.

After we spent hours outside in the snow we were cold, and so we went inside to warm up and to have some lunch. When we were sitting at the kitchen table eating a sandwich and drinking hot chocolate I asked my dad, "What did you do in the snow when you were a kid?"

"We did a lot of things. We did the same things you and Kelsie do; we built snowmen, snow forts; we had snowball fights, and we kind of went sledding..."

"What do you mean you 'kind of' went sledding?"

"I said we 'kind of went sledding' because we usually didn't have a sled and we didn't call it sledding – we called it sleigh riding. But come to think of it – we didn't have sleighs; either but that's what we called it. So we went sleigh riding, and we did some other things you've never heard of that weren't very smart."

"Like what?"

"Well, one thing we did was called skitching and the other was...umm...actually I'm not sure we ever had a name for it, but we used to ride down the sides of the city steps.

"What's skitching Dad?"

"What's skitching? What's skitching? Skitching was just the most exciting winter sport to ever be invented! It was sooooo awesome – it was a combination of skidding and hitching – as in, hitching a ride.

♪ Ride, ride, ride, [skitching] a ride
I want to get you home ♪
♪ To my baby's side [15]

Kelsie interrupted my dad and said, "Stop, Dad. No more singing – PLEASE! I want to hear the rest of the story"

My dad smiled, "I don't remember who made it up or who gave it the name, but that's what we called it. Skitching was something that could be done only after a heavy snowfall, and even then it was something we could only do for a short time – until the city snow plows cleared the streets.

Skitching was similar to water skiing but instead of being pulled behind a boat and skidding along the top of the water you were pulled by a car and you skid on top of the snowy city streets. My friends and I usually went skitching on the side streets, like Godwin Terrace, Kingsbridge Avenue or Corlear Avenue. You couldn't do it on 231st Street or Broadway because they were the first roads to be cleared and there was always a lot of traffic on these streets even during a heavy snow storm.

To skitch we waited on a street corner near a stop sign or a stop light, and we waited for a car to pull up. When the car came to a complete stop we snuck up behind it and grabbed hold of the bumper..."

"What's a bumper?"

"You know, I never thought about it, but I guess you wouldn't really know what a bumper is because most cars don't have them anymore. Well, a bumper was basically a piece of metal that was connected to the front and back of cars when I was growing up. They were intended to protect the car from getting badly damaged when a car ran into something. Wait, you know what they are. Remember when we went to Holiday World a couple of years ago and we went on the bumper cars?"

Kelsie and I said, "Yes."

"Well you know how all the bumper cars have metal all the way around them so when we ran into each other it didn't hurt too much and the part you sit in didn't get damaged at all – that's what a bumper is. Except cars only had the metal stuck to the front and back. Got it?"

"Got, it Dad. Continue."

"Yeah, okay. So we waited at the corner and when the car stopped we snuck up behind it, squatted down like a baseball catcher, grabbed onto the bumper, and held on for dear life. When the car pulled away we had to hold on tight, lean back just a little, and all of a sudden we were skitching. Usually we only held on for a block or two, then we let go and walked back to our friends who couldn't fit on or who slid off earlier, but occasionally we'd hold on for a long time, and we'd get a little tour of Kingsbridge.

It might sound dangerous, and I'm sure your mother thinks it was, but it wasn't as dangerous as skiing or sledding. I say this because the side streets were usually pretty empty after a heavy snowfall, and so we didn't have to worry too much about getting run over by cars. And since the roads were covered with snow if someone fell off they usually just slid to a stop – nothing too painful. So it wasn't life threatening, but there were some dangerous aspects of it."

"Like what?"

"Well, like the time I was skitching with a few of my friends down on 232nd Street and Corlear Avenue. We got out of St. John's early because of the heavy snow, and one of our friends from school, Nicky, came skitching with us. Nicky didn't have any gloves with him that day, but he decided to go skitching anyway. A few of us were standing on the corner when a car came by, I think it was a Volkswagen Beatle which had a big metal bumper that was easy to grab hold of, but this particular bumper had very sharp edges. We snuck behind the car and most of us grabbed hold of the bumper and started skitching. About half way down the block Nicky's feet hit a manhole cover and his feet came out from under him. He was still trying to hold onto the bumper, but he lost his grip and his hands slipped off – tearing several layers of skins off the palms of his hands. It was nasty – it was like dragging his hands across a big cheese grater."

"Dad, that's really disgusting; what's a manhole cover?"

"Kels, a manhole cover is a heavy, round metal plate that's in the middle of all the streets in New York, and I guess other places too. In New York a lot of the pipes, wires, and of course the sewers are underground, and when there are problems that need to be fixed there are people who go through the manholes to get underground to fix them. Manhole covers were a problem for skitchers because the snow didn't cover them due to the heat from underground which melted the snow.

So anyway, manhole covers made skitching a little dangerous, but for the most part it was just a lot of fun. By the way, Nicky kept on skitching that day – someone gave him a scarf to wrap around his hands.

Something else that's different between how you guys play in the snow and how I did were the clothes we wore. You guys are soft; you guys are really soft. Look at all the clothes on the floor over there – it's amazing you could even breathe with them on. You look like the little brother in 'A Christmas Story'. Name everything you wore when we were outside earlier."

I looked at my clothes and said, "I had snow boots and a snow suit on."

My dad said, "Yeah, what else?"

"Okay, I had socks, underwear, long johns, my North Face coat, North Face gloves and hat, a scarf, my snow suit, my snow boots, an undershirt, and my Under Armour shift."

"What else?"

"What? That's all?"

"Cam, what else?"

"Okay, I wore your Ski Goggles."

"What else? What about the hand warmers in your gloves and boots?"

I smiled and said, "Oh yeah, I forgot about them. They make my hands and feet nice and toasty warm."

My dad smiled and continued, "You kids are so soft now. When I was your age we didn't have all these fancy clothes. We went out in snow storms wearing only our underwear and WE LIKED IT!"

Kelsie laughed and said, "Yeah, right, Dad – not a pretty picture."

"But seriously, when you guys play out in the snow you are all toasty warm even when it's freezing outside. All your clothes are waterproof and warm on the inside – when I was growing up we didn't have these fancy schmancy clothes. When it snowed and we got dressed to play outside we didn't have a closet full of designer clothes to choose from.

We didn't have snow suits – we couldn't afford them. The rich kids could afford Long Johns, but if you were a regular working class family you put a second pair of pants on.

We didn't have snow boots – to keep our feet warm and dry (well actually only dry) we put baggies or Wonder Bread bags on our feet. After we put on the baggies or bags on our feet we put on our Chuck Taylor high top Converse or Pro-Keds.

We couldn't afford a heavy North Face winter coat – I don't even know if they were around when I was a kid – to keep our bodies warm we put on 3 undershirts, 2 long sleeve shirts, and 5 hooded sweatshirts.

And we didn't have waterproof North Face gloves – to keep our hands warm we put on wool mittens if we had them – the poor kids put tube socks on their hands to keep their hands warm…"

"No way, Dad! Don't believe him Cam! There is no way kids wore tube socks on their hands – no way!"

My dad raised his eyebrows and said, "Kels, would your daddy lie to you?"

Kelsie nodded her head and said, "Uh, yes. You would, and you are."

"The bottom line is we didn't have all the warm, waterproof clothes you have, so when we went out in the snow and especially when we went sleigh riding we started out warm but by the time we were done – WE WERE FREEZING! While we were sleigh riding we got covered with snow; then as the sun beat down on us the snow melted and soaked our clothes. We didn't notice how wet our clothes were until we walked home. The walk home was brutally cold and uncomfortable! We had to walk like Frankenstein because when the sun went down our wet clothes began to freeze! I hated that feeling!"

I asked my dad why he didn't just buy warm clothes. He said, "Because snow boots and snow suits were expensive. Remember, we had 6 kids in our family and most of the other families in the neighborhood had a lot of kids too. Back then most of the families lived pay check to pay check, and they couldn't afford to buy their kids the types of clothes you have."

"What do you mean 'pay check to pay check'?"

"Oh, um, it means when your father got paid, which was usually once every two weeks, there was only enough money to pay for grocery's, the rent, the bills – and after paying for these things – there was almost no money left over. Got it, Cam?"

"Got it."

My dad continued, "What made it worse was we couldn't go sleigh riding in our back yard like you kids do. We had to walk miles and miles to the nearest park – up hill both ways."

"Up hill both ways? I don't think so Dad."

"Well, maybe it wasn't up hill both ways, but it wasn't a short walk behind the house like it is for you two. I went sleigh riding in three different places. The first place I went was behind St. John's Middle School with Pat. The hill wasn't very big at all, but it was fun for a couple of 11 years old boys. There were also a couple of other popular hills in the area where the older kids went sleigh riding. There was the 18th hole at the Van Cortlandt Park Golf Course.

This was pretty far away from my apartment, and so I only went there a couple of times, but it was a great hill. It was a long steep hill which had some bumpy areas which were like jumps if you went over them. This hill was a lot of fun, and it could be a little dangerous because of the speed that could be built up, but for the most part this hill was safe.

The other popular hill in the area was Ewen Park hill. It wasn't as safe as the 18th Hole, and because of this I think it was the best place to go sleigh riding. Ewen Park was only a few blocks away from my apartment. To get there from my home I walked south on Kingsbridge Avenue and made a right turn on 231st Street. While standing on Kingsbridge Avenue and 231st Street if you looked to the west you could see Ewen Park. After a heavy snow fall Ewen Park looked like a huge white mountain in the distance – like Mount Kilimanjaro…"

"What? Mount Kilimanjaro?"

My dad raised his eyebrows and said, "Mount Fuji?"

"Huh? Mount Fuji?"

My dad said, "Oh, never mind. Let's just say Ewen Park looked like a huge white mountain. If you looked closely at the hill you saw little black ants moving up and down and across the hill. But as you walked down 231st Street and got closer to Ewen Park the ants came into focus, and you saw dozens and dozens of kids riding sleds, cardboard boxes, garbage can lids, and plastic bags down the hill. While standing at the bottom of the hill there were a few things that stood out. First, the hill was huge and extremely steep! But most importantly, Ewen Park didn't have a long flat area at the bottom of the hill where the sled could slow down and come to a stop. Ewen hill was long and steep but the flat area at the bottom of the hill was only 10 or 20 feet wide. To make things worse – if you couldn't slow down you rode right past the flat area into a parked car or worse – into a busy city street!

"Why do you keep calling it sleigh riding? It's called sledding, Dad."

My dad shrugged his shoulders and said, "You're right. I guess it should have been called sledding, but that's not what we called it – we called it sleigh riding. Either way, we never had a sleigh or a sled so it didn't really matter what we called it. Wait, no, I take that back. Actually, when I was 11 and 12 years old I used to go sleigh riding with Pat, and we used sleds. Pat and his sister, Mary, had a couple of Flexible Fliers, and when Mary wasn't using hers, Pat let me use it. At first we went sledding behind St. John's Middle School, but when we were 12 we brought the sleds to the big time – Ewen Park – da, da, da, daaaaaa.

When we were 12 years old, Pat and I were best friends; we loved going to Ewen Park after a heavy snowfall to go sleigh riding for the whole day. We took all the different trails, and we even created some of our own. The best trail we blazed started near the Johnson Avenue steps, next to the basketball courts, at the north/west section of Ewen. We started near the foot of these steps, and we rode south, heading toward the city steps which split the park in two. Once we crossed the steps we rode diagonally across the steepest part of the hill and zigzagged back and forth until the drop off at the bottom of the hill. Since we didn't go straight down the hill we didn't have to worry about riding into the street. These days were some of the best days of my life! Yes, even though the walk home was miserable and I had to walk like Frankenstein – it was great!

Although I loved Ewen Park when I was younger, it got even better when I was a teenager."

I asked my dad, "Why was it called Ewen Park?"

Kelsie said, "Who cares, Cameron? It's just a name..."

But my father jumped in and said, "No, Kelsie. It's okay. I actually know why it's called Ewen Park so let me tell Cam.

Okay, Cam, Ewen Park was named after John Ewen, who was a brigadier General in New York State's National Guard during the Civil War. John Ewen owned the piece of land between the low lands of the middle class neighborhood of Kingsbridge and the high lands of the upper class neighborhood of Riverdale. When he died he gave the land to his daughter, Eliza; when she died she gave the land to New York City provided they made it into a park.

Anyhow, it really was a beautiful park, and it wasn't just a great place to go in the winter after a heavy snowfall; it was great all year round. Ewen was basically broken up into several areas. There was the wide open hill where we went sleigh riding and where the girls laid out in the summer to get a tan. Steps ran through the center of the park; they were used by the Riverdale morning and evening commuters on their way to trains and buses in Kingsbridge. At night the steps were used by teenagers and transients as a place to hangout. There was a cobblestone walk path which ran through the park in a north, westerly direction. It ran through a lightly wooded area with park benches and large rocks. This part of the park was used by the teenagers in the area for some of the larger parties..."

I asked my dad, "Did you and your friends use the park for parties?"

My dad raised his eyebrows and said, "Yes, Cam. We had a few parties there. This part of the park was probably our favorite place to have parties. There was a dirt path which went from the cobblestone path to an area with a couple of park benches and a giant rock. This area was quiet and secluded – a perfect place for my friends and me to turn on the boom box to have a little party.

So where was I? Oh yeah. If you stayed on the cobblestone path it led you up to the basketball courts where Pat and I played a lot of basketball. If you stayed on the path all the way to the Johnson Avenue steps, you had to walk past the Johnson Avenue Crew – a group of 10 or 20 guys who had a reputation for being some of the meanest, nastiest guys in the area. I don't know if it's true, but I was told a few of them spent time in prison, and there were still one or two in there because they were convicted of murder. I walked past them once just to see what they looked like; they all had long hair, a lot of tattoos, and they looked mean. When I walked past them they didn't say anything, but they stared at me. I think they were trying to intimidate me – it worked."

Then my dad smiled at Kelsie and said to me, "So to answer your question Cam – it was named after a guy named John Ewen. Okay, to get back to my winter story.

Like I was saying, it was great when Pat and I were 11 and 12, but when I was a teenager things changed. When I turned 13 it was no longer cool to go sleigh riding; I guess because it was considered something little kids did, and so for a couple of years Pat and I stopped.

I don't remember exactly when this changed, probably when I was 15. I vaguely remember the day we started going sleigh riding again. All of my friends were hanging out on the stoop just up Godwin Terrace from 231st Street. When we were older this is the place all of us met for the night. We hung out there drinking beer and listening to music while we waited for everyone to come out, so we could go somewhere else, like Brandon's or one of the other bars in the neighborhood or Inwood which let young teenagers in.

Sometimes we got a little loud which bothered one of the tenants in the apartment building. I say someone didn't like it, because every so often while we were hanging out on the stoop we got egged by someone in the building."

"What do you mean, you 'got egged'?"

"Well, when we hung out here some of my friends sat on the stoop, some stood on the side walk, some sat on the parked cars, and some stood in the courtyard. We didn't think we were too loud, but you know how it is when you have a big group together; it gets loud even if nobody's yelling. I'm sure the fact some of us stood in the courtyard made it even louder because of the echo. This noise must have driven someone in the building crazy because he/she/they/it threw about 4 or 5 eggs out of their window against the wall near the place we were standing, The eggs never hit us directly, I don't think; they mostly splattered off the walls and got a bunch of us covered with raw eggs. After it happened we got mad and started yelling up at the open windows, but we never found out who did this; probably a sweet, little old lady – who knows. I actually don't think I ever got hit bad, just a few little splatters, but there were some girls who had their fancy rabbit fur coats ruined – if it's possible to ruin rabbit fur."

My dad smiled at this. I guess he didn't think rabbit fur was very fancy.

He continued, "So back to the story. I vaguely remember hanging out on this stoop one evening when it had snowed during the day. Someone, probably Scott or Danny, said, 'Hey, let's go to Ewen Park for a little while and go sleigh riding?" For some reason it was cool again to go sleigh riding because everyone there thought it was a great idea. Maybe it's like going to see Santa Claus; at 12 years old it's not cool to sit on Santa's lap but after 15 all the girls in our group got their pictures taken with him every year.

But like I said, everyone thought it was a great idea and so we walked to the O'Grady's cellar and pulled out a big piece of wood paneling to use as a sled. After we picked out the best piece of paneling we could find we walked four or five blocks to Mount Ewen Park towing our improvised sled and several bags of beer along with us.

When we reached Ewen we put our bags down on the park benches at the bottom of the hill, and we trudged up the hill to start sleigh riding. The paneling worked okay, but we just weren't going fast enough to have the kind of fun we wanted to have. So we decided to look for something better. Across the street from the hill was an auto body shop, and so several of us walked behind the building looking for something, anything that could be used as a sled.

It didn't take long for us to come up with a replacement for the paneling; there were several car hoods leaning up against the fence next to other car parts and chassis, and it seemed like these would slide pretty quickly on top of snow.

There were several hoods to choose from. Scott walked over to the first one and tried to pick it up – but it was too big. He walked over to the next one and he looked at it – but it was too small. Leaning against the fence in the corner was the car hood of a Cadillac Fleetwood. Scott walked over to it, looked at it, and lifted it up – it was just right!"

"Goldilocks, Dad? Nice."

My dad smiled and continued to tell the story, "Each of us picked up a corner, and we carried the hood across Riverdale Avenue to our other friends standing at the bottom of the hill.

When they saw the car hood everyone was excited – they thought it was a great idea! As we carried the hood past them up the hill, they put down their beers and followed us – like we were the Piped Piper of Hamblin.

A short way up the hill we put the hood down to make sure it would slide as smoothly as we assumed it would. When we put it down it was clear it was going to work perfectly because it almost slid out of our hands, all the way down the hill.

We decided to start out in the middle of the hill. When we put the hood down, three people sat on the front; these people dug their Chuck Taylor's into the snow to keep the hood from sliding down the hill as everyone else got on. There were about 12 of us ready to ride the hood down the hill, but we agreed there was only room for 6 people at a time, so we'd take turns.

For the first run three of us sat down in the front and dug our feet in the snow to hold the hood in place. The three others kneeled down behind us. Once everyone was in place and ready, we lifted up our feet – and we took off. For a split second this plan worked perfectly. I say it worked perfectly for a split second because, just as we took off – everyone else jumped on! Can you picture this? We had 12 girls and guys on the hood; 6 of us were sitting and kneeling nice and neatly – the others were piled all over us. To make matters worse, or maybe it was better, or maybe it was worse – WE WERE FLYING FASTER THAN YOU CAN IMAGINE heading straight down the hill toward people, benches, cars, and a busy street – WITHOUT ANY WAY TO STOP!!

We didn't have a way to stop the car hood and to make matters worse, and this was worse, I was one of the guys on the front and I had 2 or 3 people laying on me so I couldn't jump off. As we went faster and faster, I got more and more nervous, because I knew what was at the bottom of the hill. Luckily when we were just a few feet from the drop off at the bottom of the hill someone screamed, 'JUMP!' and everyone jumped off. I was the last one to jump off, but when I did I saw behind me dozens of my friends strewn all over the hill, and in front of me I saw dozens of my other friends scrambling to grab the bags of beer and to get out of the way of the runaway car hood.

Everyone who rode down on the hood watched it as it flew off the drop and smashed into the benches below. We all looked at each other and screamed, 'THAT WAS TOTALLY WICKED!'"

"Totally Wicked? 'Incredibles', Dad?"

"Yeah, maybe. You got a problem with that little girl?"

"Yeah, maybe."

"Okay, so where was I? Oh, yeah. For the next couple of hours we went up and down and up and down the hill – sometimes sitting down, sometimes laying down, sometimes standing up, and sometimes doing all three, but we always jumped off before we hit the final drop at the bottom of the hill. After we jumped off – we watched the car hood run into benches, parked cars, and into the street. The cars parked at the bottom of the hill looked like they had been in a demolition derby by the time we left that night."

"What else did you guys do during the winter?"

"Let me think? Oh yeah. We rode down the City Steps. Do you want to hear about that?"

"Yeah, sure Dad."

"Okay, another thing we did during the winter that you guys don't, or should I say can't do – involves snow and/or ice and city steps. We didn't really have a name for it; we couldn't come up with a catchy, memorable name that did it justice, and so we just asked, 'Does anyone want to slide down the city steps?' But I don't want to glamorize it; it was really dangerous – that's why we never did it as often as skitching or car hood sledding…"

Kelsie stopped my dad and said, "Dad! We don't even know what you're talking about. What are city steps?"

My dad smiled, "You don't know what city steps are? You are so young, so naïve, so sheltered – do I have to teach you everything?"

"Of course you do – you're the daddy." Then I smiled because I knew he liked hearing this kind of stuff."

He nodded his head with an air of satisfaction and got back to his story, "So where was I? Oh yeah, I need to teach you about city steps. City steps were all over the Bronx...wait, let me back up a little. I told you this before, but Kingsbridge is actually a valley which is located between the high lands of Riverdale on the west and Sedgwick Avenue on the east. In the middle of Kingsbridge there was a hill that Kingsbridge Avenue ran on top of. From Kingsbridge Avenue you walked down hill to Broadway on the east and Corlear Avenue on the west."

Kelsie was shaking her head and she said, "Sorry Dad, I'm not following you. Why are you telling us about a bunch of hills?"

My dad said, "Patience Dookie Doo, patience, I'm getting to it. I have to tell you about the hills so you know why there were so many city steps in the area. You see, Kingsbridge had so many hills in and around it the city planners built city steps all over the neighborhood. There were city steps leading up to Riverdale, there were city steps leading up to Sedgwick Avenue, and there were a couple of city steps leading up to Naples and Godwin Terrace.

All the steps were designed in a similar way; they all had 10 steps and then a landing, 10 steps and a landing, 10 steps and a landing. I'm sure you get my point. I guess there were landings every 10 steps so the old ladies could catch their breath. On both sides of the steps were large metal railings to hold onto, and just past the railings on both sides were decorative bricks. Actually, I'm not sure if they were really decorative, if you don't count the graffiti, but they were laid out neatly to follow the contour of the steps. The bricks flowed nice and smooth; kind of like the Jungle Racer at Holiday World."

I said, "I got you, Dad. You didn't slide down the steps – you slide down the bricks next to the steps. Nice, Dad. That sounds cool."

My dad had a proud smile on his face and then he said, "It was cool, Cam. It really was. But, but, but – it was also dangerous.

I can still remember the first day we rode down the city steps. Pat, Tommy, and I were walking to Ron's apartment to lift weights one afternoon. This is when Ron lived near the Reservoirs just past OLA. We walked up 231st Street to Albany Crescent where we passed by the firehouse. We crossed Bailey Avenue and walked up the hill until we got to PS 81. Right next to the school were city steps which we had to walk up to get to Sedgwick Avenue. It didn't cross our minds to slide down the steps at this time; at least I didn't, because there wasn't any snow on the ground. We just continued to walk; we walked through Old Fort Park, next to OLA, and past the reservoir until we made it to Ron's.

By the time we made it to his apartment it was about 12:30 p.m.; when we walked into the apartment building it was overcast, and there were a few flurries coming down but no accumulation. Ron wasn't home that day because he was on a 2 or 3 day tour with the fire department..."

I stopped my dad and said, "Wait. If he wasn't home how did you get into his apartment?"

"Well, Cam, he was one of our coaches, and he let us lift weights in his apartment. He actually made keys for Tommy and me so we could workout when he wasn't home. So anyway, where was I? Oh, yeah. When we walked in his building it was just starting to flurry, but we didn't think anything of it. We just went inside, and we lifted weights for a few hours. Afterwards, we sat down, watched TV, drank his Lipton Iced Tea, and ate all of his English Muffins. Remind me sometime to tell you the story about Ron putting a lock on his refrigerator to keep us from eating his food..."

I stopped my dad again and asked, "He put a lock on his refrigerator – are you serious?"

My dad smiled, nodded his head, and said, "Yes – I know it sounds strange, but he did."

I asked him if the lock stopped him from eating Ron's food, but he said, "No. Tommy was able to unscrew the lock but don't get me side tracked that's a whole other story."

Then my dad got back to his story, "So we worked out, watched TV, and ate and drank everything in Ron's apartment. It was getting late and Pat had to get home for dinner; I think it was about 5:00 p.m. by this time, and so we cleaned up and got ready to go..."

Kelsie stopped my dad and asked, "You cleaned the apartment before you left?"

"No, not really. I just wanted to make it sound like I was a responsible young man. No, we left the place a mess. Come on. What do you expect? We were 13 year old boys.

Okay, so by now it was after 5:00 p.m., and it was starting to get dark. We locked the apartment door and rode down in the elevator to the lobby. When we got to the lobby we were shocked by what we saw outside! While we were working out for a few hours the city was getting blanketed with a heavy snowfall. The snow was still coming down when we walked outside; I don't know how many inches of snow fell, probably 5 or 6 by the time we walked outside – it was beautiful! You can't imagine how beautiful New York City looks after a snowfall – I love how the snow glistens in the street lights, I love how it covers up the dog poop – especially before the dogs get to it, and the snow turns a fluorescent yellow. To make this snow even better it was great packing snow – perfect for snowballs.

On our way home, as we walked through the snow wearing our Chuck Taylors, we did what boys do when there's snow around – we threw snowballs at stop signs, street lights, cars, and at each other.

A short while later we reached PS 81. We stood at the top of the steps looking down at the snow covered steps. I think it would have been impossible for a 13 year old boy to look at the snow covered bricks along the side of the steps and not think about sliding down them. I'm not sure who was the first one to say it, probably Tommy, but then again I was a little bit of an instigator, and so maybe it was me. All I know is someone said, 'Let's slide down the side of the steps'. We all thought that was a great idea.

We decided to be smart, and we didn't start from the top because we had no idea how fast we would go. We started closer to the bottom; the starting point was the second landing from the bottom. This was a very reasonable approach, and honestly it wasn't too daring – all three of us slid down, and we had a good time even though we didn't go too fast. After the first run Pat said, 'Let's try it from one more flight up.' Tommy stood there for a moment without saying a word; I could see him calculating something in his head. I could only imagine what was going through his mind, 'Based on friction, aerodynamics, wind velocity, and the 2nd law of thermodynamics we will slide fast, but it will be safe starting from the top of the steps.'"

I asked my dad, "Did he really say that?"

"No, Cam. I have no idea what was going through his mind but who knows – maybe he was.

Whether he was thinking this or not Tommy said, 'I'm going to the top. Come on – let's go!' Even though Pat and I didn't talk to each other we were both on the same page. There was no way we were going to start from the top, at least not until we tried the other levels first. I said to Tommy, 'Let's try it from the 3rd level before we go to the top.' Tommy wasn't interested in the gradual approach, he said, 'If you two don't want to go from the top that's fine, but I'm going to give it a try. It will only take a minute – just wait for me – you wimps.'

Pat and I looked at each other and shrugged our shoulders. There was no way we were going to start from the top, but we also knew we wouldn't be able to talk him out of doing what he wanted to do.

Tommy walked up the steps and when he got to the top he hopped over the railing. He stood there for a few seconds examining the situation, and then he sat down on his rear. He scooted himself closer to the edge of the first drop off, and a second later he pushed like a person riding on a luge, and off he went. He started sliding down the snow covered brick hill and it was immediately apparent Tommy was in danger – his calculation must have left off the exponential increase in his velocity due to the 13th law of thermodynamics..."

"Dad, what's the 13th law of thermodynamics?"

"I don't know – I just made it up to make it sound better. There probably isn't a 13th law, but if there is one it would be 'If you slide down a steep slippery snow covered brick hill – you'll kill yourself!'

Immediately from the first drop he was flying! By the second drop off, he was both literally and figuratively flying. He was going so fast his body went airborne off every slope; as I watched him sliding down the hill, flying in the air, I was scared! I thought for sure he was going to crack his head open and die.

I'm sure Tommy was scared too; I watched him as he tried to slow himself down – he twisted and turned over to try and grab onto something – anything – but there was nothing to hold onto. All his turning over did was to cause his face to smash against the snow covered bricks as he slid and flew down the hill. When he reached the last slope he flew in the air and stopped abruptly by smashing into the railing at the bottom. Like I said, I thought he was going to crack his head wide open; at the very least I expected several broken bones and a lot of blood.

When he smashed into the rail, Pat and I ran down the steps to where he was laying motionless. When we reached him he was moaning in pain, but we were happy he was alive. After several minutes it was clear he would be okay; he had a lot of bumps, bruises, and some scrapes but thankfully he wasn't dead."

I don't think Kelsie thought my dad was being serious. She said to him, "Come on, Dad. You're not serious."

My dad nodded his head up and down as he said, "Kelsie, I am being very serious. I honestly thought Tommy was going to die. I'm not exaggerating when I say he was flying off these slopes. He flew in the air, and when he landed he crashed against the snow covered bricks – it was scary watching him, because there was nothing Pat or I could do, because it happened so fast.

I think Tommy is the only person I know who could have walked away from something like this. He was the toughest guy I grew up with.

In the future we rode down the city steps, but we never went up more than three or four slopes – never again did anyone slide down the six slopes like Tommy did this day.

So guys, that's what we used to do in the winter time. As you can see, you have it so much better than I did when I was your age; you guys have warm clothes, new sleds, safe hills, and everything is either close by or mom or I drive you. You guys don't know how good you have it..."

I stopped my dad and said, "We don't know how good we have it? Dad, you're the one who had it good! We might have more stuff than you had, but you had a lot more fun than we have – I wish I grew up in the Bronx.

A Bridge Too Far – for Roller Skating

During another one of our Saturday morning visits to McDonalds I was sitting there eating my hot cakes, and I asked my dad if he had any more stories to tell us, and he told us a really interesting story about playing hockey and crossing over a bridge.

"Well, what kind do you want to hear?"

"Do you have anymore sports stories?"

"I have a story about roller hockey. Do you want to hear it?"

"Yup, go ahead Dad."

"Roller hockey wasn't the most popular sport in the neighborhood, probably because it was the most expensive game to play. Unlike basketball where you only need a basketball and a court; hockey requires roller skates, shin guards, hockey gloves, helmets, sticks, pucks, nets, and other stuff which costs a lot of money! Although it wasn't the most popular sport and it costs a lot of money we still played it, however, we didn't use all the designer equipment the kids use nowadays. We just used old beat up roller skates and hockey sticks which were wrapped with mounds of tape to keep them from breaking in half."

"What did the goalie wear?"

"The goalie equipment was way too expensive so we had to improvise. We made goalie pads out of two thick pieces of foam cut from old mattresses; the chest protector was a pillow stuffed under a hockey jersey; and the face mask was a metal colander from my mother's kitchen with a rubber band tied around it..."

"No way! No way Dad! Don't believe him Cam!"

"Kelsie, would your Daddy lie to you? Don't answer that! Anyway, we also didn't have a roller hockey rink in Kingsbridge, so we used the PS 7 schoolyard. The schoolyard was about half the size of a football field; the school was on one side, a wrought iron fence was on the other, and on both ends were chain link fences. The concrete was cracked and uneven but it didn't have a lot of broken glass or loose gravel.

When we played hockey outside PS 7 it was frustrating because when a slap shot or pass was off line the puck often slipped through the wrought iron fence and rolled, and rolled, and rolled down Kingsbridge Avenue. The game was put on hold until one of us chased it down. The worst part about PS 7 was the cracks! It wasn't unusual to be on a breakaway with the stick and puck out in front when all of a sudden without warning – UUUUHHHH!!! The stick got caught in a crack and the butt stuck in my gut or worse – the family jewels.

PS 7 wasn't the best schoolyard for playing hockey, but it was all we had, that is, until we learned about roller hockey heaven. Tommy told us about a roller hockey rink in Inwood. 'It's an actual roller hockey rink, with real nets, real sideboards, a smooth surface, and it's free! It's in Inwood, near Dyckman Street, along the Hudson River.' It sounded too good to be true; we decided to go there on Saturday morning as early as possible.

We could have taken the bus to Inwood, but Tony came up with a short cut to get there, 'Instead of going the long way by riding on the city bus, let's cut through John F. Kennedy High School and walk across the Spuyten Duyvil Bridge.' It's amazing how this crazy suggestion sounded like a great idea to us at the time. We looked at him and said, 'Yeah, sounds great. Let's do it!'

We met on Saturday morning at 7:30 near the PS 7 steps. When everyone arrived we put on our roller skates, tied our sneakers together, put them over our shoulders, put our winter gloves on, picked up our sticks, and left. Since it was late autumn it was chilly in the morning, and we could see our breath as we talked. To keep warm some of us wore long-johns, all of us wore hooded sweatshirts, and on top we wore our St. John's Hawks jackets. When we left we skated south on Kingsbridge Avenue past St. John's Middle School, we made a right on 231st Street past Pat Mitchell's, we turned left on Tibbett Avenue past the Diner, and skated down the long road leading up to JFK.

We skated to the back of JFK which, at the time, was a large empty lot filled with weeds. We should have taken our skates off to walk through the mud, rocks, and weeds, but we didn't. Instead, we walked through the dirt and the mud in our skates until we reached the train tracks. Once we reached the tracks some of us walked on the railroad ties, and some walked on the gravel next to the tracks.

A short distance from JFK, looking over the Spuyten Duyvil section of the Harlem River was Columbia Rock. I believe it was once part of a much larger rock which was split in two when New York needed to clear a path for the train tracks which run along the Harlem River. It's called Columbia Rock because Columbia University painted a giant baby blue 'C' on the side of the rock which faces the river. The rock starts out low on one side and gradually increases in height until its pinnacle, which is about 120 feet high, and then it gradually slopes back down on the other side. A thick wire runs from one side of the rock to the other. I believe it's for people to hold onto when they walked over the rock but I'm not sure why anyone would do that..."

"Maybe it's for the people who painted the giant C."

"You might be right, Cam. One thing I know for sure is the rock was used by the kids in the neighborhood during the hot summer months. They dove off the rock into the Harlem River to cool off.

When we approached Columbia Rock, Joey said, 'I'm going to climb over it.' I said, 'What? Are you crazy? You can't climb over it – you're wearing roller skates!' But Joey ignored me and started climbing so, of course, the rest of us followed him. We climbed up the eastern side of the rock which was easy at first because it was relatively wide, but as we climbed higher and higher it became narrower and narrower.

When we reached the top we sat down to rest; it was cold, windy, and icy. Behind us were the tall Riverdale apartment buildings; to the left, in the distance, was the 225th Street Bridge; in front of us was the Harlem River, Bakers Field, and Inwood Park; to our right was the Henry Hudson Bridge. To the right, below the Henry Hudson Bridge, about a quarter mile away, was the Spuyten Duyvil Swing Bridge. There weren't many people out this early in the morning except for us and a few people from the Columbia University Rowing Club who were placing their boat into the cold Harlem River water.

If we leaned back too far we would have fallen onto the train tracks below; if we leaned too far forward we would have fallen off the rock into the cold icy water of the river. While we were sitting there Tony said, 'Hey, look at what's floating by in the river.' Timmy said, 'What is it?' 'Look it's a condom! My brother told me toilet water was let out up the river and that's proof.' We all looked down and watched it flow by along with some other nasty stuff. After a few minutes we got back up and continued our journey. Now I'm sure 120 feet doesn't sound very high to you, but as I climbed over this slippery rock, with sneakers draped over my shoulders, carrying a hockey stick, with roller skates on – it seemed REALLY HIGH! Just a little slip one way or another and we'd probably die…"

"Did anyone slip?"

"No, we were very lucky. But I'll tell you what we did do – WE CONQUERED COLUMBIA ROCK! VENIMUS, VIDIMUS, VICIMUS!"

"What's that mean?"

"We came, we saw, we conquered! We felt like Sir Edmund Hillary when he reached the top of Mount Everest."

"Who?"

"Some guy who climbed a big mountain, but he's not important. So where was I? Oh yeah. We just conquered Mount Columbia Rock or something like that. After we got to the other side we walked past the Spuyten Duyvil Train Station where there were a few people waiting for a train. They stared at us as we walked by; they probably wondered why a bunch of kids were walking along the train tracks in hockey gear but they didn't ask.

Just past the train station was the most dangerous part of our trip – crossing the Spuyten Duyvil Swing Bridge. We had never been to the bridge, and so we didn't know what to expect. The bridge crossed over the Harlem River where it meets the Hudson River. A few hundred feet above us was the Henry Hudson Bridge which connected Riverdale to Manhattan. A bridge some of the older guys in the neighborhood were rumored to have jumped off. The swing bridge looked to be about 200 yards long as it crossed over the rough waters. A few of us had second thoughts about crossing over the bridge, but we didn't say anything out loud. The bridge didn't have a solid floor; it only had thick, heavy rails which were connected to wooden crossties. The crossties were approximately two feet apart. The crossties and our roller skates were the only things between us and the frigid waters below. As we stood on the Bronx side of the river, looking at the bridge, John said, 'We came this far – we can't turn back now!' Everyone seemed to agree with John, or maybe nobody wanted to be the only one to chicken out, so we continued.

We began walking across the bridge on the front bumpers of our skates – one crosstie at a time. We didn't think about it before we got on the bridge, but then Billy asked, 'What are we going to do if a train goes by and we're on the middle of the bridge?' Tommy said, 'Either run like you're being chased by the cops or hold on for dear life.' Pat said, 'If you can't get off the bridge you better hold on because I bet it'll shake this bridge like the El train shakes my apartment building!' It's lucky we discussed our options, because when we were halfway across the bridge – you know what happened."

"A train came?"

"Yup, a train came."

He continued, "When we were halfway across the bridge Timmy looked behind us and in the distance he saw a train coming toward us. When we saw it – we started running on the bumpers of our skates, watching our steps to make sure we didn't miss a railroad tie as we were frantically trying to get off the bridge! We still had a long way to go and the train was catching up to us. It was clear we didn't have enough time to get off the bridge before the train passed, and so we decided to lay down on the crossties and hold on with all our might."

"Did you think you were going to be run over?"

"No, we weren't worried about getting run over because we had enough room on the side of the tracks but we were afraid of falling off the bridge into the water. We lay down on the cross ties and held on. A few seconds later the train flew past us; it shook the bridge so hard it felt like an earth quake. It shook Joey so hard his sneakers fell off his shoulders into the water below. He tried to save them, but as he reached for them he lost his balance and almost fell into the water himself. As soon as the train passed us, we carefully stood up and walked slowly off the bridge. The remainder of the trip was uneventful except for Joey mumbling under his breath, 'My father is going to kill me!'"

"Why would his dad kill him?"

"Because he dropped his new Converse sneakers in the river. Okay, when we got to the rink it was everything we thought it would be; it looked like a professional hockey rink. It was surrounded on all sides with boards; it had new hockey nets, the concrete was smooth, and there wasn't anyone skating on it yet. For about 30 minutes we had the rink to ourselves, and we took full advantage it; we skated all over; we shot pucks into the nets and practiced checking each other into the boards.

John said, 'Look, I can skate backwards without having to worry about tripping on a crack and breaking my back!' Mark said, 'Look, I can take a slap shot without having to chase the puck down 234th Street!' A short time after we arrived, a lot of kids showed up, and we played several rough hockey games against the kids from Inwood. We played for hours and didn't stop until the middle of the afternoon when we could barely walk, because our feet were covered with blisters and dried up blood.

It was 3:30 p.m. when we headed back home. The beginning of the trip was uneventful; we had a great day, but we were too tired to talk about it. The only thing on our minds as we approached the Swing Bridge was how much our feet hurt and how cold we were."

"Dad, why was it called the Spuyten Duyvil Swing Bridge?"

"It is called the Spuyten Duyvil because the water is very rough. I think Spuyten Duyvil is Dutch for 'Spit on the Devil'. It was called a Swing Bridge because it turned, or swung, open when boats entered or exited the Spuyten Duyvil section of the Harlem River. Okay, when we reached the bridge it was swung open. Joey said, 'Oh crap, I'm cold, I'm starving, my feet are killing me, and we're going to be sitting here for hours waiting for this $%^&* bridge to close!' Tommy said, 'No, it's only going to stay open for a few minutes. You see that boat near Bakers Field? That's the Circle Line. Once it passes us and goes into the Hudson River the bridge will automatically close and we'll be able to cross it.'"

"Dad, what's the Circle Line?"

"The Circle Line is a boat which takes hundreds of tourists around the island of Manhattan to sightsee. The boat takes off from the 34th Street Dock on the Hudson River and goes south past the Statue of Liberty and the World Trade Center, it goes around the tip of Manhattan to the Harlem River, it passes the BMW Bridges (Brooklyn, Manhattan, and Williamsburg), past the United Nations, Yankee Stadium, all the way to the 225th Street Bridge, past Spuyten Duyvil, Columbia Rock, and through the Swing Bridge, and then back down the Hudson River.

It was common for kids from the Bronx who were diving off Columbia Rock or just hanging out near the river to give the tourists on the Circle Line additional sites to see when they rode past them. Since we had nothing else to do while we waited for the bridge to close – Mark said, 'Hey guys, quick come here before the boat goes by; I have an idea!' We gathered around and listened. His idea was hilarious so we agreed, 'Let's do it!'

We all got into position! We ran as quickly as we could in our blistered feet to the edge of the river. As the boat passed by we waived our arms and screamed, 'Hey! Hey! Welcome to New York!

Welcome to New York!'

Near the bridge, the boat moved by us slowly which gave the tourists and the captain of the boat a clear view of us. When the captain saw us waiving he pulled on the boat's horn (toot, toot) as if to say, 'Hello city people, great to see you!' There were several hundred tourists from all over the world on the Circle Line viewing the sites of the city. They were carrying their little cameras and holding their children. They pulled out their cameras to take pictures of the native New Yorkers waiving to them from the shores of Manhattan. The men, woman, and children on the boat were smiling, waiving, while they were taking pictures of us – then Mark yelled, 'Guys, let's smile for the tourists!' All at once we turned around, pulled down our pants, bent over, and gave them a view of New York that wasn't on their agenda!"

"NO WAY, DAD!! You didn't moon them – did you?"

"Ask your Uncle Kenny – he'll tell you if it's true." Then he continued, "They took a picture of our rosy cheeks, but not the cheeks on our face! We got a kick out of watching the parents scrambling to cover up their kid's eyes!

After the Circle Line passed by we stopped laughing, and the swing bridge closed. We walked across the bridge, but thankfully this time we didn't have to share it with a train. When we reached the Bronx side of the river, John, Billy, Mark, and Pat were too tired to climb over the Rock again and so they walked along the train tracks but Joey, Tony, Tommy, and I decided to climb over it again because 'it was there'."

"Why would you climb over it again if it was so dangerous?"

"I have NO idea! I guess we thought it was fun or cool or something. I really don't know. So, Joey was the first one to climb up the rock, then Tommy, next Tony, and finally I began to climb. I was far behind because my feet were killing me. When Joey was about a quarter of the way up the rock – his foot slipped, he lost his balance, and he fell off the Rock into the cold, icy Harlem River – about 25 feet below. When he fell in he didn't come up out of the water right away, and so Tommy jumped into the water to help him.

Apparently Joey grazed the rock on his way into the water because when Tommy pulled him out there was blood gushing out of his head. After they climbed out of the water they plopped down on the ground – wet, cold, and exhausted.

The other guys who walked around the rock missed all the excitement and when they met up with us Billy said, 'What happened?' I said, 'Joey fell in and Tommy jumped in to save him. Hey, we need some dry clothes – let them wear our dry coats.' Billy and Mark took off their sweatshirts and gave them to Tommy and Joey. Joey wrapped his wet shirt around his head to stop the bleeding, and they stood back up, and we all started walking home again.

When we got back to the neighborhood Joey was worried what his parents would do to him? He could never go home like this; his mother would beat him with a wooden spoon and he'd be grounded for a month. We decided to go to John's apartment basement to dry the wet clothes in the laundry room. Someone else was already using the dryers so we pulled out their clothes and put Joey's and Tommy's clothes in. They both stood there in their underwear waiting for their clothes to dry.

In about thirty minutes their clothes were dry enough to wear; they put them on and we walked to the elevator. When the elevator door opened, a woman stepped out; she was on her way to pickup her dry laundry – hopefully she had a few more quarters. We quickly got in the elevator and pulled the door closed behind us.

Now we had to come up with an explanation of the gash on his head; a simply thing to do, he told his parents, 'I fell while playing hockey in PS 7…'"

"Did that really happen?"

"Would your daddy lie to you?"

After Hours...

Sometimes my dad's stories took us totally by surprise. He told us things we never even thought about and never knew existed; like the time he told us about a job he had for a short period of time.

"Well, my childhood wasn't all about fun and games; I had to work the fields, feed the chickens, milk the cows, and..."

Kelsie interrupted my dad and asked, "No way! Don't believe him, Cam – Daddy didn't live on a farm!"

"Well, maybe I didn't feed any chickens, but I did work hard. Like when I worked cleaning up After Hours places...."

"What are After Hours places?"

"In New York, at least when I was growing up, I'm not sure what it's like now, the bars were only legally allowed to stay open until 4:00 in the morning. At about 3:30 or 3:45 the bartender yelled out, 'LAST CALL' which meant you could only buy one more drink before they stopped serving alcohol. After 4:00 a.m. everyone was supposed to leave and the bar was closed down for a few hours – I think until 8:00 or 9:00 in the morning."

"Why'd they open the bars up so early?"

"I don't know, Kels...maybe so men could pour some beer on their Fruit Loops."

"Funny, Dad."

"Anyway, at 4:00 a.m. the party was just beginning for a lot of people, and so they went to the After Hour places in the neighborhood. The After Hour places were, wait Cam, do you remember watching 'Bugsy Malone' with me – the movie with Scott Baio and a bunch of other little kids?"

I remembered we had rented the movie through Netflix a couple of years ago. I said, "Was that the movie that was supposed to be a bunch of gangsters who shot each other with pies and cream puffs and they drove around in cars they had to pedal?"

"Yeah, that one! I love that movie! Anyway, that movie supposedly took place during Prohibition when you weren't allowed to drink alcohol. Remember how they had to knock on a door to get into Fat Sam's Speakeasy? And how somebody on the other side of the door opened up a little peephole to see who it was before they opened up the door to let the person in?"

"Yeah, I remember that."

"Well, that's how it was with After Hours places. They were illegal places people went to after the bars closed. Every adult in the neighborhood knew where they were, but they were hidden from sight; they were usually located in a basement, a backroom, or down an alley way near a legitimate business. You had to knock on the door, and you were only let in if they knew you or felt comfortable you wouldn't cause trouble. There were always several big bouncers..."

"What's a bouncer?"

They're big, strong guys who usually work at bars and it's their job to let people in or kick them out. But mainly they make sure people don't go crazy and start fighting and trashing the place. They are very important because remember, a lot of times when people get drunk, especially young guys, they want to fight. Clear as mud, Cam?"

"Yup, clear as mud – continue."

"Okay, where was I? Oh yeah. So, the After Hours places all had a few bouncers. Usually they had a cover charge...wait, Cam... that means people had to pay a few dollars just to get in. I'm pretty sure you had to pay a cover charge, but maybe I'm wrong. Anyway, inside it usually looked like a regular bar, but everyone I went to was pretty small..."

Kelsie sat up, "DAD! You went to places like this?!!"

"I'm sorry, I meant to say, 'everyone I heard about was pretty small'..."

Kelsie and I didn't believe him, but we didn't say anything else; we let him get back to the story.

"So they were pretty small, they had a bar for drinks, and they had gambling. Some places...um...I'm told some places had a few Black Jack tables, a Craps table, a Roulette Wheel, and some of them even had a dance floor with disco lights. I don't think they had an official closing time, but I do know...cough...because I was told...cough...when people left the sun was usually coming up outside."

"I can't believe you worked at places like this when you were my age!"

"No, Kelsie, I didn't work at after hour places when I was 13... well...actually...I did...but I didn't. I cleaned them up. I didn't work while people were there.

You see one of my best friends, John, used to help his father clean these places up. Oh wait, I need to tell you one more thing about After Hour places. Like I said earlier, every adult in the area, including the police, knew where the After Hour places were, but the cops usually left them alone. But every so often the cops conducted a raid; maybe because they received complaints from people in the neighborhood, or maybe because of loud fights outside early in the morning – I'm really not sure."

"How do you know the police knew about these places?"

"Because the cops hung out at these places too.

When the cops raided them, which was rare, they made a mess. I remember when I was...I mean...I remember being told about a time when a person I knew was at an After Hours place when it was raided. He said 6 or 8 cop cars showed up with their sirens blaring and about 15 or 20 cops broke in with sledge hammers and axes, and they trashed the place. I guess the idea was to destroy everything in the place so it would be difficult for the owner to rebuild and open up again. They destroyed everything – they busted the Black Jack tables, the Craps tables, the Roulette Wheel, they broke all the drink glasses, and they even broke the disco ball! At least that's what I was told by a friend of mine.

So you see? When the cops did this my friend's father was the person who was called to fix up the place so it could be used the next night. On several occasions, not a lot, I helped my friend and his father clean up and prepare them for the next night's party.

I can remember the first day I was asked to help. I was playing basketball in the back of St. John's Middle School. John came out to play for a little while, but he had to leave early to help his father. I'm not sure why John asked me – it might have been because his older brother couldn't help, and so his father needed someone else. John mentioned his father needed help cleaning up some place and moving some stuff, and he asked me if I wanted to help. He said his dad would pay me about $40. $40 was A LOT of money to a 13 year old – especially for a few hours of work and so I screamed, 'YES! OF COURSE I'LL DO IT! FOR $40 I'LL DO ANYTHING!!'

After we played a little more basketball, we walked to John's apartment. On the walk I talked about getting paid $40 for one day's work. John said he's been working with his father for a few years, and he had a lot of money saved up. When we got to his apartment he invited me in, and we went to his room where he had his big metal box. He kept all the money he earned over the years in this metal box. I was amazed at what I saw! It was packed with money there were tons of $1, $5, $10, and even $20 bills! I thought to myself, 'HOLY CRAP – HE'S RICH!!' There must have been hundreds, maybe thousands of dollars in there. That was the first time I realized how responsible, frugal, some might say 'cheap' John was – he had almost every penny he ever made in his life right there in this little box!

His mother told us to meet his dad at Keenan's, which was a local Irish bar he hung out in. We, or at least I, was excited about getting to work, and so we ran out of his apartment, jumped down each flight of steps, and ran outside his building. When we got outside we walked down 232nd Street and made a right on Broadway to get to Keenan's. It was a short walk; it only took us a minute to get there. When we entered Keenan's his father was entertaining the men at the bar; he was a very funny, popular guy in the neighborhood; when he saw us he said, 'Well it looks like it's time to go.' He raised his pilsner glass of Schafer beer and said, 'See you later.' Then he pushed a twenty dollar bill toward the bartender and said, 'Keenan, the next round is on me; keep the rest.'

We walked out of the bar around the corner to Broadway where Mr. J's 1964 GMC Panel Truck was parked. We got in, and he pulled away from the curb, making a left on 231st Street going toward Bailey Avenue. When we reached Bailey Avenue, he made a left turn; he drove past Cooney Grauer field on the left and the Bailey Avenue Projects on the right. He headed up the Bailey Place hill, toward Fort Independence. I quietly asked John, 'Where are we going?' John quietly told me we had to stop by the warehouse to pickup the moving van and some supplies.

After Mr. J turned onto Fort Independence, he pulled into a parking lot in front of a small brick warehouse which appeared to be abandoned. It sat back from the street; its view was obstructed by several old trees, a rusty chain link fence, and overgrown weeds which grew between the uneven, cracked, concrete squares. In the corner of the parking lot there was an industrial size trash bin. The warehouse didn't have any identifying markers on the outside, the brick was a light shade of brown, there was no building number, no sign, and you couldn't see into the building because the two or three windows it had were made of opaque glass. There were only two entrances to the building; a large overhead door which a truck could drive through and a small door with a padlock on the outside…"

Kelsie put her hand over her mouth pretending to yawn and said, "Dad, you don't have to go into so much detail. We get the point – dirty, old warehouse – you can move on now!"

"Oh, so you think I'm going into too much detail, huh? You don't know what detail is little girl. Now you're going to get it…"

"That's not what I mean! Just don't get into so much detail."

My dad smiled and said, "You can't tell your daddy how to tell a story! I'll go into as much detail as I want to go into!"

"Then I'm leaving…bye."

My dad got up and sat on Kelsie to keep her from leaving. Then he continued his long, detailed story. He said, “When he pulled into the parking lot he stopped next to a large, old, rusted moving van with two headlights, four large wheels, a muffler, a handle on the driver side door, another handle on the passenger side…”

“DAD, STOP! STOP SITTING ON ME – I CAN'T BREATHE!”

My dad sat up and said, “But Kels, you can't go until I finish my story. I'll try to give you the Reader's Digest version…”

“What's a Reader's Digest version, Dad?”

“Didn't I tell you before? It means I'll give you the short version of the story. Okay, so where was I? Oh yeah, I was telling you about the building. When Mr. J got out of his panel truck he walked over to the warehouse door, unlocked the padlock, and walked inside. A minute later he lifted open the large overhead door to shoulder height, and then he walked over to the moving van.

He got into the van and tried to turn it on. It took him a while to get it started, but once he did, he forced it into gear, and backed it up to the overhead door. He got out and told John and me to open up the back of the truck because we needed to ‘load it up’. He then walked back inside. While the door was open I looked into the dark warehouse, and I saw odd shaped, green felt covered tables everywhere, long oval table tops with cushions surrounding them, table legs piled everywhere, dozens of stools without backs, large light fixtures in one corner, brown boxes stacked on shelves along one wall, there were glasses, pitchers, and other items I had never seen before. Then Mr. J came out of a small office with a piece of paper, and he started rattling off orders and pointing everywhere, ‘We need five of these, ten of these, eight of these, fifty of these, etc. Oh yeah, and don't forget to bring a few brooms and some garbage bags!’ We worked together for about thirty minutes loading and packing all the items, listed on the piece of paper, onto the van.

When we finished, he closed the doors, locked up the warehouse; and we drove away in the van. Watching Mr. J drive the van was painful; the steering wheel was hard to turn, the breaks didn't work very well, and shifting gears was agonizing to listen to. Every time he pressed down on the clutch and changed gears there was a loud screeching, grinding sound, and the van jerked forward, backward, and side to side until the gear caught and was put in place. When we got on the highway the fastest we drove was about 45 miles per hour; any faster made the van shake so hard I thought it would fall apart.

He drove down the Major Deegan going towards the Tri-Borough Bridge, and then he crossed over a small bridge into Manhattan. It took us about 35 minutes to get to our destination; a two story building located down a dirty side street near a commercial area – sort of like 231st Street. There weren't any parking spaces, so he double parked. We got out of the van and followed Mr. J to the entrance of the building. He pulled out his large key ring and tried several keys until he found one that opened the door to the building. Then we walked up a narrow set of stairs to the second floor where there was a half opened door; it looked like it had been kicked open because the deadbolt on it was still extended and the wood surrounding the door was broken off. Mr. J pushed the door open, and we walked in.

There was broken glass and wood everywhere, there were tables which looked like they had been chopped in half with axes; there were poker chips and playing cards all over the floor – it looked like a tornado plowed through the room. When Mr. J was far enough away I asked John quietly, 'What happened here? Where are we?' But John didn't say anything. Then Mr. J said, 'It looks like the cops did a job on this place. This might take a little longer than I thought. Alright you two, I need you two to start cleaning up. Anything that looks like it can be salvaged needs to be put in that corner over there and anything small that needs to be thrown out needs to go into those garbage cans over here. Anything large that needs to be thrown out needs to be piled up in that corner, and we'll take it downstairs later.

We got right to work cleaning the place. It didn't look like there was going to be much to be salvaged because everything, except for a few stools, had been completely demolished by the police. But after several hours of hard work the room was neat and clean, except for one corner, which had a pile of wood, stools, and garbage bags with glass sticking out of them.

After we finished this part of the job Mr. J said, 'We need to bring the new stuff upstairs.' He explained to us, 'When we're outside I need you to carry everything upstairs very quickly – don't stop, don't turn around, just get in the building and up the steps! If anyone asks you anything, just ignore them and keep walking.' We followed his directions; when he gave us a table, chair, or box we moved with the speed and stealth of a Navy Seal."

"Navy Seal. Nice Dad."

"Yeah, Cam. We were smooth like SOCOM. Okay, where was I? Oh yeah. I noticed every time Mr. J handed us something, he looked down the road; I guess to see if the cops were coming.

After we moved all the items from the van to the building, we set-up and organized everything. Mr. J shouted out orders again, 'This table goes here, that table goes there. Five stools go around that table. Eight stools go around that table. Kenny, take the glasses out of those boxes and stack them on those shelves. John, place six decks of cards on those tables and put three sleeves of blue, red, and yellow chips on that table.' When we were done it looked like a small Las Vegas or Atlantic City casino. At this point all we had to do was throw away the garbage and go home."

"I can't believe my father worked at After Hours places. You tell us to never cheat or lie, and meanwhile when you were my age you broke the law and were a common criminal..."

"You're right, Kelsie – I can't believe I did it either. Actually, on the drive back I thought about what I had just participated in, and I was appalled not only at myself, but also at Mr. J for exploiting me. On the way home I thought about the words I would say to him. I planned to say, 'Mr. J, it was my understanding I was going to help you clean and move some things. I am aghast at what I now realize I participated in, and I hold you personally responsible for my actions. I had no idea I was being asked to participate in an endeavor which will facilitate the fine people of New York to break the laws of this great city of ours. If I had known this, I would have surely rejected the job offer, and furthermore, I would have done everything in my power to convince you to turn away from your evil ways!'

As I prepared to convince Mr. J he stopped the van on the corner of 231st Street and Kingsbridge Avenue to let us out. I was about to tell him, 'Repent, thy SINNER, from thy evil ways!', but just as it was coming out of my mouth Mr. J said, 'Thanks for the help boys', and he handed us $50 each! $50 each!!! I looked at Mr. J, then I looked down at the money; I looked at Mr. J; I looked at the money, at Mr. J, at the money, at Mr. J, at the money, and then I said, 'THANK YOU SO MUCH FOR ASKING ME TO HELP! PLEASE CALL ME ANYTIME YOU NEED MY HELP AGAIN!'"

"DAD! You are bad!"

"Well Kels, every man has his price, and $50 was mine."

"Sounds like you weren't a perfect boy when you were growing up."

"That's right, I wasn't. Do you two want me to tell you another 'Rebel Without a Cause' story?"

"Okay, sure."

Escape from ~~New York~~ Lake Hopatcong

"Lake Hopatcong is the name of a really nice lake in New Jersey; actually it's the largest fresh water lake in the state. Back when I was in middle school there was an amusement park located along the shores of Lake Hopatcong called Bertrand Island Amusement Park, but we just called it Lake Hopatcong."

"Lake a-what-a-kong?"

"Lake Hopatcong. It was an Amusement Park when I was a kid, but they shut it down back in the early 80's. I went there several times; the first time I went there was with my Uncle Larry, Aunt Chris, and my cousins Barbara, Denis, and Shannon. I stayed over their house for several days when I was about 9 years old – kind of like a short little vacation. One of the nights I was there we drove to Lake Hopatcong to go to the amusement park. I can remember my uncle asking me to go on the Boomerang when we first got there, but I was too afraid. But later on, when we were leaving, I got up the guts to go, and I said, 'Uncle Larry let's go on the Boomerang – I'll go on it now!' But he told me, 'Sorry Kenny, we can't. We need to leave now.' I whined and cried, actually maybe I didn't cry, but I did whine, but he never gave in. That was the first time I remember learning…"

Kelsie chimed in, "Dad, you're getting off track. We're not ready to hear about any lessons you learned from your Uncle Larry we want to hear the story about Lake Hopatcong."

"Oh, Kelsie, you'll rue the day you missed out on learning an important life lesson from my story about Uncle Larry and the Boomerang. Someday, someday, you'll be back – you'll come back, on your hands and knees, asking me to share the story with you…"

"I'm sure my life will be ruined if I don't hear that story right now – can you tell us the Lake Hopatcong story?"

"Okay, so the first time I went there was with my Uncle Larry's family, but I also went there several times with St. John's Day Camp, and it was the place my 8th grade class decided to go on our 8th grade graduation trip.

Now keep in mind, Lake Hopatcong was a great place to go; my friends and I had a great time every time we had been there. It had all the rides you expect at an amusement park; a huge wooden roller coast, the Scrambler, the Boomerang, and all the other rides you can think of. It also had a ride, I can't remember what it was called, but it was a long, slow boat ride through a dark tunnel – we called it the 'Tunnel of Love'. My friends and I talked and joked about inviting our 'girl friends' on the ride so we could 'make-out' with them in the 'Tunnel of Love'. When I was in day camp we talked about doing the same thing, but there never was any 'love' taking place in the tunnel – mostly there was a lot of rocking, screaming, and splashing.

You would think all this stuff would be enough for a bunch of 8th grade boys – but it wasn't, we needed even more excitement. I'm not sure when we came up with the idea to add a little more excitement to our trip, but I'm sure it was Tommy, John, Tony, Billy, Mark, Timmy, and me who came up with the idea. The brilliant idea we came up with involved bringing alcohol on the bus ride to Lake Hopatcong. We thought getting drunk on our 8th grade trip was appropriate, because it seemed like high school students got drunk on the weekends – so we were preparing ourselves for the future.

A couple of weeks before the trip we met during lunch to discuss our options. We agreed beer wouldn't work; the teachers would notice us carrying the coolers onto the bus, and the bus driver would notice the empty beer cans being tossed out the back window. We agreed a keg of beer wouldn't work because it probably wouldn't fit in any of our book bags. I think it was John who came up with the idea of bringing a bottle of liquor. His father had several bottles of whiskey at home and he didn't think either of his parents would notice if one was missing.

The day of the trip we arrived at school prepared for a lot of heavy, manly drinking. School started at 8:30 and by 9:00 everyone was on the bus ready to leave. The day before one of the guys said, 'Drink a lot of milk in the morning because milk coats your stomach, and it will keep you from puking when you drink the whiskey.' This made sense to me, and so I ate three or four bowls of Wheaties with a lot of milk that morning.

The bus pulled away from St. John's Middle School at 9:05. We drove down Kingsbridge Avenue, made a left on 230th Street, got on the Major Deegan south bound, to the Cross Bronx Expressway going toward the GW Bridge. On our bus there were about forty 8th grade students, two teachers (Mr. Collins and Ms. Caruso), and two chaperones. All my friends were sitting in the back of the bus; Tommy, John, Tony, and I were in the back row; Billy, Pat, Mark, and Timmy were in the next row. The parents and teachers were all sitting near the front of the bus – everything was working out perfectly.

We agreed not to open up the whiskey until we crossed over the George Washington Bridge. As soon as the bus made it safely across the bridge the party began. John pulled out the whiskey, cracked it open, and said, 'It's party time!' He took a swig, passed it to Tommy, then to John, Tony, Timmy, me, Billy, and Mark; here a swig, there a swig, everywhere a swig, swig, a gulp, gulp here, a gulp, gulp there, here a gulp, there a gulp, everywhere a gulp, gulp.

The party got into full swing when we began singing 99 bottles of beer on the wall, and Tommy put a lamp shade on his head and began hitting on Ms. Caruso."

"Come on, Dad, please don't start exaggerating again. We want to hear the real story."

"Okay, Cam, maybe Tommy didn't have a lamp shade on his head but we were passing the bottle around, and we were getting loud. We were so loud the other kids on the bus began asking, 'Hey, what are you guys doing?' It wasn't long before the teachers asked, 'Hey, what are you guys doing?' And, of course, it wasn't long before they found out exactly what we were doing.

Before we knew it Mr. Collins walked to the back of the bus to find out what all the commotion was about. He immediately knew what we were doing. How did he find out so quickly? I'm not really sure. Maybe it was his years of teaching experience, maybe it was his experience as a police officer in another life, maybe he had psychic abilities, or maybe it was the fact all us boys were arm in arm doing the 'Can-Can' down the middle isle of the bus – we'll never know for sure."

"Dad!"

"Okay, Cam – scratch the Can-Can part. When Mr. Collins got to the back of the bus he said, 'What the h#$% are you guys doing? Do you jokers have booze?' Nobody said a word. Then he said, 'Everyone stand up!' When we stood up he could see the whiskey sitting on the seat right behind my back. Mr. Collins was mad! He said, 'Give it here, Hand!' The next comment out of his mouth was, 'Sit down! I'll deal with each of you when we get to the park!'

For the rest of the ride we were able to coordinate our stories. First we'd tell him we found the whiskey on the bus under the back seat. Next, we'd tell him we opened up the bottle and took a sip because we were curious, but we didn't like the taste of it. Then we'd tell him, 'We would have told you but you never believe us. You don't like us!' Then we'd throw in a few tears for affect.

When we arrived in the Lake Hopatcong parking lot the driver parked next to the dozens of other buses which were there that day. When the bus stopped, Mr. Collins said, 'Everyone stay on the bus, in your seats, until I come back!' He went outside and had a meeting with all the other teachers for about fifteen minutes to decide our fate. When Mr. Collins stepped back on the bus he announced, 'Everybody off the bus and line up with Mr. Tursi's class outside, except for Tommy, Tony, John, Kenny, Timmy, Billy, and Mark – you guys stay seated!'

After all the free students exited the bus, Mr. Collins walked to the back of the bus, and the interrogation began. But just like we planned, the story from each of us was the same, 'Mr. Collins, we found the bottle under the back seat, sniff, sniff. We just opened the bottle and smelled it – we didn't drink any of it; sniff, sniff. We're sorry! We should have brought it to your attention earlier, but we never thought you'd believe us! We're sorry! We're soooo sorry! We'll never do it again! Sniff, sniff…can we go to the park now?'

"There's no way that worked."

"You're right, Kelsie – it didn't. Mr. Collins Kangaroo Court issued its verdict – none of us could go into the park! We were confined to the bus for the whole day! We couldn't believe it! This was outrageous!"

I stood up and said, 'Mr. Collins, this is a circus! It's a national disgrace! From my standpoint, as a young Irish American boy, this is a high-tech lynching for uppity Irish kids who in any way deign to think for themselves, to do for themselves, to have different ideas, and it is a message that unless you kowtow to an old order, this is what will happen to you!'

"Wow, that's good Dad. Who'd you steal that quote from?"

"Clarence Thomas."

"Did you really say it?"

"Nope."

"Didn't think so."

"Thanks, Kels. Alright where was I? Oh yeah, as we sat in the back of the bus fuming over this unjust verdict from Mr. Collin's Kangaroo Court – I turned to my friends and made a vow!

'As God is my witness they're not going to lick me. I'm going to live through this and when it's all over, I'll never be [on this bus] again. No, nor any of my folk. If I have to lie, steal, cheat or kill. As God is my witness, I'll never be [on this bus] again.'

"You plagiarized this one too – didn't you, Dad?"

"Yup."

"From who?"

"Scarlet O'Hara."

"Did you really say it?"

"Nope."

He smiled and got back to his story, "We wanted to get off the bus but since Mr. Collins was standing outside, in front of the bus, with Ms. Caruso – doing his best to get a little action – we couldn't walk off the bus without being noticed. Even if the teachers weren't in front of the bus, we didn't know where we would go once we got off it anyway. If we went into the park we would surely be caught by the teachers, but if we didn't go into the park where would we go? We had no way to get home, we didn't have a car, there wasn't any public transportation, and we didn't know anyone who could come to pick us up.

We couldn't figure out what to do, but then it hit me! We could hot wire a car to get home? Sure, I had never actually hot wired a car before, but Ron Meathead taught me how, and it seemed pretty simple. All I needed was something to break the ignition lock and then I'd connect a couple of wires together and then – VROOM! A rock could be used to break the ignition lock, and I knew Tommy had a pocket knife which could be used to peal the rubber away from the wires. There was only one missing piece – a car! Luckily this wouldn't be a problem because the parking lot was full of unattended vehicles.

But we still had to figure out how to get off the bus. As I gazed out the bus window I could see my school mates in the distance riding the roller coaster, the Scrambler, and the Bumper Cars – I yearned to be free!"

"Yearned, Dad?"

"Yes, YEARNED Kelsie! As I was gazing out the window yearning to be free something caught my eye – it was a little sticker at the bottom of the window, 'PUSH OUT IN CASE OF EMERGENCY'. In my life, at the time, this situation seemed like an emergency, and so I pushed, and pushed, and pushed. The other guys saw what I was doing, and they immediately knew what was on my mind. Billy said, 'I hope you're not thinking what I think you're thinking.' I looked at him and said, 'I'm not staying on this bus – I'm out of here.' I pushed one last time and the window broke free from the bus without making much noise. Since Mr. Collins was still busy trying to pickup Ms. Caruso neither of them noticed what I was doing.

Once the window swung loose from the bus I looked at the other guys and said, 'Who's with me?' Without hesitation Tommy said, 'Let's go!' The other guys were more responsible; they stayed, hoping to be paroled early for good behavior. John leaned over and held the window open for Tommy and me; it was a Liberty Lines bus and so we had to hang jump out of the window onto the gravel parking lot below. It was too high to climb back in the window and so there was no going back – we were living in the lamb!"

"Living in the lamb?"

"Living off the lamb!"

"Living off the lamb?"

"Living on the lamb! Yeah that's what we were doing. Living on the lamb. I'm pretty sure that's what we were doing."

"What does that mean?"

"I'm not sure, but we were doing it. We had to find a car to hot wire; for some reason we decided to leave the parking lot and walk to a nearby residential neighborhood. We walked out of the lot to the residential neighborhood, and we looked into the cars that were parked along the street; occasionally we pulled on a car door handle to see if the car was open. Then we saw it – the perfect car to hot wire – a Trans Am. We checked to see if the door was open – and it was! I hopped into the car and lay down on the front seat and looked under the steering column to see how easy it would be to hot wire a Trans Am.

As I was lying on the floor under the steering wheel looking for a couple of wires with notes which said, 'Connect Together to Hot Wire' I remembered we needed a rock, and so I called to Tommy, 'Can you find a big rock so I can break off the ignition lock?' Tommy left while I stayed in the car with my head under the steering wheel. He was gone for so long I started to wonder what happened to him, but then I heard a knock on the car window. I was still working under the steering wheel, and I said, 'Hey Tommy, do you have the rock?' Tommy opened the car door and said, 'Hey, Kenny, you gotta get out.' 'Why? If you give me the rock I'll have this thing started in a second.' Then I heard a much deeper voice say, 'Young man please step out of the vehicle.' When I looked up I saw Tommy and a very tall police officer. When I got out of the car I noticed several women standing on their front porches, with their young children at their feet, staring straight at us.

The officer said very sternly, 'Young men, get in the squad car!' We didn't have time to coordinate our story, so we had to improvise on the fly. We told the police officer we were with St. John's and we accidentally walked outside the park, but were trying to get back in. The officer asked me something about my head being under the steering wheel of another person's car. I couldn't come up with a coherent answer; I said something about liking this type of car and wanting one when I was older – he didn't buy it.

When we got back to the parking lot he asked me and Tommy to get out of the car, and he placed us in handcuffs. What a sight it must have been when all the kids in our school noticed Tommy and me being walked back into the park locked up in handcuffs being escorted by a police officer.

From my perspective everything was surreal – it seemed to go in slow motion. As we were led into the park like convicts all the other kids were staring and saying, 'Is that Tommy and Kenny? What did they do now? Weren't they supposed to stay on the bus? Go tell the other kids!' Minutes later it seemed like all the kids from the school were swarming around us, asking, 'What did you do? What did you do? What did you do?'

The police put up barricades to keep the crowds away from us as we walked in with our orange jump suits, shackles, and handcuffs. Tommy and I looked like Timothy McVeigh and the Unabomber. We kept our heads down as we mumbled under our breath, 'No comment. No comment. Not until we speak to our lawyer.'

"Dad, I wasn't going to say anything, but I'm sorry – there's no way you were wearing orange jump suits and saying 'no comment'. No way!

My dad cleared his throat and continued, "The police officer brought us to the main office, and over the intercom the park attendant announced, 'Can the guardian of Tommy and Kenny Hand please come to the main office?' It wasn't long before Mr. Collins came running through the crowd to the office, he was completely out of breath, and he was mad! To paraphrase Chris Rock, 'I'm not saying he should have killed us, but if he did,

I'd understand.' The police officer released us under the supervision of Mr. Collins, however, we would have preferred being placed in jail – it would have been safer.

When Mr. Collins got his hands on us, he dragged us back to the bus and locked us to the front steering wheel, he sat in the front seat, right next to us, and he gave the other boys an early release for good behavior – I guess good behavior is a relative thing.

♪ Oh Mama, I'm in fear for my life from the long arm of the law
Law man has put an end to my running and I'm so far from my home ♪
♪ The jig is up, the news is out, they finally found me
The renegade who had it made, retrieved for a bounty ♪
♪ Never more to go astray, this'll be the end today
Of the wanted man ♪ [16]

The Lake Hopatcong incident almost led to me being expelled from school. Actually, I didn't know if I would officially graduate from St. John's until I walked to the front of the church in my cap and gown and looked inside my diploma book."

"What do you mean you didn't know if you would graduate?"

"I mean, I really didn't know if I would graduate until I actually received my diploma. I'll save the rest of that story for another time."

The Great Kingsbridge Copper Rush of 1979

Maybe I shouldn't have included this next story because it might give people the wrong idea about my dad and his friends. But I decided, what the heck, why should I care if people think my dad and his friends were derelicts. Just kidding, I just think you'll like this story.

He told it to us at one of our Saturday morning breakfasts at McDonald's, when we were talking about history. I knew he loved history so I told him what we were going to learn in my Social Studies class. I said, "Mrs. Atkins said we're going to start a new topic about Westward Expansion, and it includes the California Gold Rush of 1849? Have you ever heard about it?"

He said, "Of course, I'm a daddy; I know everything! The California Gold Rush actually started in January 1848 when this guy named James Wilson Marshall discovered gold in California at a place called Sutter's Mill. People at first didn't believe him, but by 1849 it seemed like everyone in the world had heard about the gold found in California, and so people from all over the world rushed to California to strike it rich. Some came by boat, some came by covered wagon, some came by AMTRAC, and some came by plane."

"There were planes in 1849?"

"No, I was just checking to make sure you were listening to me. Okay, where was I? Oh yeah, people from all over the world. So, people came from all over the world to strike it rich; if you lived in California at this time you would have seen thousands of people all over the place searching for gold, digging for gold, panning for gold, and doing everything they could to strike it rich – California was total mayhem!"

"Dad, what's mayhem?"

"It's like it is in our house when we're late for church. People running around yelling, screaming, throwing things – you get the picture?"

"Yes, continue."

"Well, this total mayhem picture I'm trying to paint in your mind is exactly what it was like in Kingsbridge after copper was discovered in 1979. It was called 'The Great Kingsbridge Copper Rush of 1979'. I'm sure you learned about it in your Social Studies class. Right?"

"Uh…no, dad…never heard of it. Is this another one of your made up stories?"

"Made up stories?! Made up stories!! Made up stories!!! When have I ever made up a story?!!!! When? You tell me when I…!!!"

"Well, dad, there was the time…"

"NEVER MIND…let me get back to the Kingsbridge Copper Rush story! Where was I? You always make me forget where I was. Oh yeah. It began on a Thursday afternoon in August 1979 when Billy came running into the schoolyard where a bunch of us were playing soccer. He had a long green strip of metal in his hand and he was yelling at the top of his lungs, 'There's copper on them thar roofs! There's copper on them thar roofs!! There's copper on them thar roofs!!!'

"'Them thar roofs', dad? Dad, did this take place in the Bronx or in the boot heal of Missouri?"

"Yes! 'THEM THAR ROOFS'!! And YES it took place in the Bronx!!!"

My dad cleared his throat as if he was annoyed the validity of his story was being questioned. But still he continued, "So as I was saying, we were all playing soccer in the St. John's schoolyard when Billy came running in yelling EXACTLY WHAT I TOLD YOU HE WAS YELLING! We all stopped playing soccer, and we ran over to him. I was the first one to reach him, and I said, 'Calm down Billy! Calm down! Come over here and sit down!' We walked over to the short wall which looked out over the lots. Billy sat down and slumped over exhausted; his legs were spread apart, his head facing down, and he was huffing and puffing trying to catch his breath. He slowly looked up at us and said (between huffs and puffs), 'There's copper on the roofs. There's copper on the roofs!'

We turned from Billy and looked at each other; we had baffled looks on our faces wondering what in the world he was talking about. Tommy broke the silence and said, 'Yeah, so what?' Billy looked up in disbelief and responded, 'Don't you see? Don't you get it? You guys know about the Metal Factory – the one next to the Riverdale Dairy near the 225th Street Projects. Well, just a little while ago I went to the dairy with my mother, and as we were about to walk inside I noticed a sign on the outside of the Metal Factory building; it says they pay \$.50 for a pound of copper! \$.50!! When I read this I stopped, and I remembered seeing copper on Shawn's roof when we were playing Roundup a few days ago; there was copper around the sky lights, the smoke stacks, and along the ledges. I also thought I remembered seeing copper on all the other roofs in the neighborhood; I wasn't positive, but I was pretty sure.

When these two thoughts came together in my head – my mind started racing with ideas! I ran into the store and told my mother, 'I gotta go Mom! I'll be home before dinner – but I gotta go now!' I rushed out of the store, and I ran nonstop – all the way from the dairy to Godwin Terrace. Once I got here I ran up to the roof tops of every building on Godwin and I was right! I WAS RIGHT! Copper is everywhere!!! I checked ALL the roofs; the last one I checked was Robin's roof and after I saw all the copper on her roof, so I decided to walk over to the ledge to check out the other roofs in the neighborhood. See, look at my shirt it has tar all over it from leaning against the ledge.'

Billy stood up and showed us his New York Yankee shirt which was covered in tar. 'Look at all this tar. I can't believe how sticky this stuff is. My mother's going to kill me when she sees I ruined my new shirt.'

'Billy!' John said, 'Would you sit down and finish your story? We don't care about your shirt!'

Billy said, 'Oh sorry. So when I looked over the ledge I could see the roofs of all the stores on 231st Street and all over Kingsbridge; Ehring's roof, P&K's roof, Fuhrman's roof, Art Steel's roof, Northside Savings Bank's roof, EVERYONE'S ROOF!!! And for as far as my eyes could see – I saw COPPER, COPPER, and more COPPER!!!'

Billy stood up again. Pat spoke up, 'Focus Billy, focus, you're not done yet. Sit back down and finish telling us about the copper!'

'I AM focused Pat! I just need to show you something!' Billy turned around toward the lots and said, 'Look, there, and there, and there, and there! All that green you see – it's copper! You can see it everywhere; for as far as your eyes can see. Guys, we'll be rich! Rich I tell you!!'

It's funny how these words affected us and how we thought about the roofs. These roofs weren't new to us; we spent so much time on them they were almost like playgrounds or backyards to us. In the past when we looked at them all we saw was black tar, sky lights, broken glass, faded beer cans, cigarette butts, and bottle caps – but now – because of Billy's words – we saw COPPER and a lot of it! I'm not sure how James Marshall felt when he found gold at Sutter's Mill, but I can't imagine he was anymore excited than we were. Although we were excited, we didn't say anything to each other for several seconds. We just stood there looking out over the Kingsbridge landscape, our mouths slightly opened, our eyes wide open, our hearts pounding, but mostly our minds were racing with the words, 'We'll be rich! We'll be rich!' repeating over, over, and over again.

Up to this point neither Billy nor anyone else mentioned how we were going to strike it rich, but it was understood by all of us. We were going to 'mine' all the copper off the roofs of Kingsbridge and sell it to the Metal Factory."

"What? Are you kidding? Dad, are you saying you guys were going to steal the copper off the roofs?"

"Cam, 'steal' is such a harsh word – let's go with 'mine' – it's a much friendlier, albeit, less accurate, word."

After he said this he smiled at me – in a way which let me know he was joking. I smiled back, but I wasn't exactly sure what part of his story, if any, he was joking about, but I didn't ask him to clarify because I wanted to hear the rest of his story.

My dad picked up where he left off, "Although we liked Billy's idea we knew it wasn't enough – we needed a plan to make it work. We needed tools like hammers and crowbars to rip the copper off the roofs, we needed a way to carry the copper from the roofs to the Metal Factory, and we needed to decide which copper fields we should mine."

"STEAL."

"MINE. It was a simple plan – there weren't a whole lot of moving parts to consider. We decided the hammers would come from our parent's tool boxes; the crowbars came from our parent's car trunks, but we weren't sure how we would carry the copper. We expected to mine a lot of copper…"

"STEAL."

"We expected to MINE a lot of copper and so we wouldn't be able to carry it with our hands. John said, 'We need some kind of a cart – like a grocery store cart.' We both looked at each other, and I said, 'Well then – let's get some grocery carts.' We agreed three carts would be enough, and since we wanted to start mining the copper as soon as possible we decided to PROCURE the grocery carts right away…"

"Does procure also mean 'STEAL'?"

"We decided there was no time like the present to BORROW a few carts, and the best place to do the borrowing was either Waldbaums or Finest. Since Waldbaums was a little closer, we chose Waldbaums. Tommy, Shawn, John, and I decided we would be the ones to borrow the carts, so we walked to 233rd Street, down the street from my apartment building where Waldbaums was located. We split up into two groups so we wouldn't be too conspicuous; Tommy and Shawn took the direct approach, they went right into the store to borrow the carts. John and I decided we would wait in the rear of the parking lot for someone to bring their cart to us.

We stood there for a few minutes and watched dozens of shoppers walk out carrying brown paper bags full of groceries in their arms – eventually an older woman walked out of the store with a cart which she was pushing in our direction. She pushed it next to her car; she opened the trunk, and loaded up her groceries. Once she was done we walked over to her and politely asked her if we could walk her cart back to the store for her. She said, 'Why certainly you can. Thank you very much. You are two, very nice, young gentlemen.' We thanked her and promptly turned away from the store and walked quickly in the direction of Godwin Terrace.

Like I said before, Tommy and Shawn took the direct approach; they just walked into the store, grabbed two carts, walked out the door, and started running as fast as they could. When they reached the sidewalk, an employee from the grocery store noticed them and began chasing after them. The chase didn't last for long, maybe because he was overweight or maybe because the minimum wage of $2.90 an hour wasn't enough to put his life in danger by chasing a couple of punks through the busy streets of Kingsbridge – we'll never know for sure.

When we returned to Godwin Terrace we parked our BORROWED carts in the O'Grady's cellar and got back together with the other guys to finalize our plan. The final part of our plan involved deciding which buildings we would strip mine. We decided to focus on the copper fields between Broadway and Kingsbridge Avenue, from 230th Street to 233rd Street. We divided this area into four quadrants and we assigned a team of prospectors to each."

"Prospectors, Dad?"

My dad started smiling before he yelled at me, "Yes, Cam, PROSPECTORS! WHAT IS YOUR PROBLEM! THAT'S WHAT YOU CALL PEOPLE WHO DIG FOR GOLD AND COPPER LIKE WE WERE DOING!! Ok, where was I? Oh yeah, we had four teams; John, Pat, and I were assigned to all the copper fields north of 232nd Street; the biggest field being Art Steele's roof.

We decide to wait until Saturday to put our plan into action. We planned to meet on the corner of 231st and Godwin Terrace at 9:00 a.m. When we all showed up, around 9:15, we walked into Cold

Cut City and purchased Yoo-hoos and buttered rolls for breakfast; we walked outside and sat down on the stoop around the corner to eat our breakfast and to discuss the schedule for the day.

The night before we estimated each group could mine about fifty pounds of copper per hour, we planned to work for five hours (from 10:00 a.m. until 3:00 p.m.), the Metal Factory was paying $.50 per pound, and so we calculated we would have about $500 for our party. Not bad for five hours of work, especially when you consider minimum wage was $2.90 an hour at the time. We were so confident of our future riches; we told the girls the night before to be in the St. John's schoolyard at 8:00 p.m. for the party of a life time!

When we finished our buttered rolls, we walked up Godwin Terrace to the O'Grady's basement where the tools and carts were stored. We grabbed our hammers, crow bars, our…I mean...the carts, and we went our separate ways to the copper fields. The first group started on the O'Grady's roof; the second went behind St. John's and started tearing the copper off the store roofs, the third went across Broadway to Benson's roof, and my group walked North on Broadway to the back of Art Steele.

To get to the back of Art Steele we pushed our cart down the driveway between Williams Funeral Home and the Beer Distributer to a parking lot where they parked the beer trucks. Art Steele's wall was about twenty feet high so we had to figure out a way to get on top of the roof. We looked around the parking lot which was filled with broken down trucks, rotted pallets, rusty kegs, busted bottles, and other miscellaneous garbage. Against the wall there was a broken down beer truck with flat tires and a rusted out body. We figured if we piled about six pallets on the roof of the truck it would be high enough to reach the roof – so that's what we did. Pat climbed onto the truck roof while John and I grabbed the pallets; within minutes we were all on top of the roof ripping, pulling, and tearing the copper away from the skylights and the sides of the roof.

One thing we didn't consider was how exposed we were to the public; on the west side, just across from the elevated train tracks were rows of apartment buildings with windows facing Art Steele's roof. On the east side, just across from the Major Deegan, was Albany Crescent which had three apartment buildings which looked out over Art Steele. Finally, there was the 233rd Street overpass which connected Broadway to Bailey Avenue on the way to Cooney Grauer Field, at the time known as Bailey Avenue Field. At first our work seemed to go unnoticed because the streets were relatively quiet but by 11:00 a.m. there were people everywhere. The streets were packed with cars, the sidewalks were packed with people, and it seemed like everyone was looking at the three boys tearing copper off Art Steele's roof.

I was getting a little nervous, and I said, "We need to stop! Someone is going to call the cops!" But then John, said, 'People think we're working on this roof. They don't think we're stealing copper.' A few minutes later we noticed several familiar parents walking along Albany Crescent, Pat said, 'It's Mrs. Donnelly and Mrs. O'Leary.' Instead of hiding he confidently said, 'Hi, Mrs. O'Leary, Mrs. Donnelly!' Later on we found out how impressed they were with us; Mrs. O'Leary in her Irish Brogue told one of her sons, 'Oh that Kenny Hand, John, and Pat – they're hard workers they are! They were out there doing construction work in the hot summer sun – and on a Saturday no less! I'm sure their parents are so proud of them!'

Even though we spent half our day waving to friends who passed by we were able to extract all the copper from the roof. As we tore strips of copper away from the roof we stacked them near the place we climbed up on the roof. We continued to work until 3:00 p.m. like we had planned; by this time we were dirty, smelly, tired, and our clothes were soaked with sweat. When we were finished we had a pile of copper so high it looked like there was enough to resurface the Statue of Liberty.

Now we had to transport it to Godwin Terrace which meant loading up our grocery cart. Instead of carefully lowering the copper off the roof into the cart we decided to push all of it off the roof onto the ground at once. The noise of the copper hitting the ground and hitting the metal of the broken down trucks was deafening! The back door of the Beer Distributor opened up and a couple of older men walked out; one man yelled at us, 'Hey! What are you kids doing back there?' Normally we would have been scared and we might have even run, but after all the back breaking work we just finished we weren't in the mood to worry or run. We just looked at them and yelled, 'We just finished doing roofing work for Art Steele – what's your problem?!' I'm not sure why, but they both turned around and walked back in the store satisfied with our response. I guess it never crossed their mind that three young kids would be stealing copper off the roof.

We picked the copper up off the ground and loaded it into the cart – we tied it down with some rope we found in the parking lot. Our cart looked like Ted Kennedy in a bikini; yeah it fit but it wasn't very pretty!"

"Nice picture, Dad."

"Like I said, it wasn't pretty." He continued, "So we pushed our cart out of the parking lot and through the streets of Kingsbridge; every time we hit a crack in the side walk a piece of copper fell to the ground and we picked it up and stuck it back in. Apparently, we were a sight to see because people stopped and stared at us as we passed them by; we tried to ignore all the attention we received; we just focused on our destination and mumbled to ourselves, 'Nobody is looking at us, nobody is looking at us, we're invisible, we're invisible…'

When we turned the corner to go up the Godwin Terrace hill we saw the other guys drinking beer and sitting on the sidewalk near the fire hydrant at the top of the hill. I was a little concerned because I couldn't see any copper; when we got halfway up the hill with our cart I yelled, 'Where's your copper?!' As I got closer, I yelled again, 'Where's your copper, guys?!!' One of the guys pointed to the school yard and when we looked over we saw a pile of copper the size of the Eiffel Tower. We stopped and Pat said, 'Holy &#$%!, we ARE going to be rich!' We pushed our cart into the school yard and left it next to the existing copper scrap heap. Combining our pile with the existing pile it looked like we had enough copper to build a boyfriend for Lady Liberty; we estimated we had mined almost 1,000 pounds of copper – which could be exchanged for a small fortune– $500.

It was now 3:30, it had been a long day; we were hot, sweaty, tired, and our feet were killing us. We walked back across the street to our friends and sat down on the side walk, leaning against the apartment building wall. Danny passed each of us a cold drink to quench our thirst. We didn't say anything for a while – we just wanted to relax until we regained our strength and our feet stopped throbbing.

We had finished the hard work, but there was still more work to be done – we needed to transport our copper to the Metal Factory. I wasn't looking forward to carrying the copper there; I was comfortable lying on my back on the sidewalk in my soaking wet clothes. I think I nodded off for a minute until Danny spoke up and said, 'Come on guys! We need to bring the copper to the Metal place if we expect to have money for the party tonight.' Even though none of us wanted to get up, we knew Danny was right and so we rolled off the sidewalk and walked to the school yard. We stuffed as much of the copper into the carts as possible but they weren't big enough so we had to carry some of it in our arms. It was quite a sight to see – twelve teenagers pushing and carrying hundreds of pounds of copper through the streets of Kingsbridge; down Godwin Terrace to Kimberly Place – across Broadway and 230th Street to the Metal Factory.

When we reached the Metal Factory it looked like it was closed; the lights appeared to be off; there was only one car in the small parking lot, and the garage door was closed. Shawn knocked on the large metal garage door and a minute later a short, overweight, grimy, Italian guy, with a cigar in his mouth opened the door. He looked at all of us and the copper we had in our hands. He took his cigar out of his mouth with his short, chubby fingers and said, 'How ah ya? You guys looken to sell me some copper?' We told him, 'Yeah, we have about 1,000 pounds here.' He put his cigar back in his mouth and bit down on it. Through his cigar he grunted some incoherent words, and he walked back inside the building – so we followed him.

Inside the building it was dark and dirty; there were cobwebs everywhere, piles of metal all over the place, and a large rusty dump truck with *Vito's Scrap Metal* painted on the side door. In the corner there was a large scale – large enough to weigh a station wagon. Vito waddled over to the scale, pulling his pants up on the trip, and he said, 'Throw the coppa on da scale.' He walked away as we piled the copper from one of the carts onto the scale and he said, 'Ahl be back in a minute.' The weight display looked like a giant clock with only one hand; it could weigh up to 10,000 pounds, so we knew it could handle all of our copper at once.

After we loaded one cart full of copper on the scale it was clear the scale was broken because the hand on the weight display barely moved. The numbers on the scale display went in 100 pound increments; they started with 0, went up to 100, 200, 300, and so on. When Vito came back out of the office Shawn said, 'The scales broken. It's not weighing the copper accurately.' Vito said, 'No way. My scale aint neva been wrong. I'll show ya. How much you weigh?' Shawn said, '185 pounds.' 'So, push the copper off the scale and get on it.' When Shawn got on the scale the hand sprung past the 200 line and then it slowly settled back down to 185. Shawn got off the scale, and I said, 'Let's see how much it says I weigh.' At the time I weighed about 150 pounds and when I got on the scale it stopped right between the 100 and 200 pound lines. We tried this same experiment with a few more guys and each time the scale was accurate.

We didn't say much to each other, but we were shocked; we thought we had 1,000 pounds of copper, but it looked like we had drastically over estimated the weight. Vito said, 'Come on guys. I wanna go home. Put the coppa on the scale so I can get outta here.' We were all disappointed by now and so we just dumped all the copper on the scale and we watched the hand move slowly past the dashes. When the scale's hand came to a stop it didn't even reach the first number; we had only mined about 95 pounds of copper! We couldn't believe it!

Vito said, 'That looks like about 95 pounds. I'll give ya guys fifty dollars and we'll cawl it even. Alright guys? I gotta close up now.' Shawn took the money, stuffed it in his pocket, and we all walked back to Godwin Terrace dejected."

"That's all you guys made? You only made $50?? I thought this was the Great Kingsbridge Copper Rush of 1979...that doesn't sound all that great to me. Why did you call it the Great Kingsbridge Copper Rush of 1979?"

My dad looked at me like he was about to give me some sage fatherly advice. He said, "Cam, I'll tell you why I called it great. It's because we learned many valuable life lessons that day; lessons which changed our lives forever. Lessons like – never listen to Billy's ideas, borrowing grocery carts is wrong, copper is a lot lighter than it looks and..."

"Let me guess the last one, Dad. Was the most valuable lesson you learned – crime doesn't pay?"

"Hmmm…that's a good one, Cam. Not the one I was thinking of but a good one nonetheless."

"So what was the last lesson you learned?

"We learned you can still throw a great party with $50!!"

Kelsie said, "Dad, you were really bad. Did you do a lot of things like this?"

"Hmm, maybe."

"What?! What else did you do?"

"Umm, pool hopping…"

Train Surfing & Pool Hopping

The first time I heard about Pool Hopping I was eleven years old; the air conditioner in our house broke down during one of the hottest weeks of the summer. The first night it broke down it was so hot I couldn't sleep – I just tossed and turned in bed for an hour. I heard the TV in my parents room, and so I got up and walked in and said, 'Mom, Dad, I can't sleep – it's too hot.' My dad looked at my mom and said, 'I need to go buy some screens for the windows so I can turn on the attic fan.' He got up and put on his pants and said, 'Cam, do you want to go to Home Depot with me?' I was dying of heat and so I said, 'Sure.' Kelsie was also up, and so we put some clothes on, and we got in the car.

When we got into the car, he cranked up the air conditioner and backed out of the driveway. As we drove down the street on our way to Home Depot, he glanced at us, smiled, and said, "I agree it's hot, and it's hard to get to sleep. It's hard for me to sleep too, but you don't know what hot is! Have I ever told you how hot it was during the summers when I was growing up?"

"No, Dad, you haven't, but I think you're about to."

"I've told you before the Bronx had very few trees except in the parks in and around Kingsbridge – like Van Cortlandt and Ewen Park. So the brick apartment buildings and black paved roads were fully exposed to the brutal summer sun. The heat turned the buildings into brick ovens during the day baking everything and everyone on the inside.

During the hottest weeks of the summer, the scorching daytime heat carried over into the night. I can remember summer nights, lying in bed, when the heat was so unbearable, it was impossible to sleep. My family didn't have air conditioning like we have now; my family had large square metal fans which we put in each of the rooms in an attempt to cool us off. Unfortunately, during the hottest days of the summer all the fans did was to circulate hot, oppressive air – it was like trying to sleep in a convection oven. On nights like this, all I could do was lie in bed, in a pool of my own sweat, with a pounding headache, hoping somehow I'd fall asleep.

To get temporary relief from the heat I'd go to the bathroom to wash my body down with a cold, wet wash cloth. On the hottest nights I'd bring my pillow into the bathroom and I'd sleep in the bathtub on the cool porcelain – sometimes it helped to fall asleep, but usually it didn't. If I was lucky enough to catch a couple hours of sleep at night – when I woke up in the morning I felt worse; I woke up sticky, smelly, and when I peeled off my underwear it sounded like I was tearing away Velcro."

"That's nasty, Dad! Wasn't there anything you could do to cool off?"

"But seriously, there wasn't a lot anyone could do to get away from the heat, but there were things we did to try and cope with it."

"Cope, Dad?"

"Yes, Cam, COPE! Deal with, handle, or make the best of! There were things people did in order to get away from the heat, for example, many people stayed outside until late at night instead of going into their apartment. On hot summer nights the sidewalks were filled with adults sitting in lawn chairs, with coolers by their side, listening to Phil Rizzuto announce the Yankee game on their AM radio. In the poorer neighborhoods the adults were more lively and active; they also had the coolers but they sang, danced, and played their bongos late into the night. In all the neighborhoods the kids played their radios, played games in the streets, and ran under the fire hydrants to keep cool."

♪ It was a hot summer night
And the beach was burning ♪
♪ There was fog crawling over the sand
When I listen to your heart ♪
♪ I hear the whole world turning
I see the shooting stars ♪
♪ Falling through your trembling hands [17]

"So, what kind of games did you play?"

"We played all kinds of games; like roundup, stick ball, box ball, king-queen, curb ball – and all the other city games. One of my favorite city games to play on these hot summer nights was curb ball. It was a simple baseball type game played with a spaldeen. Four guys played at a time; two players on each team. The players on offense were on one side of the street standing near the sidewalk curb. One defensive player was in the street in front of the parked cars; his job was to catch grounders. The other defensive player played on the other side of the cars – on the sidewalk. His job was to catch fly balls either directly or off the apartment building wall. The offensive player who was 'batting' turned his back to the defensive players as he threw the ball down, as hard as he could, against the corner of the sidewalk curb. The objective was to spring the ball back across the street past the two players; a missed grounder was a single, a fly ball which landed past the cars onto the sidewalk was also a single, hitting the first floor of the building was a double, the second floor was a triple, and the third floor or above was a homer. This kept us busy on many nights; the only breaks we took were to cool off, either a quick run under the fire hydrant or to buy some ice cream from Mr. Softy.

Even though we knew we would eventually have to go home to the brick oven – I loved these nights with my friends while they lasted! It was like a block party or a carnival every night. But unfortunately these nights didn't last forever; the city began to crack down on kids using the fire hydrants to cool off. Apparently, during the summer, fires were common in some of the poorer neighborhoods in the city. I'm not sure why, but for some reason kids in these neighborhoods set buildings on fire just for the fun of it. Ron Klaus, a friend of mine who was a fireman, told me the kids in these neighborhoods set buildings on fire and then threw cans and bottles at the firemen as they drove by.

Well, it was because of these fires and the need to put them out, that the city asked the police to drive around the neighborhood to turn off all the fire hydrants. You see, when a lot of fire hydrants were on it caused the water pressure to be so low the fire hoses couldn't shoot the water high enough in the air to put out the fires.

I remember the first night the police drove up Godwin Terrace to the fire hydrant we used to cool off; they got out and told us, 'Sorry kids. I know it's hot, but we need to turn the hydrant off.' They turned it off with the same kind of large wrench Scott used to turn it on. After the cops drove away we waited for about 15 minutes and turned it back on. This game of cat and mouse took place on a nightly basis; the cops turned the water off; we'd wait 15 minutes, and then we'd use our wrench to turn it back on. Sometimes we turned the water off when we saw the cop car turn up the street. As they drove past us, there we stood on the side walk, next to the hydrant, in our dripping wet clothes, with water gushing down the street into the gutter – trying to act like innocent little Alter Boys who would never disobey the police.

I don't know how many times it took for the police to drive by before they finally got out of their car and searched for our wrench, but eventually they did; when they found it, they took it – and with it they took our relief from the heat. A few days later, maybe longer, the police department came out with some metal contraption which made it impossible to turn the hydrant on. This forced us to come up with alternative ways to cool off.

I think it was Tony who was the first to come up with an idea. He said, 'My brother and his friends go to the Vanny Pool at night.

There are hundreds of girls and guys from the neighborhood who go there every night once it gets dark. Do you guys want to go?' We were all hot and sweaty, and so off we went.

The quickest way to Van Courtland Park was to hop on the El train at the 231st northbound station. The northbound station was primarily used for people exiting the train since 231st Street was near the end of the line. But if you were lazy, like we were, you could pay to get on the train by putting a $.50 token into a metal revolving door entrance inside the empty station. But if you were lazy, cheap, AND BROKE there was an even better, less expensive way to ride the train; the one my friends and I preferred.

When you were at street level most, honest, people walked up the steps which led to the train station. These steps were covered with a metal roof which was in place to protect the train riders as they walked up and down the stairs from the rain, snow, and from the droppings of the hundreds of pigeons which called the train station home. When we were at street level we climbed onto the roof over the steps. We were like rock climbers, mountain climbers – NO – we were like Spiderman – NO – we were like Ninja's – NO we were like…"

"Dad, Dad, we get the picture! You climbed up on the roof, and you were cool. Continue."

"Ok. Well, it wasn't an easy climb because the roof, over the steps, was gabled and slippery: if we weren't careful it would be easy to slip off and fall twenty to thirty feet to the street. We would have splat on the ground like the pigeon droppings! Luckily none of us ever slipped or fell. Once we made it to the top of the train station roof, we waited for the train. Sometimes we hung off the roof and dropped to the train station platform and waited; usually, we sat on the roof and waited. When the train arrived, we jumped from the station roof, across a small chasm, to the roof of the train. Then we dropped down between cars and rode in the open air to the Van Cortland station; a short ride – only two stops.

Six of us rode to Van Cortland; Tommy, John, Tony, Billy, Shawn, and me. When we reached the last stop we got off the train and walked down the steps across the street from the Terminal Bar. The pool was a short distance from the station steps, but it was hidden by the thick park trees. When we walked into the park, past the trees, it was like we entered a Georgia High School Football game – it was like Friday Night Lights!

Keep in mind the pool was closed and nobody was supposed to be there, but the lights were left on; maybe to make it easier for the police to see if anyone had snuck into the pool after hours. If you came to this pool during the day you would have seen inner city kids packed into the pool wearing white, blue, and pink bathing caps. But at night it was different; when we walked past the trees, we heard heavy rock music playing, we saw hundreds of kids swimming, smoking, drinking, dancing, and making out. To make it more interesting – they were doing all of this in their underwear! It was like a scene out of Sodom and Gomorrah. I looked up waiting for the fire and brimstone."

"Nice Biblical reference, Dad."

"Thanks Kels, I thought you'd like it. Ok, back to my story. When we reached the wrought iron fence which surrounded the pool, we climbed over and looked around to see if we knew anyone there. Most of the people looked familiar but they were older; they were from 231st Street, Bailey Avenue, Johnson Avenue, Sedgwick Avenue, Fort Independence, 238th Street, and all the other neighborhoods surrounding Kingsbridge.

By now it was about 9:30 p.m.; it was still oppressively hot, and so we were dying to cool off. We were all wearing shorts so we could have gone swimming in our clothes, but since everyone else was in their underwear we decided to do the same. We took off our clothes, piled them under a bench, and walked over to the side of the pool and dove in. I have to admit I didn't feel comfortable walking around in my underwear because I had never done this before – at least not in public."

"Dad, that's just wrong. I really don't want to imagine you walking around in your underwear!"

"Well, Cam, in case you're wondering, the girls didn't think it was wrong – they thought I looked pretty cute in my little tighty whities."

"Dad, I bet they liked the skid marks in the back."

"Not bad, my little Padwan! Ok, it didn't take me long to forget I was swimming in my underwear because of how refreshing the water felt, but for some reason I wasn't crazy about being there. Most of the people were drinking beer, which was fine with me, but there were also a lot of drugs. The place reeked of pot, and every word you heard was a curse; not that I had never heard these words before or hadn't smelled marijuana but this was different – I just didn't feel comfortable."

"Dad, I thought you and your friends were tough. Why would you feel uncomfortable?"

"We were tough, but we weren't psychotic drug addicts who would kill someone for looking at us wrong or for accidently splashing us – the sociopaths at the pool would have! When I look back, I was right to feel the way I did. Several of the people from these groups ended up behind bars later in life for dealing drugs, and a couple of them actually went to prison for murder.

We were there for about an hour; we would have stayed longer but as I was diving off the high dive we heard sirens and saw flashing lights – it was the police! It was wild what happened next – it was like a scene from the *Planet of the Apes*; the scene where the Ape's on horseback chased the humans through the corn fields. Everyone started running, everyone was screaming – it was pandemonium! People were screaming, 'Run, it's the $%^& cops, run it's the $%^& cops!!' We stood there for a minute in shock, not moving at all, we were just taking it all in; we watched as the hoodlums grabbed their shorts, shoes, shirts, pot pipes, and hypodermic needles – we watched them run to the fence where they jumped over in one motion – still wearing only their underwear!

At least five cop cars drove into the park, past the trees and bushes, across the rough and pot holed ground, through the grass and weeds, right up to the pool fence. Out of their loud speakers we heard, 'Stop where you are! You are surrounded! You are under arrest! Stop where you are!' I'm not sure if they would have arrested us; I actually doubt they would have, but we didn't stay around long enough to find out. We grabbed our clothes and jumped over the fence right behind the derelicts. As soon as we made it over the fence, John said, 'Let's run to the football field and meet in the stadium stands.' We agreed without saying a word; we ran as fast as we could through the tall weeds and grass in our underwear headed toward the stadium.

Once we reached the stadium we plopped down on the concrete stands to catch our breath and to pick the weeds and grass out of our underwear. A short while later we caught our breath and got dressed; we walked back home to our steamy apartments; instead of only being hot and sweaty we were now also itchy from running through the tall weeds. In a way I was glad it worked out the way it did because it gave me a handy excuse to explain why I didn't want to go swimming at Vanny again, but we still had a problem – how to cool off at night!

We came up with a solution to our problem the next night when we all met on the O'Grady's stoop. The stoop had about five or six flights of stairs leading up to the front door of the building, on each landing there were small brick walls on both sides which we used as our chairs whenever we hung out there. By 7:00 p.m. that night the whole stoop was filled with all our friends. Scott placed his radio on the sidewalk, facing the stoop, and he tuned it to WPLJ. The big talk of the night was our trip to the Van Cortland pool the night before.

Tony led the conversation; he had an amazing gift for telling a story. Some people have this gift; they can bring a story to life so you not only hear it – you see it and experience it. Good story tellers can bring out all your emotions; they make you laugh, nervous, excited, and if they're really good they can even make you cry. Tony was one of these people; he had the girls sitting on the edge of their seats, actually brick walls, waiting to hear all the details of our thrilling night. Of course, sometimes a good story teller enhances or accentuates the finer points of the story for affect, and Tony was a master at this.

I'll never forget sitting on the stoop listening to him tell the story; the girls were captivated – AND SO WAS I! As I listened, I thought to myself, 'I don't remember standing on the roof of the train, or the girls at the pool swimming in the nude, and I definitely don't remember the police shooting at us!' The way Tony told the story I began to question whether I was there the night before, but I wasn't about to correct any of his details because the girls were amazed and in awe of us! They were all over us for most of the night – we were like rock stars and they were like our groupies."

Kelsie screamed, "DAD!!"

I said, "Nice, Dad."

My dad smiled as he slowly said, "Yes…it…was…Cam… it was sweet!"

He smiled and got back to his story, "Alright, where was I? Oh yeah, after the interest in the previous night had worn off, and the girls stopped groping us, it was still light out and so a few of us decided to play a game of stick ball."

"Can you tell me exactly what stick ball is, Dad?"

"What's stick ball? What's stick ball??!! Cam, YOU don't KNOW what STICK BALL is??? How could you NOT know what stick ball is??!! Were you raised in a cave by a pack of wolves?

"Uh, Yeah Dad, I'm pretty sure I was – and still am. So what's stick ball?"

"Hmmm…so you want to know what stick ball is? Let me think how I can explain this to you. Well, first of all, stick ball was THE greatest city game ever invented! I'm not exaggerating – I loved it – it was great! The way we played it was awesome. The game was similar to baseball, but it was different in several important ways. We didn't need a baseball, bats, or gloves; all we needed to play was a broom stick and a spaldeen. We didn't need a baseball field; our field was Godwin Terrace, from the top of the hill to the city steps across 231st Street. We didn't need nine players on a team; we could play with two or three players on each side. There wasn't a pitcher, instead the batter stood in the middle of the street at the top of the hill and threw the ball in the air and let it bounce once before he swung. The fielders were positioned in a straight line down the middle of the street, except for the deep outfielder. The first fielder was halfway down the hill; the next one stood at the bottom of the hill near the cross walk, and if we had a third player he stood across the street, on the sidewalk, near the city steps.

A batted spaldeen could be launched like a rocket high into the air with incredible velocity. If it was hit on the ground it had to get past the first fielder to be considered a hit. A fly ball past the infielder, which wasn't caught was a double; if it landed past the cross walk it was a triple; and finally if it landed across 231st Street near the city steps it was a homer. One of the key rules was a ball could be played off the cars and buildings."

"What do you mean it could be 'played off the cars and buildings'?"

"I mean that as long as you caught the ball before it hit the ground it was an out. So if the ball hit a car and bounced high in the air, or if it bounced off a building and a player caught it before it touched the ground, it was an out.

Stick ball would have been fun and exciting even if the streets were empty, but that was never the case; when we played there were cars, buses, taxis, and people all over our field. This could sometimes be annoying, but usually it added an exciting dimension of strategy to the game. Defensive players had to maneuver between, around, and over vehicles and people to catch line drives and fly balls. Many times a high fly ball turned the other defensive players into traffic cops; they had to stop cars, buses, taxis, and pedestrians to make sure their teammate didn't get run over – at least not until the ball was caught. A ball dropped as a result of being run over by a vehicle was still an out..."

"You don't expect us to believe that do you?"

My dad smiled, "You believe what you want little girl. Anyway, in stick ball you didn't run bases, instead there were imaginary runners who could only score when they were forced in. For example, if the first batter hit a triple and the next batter hit a double nobody scored because there was room on the bases for both of them. Only if the second batter hit a triple or a homer would the man on third be forced in. Does that make sense, Cam?"

"Yes, Dad, continue."

"Well, um, let me see. Um, actually, that's all I have to tell you about stick ball – it might not sound too exciting to you, but it was – it was great! Okay, now I don't remember how I got on that subject. What was I telling you about before I told you about stick ball? Oh wait, I remember; I was telling you about how hot it was when I was growing up. Okay, so after the stick ball game we all stopped in Cold Cut City for a drink.

Then we walked back to the stoop where all of the girls and a few of the guys were still hanging out listening to Scott's radio; he had a tape on, 'Bat Out of Hell', and the girls were sitting on the stoop singing 'Paradise by the Dashboard Light' at the top of their lungs.

♪ I remember every little thing
As if it happened only yesterday ♪
♪ Parking by the lake
And there was not another car in sight ♪
♪ And I never had a girl
Looking any better than you did ♪ [18]

We sat down on the stoop with the girls, and we were dying of heat – we needed to be cooled off! Tommy said, 'Scott, we need you to turn on the hydrant; I'm dying of heat.' But Scott didn't have the wrench anymore, and the hydrants were locked up so we had to come up with another plan. Billy spoke up and said, 'During the day I work as a lifeguard at 555 Kappock Street – a building right down the street from the Century. Why don't we swim there?' One of the girls said, 'Billy, do they keep the pool open at night?' He answered, 'No, but we can hop over the fence and go swimming if we keep quiet.' Based on everyone's faces it was obvious we all thought this was a good idea. I said to Billy, 'Hop over the fence. Hop over the fence into the pool. I like the sound of that – Yeah, let's go Pool Hopping!'

The girls who were sitting there said, 'We want to go! We want to go pool hopping! Can we go with you guys?' Now keep in mind, the night before we swam with a bunch of girls who were wearing nothing but their underwear – and so we naturally assumed our girls would do the same thing! None of the guys said a word. I looked around, and they were in a state of shock, their eyes were wide open, they were breathing heavy (almost hyperventilating), and drool was beginning to seep out of the sides of their mouths. I'm sure they were thinking exactly what I was thinking – 'We're going to see our girls in their UNDERWEAR! And not only underwear – we're going to see them in WET UNDERWEAR!! And everyone knows wet underwear is SEE THROUGH UNDERWEAR!! We're going to see real, live girls in WET, SEE THROUGH UNDERWEAR!!!'

♪ She's a super freak, super freak
She's super freaky, yow ♪
♪ She's a very kinky girl
The kind you don't take home to mother ♪
♪ She's a super freak, super freak
She's super freaky, yow ♪ [19]

My heart was pounding with excitement and anticipation, but I tried to keep my composure. Just like a deer hunter with a twenty point buck standing ten feet away I knew I had to move carefully – any sudden move might scare them off. And if I scared them off, you know what that meant – NO WET, SEE THROUGH UNDERWEAR! I took a deep breath, carefully measured my words, and said, 'Of course, we'd love for you to come.' Robin stood up with the other girls and said, 'Great! We need to run home to get our bathing suits. We'll be right back.' All the girls stood up ready to run home for their bathing suits.

We couldn't believe our ears. We thought to ourselves, 'What did she say? Did she say they were going to wear bathing suits? No underwear? No wet underwear?!! No wet, see through underwear?!! No 'very kinky girl'?!! No 'super freak'?!! Nooooooooooooo! They can't tease us like this!' Our hearts dropped to our stomachs – Tommy spoke up before they could get away, 'No! No! No! Don't you get it? You don't wear a bathing suit when you go pool hopping – you wear UNDERWEAR!' A couple of the girls said, 'What? We're not going swimming in our underwear! Are you guy's crazy?' Robin quickly spoke up and said to the girls, 'We need to talk.' They walked off the stoop, sat on the hood of a car, and had a meeting. We couldn't hear what they were talking about, but when they finished they came back to the stoop and said, 'Okay, we won't wear our bathing suits; so when do you want to go?'

With the underwear issue settled we were cautiously optimistic the see through underwear was back on the agenda. We got up from the stoop on our way to Riverdale; everyone, except for Scott, walked to the corner of 231st Street and Kingsbridge Avenue to the bus stop. He walked down 231st Street toward the bus stop outside of the Riverdale Liquor Store. When the bus turned on 231st Street from Broadway it stopped outside the liquor store where Scott was waiting. He got on the bus and walked to the back, near the rear exit, and he sat down. As soon as the bus pulled away he tugged on the rubber rope behind his seat and the bell rang letting the driver know someone was getting off the bus at the next stop. The bus stopped outside the Donut Shop and all the girls stepped onto the bus and paid the $.50 fare; Scott opened the back door to let the guys walk on for free. Tommy and I opted for the cool open air ride

– we rode on the outside corners of the bus.

During the 70's the city buses had large metal bumpers which were flat on top and wrapped around the corners of the buses. They were easy to stand on and with the back, side windows open they came with built in handles – it was the Bronx version of a San Francisco cable car. When the bus pulled away from the curb, Tommy and I inhaled a cloud of black exhaust and began coughing, but as soon as the bus picked up speed going down 231st Street we felt a nice breeze. The clean, cool, refreshing Bronx breeze helped cleared our lungs.

The ride up Johnson Avenue on the outside of the bus was breezy and exhilarating but also rough and bumpy. Each time we drove across a pot hole the back of the bus bottomed out; several times the bumps were so jarring I honestly thought I would be thrown off into the street.

When the bus reached the top of the hill it slowed down to make the sharp right turn onto Kappock Street. This gave Tommy and me a chance to relax; we stretched out our arms, legs, took a deep breath, and we looked around. When we turned our heads and looked back, we saw three girls in a Ford Pinto right behind us. They were smiling, laughing, and one of them even gave us a 'thumbs up' – I assume it was in appreciation for the show we had just unknowingly put on for them. From our perch on the back of the bus we smiled back and saluted them like Errol Flynn in Robin Hood when he welcomed people to Sherwood Forest."

"Dad, the Errol Flynn reference is a little too obscure for me."

"Kels, you're right – scratch that. Ok, back to the story. After turning the corner, the bus came to a complete stop just up the street from 555 Kappock Street. Tommy and I jumped down to the street, our newly made friends gave a friendly tap on their horn; they waved goodbye, and drove past the bus.

The girls and other guys stepped off the bus onto the sidewalk, and they gathered next to the bus stop sign. Tommy and I walked over to them, and we began discussing our pool hopping strategy. Our first order of business was to dispatch a reconnaissance party to survey the landscape, terrain, and the activities of any potential antagonists who might disrupt our pool hopping plans – we assigned this task to John and Shawn. A short while later they returned from their mission; during their debriefing they disclosed a great deal of pertinent information necessary for a successful operation."

"You're getting weird again, Dad."

He smiled, "The building was over twenty stories high, situated on the side of a hill, looking over the Kingsbridge valley. The pool was located in front on the west side of the building, set off to the left side. Near the front door the pool was at street level; however, the further away from the door you walked the more the pool descended below street level. Outside the front of the building there was a semi-circular driveway where vehicles stopped to unload residents and visitors entering the building. There was one doorman who assisted the residents and visitors traveling in and out of the building. Surrounding the pool was a seven foot high chain link fence with barbed wire running across the top and green metal slats woven throughout. The barbed wire was intended to keep out unwanted visitors, while the green slats were meant to provide the bathers with some privacy from the pedestrians walking by. There were two entrances to the pool; the primary entrance was from inside – through the basement. The other entrance was a fence gate located in the shadows of the building wall, about twenty feet away from the front door, near the Doorman's alcove.

Although the building layout wasn't perfect for pool hopping, we needed relief from the harsh summer heat, and so we decided to continue with our plans. From our command center, aka – the bus stop, we put our plan into action. It called for each person to clandestinely slip into the pool area one by one. The girls needed help getting over the fence, so Shawn and Tommy left the bus stop first on their way to gate near the front of the building. They walked down the sidewalk along the green fence, which ran parallel to the building. Once they reached the exit to the driveway they looked around the corner of the fence to see if the coast was clear; there was no one outside the building at this moment, and so they quickly ran to the gate. Tommy jumped onto the fence and climbed up; he gripped, stepped, and reached until he made it to the top. Once he reached the top he grabbed the tall metal pole along the wall; the pole where the barbed wire was attached. He stepped on the cross pole, and he stepped over the barbed wire – being careful not to get caught on the barbs. Once he stepped over he jumped seven feet to the pool's concrete ground.

From our command center we looked through the green slats and could see Tommy had made it in. I turned to Robin and said, 'So far so good. Robin, it's your turn. Are you sure you want to do this?' She looked at me and said, 'Kenny, don't worry about me; I'm ok. I can do this – I'm not afraid.'

"I looked back at Tommy, I could barely see him in the darkness, but I could vaguely see him giving me the thumbs up. I turned to Robin and said, 'Alright, Robin. It's time for you to go. Stay low, against the fence and Robin – whatever you do – please be careful!'"

"Dad, were you sneaking into a pool or escaping from Stalag 17?"

My dad gave Kelsie a fake mean look, and he continued, "Before I knew it, she was gone making her way around the corner of the fence. When she turned the corner, she saw Shawn, and immediately it was obvious something was wrong. Shawn was frantically waiving his hands at her; under his breath he whispered, 'Go back, Robin, go back…' Robin was nervous, but she very coolly stepped back against the fence and waited. She looked over at the front door and saw the cause of Shawn's concern – the doorman was outside smoking and walking around – walking toward the corner where Shawn was hidden! Luckily, at this moment a car drove up. The doorman flicked his cigarette butt on the ground (it rolled toward the wall and stopped at Shawn's feet) and he walked over to the car where he assisted one of the residents.

Once he stepped inside, Robin ran toward Shawn. He was squatting down like a catcher in the ready position, he had his hands cupped together; when Robin reached him she stepped into his hands, and he lifted her high on the fence. She had to step over the barbed wire without any help, but once she was on the other side Tommy reached up, and she stepped on his hands, and he lowered her to the ground. Everyone else followed Robin's lead, and within five minutes we were all inside – thankfully, we didn't lose anyone in the operation!"

"Lose anyone in the operation, Dad? Lose anyone? You are so weird. You were sneaking into a POOL – you make it sound like it was protected by men with machine guns and German Sheppards!"

Again he ignored Kelsie, "Once we were all safely in the pool, we met in the corner closest to the building. We looked around at the fence and wall that surrounded the pool and it was obvious the pedestrians walking by wouldn't be able to see us swimming in our underwear, but when we turned around and looked up it was even more obvious the WHOLE BUILDING COULD. We didn't see anyone looking out of the windows and since most people had their air conditioners on there was a chance no one would.

I looked at Tommy and said, "I'm hot – I'm going swimming." I took off my shirt, shoes, and shorts; then I dove into the deep end of the pool. All of the guys followed my lead, and in a minute we were all cooling off in the refreshing water.

The girls were still in the corner, but then they gathered in a circle. We knew what they were doing; they were getting ready to take off their clothes so they could go swimming in their UNDERWEAR!!

♪ She's a super freak, super freak
She's super freaky, yow ♪.[19]

We swam around the pool like alligators with only our eyes exposed from the water – trying to get a sneak peak of the girls taking it all off.

♪ She's a super freak, super freak
She's super freaky, yow ♪[19]

The girls started moving around doing something; I could tell they were starting to take off their clothes. First, they kicked off their shoes…then they leaned over and took off their socks…

our hearts were pounding waiting for the next article of clothing to be stripped off...we waited and waited...the anticipation was building!!! All of a sudden the girls broke out of their huddle and they started walking toward us – with ALL their clothes on – except for their socks and shoes!!!! Tommy was the first one to speak up, he yelled, 'What are you doing??? You can't swim in your clothes!!!' Jennifer said, 'Why not?' I yelled, 'Because you said you were swimming in your underwear!' Beth said, 'We didn't say that. We said we wouldn't wear our bathing suits!' Shawn said, 'You can't do that! We're pool hopping!' Jordan said, 'Yes, we can! Watch us!' Then Robin dove into the pool with all her clothes on.

Billy yelled, 'No way!! There's no way you girls are going to do this to us!' He jumped out of the pool and started running after Jennifer – I'm not sure what he was going to do, but he was chasing her. Jennifer ran away from Billy, and while she was running she let out the loudest, blood curdling scream I had ever heard! It must have been the loudest scream everyone in the building had ever heard too because several people opened up their window and stuck out their heads to see if someone had just been murdered outside their building.

One lady on the sixth floor opened her window and started yelling, 'Hey ya kids whut awe ya doen in da pool?'

John said, 'We're swimming lady. What are you doing?'

She responded, "You wa not supposed to be in da pool afta 9:00!

Tommy said, 'Hey lady, we live here. I rented the pool for my birthday party!'

'Listen ya little wise a@#, I'm not a schmuck! Where do ya live?'

Billy said, 'I live in 26D!'

She said, There's only 25 flaws in da builden – if ya don't leave I'm cawlen da super!'

John said, 'Give us a break lady – we're having a birthday party!'

She yelled even louder and in disbelief, 'Yaw haven a birthday pawty in ya underwear – I don't think so!! I'm not cawlen the super – I'm goen to cawl the police!' She slammed her window shut and went inside.

At first nobody was sure what to do. Tommy said, 'I'm still hot – I'm not going anywhere!' This was good enough for me, and so I dove under water again and started swimming. When I came up for air in the deep end I heard a siren, and it sounded like it was getting closer. We looked at each other, and the mad rush was on!

Everyone frantically swam to the edge of the pool and jumped out. We ran to our clothes which were in a couple of big piles near the building; it was dark, and so it wasn't easy to find our own clothes. I grabbed the first shorts I got my hands on and put them on; they were a little tight around the waist so I was sure they weren't mine, but I didn't care – we had to get out fast! As soon as we had shorts on we grabbed our sneakers; we hopped on one foot then the other trying to get them on as quickly as possible. Once our sneakers and shirts were on we were ready to go; no one cared about tying their shoes or putting on a shirt – we just had to go! Even though we were frantic, it wasn't every man and girl for him or herself; chivalry was not dead – the guys took care of the girls."

"Chivalry, Dad, what's that?"

"Chivalry kind of means the men take care of the women. To take care of the girls we reversed the plan we used to get into the pool; Tommy climbed outside; Shawn ran to the gate; Jennifer hopped out first, then Jordan, next was Robin, and Beth. After the girls made it safely outside the pool we implemented the 'everyman for himself' strategy – all the guys jumped onto the fence and climbed over at the same time. The girls and Tommy were waiting for us at the bottom of the fence; we could still hear the sirens, but they now sounded further away but this didn't matter – as soon as we were all out we started running. We ran out of the driveway, made a right on Kappock Street, and then a right on Netherland Avenue just down the street from the Century.

When we passed by the Century we all stopped running because we no longer heard the sirens, and we had to get dressed again.

We swapped shorts and shirts so everyone was wearing their own clothes, and we tied our sneakers.

There were other nights when we hopped from pool to pool in Riverdale but not this night; we decided we had enough fun for one night. So, all of us walked down Netherland Avenue laughing and joking in our sopping wet clothes on our way back to Kingsbridge.

When we reached 232nd Street we made a right turn and walked down a side street which led to Ewen Park. It was about 10:30 p.m. by the time we reached the top of Ewen Park; we stood there and looked out over our home – Kingsbridge.

As we stood there at the top of the hill we felt a nice breeze – Tommy said, 'Come on – let's go home.'

Cam, did my story teach you anything?"

"Yeah Dad – it did. It taught me how different your childhood was compared to mine; it taught me about friendship; but mostly it taught me if I ever go swimming with you at night I better wear clean underwear."

♪ It was long ago and it was far away
It was so much better than it is today ♪
♪ It was long ago and it was far away
It was so much better than it is today ♪" [18]

Kelsie said, "You know Dad, swimming at night is dangerous. You might have been killed if you dove into the shallow end."

"Kels, you know you're right but you know you can also get killed playing practical jokes on people."

"What?"

Ron's Hole

"Okay, sit back and relax; this is a story about me almost getting murdered when I was 12 or 13…"

"MURDERED?!"

"Yup Kels, murdered! Hey, I'm from The Bronx – what do you expect? Anyway, when I was growing up one of my coaches was a guy named Ron Klaus. Some people called him Meathead because they thought it was his nickname, but actually it was a name that really ticked him off. Ron was a New York City Fireman, an avid weight lifter, a race car driver, and in his spare time he helped coach baseball and football in the neighborhood."

"Wait, Dad. Why did people call him Meathead?"

"A guy named Pat Leo gave Ron the nickname Meathead. Most people didn't realize this; they thought people called him Meathead because he had a crew cut. But actually Pat Leo gave him the nickname as an insult, and unfortunately it stuck. The name came from a show called *All in the Family*. In the show, when the son-in-law said something stupid, the main character, Archie Bunker, called him Meathead. So the name was an insult to Ron, and that's why it got him so mad when someone called him that. There were many people who didn't know this was an insult, and so they innocently referred to Ron as Meathead. Okay, Cam?"

"Yes, continue."

"Okay. Ron was a great coach and a good guy. He taught me how to play baseball, and I became pretty good. He also let me and a few of my friends hangout in his apartment and lift weights. He treated me and my friends really well, but he did have a few idiosyncrasies."

"What's that?"

"It's things that a person does that are strange. Like when we were watching the US Open Tennis and Rafa Nadal kept picking his butt before he served. Got it, Cam?"

"Got it. Continue."

"Alright, like I said, he let me and my friends lift weights and hangout in his apartment; we even had keys to his apartment so we could go up there anytime we wanted. Since he was a fireman he worked three and four day shifts, and so there were many times when it felt like Tommy, Pat and I had our own apartment.

One of his idiosyncrasies was he was a NEAT FREAK! Now, as you know I like our house clean, but Ron was over the top. If you looked in his closet you'd find ALL of his hangers were EXACTLY 1.5 inches apart. Also, he only wore white socks and to make sure he wore the correct matches he wrote L1 and R1, L2 and R2, etc., on his socks…"

"Why did he write that on his socks?"

"L1 and R1 stood for left sock 1 and right sock 1. He wrote this on his socks because he didn't want to wear two different socks; keep in mind all his socks were white and they were the same style. Another idiosyncrasy was when he left his apartment, he made sure the dining room chairs were facing the correct way. When he vacuumed he made sure the carpet fibers faced in the same direction. In his refrigerator, he had specific places for the milk (and only the milk) and for the juice (and only the juice). He carried a money clip and he faced all the money the same way which I know isn't really unusual but still you get my point. I think Felix Unger from *The Odd Couple* was based on Ron. If any of the things I mentioned were ever out of place…IT DROVE HIM CRAZY!

Something else you need to know is Ron also liked guns. He enjoyed going to firing ranges and shooting several rounds of ammo. Tommy, Pat, and I occasionally went to the gun range with him and he taught us how to shoot a gun. He usually carried his gun with him wherever he went and when he came home, he placed the gun neatly on his dining room table. I can remember one afternoon Tommy was playing with one of Ron's guns and he was trying to pull the trigger, but he couldn't. He thought the gun was empty, but it actually had one bullet loaded, ready to be fired. Tommy put the gun to his head for fun…"

"What do you mean for fun?"

"I don't know. Maybe I shouldn't say for fun, but my point is he was trying to pull the trigger. When he couldn't pull it he put it to his head, and he continued to try and pull the trigger. He didn't know the reason he couldn't pull it was because the safety lock was on. Luckily he didn't know how to take the safety lock off, or I'm sure he would have blown his head off that day.

Well, Tommy and I liked to play practical jokes on Ron. I might have gotten a bigger kick out of it than Tommy, but we both did it. What made it funnier is Ron got so mad when we played these pranks on him. Whenever we visited Ron's apartment we, or I, moved his hangers so that they weren't 1.5 inches apart. We mixed up his socks so that L1 would be with L2. We'd move his drinks around in his refrigerator. We'd also eat his food and drink his ice tea, juice, etc. Ron eventually placed a lock on his refrigerator to keep us out…"

"A lock?"

"Yeah, a lock. Like the one you put on a shed or your locker. Tommy was good at unscrewing the lock so we could still get into his refrigerator. We'd play these practical jokes on Ron; he'd get mad; we'd apologize, and then we'd do it again – life was good."

"How does this have anything to do with you almost getting killed?"

"Oh, yeah. There was one day when the practical jokes went a little too far, at least for Ron. Tommy and I were working out one day, and Ron came home from a three day shift. He placed his gun and his money clip on the table, and he started making his dinner. Tommy and I thought it would be funny to hide his money clip underneath his lamp, so we did. Then we left and went home for dinner.

After dinner we'd forgotten all about hiding Ron's money. That night Ron came driving up the block and asked Tommy and me to come with him to go somewhere – I think Carvel. Tommy got into his El Camino first, and then I got in. Tommy was sitting next to Ron and I was next to the door. We didn't know where we were going – he didn't say a word as he drove us on the Henry Hudson Parkway going toward Yonkers. Then before we knew it, he pulled off the road into a dark grassy area where it was totally pitch black. Ron referred to this area as 'Ron's Hole.' When we came to a stop he reached on the floor and he pulled out his 45 caliber handgun, pointed it at our heads, and said, 'Where's my &#$%ing money!?'

I thought to myself, 'Oh no – he really is crazy. We're about to get murdered right here. Our names are going to be in the Riverdale Press, 'Two boys found shot in head off the Henry Hudson Parkway.' Tommy on the other hand began laughing. I'm still thinking to myself, 'Tommy, this guy really is nuts. We're about to die. Stop laughing!' I started pleading with Ron, 'Don't shoot! The money is under the lamp! Please Ron – don't kill us! The money is under the lamp – I swear!' I pleaded with him for, what seemed to be hours, and I was close to tears, but then Ron looked at us and put the gun away. He started laughing, and he said he was just trying to teach us a lesson.

To this day I wonder if he really was just trying to teach us a lesson or if he had other thoughts when he pulled off the road...

Right:
222 West 233rd Street –
Moving On Up

Left:
The Great Kingsbridge
Copper Rush

Right:
The Van Cortland Flats –
Are you My Mother Coach?

Left:
Columbia Rock –
A Bridge Too Far for
Roller Skating

Right:
3249 Corlear Avenue –
A New Beginning

Left:
St. John's Middle School –
Love Machine

Right:
St. John's Catholic Church

Left:
231st Street

Right:
Mom and Dad's wedding
July 27, 1985.

Left to Right: The Evil Aunt Chris, Dad, Mom, Uncle Philip, Grandma Hand, Aunt Gena, Grandpa Hand, Uncle Richie, Aunt Patricia

Left:
Bobby Krokus, Grandpa Hand,
Great Uncle Ray,
Great Great Uncle Bob (Bob Hartford)

Right:
Great Grandpa and
Great Grandma Doyle

Left:
Left to Right, Great Grandpa Doyle (William Doyle),
Great, Great Aunt Catherine Alma,
Great, Great Grandpa Doyle (Gene Doyle),
Great, Great Uncle Gene,
Great, Great Grandma Doyle (Annie Beglin),
Great, Great Aunt Anne

Yup – they're all Great

SECTION VI
Another One Flew Over the Cuckoo's Nest

♪ Sit down – take a look at yourself
Don't you want to be somebody ♪
♪ Someday somebody's going to see inside
You have to face up, you can't run and hide ♪
♪ Have you heard about the lonesome loser
He's a loser, but he still keeps trying ♪ [20]

High School Dropout

I don't remember exactly why he told us this story; I think it was when I asked him where he went to high school. This story didn't take place at McDonald's; it was when Kelsie and I were riding in the car with him. At first it was interesting, but later in his story I got to see a side of my dad I'd never seen before – it was sad.

"Are you sure you want to know the whole sordid details of my school years?"

We weren't sure what sordid meant, but we wanted to hear about them and so we said, "Yeah."

"Before I continue I need to explain some things to you. As you can tell by the Lake Hopatcong story I thought I was pretty cool in 8th grade – I thought I was the man. For a 13 year old boy my life was good; I was athletic, a chick magnet…"

"Chick magnet – I doubt it."

"Well maybe not a chick magnet, but I was athletic, I liked to have fun, and I hung out with a popular group. Life was good.

But the transition from middle school to high school was difficult for me. It shouldn't have been, but it was."

"Why?"

"Cam, do you remember how Jewel acted when we moved from St. Louis to Georgia?"

"Yeah, she flipped out. I remember bringing her on the plane with us. We gave her a tranquillizer pill we got from the vet, and she started to bug out. Her eyes were all glassy, and she made the weirdest noises I've ever heard."

Kelsie chimed in, "Yeah and when she got to our new house she ran under your bed, and I don't think she came out for 3 months – except to eat and go to the bathroom.

"Exactly, Jewel freaked out when we moved, and she acted really strange for a while, but now she's back to normal – she's back to her nice, friendly cat self."

Well, when I was a kid I was kind of like Jewel. When I was put in a new situation, since I was sensitive and self conscious, it freaked me out too. The only difference between Jewel and me is when I was put in a new situation I didn't lick myself – but that's only because I couldn't."

He laughed. I guess he thought this was funny – we didn't get it.

He continued, "When I moved from Suffern to the Bronx, I was 8 years old, this was difficult for me, but eventually I got comfortable with it and, as you know, I came to love the Bronx, my school, and my new friends."

"But what do you mean you were sensitive and self conscious?"

"Well, it's like that dream everyone has, you know, the one where you're out in a public place like school, work, playing baseball, or walking your dog, and then you suddenly realize you're only wearing your underwear. And then, to make matters worse, you realize everyone is looking at you and then…"

Kelsie and I were confused. She said, "Uh, Dad. What are you talking about? Are you saying you have dreams that you're walking around in public with just your underwear on? That's really weird! I've never had a dream like that."

"Yeah, Dad. I've never had a dream like that either. Are you serious?"

Now my dad was confused. He said, "Are you kidding me? Neither of you have ever had a dream about being in your underwear while you are in a public place?"

"NO, NEVER!"

My dad said, "Oh, well, neither have I, cough, cough, I was only joking. You guys fell for it, cough, cough. Okay, so where was I? Oh yeah, I was telling you why I was so sensitive and self conscious. Let me think, let me think, poo, socks, pajamas, hmmm, let me see. Oh yeah, I used the silly example of dreaming about being in public in only my underwear. What I really mean is, I got embarrassed very easily, and I felt like people were looking at me like I was different. Do you see how the underwear dream fits in? You get it?"

"Nope."

"Well my point is I went from a small school to a large school and I didn't handle the transition very well. Because I'm so...sniff, sniff, sniff...sensitive. But another problem was I went from St. John's Middle School, a small Catholic school where I was well known, to a huge school, John F. Kennedy, where only a couple of my friends were going, and where I was a 'nobody'.

"So why didn't you just go to a Catholic school with all your other friends?"

"The main reason is because Catholic schools cost a lot of money, and since there were six kids in my family it was out of the question for me to go to a Catholic school. That's the main reason, but also my parents, mostly my mother, believed Kennedy was a good school and a person could get a good education there if they applied themselves. My mother pointed to the fact my brother Richie graduated from Kennedy, and he did well.

While I was in 8th grade we had to choose which school we would attend. By March or April everyone knew which school they would go to in September. I don't remember arguing with my mother about this – I'm not sure why. Maybe it was because I didn't have a desire to go to any particular school. Or maybe it was because my brother seemed to do pretty well at Kennedy, and I thought my mother was right. Or maybe it was because I knew we didn't have enough money for me to go to Catholic school, and I thought it would be selfish of me to fight for it. I'm really not sure, but I do remember the other kids talking about going to their new schools and being excited about it. I wasn't excited about Kennedy, but I don't remember dreading it either.

Where was I? Oh yeah, I was telling you how the transition from grade school to high school was difficult for me. Alright, let me tell you about my first day in high school. Remember, I was not only shy, self conscious, and sensitive but now without the safety and control of St. John's Middle School my days now included – stress and anxiety.

Remember how I mentioned Underdog's energy pill?"

"Yes, but I didn't really understand what that meant."

"Well, Underdog was quiet and shy, just like me, but when he took an energy pill he became a new dog – someone who was outgoing and confident. Going to Kennedy I felt lost and uncomfortable and so I looked forward to taking my energy pill – beer – more and more so I could feel confident and comfortable again."

"I still don't understand."

"Well, let me tell you about high school maybe it will become clearer."

"Sounds good Dad."

"Okay, high school started at 8:35 a.m. and so every morning my mom woke me up at 7:15 a.m. My mother was like an alarm clock for all my brothers and sisters. Just like an alarm clock she called me quietly at first, but with every, 'Kenny it's time to get up' she became louder and louder until she reached a high pitched scream! And just like an alarm clock I could hit the snooze button to get another 5 minutes of uninterrupted sleep by saying, 'I'm up Mom, I'm up.' My mornings were loud and hectic. My mother had 5 kids to wake up; she had to make sure we showered, got dressed, ate, and left the apartment on time to make it to school.

With 5 kids to get ready and only one bathroom, the apartment was filled with yelling and screaming each morning; 'Chris, get out of the bathroom! I need to take a shower!', 'Kenny won't get out of the bathroom!', 'Mom, tell her to get out!', 'Mom, tell him to get out!', 'Chris, GET OUT NOW!', 'Kenny, GET OUT NOW!', 'Mom, I don't have any clean clothes!', 'Mom, Philip drank all the milk!', 'We're out of Cheerios!'..."

"Dad, that sounds like me and Kelsie in the morning. What's the big deal?"

"I'm sure it's how most kids started their day but for me it stressed me out. Because of the yelling and partly because of the 25 tablespoons of sugar I put in my cereal, my heart was pounding and my body was shaking every morning by the time I left for school.

I walked to school every morning; to get there I walked up 233rd Street and made a left on Kingsbridge Avenue walking toward 231st Street. In the mornings the streets were crowded with kids walking to school and adults walking to work. I put my book bag over one shoulder and held onto it with my left hand, I put my other hand in my pocket, and I put my head down and walked.

I walked up Kingsbridge Avenue until 231st Street where I made a right turn heading towards Ewen Park. I could see some of the kids I went to St. John's with walking to their bus stops with their friends. I didn't want them to see me walking to school by myself; I kept my head down and tried to avoid eye contact with them. When I reached Tibbett Avenue I made a left and walked past Jack LaLanne's on my left and the diner on my right. In front of me, in the distance, was my new school.

All around me were kids walking towards Kennedy; most of them were walking with friends; some were walking alone, but they all seemed to walk with a purpose. As I got closer and closer I felt more and more awkward and my heart began pounded harder and harder – maybe it was the sugar rush kicking in. I felt like everyone was looking at me wondering why I was walking to school by myself – I was used to walking with a big group of people at St. John's.

Although I didn't realize it at the time – I'd experienced this before – and everything worked out fine. I felt this way when I moved from Suffern to the Bronx. I moved from Suffern to the Bronx only a few years earlier, I didn't know anyone then either, I felt uncomfortable then too, but before I knew it I had tons of friends, and I fit right in. If I thought about it I might have realized this situation was the same as the first day at St. Johns, but I'm not sure it would have mattered. All I knew now was I had gone from a small school where I was a 'somebody' to a huge school where I was a 'nobody'. I tried to push the negative thoughts of being a 'nobody' out of my mind, I tried to ignore my feelings, but it was hard. I just put my head down and kept walking while I repeated to myself, 'I'll be okay, I'll be okay, help me, God…'

Once I made it across 230th Street I took a deep breath and began walking the last quarter mile to the front door of the school. I looked down the road and saw guys sitting on and leaning against the parked cars which lined the street. That usually meant drug dealers. When I walked past these guys I tried my best to keep my eyes down or straight ahead but no matter how I tried to ignore them I heard, 'Yo man. Hey man. You want some Cheeba, Cheeba man, joints, nickel bag, dime bag, you want some Ludes man, hey man, you want some Cheeba, hey man, hey man, come on man, Cheeba, Cheeba'."

"Dad, what's Cheeba and Ludes?"

"Cheeba was marijuana and Ludes were short for Quaaludes, which is some kind of illegal drug."

"Oh, wow."

"Most of the stress I felt while I walked to school was in my mind; something I conjured up myself; but the drug dealers were real, and I didn't like walking past them. Some of these guys who dealt drugs outside Kennedy were hardcore – they weren't just punks looking to make a few extra dollars. I was nervous walking past them, and I should have been – no 13 year old little boy should have to experience this everyday on his way to and from school, but I did."

"What do you mean by 'hardcore people'?"

"Kelsie, what I'm saying is some of these guys were really bad people. Hmmm, let me see how I can help you understand. Okay, I got it. I'm going to tell you a sad story about a friend of mine.

Joe

When I was growing up I knew someone I would consider a friend – his name, was Joe. Joe went to Our Lady of Angels, a Catholic school located near the Jerome Avenue Reservoir. I met him for the first time when we both were trying out for the Bronx Catholic School All-Star Team. This was an all-star team that was supposed to tour across Canada and play against the Catholic schools in Canada. Joe and I both made the team, and we got to know each other pretty well during the tryouts and practices."

"You traveled across Canada playing basketball?"

"No, we were supposed to, but it got cancelled when we had trouble raising enough money, and then later on one of the coaches sexually molested a couple of the players – I'm sorry – he allegedly molested them. By the way, I wasn't one of them. But that's a whole other story – I'll tell you about it someday when you're both older.

Well, I got to know Joe at this time, and he was without a doubt the most outgoing, friendliest guy I had ever met. He was a great basketball player, but more importantly he was a great guy – everyone liked him. I didn't see him too much over the next couple of years, but when we needed another player on our St. John's CYO team we asked him to play, and he said yes. So we started hanging out together a little more. By this time in his life he had started smoking pot; I don't think he smoked a lot, but he smoked it. He was still a great guy, but you could tell he was going down a road he never should have started down. When he was about 17 years old he started smoking it more and more; one thing led to another, and he started dealing pot."

"What's dealing pot mean?"

"Cam, it means he started selling marijuana. I can still remember seeing Joe one night. I was hanging out with a few of my friends outside of Cold Cut City, and Joe walked up to us to say hello. He was still outgoing and friendly, but he was also obviously high, and he wasn't as neat and clean as he used to be. His hair was longer and messy, and he had a dark, heavy coat on – it was some kind of green, military jacket. It had a lot of pockets to keep his pot and his money. I can remember him telling us he was selling drugs, and he was making a lot of money, and then he whipped out a giant wad of money to prove it. I don't know how much money he had, but it had to be several thousand dollars. It was pretty impressive for him to have that much money, but we all knew it wasn't good. I don't think we said too much to him; I'm pretty sure we didn't try to talk him out of what he was doing. I don't know why; we should have.

Even though he was selling drugs I could still see he was a good guy; a good guy who was making some bad decisions. I believe he would have turned his life around if he had more time. Unfortunately for Joe, his family, and his friends – he ran out of time. He never had the chance to turn his life around. I don't know why some people are given the chance to turn their lives around and some aren't – it's a shame.

I think it was a couple months after we saw him that night that it happened. I'm not sure if anyone ever figured out why it happened or who did it – I'm really not sure. Joe was found in an empty apartment with a gun shot to his head – dead. The person or people who did this to Joe were hardcore bad people.

Now do you understand what I mean by hardcore bad people?"

Kelsie and I were both shocked by this story, but then Kelsie said, "Yes, Dad. Are you serious? Did that really happen?"

My dad looked a little sad. He continued, "Yes. Unfortunately, yes. And these were the types of people I had to walk past everyday on my way to and from school.

After I made it past the drug dealers there was a large school yard I had to walk across. During the warm days the schoolyard was filled with students – most of them drinking beer and smoking cigarettes or pot out in the open. Radios played Led Zeppelin or Jethro Tull songs, and there was always a Frisbee or a football being thrown around. It might have been a fun atmosphere except for the fact all these kids should have been in school.

Early on in the school year I kept my head down as I walked through the schoolyard; I only looked up to make sure I didn't get hit in the head by a flying football or Frisbee. Before I entered school I had to walk past the security guards. I didn't really understand their roll; it seemed to me it was their job to make it difficult for students to get into school. Before I could enter the school I waited in a long line as the kids in front of me showed the guards their I.D. and school schedule. I wondered why the school didn't use these guards to tell the kids on the cars to get off the school grounds or why they didn't stop the kids from drinking beer, or why they didn't stop the kids from smoking pot. I wondered, but I didn't ask – maybe there was something I didn't understand – after all I assumed the adults knew what they were doing. I didn't like walking past the security guards; they rarely talked to the students, and when they did it was usually to accuse them of stealing someone else's school schedule.

When I entered the school it was overwhelming – it was like Times Square at lunch time. There were kids everywhere, and they all seemed to know what they were doing; they all seemed to know where they were going, and they all seemed to know how to get there, all of them, except for me. I stood there with a glaze over my eyes, my heart was still pounding, and my body was still shaking. I remembered feeling like this before, and I didn't like it – it's how I felt when I was 9 years old."

"What happened when you were 9?"

"Didn't I tell you the "Are you my Coach Story?"

"Oh, yeah. Gotcha."

"This is how I felt the first day I walked through the doors of Kennedy; I felt lost; I felt overwhelmed, and I felt alone even though I was in the middle of a sea of people. I'm not sure how, but eventually I learned how to get around this huge, intimidating school.

Inside the school it was actually very nice; the classrooms, hallways, and bathrooms were always neat and clean. After walking past the drug dealers, the inside of the building felt like a safe haven. When I sat at my desk, in my classrooms, I felt better. It's funny, the first thing I noticed when I sat down inside my classrooms were the desktops. They were made of wood, and so kids carved their initials and other interesting sayings into them. Many of the sayings were similar to ones you'd find on bathroom walls at sleazy truck stops around the country, but some were funny. My favorite saying was one I read in my English class. One of the teachers who also used the classroom was Mr. Lipchitz. Carved on several of the desktops in the room was the saying, 'Mr. Lipchitz, if your lip Schitz, my ass whistles.' I always thought this was funny.

Other than this, in many ways my classes weren't a whole lot different from my classes at St. Johns. The teachers were all nice as I remember. One thing I do recall being different is when the teachers called roll; there were always several kids absent, but it didn't seem to concern them. In St. Johns, the teachers would ask, 'Does anyone know where Johnny is today or Bobby or Jane?' If you missed a day of school somebody noticed, and if you missed more than one day they called your house. But they didn't do this at Kennedy. Maybe it's because they assumed the rolls were wrong. Or maybe they had too many kids to keep track of. Or maybe they assumed 13 of 14 year old kids were mature enough to take care of themselves. Or, most likely, it was because they assumed the kids were cutting school, and this was so common it didn't raise any concerns. I'm really not sure – I just know it was different.

I'm not saying the teachers didn't care about the students – I'm sure most did. The teachers I had seemed to care about the kids when they showed up to class. There was my Social Studies teacher, Mr. Levine, he was an excellent teacher – he really made history interesting. I remember him talking to me several times about missing class and how I had to make up my work after school. He didn't seem to take cutting class for granted; he seemed to want the kids to show up to class, and he wanted them to succeed. Then there was my English teacher – I can't remember his name, but he reminded me of Gabe Kotter from 'Welcome Back Kotter'. He made prepositions and dangling participles as interesting as they can be, but I also felt he cared about his students. He used to break away from teaching English many times to tell us stories about life. I know he did this because he wanted to help us, and specifically he wanted us to stay in school. There were other teachers I can vaguely remember and all the memories I have of them were good. I didn't have a teacher at Kennedy I didn't like.

The guys in my classes at Kennedy were a lot more diverse than my classmates in St. Johns, but they were all good guys. There was James Road who was in my English class. He played football for the 'Flow Sweet Tigers' – I joked with him mercilessly about playing for a team named 'Flow Sweet'. But actually he was a very good athlete – a few years later he played on the Bronx Steelers when we won the Bronx Championship. There was also Duane Williams, also in my English class; he played football for the Warriors when I played quarterback for the Bronx Spartans. He joked with me unmercifully because his team killed us both times we played them. I got to know a few other guys a little but not enough to become good friends with any of them; probably because I wasn't there long enough to get to know them.

The girls, on the other hand, OH MY GOSH – they were out of control!"

I was curious so I stopped him, "What was wrong with the girls?"

"Like I said, they were out of control! You guys know how good looking I am and how women throw themselves at me…"

"Yeah, Dad, you're a chick magnet." I only said this because that's what he told me many times in the past – especially as he was putting on his sun glasses.

My dad smiled, "You got that right, homey!" Then he continued, "Well, I was a chick magnet in high school too – the chicks were all over me! I was the only 13 year old boy at Kennedy with groupies! I was like a rock star with girls hanging all over me! In between classes it was like 'Girls Gone Wild' in the hallway. I had girls flashing me left and right..."

Kelsie was shaking her head when she said, "Oh brother. Don't believe him, Cam! There is no way that's true!"

"I wish it wasn't true, but they were all over me – it freaked me out! I remember girls fighting over who would sit next to me. I remember girls in my dance class fighting over who would dance with me. It was like a school full of Jamie Finley's!"

Kelsie asked, "Who was Jamie Finley? I bet she was a girl who thought you were a chick magnet, huh?"

My dad smiled at Kelsie and said, "Bingo! You're finally catching on Dookie Doo!

Jamie was my first groupie. She went to St. Johns with me and she was all over me – day and night. She was a cute, strawberry blond, freckle faced little girl, who wasn't shy about telling me she wanted to be my girlfriend. Now keep in mind she started this when I was in 4th grade, and it lasted until 6th or 7th grade! I didn't like girls back then – I thought they were gross – just like you, Cam! I was much more interested in the Yankees, Giants, Knicks, Rangers, and sports in general – I couldn't care less about girls.

But for some reason Jamie really liked me – oh wait – I didn't mean to say 'for some reason' – I meant to say she liked me because I was a chick magnet!"

My dad smiled as he continued, "I think she must have liked me for my body because I never talked to her. But then again maybe part of the reason she liked me so much was because I was shy and

I never talked to her. It embarrassed me when she wrote me letters and when she called to me, 'Hi Kenny, hi Kenny, hi Kenny…' The fact I was shy and ignored her probably made her like me more. You know how chicks are, Cam – they want what they can't have…"

My dad and I were both smiling as I said, "Yup, Dad – don't I know it."

"My family teased me mercilessly because of my 'girlfriend' and just like I felt uncomfortable with all the attention Jamie gave me – I also felt uncomfortable with all the attention the girls at Kennedy gave me. I was not prepared for this; I wasn't smooth or sophisticated enough. Even though on the outside I acted cool, on the inside I was still an innocent little boy who got nervous when I walked my girlfriend to the bus stop. Oh by the way, I'll never forget one letter Jamie wrote to me when I was in 5th grade. I don't remember everything it said but part of it said, 'Your dimples give me goose pimples.'

Kelsie got up and said, "Oh no. I can't take this anymore! I'm leaving!"

My dad said, "Okay, but you're going to miss the story about Bronwyn…"

Kelsie sat back down with a confused look on her face and said, "What's a Bronwyn? Is that a girl's name?"

"Yes, it was a girl I met at Kennedy. I think Bronwyn is a German name which means 'Psychotic Stalker'! Bronwyn was in a couple of my classes, and she was obsessed with me. At first the attention was kind of nice, but it got weird very quickly. She never left me alone; she was always there – she waited for me outside in the hallway before class; she sat next to me during class, and she waited for me in the hallway after class. I told her I had a girlfriend, but she didn't care – she kept asking me out – again and again and again. Finally, I made it clear I couldn't go out with her, and she flipped – she was like Glenn Close in 'Fatal Attraction' – she was evil! It started with her giving me dirty looks in class. Next she told everyone I was 'jerk'; then she made fun of my clothes; finally she put a horse's head in my bed and boiled my pet rabbit – it wasn't pretty, not pretty at all!"

♪ She's just a devil woman
With evil on her mind ♪
♪ Beware the devil woman
She's gonna get you from behind ♪ [21]

I interrupted my dad and said, "Nice song, Dad. I know you're joking about the horse and the rabbit, but did she really make fun of your clothes?"

"YES! She was nuts! Back then the only clothes I had were football jerseys and jeans. She made fun of my clothes. She'd ask me, 'Why do you wear football jerseys? My baby brother wears football jerseys. Don't you think you're a little too old to wear them?' It was ridiculous, but it bothered me.

The whole chick situation at Kennedy was just one more headache for me. Bronwyn and having groupies following me around school wouldn't have been a big deal if I had friends at Kennedy, but I didn't. With some of the other things going on in my life, it was just one more thing that stressed me out.

I'm not really sure why but as the days passed my stress and anxiety level increased. I just never felt comfortable.

But there was still one thing I looked forward to which might help me connect to my new school – sports. As an eighth grader, I was a sports fanatic; I wasn't big, but I was fast, coordinated, and I was good at sports. I was the all-star quarterback on the St. John's Eagles; I made the Inwood All-Star baseball team as a 13 year old; and I made the Bronx Catholic School All-Star Basketball team. I didn't necessarily expect to be an all-star football or basketball player in high school because high school players were huge compared to me, but I did expect to make the teams. Baseball, on the other hand, was my best sport and I did expect to be an all-star. My brother Richie played baseball for Kennedy, and he was excellent; he pitched and played third base. I thought this would help the coach, Coach Baskin, notice me, and I was confident once he saw me play he'd be impressed. Playing sports was the one area of my life I had confidence in myself."

"So Dad – did you? Did you play sports for Kennedy?"

My dad looked sad again when he answered my question, "No Cam. No. I tried to. At least I think I tried to, but it just didn't work out the way I had hoped.

I don't remember which sport I tried to tryout for first, but neither worked out the way I had hoped. First of all, it wasn't easy finding out when basketball or baseball tryouts were or where they were. There was nothing posted, nothing announced, nothing.

I don't remember how but somehow I found out about a Freshman Basketball practice taking place after school. I remember going up to the coach, and he told me, 'We already have our team.' I knew this couldn't be true, or at least I didn't think it could be, but it was clear he didn't want me to play on the team. I watched his 'team' run up and down the court – everyone on his team was black. Maybe I was being paranoid, but it seemed like he didn't want a short, white kid on his team – maybe not – I'm not really sure. But I couldn't figure out why I couldn't try out. This was something I dealt with whenever I played basketball, especially when I was 14, 15, and 16."

Kelsie said, "What do you mean? What did you have to deal with?"

"I dealt with stereotypes and racism. People didn't think white kids could play basketball. They especially didn't think a short white guy could play basketball. I can't tell you how many times I played in the parks and was told, 'No man, white boys can't play' but once they saw me play they'd say, 'Yo check it out – little white man can play!'

Again, I don't remember when I asked about baseball tryouts, but I do remember it being difficult to find out when practices were. I asked my teachers, and they didn't know; they suggested I ask Coach Baskin. His office, or at least one of them, was near the weight room in the gym. When I got to his office the door was partially opened. I quietly knocked on the door and said, 'Um, Coach Baskin do you have a minute?' He gave me a quick look, he put his head back down, and resumed writing; he then said, 'What can I do for you?' I said, 'I'm Richie Hand's brother and I want to find out when baseball season starts. I'm pretty good, and I want to try out for the team.' Without looking up he said something about it being tough to make the team because he had most of his players coming back. Then he told me he hasn't decided when practices would be yet.

Maybe it was me, maybe I was too sensitive, but I expected more from Coach Baskin. I expected him to care or at least to pretend to care. Maybe he did care, but if he did he covered it up pretty well. But then again maybe he treated everyone who walked into his office this way. Later on in life I was told Coach Baskin favored the Hispanic kids because he thought they were better baseball players. Maybe this was true – maybe it wasn't – but it was clear he didn't favor me that day. The least he could have done was look at me when he talked to me.

I wasn't used to being treated like this, like 'a nobody', like I wasn't important – at least not when it came to sports.

In both situations I walked away with my head down – hurt and dejected. I wanted to yell, 'Don't you see? I need help! Don't you understand? If I don't get involved in sports, I don't know what will happen to me! I don't want to drop out, but I need to fit in somewhere! I know on the outside I act like I'm confident – but I'm not! I know I pretend I'm not afraid of anything – but I am!

When I look back on this time in my life the one thing I wish more than anything is that I could have been honest about how I felt. I wish I could have been honest about how uncomfortable and scared I was at school. I also wish other people were honest with me. I wish I knew what I know now; everyone has some self doubt, some more than others, but everyone has it. Maybe it wouldn't have helped, but I think it would have. Just knowing other people weren't perfect, like they appear to be, would have helped me to know I wasn't so different, so weird, and so alone.

With this latest let down – my life hit a new low. Compared to a year ago when I was a 'somebody' – I was embarrassed of what my life had become. I needed advise, support, love, and understanding, but it was nowhere to be found."

I felt bad for my dad. I asked him, "Why didn't anyone help you?"

"Because nobody knew about my anxiety, my self doubt, and my low self esteem – I pretended like everything was fine. I'm not exactly sure why I didn't tell anyone; maybe I was too embarrassed, maybe I felt pressure to be cool, or maybe I thought people would laugh at me – all I know is I put on a mask everyday to hide my true feelings.

♪ Masquerading as a man with a reason
My charade is the event of a season ♪
♪ And if I claim to be a wise man, well
It surely means that I don't know ♪
♪ On a stormy sea of moving emotion
Tossed about I'm like a ship on the ocean ♪ [22]

Kelsie asked, "Why did you put on a mask?"

"I don't know – I wish I didn't, but I think a lot of people probably do this – on the outside they pretend everything is okay, even great, but on the inside they are hurting. I'm sure my family and friends would have helped me, but they had no idea what was going on in my mind."

Kelsie and I didn't say anything for a little while. I felt bad for my dad, or maybe I should say I felt bad for that little boy. Then I quietly asked him, "So what happened next? What did you do?"

"Well, things actually got worse. When I look back on this time it doesn't sound that bad to me. I wonder why all these things bothered me so much – I really do wonder."

My dad looked away; almost like he was talking to himself and not Kelsie and me. He asked a bunch of questions – I think he was asking himself.

- "I went from a small Catholic school to a large public school – so what – why was that such a problem for me?

- I had to walk past drug dealers on my way to school – so what – why couldn't I walk past them without letting them bother me?

- I didn't have friends in Kennedy – so what – I had a lot of friends in the neighborhood, and eventually I would have made some friends at Kennedy?

- I had to deal with some girls at school which made things a little uncomfortable for me – who cares – why couldn't I just ignore them?

- I didn't play sports for Kennedy – so what – I was still able to play on the neighborhood teams?

- None of these things were a big deal. Why did they bother me so much with all the other things that bothered me? Why did I feel so nervous and uncomfortable? Why didn't I have more self confidence? Why did I start drinking so much?

- I really wonder why? I really do."

"Why did you let these things bother you so much?"

He had a sad look on his face when he said, "I don't know. I really don't. But I guess it goes back to what I said earlier. Maybe it was because I was just so sensitive and so stinking self conscious – and immature. I guess I just didn't know how to deal with all these changes…I just didn't know how. I really wish things could have been different – I feel bad for that confused little boy."

My dad stopped for a minute. His eyes were looking down toward the ground, but they weren't focused. His mind seemed to be somewhere else.

Then my dad quietly said, "One of my favorite movies is the Shawshank Redemption. Kelsie, that's the movie you and I watched a few weeks ago together. There was a part where Red talks about the 'young stupid kid who committed that crime' and how he wants to 'talk some sense to him.'"

My dad stopped again for a few seconds and then he said, "Well, just like Red, I wish I could go back to this time in my life and be a friend to that bewildered little boy. I wish I could teach him how to deal with the stress he felt. I would tell him things really weren't bad. I would tel him everyone has doubts sometimes, everyone feels different sometimes. I wish I could walk with him; I would walk with him past the drug dealers and tell him, 'Don't worry – just ignore them.' I wish I was there with him on the first day of school. I wish I was there to show him around the school. I wish I was there with him in class. When he felt uncomfortable I'd whisper to him, 'Don't worry. Focus on your school work. Don't worry about anyone else.' I wish I could have been there to encourage him. I would have encouraged him to become friends with a few of the kids in class. I wish I was there with him when he talked to the basketball coach – I would have told him to be more determined, more persistent. I would have told him, 'Don't give up so easily!' I wish I was there with him when he talked to Coach Baskin. I would have told him, 'Be confident, Kenny! Speak up! Tell Coach Baskin he needs to let you try out because you're good, and you'll be the best player on his team!' I never would have let that little boy give up! I never would have let him turn around with his head down!

I would have told that little boy, 'When that little voice in your head tells you 'you're different', 'you're dumb' or 'you're no good' – don't believe it! You're a good boy, and I'm proud of you!'

Then I'd put my hands around his face, and I'd look him straight in his eyes, and I'd tell him – if I had to pick out a little boy for my own I would go to 'Kid's R Us' and I'd walk to the Kenny Hand aisle and I'd pick you! Don't ever forget this! You're a good boy Kenny!"

I stopped my dad and said, "Hey Dad! That's what you tell me. You've been telling me you'd pick me out at 'Kids R Us' since I was a little boy."

"Yeah Dad. You've told me you would go to the Kelsie Lyn isle to pick me out too."

When I looked in my dad's eyes they were glassy. He slowly and quietly said to us, "Yes, I tell you that all the time because you are both great kids. I really mean that. If I was a kid I would want both of you as friends. I say that 'Kids R Us' thing because I want you to know how much I love you, and I also never, ever want you to have the same self doubts I had."

"But Dad, when did things get better for you?"

"Things eventually got much better, but not at this time; in fact, several other things happened which made things worse for this poor little boy.

He started quietly and slowly, "You know guys, Parents aren't perfect. Parents have problems, challenges, emotions, needs, wants, desires and everything else – everyone has. They're not perfect, and they make mistakes and have regrets just like you. So if I say something out of anger to you, Kelsie or Cam, I hope both of you can forgive me because, trust me, I love you more than either one of you will ever understand. You won't understand until you have children of your own."

He then proceeded to tell us about an argument he overheard between his father and mother when he was struggling during his high school freshman year. He said, "My father, to this day, probably doesn't know I overheard their argument, and he probably doesn't even remember it. I'm sure he didn't mean it, but like I told you before parents sometimes say things they don't mean.

I don't remember ever saying anything to either of you that would hurt your feelings but…"

Kelsie said, "OH, YES YOU HAVE!"

"Really, I don't remember ever saying anything mean to you or anything that might hurt your feelings."

"Oh well, then you don't have a very good memory!"

"Kelsie, if it's about the time I told you that you are the worst soccer player I've ever seen that doesn't count. You ARE the worst soccer player I've ever seen!"

"Dad! That's not it, but it's like that."

"Well, you'll have to tell me about it sometime, but right now I want to tell you this story. Where was I? Oh yeah."

"See, I told you Dad! I'm scarred for life!"

"I don't have to worry about you, Kelsie. You're resilient – you'll get over it. You're not sensitive like me. So do you want to hear the story?"

I sat up and said, "I do!"

The Lonesome Loser's Wonderful Life

This story is about a conversation my dad overheard his parents having about him. He discussed this with his parents when he was older, and they are convinced it never happened. He told me maybe they're right, but as a teenager he believed he heard it, and it confirmed and exacerbated his own self-doubts, so whether it happened or not, this story had a dramatic impact on his life.

"Okay, so it happened on a Saturday when I spent the day at my grandmother's house on Corlear Ave with my family. At the time we were living in our apartment on 233rd Street, and occasionally we spent the afternoon at her house BBQing, playing Whiffle ball, and enjoying each other's company in the back yard. Actually, I guess we didn't really BBQ – we made sandwiches, homemade potato salad, macaroni salad, and chips. We spent the afternoon and part of the night outside on lawn chairs eating, drinking, playing, and talking.

To get the backyard in shape for the family the grass had to be mowed, the branches, leaves, and grass had to be racked, and so I offered to help. My grandmother had an old gas powered mower which I had never used even when I lived at her house. I can't really remember, but I assume Richie mowed the grass when we lived there. But now since I was older, I wanted to help, and so I volunteered to mow the lawn while my dad did the other yard work.

Since it was an old lawn mower, it conked out on me numerous times. When it conked out I called my dad and he got down and wiggled this and waddled that. Then he'd ask me to pull the starter again and, like magic, the mower started up. I didn't know what he did to get it working again; he didn't tell me; he just did something that got it working. So when it conked out on me again and again, I asked him for help again and again. Even with this little lawn mower problem I was very proud of myself for being such a helpful son.

After all our hard work, the backyard was ready for everyone to come outside to enjoy the afternoon with the whole family.

While my parents were sitting eating, drinking, and talking I played Whiffle ball with Philip. Darla Franzetti and Patricia played together. Gena listened to her radio. Richie talked and played basketball with his friend Billy McKnight. Christine showed up later with her friends Nancy, Suzette, and Katie. Later on my friend Pat showed up and we played stick ball. After the games we sat around for several hours talking, laughing, eating, and drinking. It was one of those days where you lay in bed thinking, 'This is what it's all about, working hard, good food and drink, and spending time with the people you love – your family and friends.' Unfortunately, this is not what I heard when I went to bed. Instead of hearing what a great son I was I heard something else – I heard my mother and father arguing.

In the apartment, my room was about ten feet away from the living room where they were arguing. I didn't know what they were arguing about so I walked to the door and put my ear to it. All I could hear was my father saying the words, 'idiot', 'stupid', and 'dumb'; however, I didn't know who or what he was referring to so I opened my door. It usually made a creaking, squeaking noise when I opened it so I was very careful not to let my parents hear me. When I opened the door a crack I heard my mother say, 'He is not! He just never did it before.' I couldn't hear everything my father said, but I did hear him loud and clear make his main argument, 'Annie, he's just plain dumb – just plain dumb and stupid!' I wondered who they were talking about. My dad obviously thought the guy was really stupid, but I couldn't understand why they were arguing about him. Then I thought to myself, 'Maybe they're talking about a politician; they're always discussing politics. Or maybe they're arguing about one of my father's bosses; he didn't always see eye to eye with his bosses.' I then thought, 'Okay, they're arguing, but I'm sure they'll stop pretty soon, after all, they're just having a silly argument about some stupid guy, but then I thought I heard my name – 'Kenny'.

After hearing my name I listened closer and I realized they were talking about me. My dad, the person I just worked with the whole day mowing, raking, and cleaning my grandmother's yard with – was arguing with my mother about how dumb I was. He yelled, 'Annie, he's stupid, why is it so hard for you to accept that we have a stupid son? We have two other children who are handicapped, why is it so hard for you to accept Kenny's stupid! I mean, you should have seen him today; he couldn't even mow the lawn without asking me to start the lawn mower up for him every 5 minutes! All I'm saying is that he is not as smart as most kids his age – why do you find it so hard to believe?' My mother argued he was wrong, and then I heard her say, 'Richie, keep your voice down – he might hear you.'

The argument subsided and I quietly got back into bed; my chin quivering, my stomach nauseous, and my mind in such a bewildered state I couldn't explain what was going through it. It's hard to describe how you feel when the man who raised you, the man you look up to, the person you want approval from – thinks you are stupid. All I know is it hurt inside, and I couldn't hold back my tears. I looked out my window, up at the street light, and the tears began streaming down my face. I heard someone walk from the living room to my bedroom door (which was still cracked open) and so I held my breath to keep them from seeing I was awake and crying.

I stayed up crying that night for hours. I thought about school, sports, Camp Venture, Gena, Philip, and many other things. Up to that point in my life I never thought about my intelligence – I just never did. If I did poorly at school I always attributed it to 'not trying' or 'poor teachers'. I never attributed being a C+ student to being stupid – it just never crossed my mind. Yes, I was never in the class with the 'smart' kids but I also was never in the class with the 'dumb' kids; then again maybe I was. Maybe I was just a little smarter than my sister Gena; at Camp Venture there were many different levels of mentally handicapped kids, from barely functional to highly functional – to the point they could almost attend a typical public school – maybe I was one of these types of kids.

When I woke up the next morning I didn't say anything to anyone; maybe this proved my dad was right. Wouldn't a smart person say, 'Dad, I heard what you said about me last night, and I want to tell you I'm not dumb! I'm smart! I just didn't know how to fix that old piece of crap lawn mower! Why didn't you show me what you were doing so I could fix it without your help?' Then again, why didn't I ask him to show me what he was doing when it kept breaking down? That's what a smart kid would have done. For many years whenever I did something stupid, which everyone does,

I figured it was because I was dumb, not a mistake, not because I hadn't learned it yet, not because I wasn't shown correctly. When I did something dumb, it was because that's what I was – DUMB."

♪ Have you heard about the lonesome loser,
Beaten by the queen of hearts every time ♪
♪ Have you heard about the lonesome loser,
He's a loser, but he still keeps on trying' ♪
♪ "It's okay", he smiles and says
Though this loneliness is driving him crazy ♪
♪ He don't show what goes on in his head,
But if you watch very close you'll see it all…♪ [20]

"That's sad, Dad. I'm sure he didn't mean it."

"Well, maybe he did mean it at the time because I'm sure he thought, I thought, I was cool. By this time in my life I was drinking all the time and so I put on an air of confidence most days. I'm sure he didn't know how lost I was inside. I put on a good act for a lot of people. But thankfully, 30 years and thousands of hours of therapy later I'm over it…sniff, sniff."

"It'll be okay, Dad. We don't think you're dumb!"

"Thanks, Cam! Alright, now don't get me wrong my dad is a great guy, but I don't think our relationship improved until I got older. Someday I'll tell you about the trip we went on together to Atlantic City and the many nights we went to the Meadowlands racetrack and several other racetracks in the city. Oh wait, I need to tell you a story about the first time I realized my dad had a soft side. It's the time I was first introduced to my favorite movie."

"What movie?"

"Hold on, be patient, you'll find out."

Now Kelsie and Cam, as you know, everybody loves my dad and they especially love being around him. He's always the life of the party, but he also has a softer, feminine side – as you'll see.

Every year around Christmas time I saw my father in front of the TV watching a black and white movie on channel 9, WPIX. Without exception toward the end of the movie he had tears streaming down his face. I wondered, 'What the heck is up with this? Why does he cry every time he sees this movie? I can't believe he cries watching some silly black and white movie with some cheesy old time actors.'

One particular night my father was sitting on the couch in his pink fuzzy slippers, his boxer trunks with hearts on them, and a white v-neck undershirt. I also I noticed him holding an empty box of tissues. I could tell it was empty because there were about two dozen rolled up used tissues sprawled on the couch, coffee table, and floor as my dad sat on the couch with both his legs folded underneath his thighs. When I looked at his face I noticed his nose was running and his eyes were wet and blood shot – he'd been crying again!

I walked into the living room and saw this pitiful sight of a father and said, 'Mom…I mean Dad, I don't mean to be insensitive, but what do you think the guys from the garage would say if they saw you sitting here like a woman weeping because your favorite panty liner has been discontinued? Come on, suck it up, be a man, rub some dirt in it!' My father said, 'Sniff, sniff, why don't you try to sit down and watch this movie from beginning to end and tell me what you think about it, sniff, sniff. See if you can keep from crying!' 'Dad, you wouldn't catch me dead watching this movie, but what's it about?' 'Just watch and see for yourself – I can't tell you right now – I'm too emotional! You can watch it any night this week because it's on every day until Christmas.' As luck would have it I came down with a case of the flu a few days later, and so I decided to watch the movie from beginning to end while I was curled up in my bed trying to 'sweat out' the flu. As I was laying in bed wearing three pairs of sweat pants, four sweat shirts, a winter hat, and scarf, it came on, my father's favorite movie, *It's a Wonderful Life*.

This particular year *It's a Wonderful Life* was on every night between Thanksgiving and Christmas day. The movie started out slowly. It's about a young boy who dreams about growing up to become an engineer who builds large exciting structures, in grand exotic places, while his dad ran the local Building and Loan which helped people to build homes and participate in the American Dream. Well one thing leads to another and before he knows it he has given up on his dreams of fame, fortune, and getting away from his small home town of Bedford Falls. Then after running into financial difficulties due to a simple minded Uncle – he thinks it would be better if he 'had never been born', and so he attempts to commit suicide. Before he has a chance to jump off the bridge his guardian angel, Clarence, stops him by jumping off the bridge into the icy water himself – a move he knows will cause George to jump in to save his life. After Clarence and George get out of the water and they dry off – Clarence gives George a gift to help him see how worthwhile and important his life is. The gift was showing him what the world would be like if he had never been born. He gets to see all the people whose lives he impacted and how much better their lives were because of him. The things he did for them, although not exotic or exciting were, just like my dad, the things that help make people's lives better – kindness, help during troubled times, and looking out for family and friends.

After running around Bedford Falls looking for people who knew him (since 'he had never been born' – no one knew him, not even his mother) he only found people whose lives were dark and dreary because he wasn't ever born to brighten and improve their lives. As George was again at the end of his rope – his guardian angel pointed out to him, 'You see George, you really did have a wonderful life.' At this point George tells Clarence, 'I want to live again, I want to live again…' and Clarence answers his prayer and George is back in the world where he existed.

Back in his world he runs home excited to see his family with a better appreciation for how wonderful his life was. The climax of the movie was the final scene which takes place at his home. His family and friends who love him come pouring through the door showering him with money to help him with his financial difficulties because of everything he did for them.

Then his younger brother, who is a military hero, walks through the door and gives a toast, 'To my big brother George – the richest man in town!' Along with all the festivities George opens a book which was left for him on top of a basket piled high with money and he opens the cover and it read, 'To my friend George, Remember no man is a failure who has friends. Clarence PS Thanks for the wings!'

By the end of the movie I was blubbering like a little baby – just like my dad. It was at the same time the saddest movie and the most uplifting movie I had ever seen – but most importantly it was the most accurate portrayal of human nature I had ever seen.

From this movie I think I got to know my dad a little better; I guess he's just like everyone else. So maybe the time I heard him talking about me was like the time George Bailey yelled at his children; maybe it was a time when he was at the end of his rope. Maybe I heard a man who was going through a tough time in his life. Or maybe I was wrong and he wasn't talking about me; maybe I dreamt the whole thing. Who knows for sure? All I know is my dad is just like George Bailey – if he needed help he would realize how many people he has touched – family and friends would pour through his door to be there for him! But more than anything – I hope he realizes he is living a *Wonderful Life* too!"

"That's nice, Dad."

"Well I hope you'll think the same about me when you're older.

Okay, so where was I when I was telling you about my pitiful life? Oh yeah. I wish I could say things got better for me while I was in high school, but they didn't. I mentioned to you earlier I started drinking beer after my 8th grade graduation, well, as my hopes to 'connect' at school faded and I lost more confidence in myself, I began to drink more and more because it made me feel better. I should have reached out for help, but I didn't; instead I slowly but surely stopped going to school. I pretended to be sick, I argued with my mother; sometimes she gave in and let me stay home because she was tired of fighting with me, but mostly she forced me out the door.

When my mom forced me out I rarely went to school; I usually found something to do and somewhere to go. I'd workout at Ron's; I'd hangout with friends; I'd play basketball; I'd drink beer – I'd do anything to pass the time until my friends got out of school."

"So when did you actually drop out of school?"

"I'm really not sure. I suppose I officially dropped out when I was 16, but I stopped going to school off and on long before that. I'm not even sure how much time I spent in school. I probably spent about 6 months in school my 1st year and maybe 5 or 6 months in school the other two years.

A lot of my life during this time is blurry, and so it's hard for me to remember exactly when certain things happened. Like the first day the Truant Officer came to my house. I don't remember if this happened during my freshman or sophomore year, but I do remember when he knocked on our door early one morning while I was still laying in bed. I heard him tell my mother at the door, 'Mrs. Hand. Your son has stopped going to school'. This led to me going back to school for a while, but it didn't last for long. Later, maybe months later, when the Truant Officer returned, he made another recommendation. He recommended I enroll in the 'Out of School Program'; a short time later – I did."

"What's the 'Out of School Program'?"

"It was, and might still be, a New York City program where kids worked in the public or private sector and gained high school credits – high school credits which allowed them to graduate from high school. As I remember it, the jobs could be anything from working in a restaurant to working in a school. These jobs didn't necessarily develop important skills which helped kids later on in life – they just kept them off the streets.

I believe I had two or three different jobs, but the one I remember clearest was working as a kindergarten teacher's assistant in PS 7. PS 7 was just around the corner from my apartment building, and so I kind of liked it – at least at first. But just think about this; the City of New York allowed a teenage juvenile delinquent with emotional problems and a drinking problem to work with 5 year old children! That was so insane! If that's not crazy enough, consider this, by teaching little kids to color inside the lines and by reading them *The Little Engine That Could* – I could have received a New York City High School Diploma!

But like most things I did at this time in my life – I didn't follow through with this either. I stopped going to my job at PS 7 after several months."

"Wow, Dad. Is that really true? Could you really have graduated from high school by working at PS 7?"

My dad nodded his head, "Yes Kels, it's true. It made no sense to me then, and it makes less sense to me now, but that's how it was. After I stopped working at PS 7, I don't think I ever returned to school – I must have been close to 16."

Kelsie asked, "So what happened after you dropped out? What did you do? Did you get a job? Did you continue to drink beer?"

"After I dropped out of high school I did a lot of different things, some good, some bad, but I'll tell you about them another time. But I do want to tell you one more piece of the high school drop out story. Do you want to hear it?"

"Yeah, of course we do."

As I approached my 16th birthday I started to feel the consequences of dropping out. There were a couple of experiences which made me realize I was going in the wrong direction.

First of all, at this time in my life I spent a lot of time playing basketball with a couple of my friends – Shawn and Bobby. We played basketball all over the neighborhood together, but during the summer of 1980 we played a lot of basketball in Manhattan College's Draddy Gymnasium. I always considered Shawn and Bobby to be very smart. They both took school seriously; Shawn went to Cardinal Spellman and Bobby transferred from Sacred Heart to Fordham Prep. Both schools had excellent academic reputations. All three of us got along, especially on the basketball court, but off the court I couldn't keep up with them. Shawn and Bobby spent a lot of time discussing school, history, politics, current events, and the college they wanted to attend after high school. Needless to say I didn't participate in these conversations; I didn't understand these subjects.

This was very uncomfortable for me but looking back on it I'm thankful it happened because it eventually helped me realize the consequences of dropping out.

♪ Sit down, take a look at yourself
Don't you want to be somebody ♪
♪ Someday somebody's gonna see inside,
You have to face up, you can't run and hide ♪ [20]

Deliver Me From Evil…

This next story taught us how important it is to listen to our parents when they say things like 'Don't talk to strangers'. It also showed us Kingsbridge, like most places, had its share of deviant people. One more thing, it happened around the time he stopped going to school and was drinking heavily. He didn't say it to us, but I imagine this experience disturbed him on a number of levels – I know it would have disturbed me.

"Doubledays was a new neighborhood restaurant located a few miles north on Broadway near the city line between the Bronx and Yonkers. Like all neighborhood restaurants it was a place to bring your wife for a nice meal or to meet your friends for a few drinks.

A short time after it opened I applied for a job there, and because a friend of Richie's managed the kitchen I was hired on the spot to work Friday and Saturday as a dish washer. During the dead time the cook, Kevin O'Sullivan, smoked and had a few beers to relax. Even though I was only around 15 at the time – this was also one of the perks of the job for me. Working here on weekend nights saved me a lot of money; not only did I earn a few dollars – I also saved a lot because the beer was free.

On slower nights I finished at midnight and still had a few hours to meet up with my friends for a few drinks. The job was convenient and easy to get to because it was located on Broadway; a 15 minute ride on the #20 bus. I got on the bus on the corner of Broadway and 234th Street; I got off the bus outside the front door of Doubledays. This commute worked perfectly most of the time because the buses ran every 15 to 20 minutes, and they were very punctual, however, if I got off work after midnight the buses only ran once per hour – maybe less.

Do you guys want to hear one of the scariest stories of my life?"

"Of course!"

"Okay but don't tell your mother, she probably wouldn't approve of me telling this story."

Kelsie crossed her fingers and said, "Okay, we won't."

"Alright, it happened on a Saturday night when I worked late; I didn't get off work until 2:00 a.m. Because of this I assumed most of my friends were either home or wouldn't stay out much longer so I decided not to rush back to the neighborhood. As I walked out of the front door of the restaurant I saw the #20 bus pull away from the curb. I knew this meant I'd be waiting for the next bus for a long time! I had a decision to make; should I wait for another bus, should I ask Kevin for a ride, should I pay for a cab, or should I just walk home? I decided to walk home.

My feet were sore from standing up all night so as I walked, and walked, and walked, my feet hurt more, and more, and more. I walked past the Van Cortland horse stables, past the Van Cortland Motel where I heard a lot of heavy breathing..."

"Why did you hear heavy breathing?"

"I'll tell you when you're older, Cam. Anyway, I walked under the Henry Hudson Parkway near the Vanny Flats, I passed by Riverdale Country School, and I continued to walk and walk and walk. By this time my shoes were ripping into my Achilles heels; I was in so much pain I was almost in tears.

I walked past Pat's grandparent's apartment, past the Riverdale Press, some bars, and a few stores. As I approached a dark wooded area across from the Flats, I was nervous because it seemed like a perfect place for a mugger to wait for unsuspecting victims. To avoid being mugged I moved into the street under the street lights. I was in the street for about 50 yards when a car pulled up next to me. This scared me at first, but when I looked into the open car window I breathed a sigh of relief – it wasn't someone looking to mug me – it was a nice older gentleman.

It was difficult to tell but I thought I recognized him; it might be one of my friend's father or maybe somebody from Doubledays. The man leaned over to the passenger side window and with a kindly smile he said, 'Do you need a ride?' I thought to myself, 'Yes! I don't have to walk the rest of the way home!' I smiled and said to the kindly man, 'Yeah, I just got off work, but I missed the bus and so I had to walk home. I've already walked a couple miles and my feet are killing me! I live on 233rd Street, and so if you could drive me home that would be great!' The gentleman smiled, 'Sure, hop in, I'll give you a ride.'

I opened the passenger door and got in. When I sat down my feet felt so much better; I leaned back and relaxed. The nice man pressed a button on his door, my window rolled up, and he pulled away. When he got on the road going south he said, 'So, how are you doing?' I said, 'My feet are killing me, but they feel better now.' The man reached his hand over and put it on my knee and said, 'No, I mean – how are you doing?'"

Kelsie jumped up from her seat and said, "WHAT?! He touched your leg!! Why'd he do that?"

"Yes, Kelsie. I'm sure you know why he did it, and it terrified me! A million terrible thoughts ran through my mind. I pictured myself being abused, stabbed, shot, or killed. I couldn't believe it was happening – I had been taught never to go with strangers when I was a kid, but this wasn't a REAL stranger – it was a 50 year old man who looked familiar. He didn't look mean, evil, and he didn't look like a pervert, but he was, and I thought for sure I was about to be molested and killed. When he touched my knee I grabbed the door handle and started shaking it but the door was locked so I pounded on the window with my fist! I was ready to do anything to get out of there, but the man yelled, 'No! Stop! Stop! I'll pull over and let you out right here! Take it easy!' He pulled over and let me out on Broadway near the entrance to Van Cortland Park, near the mansion.

It was the scariest experience of my life; here was a man who was probably married with children yet he stalked young teenagers in my neighborhood. Just like the TV show, 'To Catch a Predator', here was an apparently nice man who preyed on innocent young kids to fulfill his disgusting, deviant, sexual desires."

His stories seemed to be getting sadder and sadder. At one of our Saturday morning breakfasts Kelsie asked, "So Dad, are you going to tell us when your life started improving?"

Trashing the Planet

"Like I said before, things eventually got much better, but not anytime soon. I had people all around me who would have been happy to help me but I never asked for it.

For example, when I was growing up there was one person, more than anyone else, who I looked up to – my brother Richie. As you know Richie is 5 years older than me, and he was successful at everything he did.

He was good at school, baseball, football, basketball, hockey, swimming, and everyone liked my brother – nobody had anything but good things to say about him. He was a typical first born son; mature, level headed, and smart. So, of course, I wanted to be like him, and I wanted him to be proud of me.

When Richie was 18 years old he worked for a privately owned trash company named Trippi; Richie jokingly referred to himself as a 'Sanitation Engineer' as opposed to a 'Trash Man'. He worked in Rockland County near my Uncle Bob's bar in Congers, NY. At this time Richie still lived in our apartment and so 5 days a week he woke up at 5:00 a.m. and made the 35 minute trip to Congers to pickup trash. I can still remember the day Richie asked me if I wanted to help him on his garbage route.

Another thing, he worked 5 days a week except when a holiday fell during the week. It was nice to get a day off, but it came with a price. The garbage piled up which made for backbreaking work on the days following the holiday. One day, I think it was around Thanksgiving, Richie asked me, 'Hey, Kenny, do you want to make a few extra dollars working with me on my route? I need help on Friday after Thanksgiving.'

On the inside I thought, 'Help you? Of course! I would do anything to hang out with my big brother! I'd love to!' but on the outside I said coolly, 'Yeah, sure. What time do we leave?'

Richie said, '5:00 a.m.'

'Okay. Can you wake me up when you get up?'

I was so excited the night before, I laid out my clothes and thought about how hard I would work for Richie – I'd show him what a great worker I am. On Friday, the alarm clock rang and I jumped out of bed without my brother having to wake me up. I put on the oldest, dirtiest clothes I could find, and then I brushed my teeth, hair, and I put on my construction boots and waited by the front door for him. When we walked out of the building it was still dark outside. We got into his van and drove down Kingsbridge Avenue toward 238th Street. We made a right on 238th Street, and then we made a left on Bailey Avenue driving towards the entrance to the Major Deegan near the Van Cortland Golf Course.

♪ You get up every morning
From you alarm clock's warning ♪
♪ Take the 8:15 into the city
There's a whistle up above ♪ [23]

We got on the Deegan and drove past Yonkers Raceway, dropped 10 cents in the toll booth near Dobbs Ferry, drove across the Tappan Zee Bridge and got off at the Conger's exit. There wasn't much discussion on the drive, but I wished there was. Like I mentioned to you when we talked about school – the past few months, maybe the past year, were some of the toughest times of my life, and I needed some guidance, some help – I needed someone to help me deal with all the new situations I found myself in. I wanted to ask my big brother for advice about school, girls, work, and how deal with all the pressures I felt. Richie was one person I would have listened to; he was the one person I respected and wanted to impress – I wanted to ask him for his help…but I didn't. I just sat quietly on the trip trying to act like I was cool.

When we pulled into Trippi's parking lot we got out of the van and climbed into the sanitation truck. Richie turned on the radio to WPLJ, and we listened to some rock music as we drove from house to house. Since I was in the passenger seat I was responsible for picking up the trash cans on the right side of the street while Richie took care of the left side of the street. In certain areas where the truck couldn't make it down the street I was given a large plastic garbage bin which was big enough to handle the contents of about 4 garbage cans. Once the plastic bin was filled I carried it back to the truck and emptied it. This was an efficient way to do the job but extremely hard – THE PLASTIC BIN WAS STINKING HEAVY! Richie told me to pick it up and put it on my shoulder, but that was easier said than done – but I did it without complaining – it didn't matter how tough it was because I wanted to impress him.

After about 4 hours of work we stopped off at the local diner for breakfast where we sat down at the counter. Richie asked me, 'What do you want – it's on me?' I said, 'I'll have whatever you're having.' The waitress walked over and he said, in his typical friendly, unassuming way, 'Hey Barb, how are you? We'll have two orders of scrambled eggs, bacon, toast, home fries, and some juice.' Barb seemed to be flirting with Richie when she said, 'Sure Rich. Who's your helper?' Richie smiled and responded, 'My brother, Kenny.' I smiled and gave a friendly nod. A couple of minutes later the food was on the counter, and we woofed it down. Just a few short minutes later we were done and ready to leave. Richie grabbed the check, left $5 on the counter for Barb, and he walked to the cash register and paid the bill.

We climbed back in the truck with my feet killing me. Yes Kels, my feet were killing me again because I was wearing uncomfortable construction boots. Although my feet hurt and I wanted to take a nap we got back on the road to finish the job. We were done a few hours later; by the end of the route I was tired, my muscles were sore, and I smelled worse than Kelsie after cleaning out the horse stables."

Kelsie smiled, "Nice Dad. But did you smell as bad as the bathroom after you've been sitting in there for an hour?"

"If you're asking if I smelled like flowers? No, I smelled bad."

Then he got back to his story, "After we finished collecting the trash, we drove the truck to the Nyack trash dump where we drove to the top of a mountain of trash and emptied the garbage truck on Garbage Mountain. After this we drove back to Congers and exchanged the truck for the van, and we were on our way back to the Bronx. We listened to WPLJ on the way back; again we had very little conversation, but this was fine with me because I was exhausted!

When I got back to the Bronx I hobbled up the stairs of the apartment, and I took off my smelly clothes. Then I put on some gym shorts and collapsed on my bed ready to go back to sleep. I laid there in bed exhausted, but I felt proud of the job I did for my brother, and although he didn't say, 'Thanks Kenny, you did a great job, I appreciate your help' – I hoped he would. A few minutes later Richie walked into the bedroom and dropped $30 on my chest and said, 'Thanks.' I loved getting paid $30, which was a lot of money especially in 1979 but I hoped 'Thanks' meant more than just 'Thanks' – I hoped it meant, 'Thanks Kenny, you did a great job' but I wasn't sure. I said, 'Thank you' in return, and I rolled over and went to sleep.

When Christmas and New Years rolled around I hoped Richie would ask me again for my help, but that didn't happen. Richie was dating a girl named Dawn at the time and she had two brothers who were close to my age. Instead of asking me for help he asked Scott. The day after he got help from Scott, I heard my brother telling my mother, 'Wow, Scott was great! He's hardworking, smart, and has a great personality. We had a great time, and we got done a lot sooner than I thought we would.' I sat there and listened to the conversation and pretended it didn't bother me – but it did. Richie didn't say anything wrong – I just wished he thought I was hardworking, smart, and had a great personality too."

"Dad, you are sooo sensitive!"

"Kelsie, you need to keep in mind all little brothers look up to their older brothers even if they don't act like it. And in case you don't realize it little girl, Cameron looks up to you too!"

"Dad! No I don't. Kelsie's annoying!"

Midnight Express to Connecticut...

My dad told us the next story over several weekend breakfasts at McDonalds. He claims he told us this story because he was trying to talk Kelsie out of dating a boy but I think he wanted to tell us this story for other reasons. I think he wanted to tell us this story because he thought it was cool. Sure, he sprinkled the story with some fatherly advice but I don't think that was his main purpose – I think he thought this experience defined him in some way – but maybe I'm wrong.

"Kelsie, when I was your age I dated a girl who went away for the summer to visit her grandmother in Connecticut. If I was a sensible young boy I would have let her enjoy her summer with her grandmother, but I was never accused of being sensible."

"What did you do?"

"Well, I was so captivated by her charm I thought I couldn't live without her even for a few short weeks."

"Dad! I don't want to hear about your girlfriends! Especially girls who you thought were charming!"

"Kelsie, you need to understand this isn't about me and a charming girl. It's about how cute, innocent relationships can cause young kids, like I was, to make bad decisions. Are you with me?"

"I'll listen for a while, but you better not talk about any lovey, dovey stuff!"

"Oh would you stop and just listen. Okay, after she went to her grandmother's house I was so distraught I frantically tried to devise a plan to see her. After sitting around one afternoon, discussing it with a few of my friends, we came up with a plan – The Midnight Express to Connecticut!"

"Did you really call it that?"

"Well, not really, but sort of. You guys need to sit back and relax, this might take a while. It was a Saturday night during the hottest month of the New York summer – August. The plan was for me to pickup John, Tommy, Robin, and Jennifer very early in the morning. John slept over Tommy's apartment and Jennifer slept over Robin's; I had two pickups to make prior to the Midnight Express taking off.

I arrived home close to 10:30 at night; my parents, Gena, Tricia, and Philip were all awake watching TV in the living room. I said, 'Hello', and I sat down on the couch next to my father and Philip. The TV was turned to channel 11, WPIX, my father's favorite sitcom was on – *Barney Miller* – a show he watched every night before going to bed. I kicked off my sneakers, put my feet on the coffee table, and I tried to be calm, cool, and relaxed.

Time dragged by as I sat there with my family watching one re-run after another. I leaned back thinking, 'Is anyone ever going to go to bed?' Eventually they did, one by one. Tricia went into the bedroom first; it was about 11:30. A few minutes later Gena got up, and a short time later Philip stood up and went inside.

My mother and father were night owls; they could be up all night, so I needed to be patient and calm. In time my mother got up, said, 'Good night', and walked to the back bedroom – it was 1:30. My father, as normal, stayed up the latest; after we watched an episode of *The Honeymooners* he got up and announced, 'I'm going to bed. Good night.' I said, 'Good night. I'm going to stay up for just a little while longer.' I looked at the clock and it was 2:00 a.m.

When he left the room I looked down on the coffee table and there they were – my father's keys. My plan was to wait an hour to make sure everyone was in a deep sleep before I left, so I lay down on the couch and waited. *Dance Fever* was on TV; my eyes were watching but my mind was on other things. There were a million things running through my mind but if you're wondering if I had any second thoughts, I didn't, I couldn't wait to leave.

The hour finally passed; I looked over at the clock and it said 3:00 a.m. Although I was dying to leave I knew it was too early; I needed to give my parents more time to fall into a deep sleep, and my friends probably needed more time to rest. The time seemed to stand still for the next 45 minutes; I was like an 8 year old waiting for Christmas morning to come..."

"Dad, you used that line before, in a different story."

My dad ignored Kelsie and continued, "When the clock finally flipped to 3:45 I stood up and quietly walked to the back hallway to listen for signs of life. It was very quiet except for an occasional snore from my parent's bedroom. The last thing I checked before grabbing the keys was my wallet; I had about $80 for the trip, I thought to myself, 'This should be plenty of money.'

When I grabbed the keys Pepper jumped up from his spot between the couch and chair. I thought to myself, 'Shoot! I didn't think about Pepper!' Whenever he heard the jingle of keys he hoped someone was about to take him for a walk and he ran to the front door, barked, and spun around. If he did this he'd wake up my family for sure. Before he started barking and spinning I quietly put the keys into my pocket and I slowly sat back down on the couch. With a hushed voice I said, 'No Pepper, I'm not taking you out.' He calmed down, but I had to come up with a different plan.

Originally, my plan was to walk out the front door and gently shut it behind me, but with Pepper my plans changed. My other option was to climb out the bedroom window. The fire escape was located outside my bedroom window and we always had our windows open during the summer. The window to the fire escape had a screen in it and the other one had a big metal fan. I knew the fan would help cover up the noise I'd make pulling out the screen; plus Gena, Philip, and Tricia were deep sleepers, so I was relatively confident I could sneak out without waking them.

When I walked out of the living room Pepper jumped up again and followed me hoping I'd turn right toward the front door, but when I didn't he calmed down. I opened the bedroom door and shut it behind me so he couldn't follow me in.

I tippy toed around the beds over to the window where I carefully pulled out the screen and placed it on the floor behind me. I climbed out the window and once I was on the fire escape I reached back and pulled the screen back in place. The fire escape was old and dirty but most of all it was creaky. When I moved, it shook which caused the latter to rattle against the other metal bars; it wasn't too loud but it was loud enough to concern me.

We lived on the first floor which is one story above the ground floor. The latter to our fire escape was pulled up and suspended 10 feet off the ground to keep burglars from being able to climb up. Lowering the latter to make it easier to climb down was out of the question because of the noise it would make. I had to climb down the latter and once I made it to the bottom rung I'd have to jump the last 10 feet.

After I put the screen in place I grabbed hold of the latter and reached around it with my leg to the outside of the fire escape. I quietly climbed down one rung at a time trying not to rattle the latter but it wasn't easy. I hoped Mrs. Pasamonte, our neighbor downstairs in apartment D, wouldn't hear me climbing down. When I reached the bottom rung my shirt and hands were filthy from rubbing against the dirty metal. I carefully maneuvered my body until I found myself dangling from the latter – I let go and fell to the ground.

When I came home earlier I didn't notice the car parked on the hill so most likely it was parked on Broadway. I walked down the hill, around the corner, past the Liffy, and there it was. It was parked outside the fruit stand, next to Salamarias. Next to it were dozens of boxes and bags filled with old fruit and vegetables waiting to be picked up by the Sanitation truck the next day.

The smell of the trash was nasty so I stepped off the sidewalk and into the street. As I walked to the driver side of the car I slipped on a piece of rotten lettuce or maybe it was a cabbage.

My brother's car was a 1973 Chevy something, I'm still not sure what, but it was a nice looking car but not too flashy. Not a car which would generate a lot of attention even with six young kids driving around in it. I opened the door, sat down, and pulled the door closed behind me. My feet couldn't touch the pedal so I reached under the seat, moved a lever, and scooted the seat forward. The keys were in my hand ready to be put into the ignition but first I sat back. I looked out the window toward the William's Funeral Home clock – it flashed 3:45 a.m. and 87 degrees."

"Dad, what were you thinking?"

"I don't know. In the quietness of the moment maybe I considered stopping but if I did – I didn't consider it for long.

After my short pause I put the key in the ignition and started the car. Since the car was on the corner I pulled forward and made a right turn onto my street and drove up the hill."

"Why'd you do that? Weren't you afraid your parents would see you?"

"I'm not sure why, I just did. My parents didn't see me but when I drove past my windows who do you think I saw?"

"Who?"

"My brother Philip. I'm not sure if I woke him when I climbed out or if he normally got up in the middle of the night; all I know is he didn't seem to notice me when I drove by. Maybe it was too dark to see my face or maybe he wasn't familiar with Richie's car; I'm not sure.

The streets of Kingsbridge at this time in the morning are quiet and serine, except for an occasional train, bus, or drunk passing by. It was a strange feeling walking and driving on the empty streets past the store fronts with the metal security gates pulled down for the night. I felt like the Omega man.

My first stop was Tommy's apartment; his building was around the corning, just a short distance away. He lived in the basement apartment on the corner of 234th and Kingsbridge Avenue. His windows were at knee level and were partially covered by a wrought iron fence and manicured bushes which surrounded the building."

"His windows were at knee level? Could people see in?"

"No, unless of course the bathroom window shade fell down, but that's a whole other story.

So where was I? Oh yeah. I drove up Kingsbridge Avenue and double parked outside Tommy's basement apartment. I got out of the car, walked to his bedroom window, stepped over the short wrought iron fence, leaned over the shrubs, and I tapped on the window.

I tapped several times before there was any sign they heard me. But then I heard a loud yawn and groan, 'Ahhhhh, Tommy, Kenny's here, come on, get up.' A minute later I heard a loud thump and a few curse words; it sounded like Tommy stubbed his tow on the barbells lying on his bedroom floor. A second later the blinds were pulled up and there was Tommy standing in his underwear with his eyes half closed; he motioned they'd be out in a minute.

I went back to the car, sat down, and listened to the radio. A few minutes later the window open; John stepped out and Tommy handed him a bag which had some clothes in it. When they were both out he turned around to pull down the window. They stepped over the bushes and the fence and walked toward my car. They didn't say much when they got in they just plopped down and groaned like they were exhausted. Tommy sat in the passenger seat because he looked older than John and me. We thought this was important if we drove past the police. Before we pulled away Tommy said, 'Are we sure we want to do this?' Both John and I said, 'Yeah. Let's do it. It'll be fun!'"

"Dad, you're story is not setting a good example for Cameron!"

"You're right Kels. I'm going to stop right here."

We both screamed, "NO KEEP GOING!"

"Okay. When we were all in the car I turned and told Tommy and John to put on their seatbelts..."

"Really?"

"No Cam, I just wanted to set a good example so Kelsie will get off my case. Anyway, our first stop was around the corner to Robin's apartment building. Her building was just a minute away; we went up Kingsbridge Avenue, made a left on 231st Street near the Donut Shop, and a quick right past Cold Cut City. Once I was on Godwin Terrace I drove past Ehring's and double parked outside Robin's alleyway on the left side of the street.

We got out and walked through the alleyway to the back of the building where Robin's bedroom window was. Inside the window it was dark but we could still see the girls sleeping with a bag of clothes next to the bed. John quietly tapped on her window and they slowly woke up and rolled out of bed. Unfortunately, they didn't come to the window like Tommy did..."

"What do you mean?"

My dad smiled, 'You know, in their underwear!'

Kelsie sat up, "What!?"

"I'm kidding! I mean I'm kidding about wanting them to come to the window in their...oh never mind...you get what I'm saying. Anyway, Robin came over to the window, opened it, and whispered, 'Are we really going to do this?' We quietly said, 'Yes, of course, come on.' A few minutes later the girls climbed out the window with our help and all of us walked to the car in silence. I got into the driver seat and Tommy opened the passenger side door. My brother's car was a two door sedan so Tommy pulled the passenger seat forward and let Robin get in, then John, and finally Jennifer. When they were comfortably in the back seat Tommy stepped in, closed the door, and we pulled away.

It was about 4:30 or 4:45 now; the streets were still quiet but they were waking up for the new day. Early in the morning on 231st Street and along Broadway the security gates are lifted up or slid to the side as the donut shops, bakeries, deli's, diner's, and convenience stores begin preparing for the busy day ahead.

We drove up then down Godwin Terrace, past St. John's and the Bodaga. We turned left on 230th Street, near the Projects, and continued past the Getty Station on our way to the northbound entrance to the Major Deegan.

Jordan's Grandmother lived in Fairfield, Connecticut, a quaint middle class suburban town along the Long Island Sound. Looking back on it Jordan's grandmother didn't live far away but to us it felt like we were embarking on an epic journey.

The Major Deegan Expressway was quiet and relatively empty compared to the normal daytime traffic. We drove north past Stella Dora, Van Cortland Park, past Yonkers Raceway, Cross County Mall, and eventually we merged onto the Cross County Expressway. The

Cross County would take us to the Hutch, 287, and ultimately to I-95. For most of the early part of the trip we didn't talk too much."

"Why not?"

"I'm not sure. Maybe we were nervous, maybe we were having second thoughts, maybe we were still half asleep, or maybe we were reflecting on what we were doing – who knows.

Tommy was my copilot with the map and directions. He sat up and said, 'Okay, we're going to get on the Hutch and we'll stay on it until we get to the Cross Westchester Expressway. Once we're on the Cross Westchester we need to get on I-95 but the signs might say the New England Thruway. Are you okay Kenny? You're not going to fall asleep are you?' 'No, I'm fine. My heart is pounding so hard I couldn't fall asleep if I wanted to. I'm sure I'll crash later..."

"YOU SAID YOU'D CRASH!?"

"Cam, that's a figure of speech. It means I would be so tired I'd fall asleep. Anyway, I told Tommy, 'I'm not tired now.' On the Hutch we drove past exits for Mamaroneck, Harrison, Rye (where Rye Playland is located), and pretty soon we approached the Cross Westchester or I-287. I said, 'Hey Tommy is this it?' 'Yeah, this is it.' 'Do I go east or west?' 'Let me see, we want to go right, towards the Atlantic Ocean, so we go east. I always remember my directions by 'WE', west is on the left and east is on the right. Yeah, take this next exit and it'll take us on I-95 north.' 'That's a good way to remember west from east; how do you remember north from south?' 'That's easy, north is up, and south is down.' 'Really?' 'Yeah.' 'Hmmm, hey John, you awake?' 'Yeah. What?' 'I might need your help when we turn north or south.'"

"But Dad, isn't that true? Isn't north up?"

"Cam, we'll discuss directions when we have more time but for now let me get back to the story. Where was I? North, south, co-pilot, okay now I remember. After we drove on the Cross Westchester we reached the main road on our journey, I-95, also known as the New England Thruway. After being on the thruway for several minutes we crossed a bridge which spanned an inlet of the Long Island Sound. Above the bridge was a sign, 'Welcome to Connecticut'.

It was about this time John said, 'Hey Kenny, let's stop and get something to eat – I'm starving.' 'Okay, where?' 'I don't know. Let's find a deli.'"

"Dad, why didn't you go to McDonalds like we do?"

"Cam, I don't think McDonald's had breakfast at the time. Well, maybe they did but I'm sure there weren't many 24 hour McDonalds and they definitely weren't off of every exit like they are now.

I said to John, 'Well I don't know if we'll find a deli here but let's pull off the highway up here.' A quarter mile up the road was exit 2, Delavan Avenue; I pulled off the highway and made a left at the end of the ramp. We were in a town named Greenwich, which was pronounced 'Gren-itch' which we incorrectly referred to as 'Green Witch'. We searched around the town for a while but we couldn't find a deli or any open store. There was a small convenience store which appeared to be open but when Tommy and I knocked on the door a man told us, 'We don't open until 7:00.'

When we walked away from the store, we noticed a police car driving slowly by eying us as we walked back to the car. John quietly said, 'Keep walking toward the car and don't act suspicious.' We nonchalantly got in the car I pulled away in the opposite direction..."

"Did he come after you?"

"I don't think so but we didn't stick around long enough to find out. I turned back on Delavan Avenue and got back on the Thruway as quickly as I could. We weren't on the road for long before we saw a sign for a restaurant off the Arch Street exit. It was a beautiful restaurant which looked over a fancy, upscale cove located near Steamboat Road. I pulled into the parking lot and we all got out. When I look back I don't understand why I'd think a nice restaurant like this would be open at 6:30 in the morning but I did – we all did.

We got out of the car, opened the restaurant door, and walked in. I don't remember its name but inside there were dozens of pictures of celebrities hung all over the walls. It appeared to be empty but there was music playing and we heard the sound of dishes clanging together so we continued strolling in assuming it was open for business.

We walked into the empty dining room and there was a man walking towards us but he didn't notice us at first. When he looked up, he saw us, and he was startled. The water glasses he was carrying slipped from his hands and shattered on the floor. In broken English he said, 'What you doing here? I call police if you no leave now!' Tommy said, 'Calm down, we're looking for a place to eat and we thought you were open.' 'It 6:30 in morning what kind restaurant open this time? Get out or I call police!' All of us slowly stepped back and I put up my hands and said, 'Sorry sir, don't call the cops, we're leaving right now'. We turned and ran back to the car and I raced to get back on I-95."

"Did he call the cops?"

"I don't know. Probably not but again we didn't wait around long enough to find out."

"So, did you guys get any food?"

"No, we never did but after all the excitement we were all awake and in a more talkative mood. John said, 'Let's forget about the food, I'll eat later when we're sure places are open.' As we got back on the Interstate Jennifer asked me how I learned to drive. I smiled, 'My first experience driving a car came with my father when I lived in Suffern; he let me sit on his lap and steer the car while he drove around town. And then when I was older he brought me to Spook Rock Golf Course where he let me drive the golf cart while he played golf.' 'Funny.' 'But I guess it was Ron Klaus who really taught me how to drive. A couple of years ago he took Tommy and me to the Van Cortland Golf Course Parking Lot and he taught us how to drive his El Camino.'"

"Dad, why did teach you how to drive when you were so young?"

"I'm not sure but we were glad he did. Anyway, I continued to tell Jennifer, 'After he taught us I took every opportunity to drive my parent's or brother's car, no matter how short the trip was. Most of my driving was at Camp Venture or after my Inwood Baseball League games.

My mom usually drove me to my games and afterwards I'd ask her for the keys to the car. I'd run to the car and when I got there I'd drive back and forth in the parking space; forward 5 feet, backward 10 feet, forward 10 feet, backward 10 feet – I'd do this until I saw my mother and then I'd stop the car and put it back in park. I don't think she knew I did this until one day when I had an unfortunately experience – a little fender bender.'"

I interrupted, "What's a fender bender?"

"An accident..."

"You got into an accident driving in a parking space?"

"Yup, I was a rookie. Anyway, I was telling Jennifer, 'This day when my mother drove me to my game she parked the car outside Inwood Park. Across the street was a small park where several old men were feeding pigeons and playing chess. After the game I got the keys from my mother and I ran to the car. I did my normal maneuvers; 10 feet forward, 10 feet back. As I was cruising in my parking space the old men were watching me; I assumed they were really impressed with my driving skills. But it's more likely they were wondering why this young knucklehead, in a baseball uniform, was driving back and forth in a little parking space.

Then, as always, I saw my mother walking toward me so I lightly put my foot on the brake but it didn't stop – it actually picked up a little speed. Instead of being calm I got nervous and I slammed my foot on the brake but, being the rookie I was, I didn't realize my foot was actually on the gas pedal and so you know what happened next. I slammed into the parked car behind me! I'll never forget the sound of the tires screeching and the loud BANG!

Within seconds my mother, the old men, and every other person in the park were standing around the back of my car. It was one of the most embarrassing moments of my life but look on the bright side; I learned a valuable lesson that day.'"

"What lesson did you learn? Did you learn never to drive back and forth in a parking space?"

"No Kels, I learned, brake on the left, gas on the right. Anyway, so we continued to talk, 'Robin asked, 'Whose idea was it to steal your brother's car to see Jordan? 'I guess it was my idea.' 'But why?'

'Well let me ask you why you came with us.' She said, 'Well, first of all, I wanted to see Jordan, she's my best friend, but also you guys are a lot of fun. Most girls in the neighborhood would have said yes if you asked them to go – you guys know that.' I said, 'Maybe Tommy and John know that but I didn't.' She said, 'Yes you did. You guys are a lot of fun to hang out with.'"

"Dad, she didn't say that to you – did she?"

"Maybe she didn't but I'm pretty sure she did. Anyway, after she said something like that I said, 'Robin, that's nice to hear but I think all of our friends are fun to be around. We're really lucky to have such good friends. When I go out on a Friday or Saturday night and walk into the school yard it doesn't matter who's there – it could be any of the girls or guys and I'd have a good time. We have a lot of good friends. How many people can say that? How many people can say they have forty or fifty good friends?' Jennifer said, 'He's right Robin. The first time I came to one of your Godwin Parties it was in Ewen Park and I couldn't believe it. You guys all got along so well. I couldn't believe how many people were in your group but I really couldn't believe how nice everyone was, except for Lori, she told me she would kick my ass all the way up Ewen Park back to Johnson Avenue if I didn't leave. But even she turned out to be nice once we got to know each other.

In some groups the guys and girls don't really talk to each other but you guys really seemed to like each other.' John said, 'We do really like each other – what's not to like about us?'

Jennifer said, 'But seriously – you guys never argue or fight with each other and when you get loud it's only when you sing a song, like Free Bird or Paradise by the Dashboard Light – it's really funny. How did all of you become such good friends?' I said, 'I'm not really sure. Robin, do you remember?

She said, 'The way I remember it is I was in the original group, along with Lori, Maureen, Shawn, Scott, Mary, Billy, Joanne, Jackie, Brigit…um who else? Oh yeah, Chris. It wasn't until we all went skating, remember when you boys took us skating at Kelton's.' I laughed and said, 'I remember, that was the first time I kissed a girl. Do you remember Robin? You know you were the first girl I ever kissed?' 'You kissed me? Is that what that was? No, I'm just kidding Kenny. I think I remember it.' Jennifer said, 'Really, I thought Jordan was your only girlfriend – you two actually dated each other?' 'Yeah, Robin was crazy about me. She couldn't keep her hands off of me in 7th grade. I was quite the hunk – right Robin?' She rubbed her chin and said, 'Ooooh boy! Is that how you remember it? Kenny, why don't you tell Jennifer the story about our', she cleared her throat, 'our first kiss.' Uh, Jennifer – I use the word kiss very loosely – I think it was a kiss but it happened so quickly it was more like a hit and run something.' I spoke up, 'Hey, easy, Robin, I was a rookie, I've improved since then – I think.

The Love Machine

Okay Jennifer sit back and relax and I'll tell you this romantic story about my passionate love affair with Robin. But let me tell you our relationship was purely a physical one. And Robin, don't interrupt me, this is how I remember it and I don't want you arguing with my memory.' Robin said, 'Jennifer, you better relax, have you ever heard one of his stories? They can get long.' I chimed in and said, 'Hey, they're long but they're good – right?' Robin laughed, 'Sure, I guess – go ahead.'

'Okay, I'm going to start from the beginning. As you know when we were younger there were a lot of rules; there were rules in school, rules in sports, rules in church, and there were rules for dating. First, only boys could ask a girl out and they had to specifically ask, 'Will you go out with me?' If she said yes, they were going out – if she said no he was humiliated. To break up with a girl you had to say, 'It's quits.' You didn't say, 'I don't want to go out with you', you didn't say, 'I don't like you anymore', you said, 'It's quits' – period. Technically you didn't have to say it in person, you could say it over the phone, you could write it on a note, you could tell your friend to tell your girlfriend, or you could even scream it across the school yard – but you had to say, 'It's quits.'

Robin said, 'Yeah but you were supposed to say it to their face – at least real men did.'

I smiled, 'Robin, did you just interrupt me? I'm just kidding. I agree with you, the nice way to break up with someone was to say it to their face but a lot of people didn't do that. I remember when Pat was going out with Kelly. When Kelly decided to break up with him she told Susan to tell Pat, 'It's quits.' I remember how mad Pat was. As soon as Susan told him, he looked for Kelly and when he saw her he yelled across the school yard, 'Hey Kelly – it's quits! It's back to the pound for you!'

Jennifer said, 'Wow, back to the pound, that's mean.'

I laughed, 'I'm sure Pat didn't mean it, well back then he did, but they're good friends now so they both got over it. Where was I? Oh yeah, I was telling you about going out with Robin. She was in my 7th grade class at St. John's and, Robin, cover your ears, I thought she was cute. You can uncover your ears now. She knew I liked her because she was the target of my daily teasing and I thought she liked me too because she teased me right back. In 7th grade, some of us guys began thinking seriously about girls and dating. We started talking openly about the girl we liked and about asking her out. It took me a while but with the help of Tony, John, and Timmy I asked Robin out.'"

"What do you mean they helped you, Dad?"

"Cam, I'm saying they kept asking me, 'Are you going to ask her out? Are you going to ask her out? Are you going to ask her out?'"

"Gotcha. Peer pressure."

"Yes, peer pressure. Anyway, I told Jennifer, 'I eventually worked up the nerve to ask her. On a Friday afternoon at school, prior to the last period, I asked Tony to ask Jordan to ask Robin if she would meet me in front of school after the final period so I could ask her out. Seems pretty complicated – I know. Even though I liked Robin and teased her every day I never really had a conversation with her unless asking her for the answers to a test constitutes a conversation. So really talking to her terrified me. Wait, hold it – I also asked her if I could copy her homework but I don't think that counts as a conversation either.

When the school bell finally rang at 3:00 p.m. all the students ran out of school except for me; I purposely meandered through the hallways because I was afraid to ask her out. Eventually I walked down the stairs closest to the south exit of the school, you know, where all the girls smoked cigarettes. My heart was pounding so hard I thought I was having a heart attack; I considered going out the back door of the school to avoid the whole situation but I didn't want to back out because I knew all the guys would call me a wimp if I did.'"

"Peer pressure Dad. You always tell us not to give into peer pressure!"

My dad smiled, "Yeah, yeah, yeah, do as I say, not as I do.

Anyway, when I reached the bottom floor I decided to walk out to face my destiny and there was Robin standing outside the school gate, on Kingsbridge Avenue. She was on the sidewalk, next to the curb, with Jordan, Kelly, Lori, and everyone else watching closely from down the block. I have to admit she looked cute, her hair was in pig tails, she was wearing her stylish rabbit fur coat, underneath she had on her St. John's uniform; a yellow blouse, brown vest, brown plaid skirt, tube socks with white, red, and blue stripes, and her brand new Pro Keds (with her friend's names written all over the sides). Pro Keds weren't part of the official school uniform; most of the girls wore their brown school shoes like Earth Shoes, Lil'Abners, Hush Puppies, or Clogs until they got out of school and then they changed out of their shoes into their sneakers.

When I saw Robin I walked towards her and stuttered a barely audible, 'Hi', and Robin said, 'Hi' – I think she was nervous too. I thought to myself, 'When should I ask her?' and I bet she was thinking 'When is he going to ask me?' We both smiled a lot and shuffled our feet back and forth and then I got up the nerve and I blurted out, 'Will you go out with me?' At that precise moment Robin stepped back and stumbled off the curb. Before she was able to answer she stepped into the biggest load of dog poop I'd ever seen.'"

"Dad, does every story you have include poop?"

"Yes Kels. You got a problem with that?"

"It's kind of disgusting but you can continue."

"Okay, where was I? Oh yeah, I was telling Jennifer, 'Kingsbridge Avenue hadn't seen poop this large since the days dinosaurs roamed the earth and there was Robin – ankle deep in a 5 pound monstrous turd. I thought to myself, 'What a perfect ice breaker, now maybe we'll loosen up!' I didn't consider Robin's feelings, I just thought it was hilarious.'

Robin smiled, 'Yes Kenny, I was so embarrassed and you just laughed.' 'Well, what could I do?' 'I don't know, you should have done something.' 'So Jennifer, here was Robin being asked out by the man of her dreams and she was ankle deep in crap; probably not how she had this special moment envisioned in her dreams was it Robin...'

Robin laughed, 'Keep on going, you're not doing a bad job, I'm not saying anymore.' I said, 'Okay, so Jennifer it was kind of like a bride walking down the aisle on her wedding day with a long stream of toilet paper stuck to her shoe – not what you girls dream of on your special days. As Robin stood in the street scraping her Pro Keds against the curb trying to get the poop off she eventually said, 'Yes'. I then asked her to go on a date with me. A skating date on Saturday Night at Kelton's Ice Skating Rink – Robin said, 'Yes.'

Asking Robin to go skating was a part of a bigger, well thought out, plan by us guys to bring our relationship to the next level before we got to the first. We agreed to ask out the girl we liked and if she said yes we'd ask her if she wanted to go to Kelton's Ice Skating Rink the following Saturday Night. But the plot was even thicker and more diabolical than this. The plot included walking our girlfriend home after skating and planting a wet one – BAM – right on her lips!'"

"Dad! I don't want to hear about this!"

"Relax Dookie Doo!"

"Okay but I'll leave if it's about kissing!"

"Okay, where was I? I was telling Jennifer, 'Our plan was to do a little kissy poo with our girlfriend. A maneuver some of us, not me but some others, claimed to have done before but which, I know, none had ever had the guts to do. To prepare for Saturday night we needed to have money to pay for both us and our girlfriends, we needed to decide what to wear, and we needed to work on our pucker – I'm sure all of our forearms and our mirrors got quite a workout in the preparation for the big night."

"Dad, I hope you're joking. You didn't really kiss your forearm – did you?"

"Well, all I can say Kels is that in some primitive Middle East and African cultures I would have been required to marry my forearm."

"Dad, you're really weird."

"Yes, I know Kels. So where was I? Oh yeah. I was telling you about telling Jennifer about our Kelton's date. So I said to her, 'All of us, both the girls and boys, agreed to meet on 231st Street and Godwin Terrace and then we'd walk to Kelton's together. We were standing together on the street corner about 15 feet away from the girls when everyone arrived and then we walked to Kelton's in our two herds. When we got there we had a great time skating. There's nothing better than an activity to loosen things up; especially an activity where you don't have to talk. We spent a lot of time showing the girls how fast we could skate in and out of the slower people. The girls, on the other hand, spent a lot of time giggling and holding hands while they skated around. They also spent a lot of time in the bathroom – together. I'll never understand what the deal is with girls and bathrooms.

Part of the plan was to bring enough money to buy the girls something to eat and so when the Zamboni came out to clean the ice I asked Robin, 'Can I buy you something from the snack bar?' She said, 'Sure, I'll have a Coke and some M&M's.' I turned and went to the snack bar for her snack – the plan was working out perfectly. We wanted the girls to feel obligated to give us a kiss after we spent so much money on them. I had my best lovey, dovey line all prepared, 'Come on baby give me some sugar. I bought you M&M's and a Coke baby doll won't you give me some loving. You know all the other girls are doing it. Come on baby don't you love me…?'"

Kelsie said, "Weird Dad!"

I asked, "Did it work?"

"Keep listening Cam and find out. I continued telling Jennifer, 'After the skating was over we decided to leave and go back to the neighborhood. As we walked back we again separated into the boy herd and the girl herd. The boys walked behind the girls and talked about the next part of their plan, 'Are you going to kiss her?' 'If you don't kiss her, you're a wimp.' The pressure was on us to either kiss our girlfriend or lie about kissing them. I wasn't about to lie about it. I committed to myself I would kiss Robin but I was TERRIFIED! I wasn't a kisser! I didn't even kiss my aunts or grandmothers at family get-togethers! Even worse, when I practiced on my forearm my 'forearm kisses' never made the 'smack' sound I heard on TV and in movies when a man kissed a woman. Even though I needed more forearm practice I couldn't go back to the guys the next day without giving it a try.

When our two herds got back to 231st Street and Godwin Terrace the girlfriends and boyfriends paired off and the boys asked the girls, 'Can I walk you home?' Robin said, 'Yes' to me and so we said, 'Bye' to the others and we walked up Godwin Terrace to Robin's apartment. You know where Robin lives and I knew her hallway was a perfect place to give her a kiss – it was secluded and romantic. As we walked to her apartment we could hear the soft rumble of the El train and city buses along with the sound of police and ambulance sirens in the distance. We could also smell the aroma of poop and urine mixed with engine exhaust – there was certainly love in the air that night.'

♪ Love is in the air
Everywhere I look around ♪
♪ Love is in the air
In every site and every sound ♪
♪ And I don't know if I'm being foolish
Don't know if I'm being wise ♪ [24]

Robin said, 'Oh boy, now you're going a little too far but go ahead Prince Charming.'"

"Why'd she call you Prince Charming?"

"Probably because I played Prince Charming in a St. John's Day Camp presentation of Cinderella when I was 12 – remember I told you that before!"

"Don't listen to him Cam. He's so fully of baloney!"

"It's true my cynical little girl. Anyway, I was telling Jennifer, 'As soon as we walked through the alley my body was shaking, my stomach was turning, and my heart was beating so hard I thought it was about to explode but I wasn't about to stop now! We walked through the hallway door to Robin's front door, I could hear Brownie behind the door growling – ready to attack any intruders, and then Robin turned around and gazed into my eyes…'"

"Gazed dad?"

"Yes, gazed Kelsie. She gazed into my eyes. Well, actually, maybe 'looked' would be more accurate than 'gazed' but hey – I'm trying to make it sound romantic.

Okay, I was telling Jennifer, 'When she looked into my eyes I thought to myself, 'Oh my gosh! What do I do now? Do I ask her to kiss me? Do I just wrap my arms around her and lay a wet one right on her lips – BUT WAIT – even if I want to do this – I don't know how to! Oh no!' Finally, I took a deep breath and decided to go for it! I puckered my lips, closed my eyes, leaned forward, and I kissed something, I was aiming for her lips but I wasn't sure if I kissed her lips, shoulder, cheek, forehead, or the wall. Not because you weren't a good kisser Robin. You probably were – it's just because it happened so fast. After I 'kissed' her I turned around and ran! I didn't even say goodbye, maybe I did, I can't remember. Robin said, 'You didn't say anything. You just ran!' I smiled and said, 'Thanks for clarifying that for me.'

'When I ran out of her hallway into the alleyway I jumped for joy because I finally 'kissed' a girl!! But at the same time, even though I think I kissed her I was disappointed because I knew the execution wasn't exactly flawless.' Robin smiled and said, 'That's an understatement if I've ever heard one. No, I'm kidding Kenny.' No matter what you say Robin I think it was a good try. If I received a grade on the kiss I would have been given an 'E' for effort and an 'N' for needs much improvement. When I walked home I sang a song to myself which I thought was appropriate for the night.

♪ I'm just a love machine
And I won't work for nobody but you ♪
♪ I'm just a love machine
A hugging, kissing fiend ♪
♪ Na, na na na na, na na na na, woo-woo-wooo…' [25]

Okay, let me take a break from this story. So you see Kelsie? This is why I don't want you dating Snickle Fritz."

"His name is Dylan!"

"Yeah, yeah, yeah. So you see what happens when you start dating when you're young – you step in a mound of poop, you go out with boys who kiss their arms, they expect a piece of booty just because they buy you a Coke and a bag of M&M's, and when they try to kiss you it all happens so fast you don't know if you've been kissed or head butted. Is this what you want? YOU WANT TO BE A POOP STEPPING, ARM KISSING, COKE DRINKING, M&M EATING, HEAD BUTTING LITTLE GIRL! Is this what you want?"

"You're so weird dad!"

My dad ignored Kelsie and continued his story. He said, "So Jennifer said to me 'That's too funny Kenny! So when did you and Jordan start dating? You know when I first came around I asked if you were going out with anyone and it was made very clear to me to stay away from you – you were Jordan's boyfriend. When I was told this I said, 'Okay, I was just asking, I'm not about to make a move on him.' So how did you and Jordan become such an item?' Robin said, 'Jennifer, don't ask him that! You saw how long the first kiss story was, the story about Jordan is longer, much longer!' 'Well, I thought that story was cute and what else do we have to talk about?' Robin said, 'I know, I'm just kidding. Go ahead Kenny tell us your Jordan story.'

I said, 'Okay, but remember I'm only telling you because you asked me don't blame me if I go on too long.

Well, I knew Jordan from 7th grade when she was dating Tony and I was dating Robin. As you know she was Robin's best friend. Even though I knew her I never really noticed her until our preparation for 8th grade graduation. For our graduation all the students had to walk down the center isle of St. John's Church in two single files – one line of girls and one line of boys. Jordan and I were lined up next to each other and had to walk down the isle together so during every rehearsal we were with each other. She was never in my homeroom class or any of my other classes; she was in one of the smarter classes. Still I was surprised I hadn't noticed her before school, during lunch, or after school but I didn't – at least not like I noticed her now."

"Dad! You're doing it again! You're talking about girlfriends!"

"Kelsie, would you stop and relax. I haven't told you any lovey, dovey stories yet but you're asking for it…" My father smiled and raised his voice, "…WHEN I LOOKED AT HER DURING OUR REHEARSALS I THOUGHT I WAS LOOKING AT AN ANGEL, SHE HAD BEAUTIFUL EYES, HAIR, AND THE MOST BEAUTIFUL SMILE I HAD EVER SEEN!"

"Dad!"

He smiled and lowered his voice, "Okay, so I was telling Jennifer, 'During graduation practice her ongoing joke with me was, 'Before you practice for the graduation ceremony shouldn't you be sure you'll be graduating?' She, of course, was referring to the Lake Hopatcong affair and how I still didn't know if I was going to be allowed to graduate. She joked with me, 'When you receive the book your diploma is supposed to be in you better check inside to make sure there's not a blank sheet of paper in it.' I also teased her but I can't remember about what. We teased each other every day we had our graduation rehearsal and this became the highlight of my day. At school I made sure to 'accidentally' run into her between classes so I could see her and talk to her.

When graduation day finally came, we were all dressed in our caps and gowns, waiting at the back of the church to enter and walk up the isle. Oh, by the way, Jennifer have you ever been in St. John's church?' 'No, I've never been in it.' 'Okay, well St. John's is large it holds about 2,000 people comfortably and on graduation day it was filled with the family of all the graduates. When the organ music started everyone began walking down the isle, Jordan asked me, 'Do you know yet if you'll receive your diploma?' I told her, 'I haven't asked – I'm afraid to.' We smiled at each other and began walking down the isle, past our parents, brothers, sisters, friends, and teachers. When we arrived at the front of the church the monsignor called our names, handed us our book, which was supposed to have a diploma inside, shook our hands, and then we sat in our assigned pew. When Jordan and I got back to our pew, she leaned over and asked, 'Well, did you receive your diploma?' I tried to act nonchalant about it but inside I was worried. I opened it slowly and there it was, 'Kenneth M. Hand, Graduate of St. John's Middle School, 1978'. She looked at me, gave me a smile and reached over and squeezed my hand. This took me by surprise and gave me a warm fuzzy feeling inside..."

"Dad! I'm telling mom!"

He was still smiling when he started singing another one of his oldie songs;

♪ I can't fight this feeling any longer
And yet Im still afraid to let it flow ♪
♪ What started out as friendship, has grown stronger
I only wish I had the strength to let it show ♪ [26]

"Dad, please stop singing. It's weird."

"Okay, so where was I? Oh yeah. So I continued to tell Jennifer the story, 'After the ceremony we went outside with our family and friends to have our pictures taken. After the pictures and congratulations were done all our friends made plans to meet for a party in the back of St. John's Elementary School later that same night. We planned on having a party with a lot of music, food, and drink. The plan was for the boys, Tommy, John, Billy, Mark, Pat, Tony, Scott, etc. to buy the beer. We planned to buy it from the Bodega on the corner of 230th Street and Godwin Terrace across the street from the projects.'"

"Dad, what's a Bodega? You might have told me before but I forget."

"Cam, a Bodega is a small Spanish grocery store which didn't mind selling beer to underage teenagers, at least when I was a kid, and so that was the place my friends and I bought beer. Okay, so where was I? Oh yeah. I was telling Jennifer about the night of graduation. I told her, 'That night we bought some Budweiser;

we picked up the beer at 6:00 p.m., the girls brought the food, and Scott brought the music. By 6:30 everyone started piling into the schoolyard; the schoolyard was locked up and so Tommy had to break out an industrial strength wire cutter. He cut a nice clean hole in the fence to make it easy for the girls to enter into the schoolyard; he was always quite the gentleman. Right Tommy?' Tommy put his head back down earlier and he was now half asleep. He groaned, 'Yeah, sure, is your boring story over yet?' I said, 'Go back to sleep. I'm almost done. So to get back to the story Jennifer – the beer, girls, and music were all there by 7:00 p.m. and the party was officially started.

Since I had never drank beer before, except when my uncles allowed me to take sips of their Schafer Beer at family get-togethers, I never acquired a taste for it. Actually, I hated the taste but I had to learn to like it because I was going into high school. The way I developed a taste for beer was unusual. I bought some bags of M&M's to cover up the flavor of the it. I put 4 M&M's in my mouth and then took a sip of beer. I probably drank two cans of beer that night but I ate more than 25 bags of M&M's. Even though I didn't drink a lot that night the beer gave me the nerve I needed to do something – something I was thinking about doing for several weeks."

"Dad, so this is when you started drinking?"

"Yes, this is the Underdog energy pill I mentioned to you before. This was the first time I realized beer could help me to relax and be more outgoing but it came with a price. Because of this I didn't need the peer pressure of my friends and in fact they didn't even know what I was thinking about doing.

The party had been going on for a couple of hours when a few of the girls came back from a trip to the bathroom together. I walked up to Jordan and asked her if I could talk to her. She teased me and said, 'Sure, but we've been talking all night.' I said, 'No, I want to talk to you by yourself, can we go for a walk together?' She said, 'Ok, but why?' I said, 'Because I want to ask you something. Do you know what I mean – I want to ask you something?' She reached for my hand and pulled me toward the fence opening and said, 'Sure, where do you want to go?' I told her, 'Nowhere in particular, just a walk.' We turned and walked out of the schoolyard, down the hill, toward 231st Street and we stopped and sat down on Robin's stoop.

When we sat down on the steps, I said, 'You know what I'm going to ask you don't you?' She said, 'Yes, but I want to hear it – you're not getting off that easy.' I said, 'Ok, will you go out with me?' 'What do you think my answer is?' 'I'm pretty sure you'll say yes but I'm starting to wonder. I hope you're going to say yes – I wouldn't have asked you if I thought you might say no!' She said, 'Well, I really like you – of course I'll go out with you.' She smiled, leaned over, and kissed me all over my face!'"

"DAD!! Stop or I'll tell Mommy!"

My dad was smiling, "Kelsie, I just said she kissed me all over my face. Can you blame her? Millions of women in this world would kill to have an opportunity to kiss me all over my face and she took full advantage of it…"

"DAD!!!"

"Okay, where was I? Oh yeah, I was telling you about a story I was telling Jennifer about a girlfriend of mine – I'm getting so confused. So I told Jennifer, 'She was sleeping over Robin's apartment that night and so we had a short walk to Robin's apartment – it was like 'déjà vu' all over again, only this time I was going to give her a kiss because I wanted to – not because of peer pressure – sorry Robin – no offense intended.' Robin smiled and said, 'None taken.' That was a Clint Eastwood movie reference but I'm sure you missed it Kels. Okay, when I walked her to Robin's door I leaned forward and this time I'm sure I kissed her – it was very romantic! But don't ask Jordan – just take my word for it. And by the way, I was singing again as I walked out of Robin's alleyway;

♪ When I need you
I just close my eyes and I'm with you ♪
♪ And all that I so want to give you
Is only a heart beat away ♪ [27]

Tommy said, 'Kenny, would you stop singing? I'm trying to sleep and I can't sleep with you singing that girly man song.'

Jennifer said, 'If you're so crazy about Jordan how come you two have broken up so many times? Robin chimed in and said, 'I'll tell you why – it's because Kenny's a flirt. When he has a few beers he likes to flirt with all the girls.' 'What!? What are you talking about? I've never flirted with anyone. Jennifer don't listen to Robin; this is an unfair rumor started by all the women I've scorned over the years! I don't deserve this reputation! Watch this…hey John…do I flirt with other girls?' 'Yeah, why?' 'Shut up John and go back to sleep! John doesn't know what he's talking about! I'm a one woman man! When I have a couple of beers I do become a little friendlier but that's it, just friendly, I don't flirt!' Robin said, 'Kenny, you ARE a flirt. Maybe you don't realize it but you are.' 'What are you talking about? Hey, Tommy, wake up! Tommy, do I flirt with girls?' 'Yeah, why?' 'What??? Go back to sleep! What are you guys talking about?'

Robin said to me, 'Alright Kenny – what about that Spanish girl from Kennedy who came to the party in Van Cortlandt park near the lake?' 'What girl?' 'The one you sat next to the whole night.' 'You mean the girl in my Spanish class?' 'Kenny, I don't know much about her all I know is you were flirting with her the whole night.' 'Well, I kind of remember her, a very smart girl as I recall. Why do you ask? Did I ask her out?' Robin said, 'No, I don't think so.' I said, 'If I'm thinking of the correct girl she helped me in my Spanish class. I was struggling and she helped me in 'Escuela'. You shouldn't confuse my need for help in school with flirting.' 'Oh yeah right, I saw her, she was very pretty. If she was a guy would you have asked for help?' 'Of course, if he could help me with Espanol!' Robin rubbed her chin and said, 'Oh boy Kenny!'

Then she said, 'Okay, how about that girl in your English Class, I think her name was Donna.' 'I'm sorry I don't remember a Donna.' 'Well Lori does, she says you sat next to her in English Class and you sure acted like you liked her.' 'Okay, let me ask you this – was she smart?' 'Kenny, I don't know!' 'Well now it's coming back to me – she was smart. She helped me to conjugate verbs. I needed help and she was a member of the English Club.' Robin raised her eyebrows and said, 'English Club…there's no such thing as an English Club in Kennedy!' I said, 'Yes there was and she was the leader of it. I needed help and she was kind enough to provide it to me. Our relationship was purely platonic!'

Then Robin asked me, 'And what about that girl named Linda? Was she your baseball coach?' 'No, what, hold it, who? You're confusing me now.' Robin said, 'I'm talking about a girl named Linda in your History class. Do you remember her?' 'I have to say the name doesn't ring a bell. Who is she?' She said, 'She was a girl from Riverdale who swore you were going to ask her out.' 'Wait, hold on! Was she the girl who was an expert on the French Revolution in my History Class?' Robin laughed and said, 'I don't know. All I know is the girls from Riverdale thought Linda and you were going out together.' I said, 'I have no idea what you're talking about. All I know is she was a history buff and we both agreed Robespierre was a tyrant. You see I've shot down all your claims of me being a flirt!'

Robin said, 'Oh wait I have more. What about Bronwyn?' I was exasperated and said, 'Okay, that's enough. I can tell you're going to continue to make up names of girls who I supposedly flirted with but you don't have a shred of evidence – let's change the subject!' 'Kenny, I never said you cheated; I'm just saying you're a big flirt.'"

"Dad, you don't still flirt do you?"

"Kels, I DON'T FLIRT! Not too long ago I was told I'm charming but that's very different from being a flirt – charming is good, being a flirt is bad.

Anyway, where was I? Oh yeah. As we talked in the car we continued to drive north on the New England Thruway; also known as 'up' to Tommy. During our conversations we drove past exits for Greenwich, Stamford, Darien, Norwalk, and Westport. Up ahead was exit 19, the Center Street exit going toward Southport. Tommy said, 'Get off here. This will take us to US-1, Post Road, and then we'll turn right on South Pine Road. It's not far from there, it won't be long.'

We got off and made a right on South Pine Road; it was a nice middle class neighborhood with tree lined streets and beautiful houses on both sides. We passed by a nice par 3 golf course as we got closer to Pine Creek Road where Jordan's grandmother lived. When we made a left on Pine Creek Road we could see the Long Island Sound through the trees, just past the houses. Pine Creek was a quaint neighborhood with smaller, well maintained one and two story houses with neatly manicured yards. The type of neighborhood young professionals discovered in the 80's turning many affordable middle class neighborhoods on the outskirts of the city into unaffordable Yuppivilles by the late 80's and early 90's.

Her house was a short distance down the street; it was a cute one story home maintained with meticulous care. The front yard had a small patch of green grass and several bushes including a large rose bush which leaned across the front windows. The driveway was eye-catching; instead of being paved it consisted of millions of tiny sea shells gathered from the Long Island Sound. We drove slowly by her house hoping Jordan would be outside or looking out the window; we didn't see her so I parked at the end of the street and we discussed how to tell Jordan we were here."

"Why didn't you text her?"

My dad smiled, "Cam, remember, we didn't have cell phones when I was growing up."

"Oh yeah, I forgot. Continue."

"It was about 8:30 in the morning when we parked down the street. Although we had only been on the road for a few hours it felt like much longer – in a good way.

Since it was early in the morning and her grandmother didn't know we were visiting we decided it would be best for Jennifer and Robin to go up to the door and ring the bell. Tommy, John, and I got out of the car, sat on the hood of the car, and waited. From where we sat we could see everything. After the girls rang the doorbell we saw the door open and out walked Jordan onto the front porch. I could read her lips, she said, 'Oh my gosh, I can't believe you really drove here!' There were a few hugs, some laughs, and then I saw her say, 'Where are the guys?' Robin pointed down the street toward us and when Jordan saw us she put her hands over her mouth, as if to say, 'I can't believe it!' She waved to us; my heart started going pitter patter."

"NO DAD! No more lovey dovey stuff!"

"Just a little more Kelsie – not too much. Alright, although I was tired from not sleeping the night before I now got my second wind. The girls gave us a wave inviting us to join them at the house. We got off the car and walked toward them. When I got to Jordan I gave her a hug and a big wet…"

"Dad! I'll leave if you tell me you kissed her again!"

My dad smiled as he said, "...I gave her a big, wet...high five. She said, 'Kenny, I can't believe you really did it. I can't believe you came to see me. I know you told me you would but I didn't think it was possible. I've missed you so much – it's not easy being away from my man, my strong, viral man…"

"DAD! First, I know she didn't really say that and I don't want to hear anymore lovey, dovey stuff! And by the way, don't you mean virile?"

"Viral, virile – what's the difference Miss Smarty Pants?"

Kelsie smiled and said, "I guess if YOU don't think there's a difference between a virus and being manly there's no difference."

My dad ignored her and continued, "So now that we made it to Connecticut we didn't know what to do. The whole time we focused on preparing for the trip and the trip itself; we never talked about what we'd do once we got there. Jordan pointed out there was a nice private beach down the road and we could spend the day there. This sounded like a good idea so we walked down the road to the beach.

We spent about an hour at the beach hanging out and we had some fun but at this time in my life I felt uncomfortable unless I was drinking beer..."

"Why did you always have to drink beer?"

"I don't know Cam. It's ridiculous but that's how I was. Like I've said before, I'm by nature a quiet, reserved person and at this time I didn't have a lot of self confidence. When I drank it took away my inhibitions and made me feel more outgoing and confident but, like I've told you before, it came with consequences."

"You don't drink now and you seem to be confident."

"Yeah well, God helped me a lot with that and I also think as you get older you learn to deal with your problems a little better. I read an inspirational prayer once, 'Lord grant me the serenity to accept the things I cannot change, the courage to change the things I can, and the wisdom to know the difference.' As a young boy I didn't have this attitude. I wanted to be more outgoing and confident and beer helped me do this. So, of course, it didn't take me long to say 'let's get some beer'. Before long we were all walking along the sandy road back to the car; to buy some cold beer.

Now keep in mind we were all 15 years old and unlike the Bronx where you could buy beer at the nearest Bodega without any I.D. we didn't know where to buy it in Connecticut so we all hopped into the car except this time it was with an additional passenger – Jordan. She showed us where the nearest store was – a left here, a right there, and about 15 minutes later we were at a medium sized grocery store.

We decided the guys would go into the store to purchase the beer. We walked up and down each isle not once or twice but three times but the beer was nowhere to be found. We didn't want to ask anyone because it might make us appear like we weren't old enough to buy it. On our fourth trip up and down the isles we found it.

Why couldn't we find it before? It was because the beer case was covered up by a large blue tarp. We thought this was a great idea; this grocery store covered up the beer case with a tarp to make sure the beer would stay cold. Tommy said, 'Tarps over the beer case – genius' these culchies.'"

"*Harry Potter* Dad?"

"Yeah Kels but with an Irish twist. Anyway, when we reached in and touched the beer it was ice cold. We decided to buy two cases of Budweiser, some ice, and a Styrofoam cooler. We loaded up the beer in our arms and marched through the store on our way to the cash register. As we walked through the store there were several old ladies who gave us disapproving looks. We thought the ladies might have thought we looked too young or maybe they were just morally opposed to alcohol. Whatever their problem was, it was their problem not ours, so we kept marching to the register.

We placed the beer on the conveyor belt and the woman at the cash register gave us a weird look and said, 'I'm sorry young men, we don't sell alcohol on Sundays.' I said, 'X-squeeze me – you don't do what? Come on now – am I on *Candid Camera*?' 'I'm sorry we don't sell alcohol on Sundays.' I said, 'Well, can you tell us where we can buy beer on Sunday?' 'You will have to buy beer in New York, we have the blue laws in Connecticut and no one can sell beer on Sunday.' Tommy said, 'WHAT? Are you kidding? Is this some type of a cruel joke? What is this world coming to when six, fifteen year old kids can't buy beer on a Sunday?' The woman just shrugged her shoulders so we had to carry the beer back through the store. On our way back we received more disapproving looks but we ignored them and we stacked the beer back in the case.

When we regrouped outside with the girls we had an important decision to make; do we go back to the beach without beer or go back to New York? We decided to go back to the Bronx but first we had to convince Jordan's grandmother to allow her to go back to the city with us. Jordan's grandmother was a German Immigrant with a thick German accent who loved the beach and couldn't understand why anyone would want to go back to the city instead of laying out at the beach. But eventually she agreed to allow Jordan to go back to the Bronx with us.

As we drove back Robin asked me, 'Kenny, what do you think your mother is going to say about you taking your bother's car?' 'I don't know, she likes Jordan so maybe she'll understand why I stole it. You know – I bet she won't say too much. My brother and father will be the one's who are upset.' 'So, why won't your mother be mad?' I smiled, 'Because I'm her favorite. She'll act like she's upset with me, because she has to, but she won't be.' Robin said, 'You're your mother's favorite – how do you know that?' 'I just know it. I can tell by the way she talks to me. Tommy and John are their mother's favorites too. I can tell I'm my mother's favorite for a lot of reasons. She's never missed any of my baseball, football, or basketball games. If you asked her she'd say she goes to all her kid's games and she loves all of us equally but she's just saying that. Just ask my brother's and sisters – they'll tell you I'm her favorite. Really, they'll tell you but another way I can tell is when I talk to her. You know when I get home from hanging out all night my mother usually waits up for me and when I get home we'll stay up and talk. My mom is very easy to talk to and I can tell she enjoys talking to me. I've told her I'm her favorite but she denies having any favorites; but like I said, she has to say that.'

Then Jennifer asked, 'But Kenny, what about Gena and Philip – aren't they your mother's favorites?' 'Well, they have a special place in my mother's heart but that's different.' 'Kenny, can I ask you a question, just a question, I'm curious – I hope you don't mind. What's it like having a handicapped brother and sister?' I said, 'No, that's okay, I don't mind you asking. Hmmm, I don't know, I've never really thought about it. I guess at home I don't think too much about it – they're just Gena and Philip to me. Actually, I guess it's great having them around at home because they keep things interesting. Gena is usually happy – but she does get mad sometimes – but she's still fun to be around. Philip is always a lot of fun to be around. Everyone in the neighborhood knows Philip. He spends a lot of time looking out the window watching people, waving at them, and saying hello.' 'Kenny, can he talk? I've never heard him talk.' 'Uh, I guess I'd say he can communicate very well but he can't really talk very clearly. Philip uses a lot of hand gestures, some sounds, and a lot of pointing. Living at my house is like living in a non-stop game of charades.' 'Whenever I see him at one of your games he always comes over and gives me a hug and kiss.' 'I know Robin. He has more girlfriends and gets more action than any guy I know. I think he's kissed Jordan more than I have. He's the real flirt in the family.'

Then Jennifer asked, 'What about Gena, I don't see her as much as Philip?' 'I know. Many people are surprised I even have a sister other than Chris and Tricia. But Gena is great too. She would rather spend her time in the apartment watching her soap operas. Gena is like a living 'Soap Opera Digest' – no matter how long you've stopped watching one of her soap operas if you're curious about what you missed she can get you caught up with all the details in a matter of minutes – she's extremely smart. She actually went to a regular school until she was in 3rd grade. I'm pretty sure it was 3rd grade. There's really nothing she can't do.' Jordan said, 'I'm sure she will be able to live on her own when she's older without a lot of help.' I nodded and said, 'Yeah, I think you're right. I think my mom said her intelligence and her ability to learn is at the level of a nine or ten year old but unlike other kids that age she'll always stay at that level – at least that's what the experts say but I don't always think the experts know what they're talking about.

The sad part about Gena, and this makes me cry if I think about it too much, is Gena realizes she's mentally handicapped. She doesn't say it all the time but just like all of us she gets down and depressed a little sometimes; when she does she talks about being 'retarded'. I think it happens on a monthly basis – it's probably one of those girl emotional times of the month things. We don't use the word 'retarded' in our family but Gena hears it at school and that's the word she uses to describe herself when she feels like this. She'll say to my mother, 'Why am I like this? I don't want to be retarded. Why can't I be normal like Chris and Tricia.' If Tricia is around when she feels like this she'll yell at Tricia and say things like, 'It's not fair you get to go out with your friends and I don't! It's just not fair!' It's very sad but she eventually gets over it – sometimes it takes longer than others but she always does.' Jordan asked, 'What do you do when she says it?' 'I guess I try to get her mind off of it. I try to talk to her about other things like Michael Jackson or her shows. She calls the soap operas she watches, 'her shows', and so I try to ask her what's happening on them. Sometimes it works but sometimes she says, 'Kenny, I don't know. Mom, why am I like this…' When that doesn't work I ask her if I can buy her a bottle of Coke because she loves Coke. She has a big plastic cup she fills up to the top with ice, she then fills it with Coke to the very top and she nurses it for the whole day while she's watching her shows. It's very sad and it makes me wonder why God allows people to be like this – not smart enough to be normal, whatever normal is, but smart enough to realize she's not normal – it just doesn't seem right. But, like I said, she's not like this all the time.

A Place in the Sun...

She is a lot of fun to be around most of the time – especially at Camp Venture. And if you ever see her at a wedding she is the life of the party.' Robin asked, 'What's Camp Venture?' I said, 'It's a day camp for mentally handicapped kids. My mother works there and was actually one of the original founders back in 1970 along with a bunch of other parents of handicapped children. Do you want me to tell you about it?'

"All three girls said, 'Yes', so I did."

Kelsie interrupted my dad's story and said, "So are you going to tell us the story about Camp Venture?"

My dad smiled and said, "Of course I am – it's part of my Connecticut trip story – so sit back and relax. So where was I? Oh yeah. I started telling them about Camp Venture. I said, 'Alright girls but first I need to kind of set the stage. You see before I moved to the Bronx, when I still lived in Suffern, I spent most of my summer days and my winter Saturdays at Camp Venture and Club Venture. These were places set up specifically for kids who were mentally handicapped.

From as early as I can remember Camp Venture was around but actually it was started in 1969 when I was about 5 years old. It was started by a few dozen parents of handicapped children in the Rockland County area – including my parents. They got together and started it because there weren't many places for handicapped kids to get together with each other to have a quote, unquote 'normal' life. Camp Venture's motto was *A Place in the Sun* and it really was – especially compared to the places the state had set-up for most mentally handicapped people at the time.

I can still recall the summer days when my mother, Richie, Gena, Philip, Christine, Patricia, and I loaded up into our car to drive to Camp Venture. We drove up Route 59 to the New York Thruway South, then we took the Palisades Parkway north to County Route 98, and finally we made a left on East Kirkbridge. When we made the left on East Kirkbridge we drove through Letchworth Village which was an institution for mentally handicapped people. Letchworth had a lot of trees and so when we drove through it, even on sunny days, the sun never shown through the trees. It was a very dark, dreary, and depressing place. It was very disturbing to drive through Letchworth Village, especially for me when I was five, because all I saw were handicapped men and woman sitting on benches rocking back and forth or groups of handicapped adults being walked, in single file, from one building to the next. It was at about this time the movie *Night of the Living Dead* came out and this short drive through this horrible place reminded me of the zombies who roamed the countryside in the movie.

Although the drive was short it made a lasting impression on me because these special men and women seemed to be going through the motions of life without living. I never saw any 'normal' people, except for the workers who were dressed in white uniforms, and I never saw anything that could be mistaken for happiness or joy.' Jordan asked me, 'What do you mean?' 'I mean nobody smiled, nobody laughed – they were like zombies. I have no idea why human beings would create such a horrible place like this. Maybe it was a good place when they started it but when I drove through it – it was a sad, depressing place.

Letchworth village was in stark contrast to Camp Venture. Once we passed through Letchworth village the trees opened up, the sun shown through, and you came to a sign which read, *Camp Venture – A Place in the Sun*, and it was a place in the sun – both literally and figuratively. There were people everywhere; boys, girls, young kids, teenagers, older kids, counselors, mothers, fathers, and they were all alive, vibrant and having a great time! The camp had three swimming pools; two in-ground and one above ground. They had a main building where the offices were, and there were several pavilions where they held arts and crafts, finger painting, sang songs, practiced for the camp play, played sports, and did all the things 'regular' kids do at camp. It was truly an inspirational environment; I was inspired by the counselors who always seemed so smart, strong, and nice – even in the most difficult circumstances.' Jennifer asked, 'What do you mean? What did they do?' I laughed and said, 'I don't know if I should tell you girls this story. I don't want you to get the wrong idea.' Jordan said, 'Well you have to tell us now.' 'Okay, I'll tell you but I'm not making fun of anyone; the point of the story is how loving and caring the counselors were and how innocent the campers were.' 'Okay, we'll keep that in mind.'

'Alright, here it goes. It happened one day at Camp Venture when Chris and I were on the swings in the playground. Chris and I saw several of the counselors running to the pavilion where the campers got dressed to go swimming. The pavilion had a bathroom in it and so it was also used by the campers to go to the bathroom and like I said the campers were always laughing and so happy but some of them were also curious – some more than others.

This one particular day one of the more curious campers just finished finger painting in the Arts and Craft Pavilion and apparently he enjoyed finger painting so much he decided to continue while he was in the bathroom. But this time instead of using paint and paper – he used his poop and his body..."

Kelsie stopped my dad and said, 'This proves it Cam – daddy doesn't have any stories which don't include poop."

My dad laughed and continued. So I was telling the girls, 'After he was done finger painting he was covered from head to toe in his own poop.' Jennifer said, 'Ewe! What did the counselors do?' 'The counselors had to clean him off. If I was one of the counselors – I would have handed back my minimum wage check and walked home but not the Camp Venture counselors. They had so much patience and strong stomachs they cleaned the camper from head to toe. When I watched them hosing him down they laughed and joked with the camper BUT they did it in a really nice way. They did it in a way that didn't take away his dignity.' The girls laughed and Robin said, 'How does a person covered in their own poop keep their dignity Kenny?' I nodded my head and said, 'I know what you mean but you know what I mean. The counselors had an amazing ability to make these campers feel like someone special – even when they were covered in their own poop."

"Dad, can I interrupt you?"

"Sure Kelsie."

"I need to ask you something. Do you have a poop fetish?"

"No. Do you know what fetish means Kelsie?"

"No, not really, but I think you have one."

My dad shook his head and continued with his story, "I told the girls, 'Even at such a young age I was inspired by the counselors but I was also inspired by the campers because they didn't have a hateful bone in their bodies. They only knew two emotions – happiness and love. My brother Richie, Chris, Tricia and I could expect to be hugged and kissed every time we ran into one of the campers who were, 'just happy to see us'. Everyone from the person who cleaned the camp, to the counselors, to the Camp Administration, to the parents, to the campers were 100% behind Camp Venture and it showed. So that's Camp Venture or at least what I remember about it.' Jordan said, 'That's a really nice story Kenny. You obviously really liked Camp Venture and I can see why.'

After we finished talking about Camp Venture we were still driving down I-95 on our way to the Bronx. It was at this point I noticed the gas tank was near empty. In 1979 there was an OPEC embargo which caused there to be long lines at gas stations and some gas stations ran out of gas and had to shut their doors. This made the search for gas difficult as we drove around town looking to fill the tank.

The first gas station which appeared to be open was a Shell Station; there were lights on and people appeared to be working and so we pulled up to the pump. At this time there was no such thing as 'Self Service' gas stations. So I parked the car and waited for the Gas Attendant to come up to the car and pump gas; we waited, and waited, and waited. I got out of the car and walked inside and asked, 'Are you guys open?' The attendant said, 'We're out of gas but the station across the street might still have some.' I said, 'Thank you' and I walked to the car and told everyone, 'Get in, we're going across the street.' I pulled away for the pump a little too quickly and before I knew it I had a problem! Around most gas pumps are concrete pillars to protect them from being hit by vehicles and this day they did their job. When I pulled around the pump I cut the steering wheel too sharply and the car side swiped one of the pillars making a nasty screech – it sounded like finger nails scratching a chalkboard. I cringed and didn't want to get out of the car to look at the damage. John and Tommy got out and looked at it; when I saw their faces I knew it wasn't good and so I got out, took a deep breath, and peeked through my fingers. The pillar ripped a gash in the door about two feet long and 4 inches wide. There was no way to fix it; I'd have to buy a new door.

I was distraught and sick to my stomach when I thought about what I'd done. How would I explain this to my mother and father but most importantly – how could I ever explain this to Richie? The girls got out of the car and they all rallied around me and tried to comfort me but there wasn't any comforting me at the time. This was the first time I thought this trip might not have been the greatest idea I ever came up with. We all got back in the car and I carefully drove across the street and before we were able to pull up to the pump an attendant walked toward us waving his arms saying, 'We're out of gas!' So our search for gas continued.

We decided to get on the highway because we noticed gas stations along the highway on our way to Connecticut. A few miles down the I-95 we saw a sign along the highway for a gas station so we pulled off the interstate. As we approached the exit we could see cars lined up for as far as our eyes could see but we had no choice we needed gas. We waited in line for about 45 minutes and when I finally pulled up to the pump I was about 8 feet away from it. For some unknown reason I was nervous about pulling too close to those little pillars. A nice older African American gentleman was the gas attendant and he had a look on his face which indicated he doubted whether we were old enough to drive. He came close to the car and looked inside the window at all of us and said, 'There's no way anyone in this car is old enough to drive but how much gas do you want?' I said, 'Fill her up Sir.' The gentleman was shaking his head as he pumped gas into the car. When he finished I said, 'Thank you' in my most sincere voice, I paid him, and we quickly pulled away nervous he would call the cops on us.

When we got on the highway I was still worrying about what happened to the car door and how I would explain it to my brother but then a song came on the radio which helped me forget my problems at least for a few minutes. Tommy turned up the radio and we started singing to Lynyrd Skynyrd's Free Bird…

♪ If I leave here tomorrow, would you still remember me?
For I must be traveling on now ♪
♪ There's too many places I haven't seen
And if I stayed here with you now ♪
♪ Things just wouldn't be the same
Well I'm as free as a bird now ♪
♪ And a bird you cannot change [8]

As we got back to New York we reconsidered going back to the neighborhood – instead we decided to go to Tibbett's Brook Park where we knew our friends would be. When we arrived in the park we had to drive past the Park Rangers so we had to be careful not to arouse any suspicion otherwise they might call the police. We got in without any problems; we parked the car, walked through the park, and entered the pool at about 1:30 p.m. When we walked into the pool we were greeted by our friends like rock stars. I didn't enjoy the rock star life for too long because I was exhausted. I fell asleep on one of my friend's towels and I didn't wake up until later that afternoon.

After I got some rest I went swimming for a little while and then we decided to drive back to the neighborhood. When we reached Godwin Terrace I dropped off the girls and Tommy at the top of the hill and John and I parked the car around the corner. When I pulled around the corner I drove directly into a space on the left side of the street – in other words the car was facing all the other cars parked on the street. John told me, 'Kenny you can't park like this.' I said, 'Why?' 'Don't you know you can't park facing the other cars. Look at all the other cars – none of them are facing the same way you are.' So I said, 'Okay' and I made a u-turn and pulled back up the street and I again pulled directly into a space on the left side of the street. John said, 'Don't you get it? You can't park like this. You have to face in the same direction as all the other cars on the side of the street you are parked on!' 'That's ridiculous. Who told you that?' 'Kenny, it's just the way it is.' He got out and pointed me in the direction I was supposed to park.

After I parked the car we walked back up the street, past the front of St. Johns up to the O'Grady's stoop. I was sitting there for a few minutes and then someone suggested we walk down the street to the Bodega for a six pack of beer. But before we could do anything my brother pulled up outside the stoop. He raced out of his van and screamed, 'Kenny, where's my car?' I used the calmest voice I could muster and said, 'What do you mean? I haven't seen your car.' My brother gave me a look like there was no way he believed me but he got back in his van, drove down the hill, and made a left on Kimberly Place where I had just parked his car. I told everyone sitting on the stoop, 'When he comes back tell him I ran down the hill' and I proceeded to race into the building, up the steps, and on top of the roof so I could watch my brother from the safety of the building's roof.

As I stood on top of the roof, looking over the ledge, I saw my brother's van screech around the corner, right back to the stoop. I saw Richie jump out of the car looking to catch me. I watched him but couldn't really hear what he was saying but based on his gestures and his facial expression he had murder on his agenda. As I watched him pull away in his van I knew I couldn't go home – I'd have to wait until my brother's anger subsided which might take one or two…decades…"

"Dad, were you eating the lamb again?"

My dad smiled, "Yup Cam, I was eating the lamb or as some people put it – I was living on the lamb.

When Richie pulled away in his van I knew it was safe to come down from the roof to join my friends again. By now, the story of our road trip to meet Jordan in Connecticut had spread throughout the neighborhood like wildfire and so no parent was willing to provide sanctuary for me. Luckily for everyone else they didn't need a sanctuary; the girl's parents never found out about the trip and Tommy and John, although they received a verbal scolding from their mothers they didn't get in big trouble – 'At least [they] didn't steal a car.'

On the other hand, I had major problems; I didn't have clothes to wear, money for food, a shower, a bathroom, or a place to live and since it was getting late I needed to come up with an idea fast! Everyone sitting on the O'Grady's stoop tried to come up with solutions. Jordan said, 'What about Ron Meathead's house – won't he let you stay there?' I said, 'I'm not staying there after the 'Ron's Hole Affair'!' Then Jennifer asked, 'Do you have any relatives?' I said, 'Yes, but how am I going to explain to them why I need to stay at their house? Plus, none of them live nearby.' Then it hit me, 'Hey, what about the O'Grady's cellar?'

Mr. and Mrs. O'Grady were the Supers of the building directly across the street from St. John's Grammar School – they were both Irish immigrants who both still spoke with noticeable brogues. Since the O'Grady's were the Supers they had the unpleasant job of chasing us off the stoop when they received complaints from the tenants. Early on we complained about being chased off the stoop and being told to turn off the radio but once we got to know the O'Grady's we began to love and respect them. Mrs. O'Grady was like a second mother to the girls in the neighborhood and to me. She called me 'Her adopted son' and so maybe, just maybe, she could find it in their heart to let me live in one of the storage rooms in the apartment building basement?"

"You lived in a storage room?"

"Hold on Cam. I'm getting to it. Where was I? Oh yeah. Now, a storage room in the basement isn't exactly a room at the Waldorf Astoria; it didn't have carpeting, air conditioning, or a window; it did have cracked concrete floors and walls, sweating pipes and corroded wires running along the ceiling, cobwebs in every corner, cockroaches the size of small mice, and mice the size of small dogs. But there was one room which would be perfect to double as a bachelor's pad – it was Mary's club house. Mary and some of the other girls occasionally hung out in the room, especially during the winter months, and drank beer, smoked cigarettes, and listened to music. Mary and Bernadette were Mr. and Mrs. O'Grady's daughters. Mary attended school at St. John's with me and we were good friends; Bernadette lived most of her life in Ireland with relatives but she came back during her teenage years to live with her parents and Mary. Her room was furnished in the finest 1970's clubhouse décor; it had a recliner chair, a roll away bed, TV, fan, and a record player. If Mr. and Mrs. O'Grady were kind enough to allow me to stay in the basement maybe they would also let me use their shower in the morning. If they gave me the okay, I would be set; I'd have a shower, bathroom, a place to live and money – wait, I haven't told you how I would get money. You can't live in a bachelor pad without money. Hold it. Did I tell you about the 'The Meat Market Scam.'"

"No."

"Okay good. So let me move on to the next part of the story. Alright, I was able to be totally honest with Mrs. O'Grady. I told her the whole story about the trip to Connecticut, the accident, my brother, and the bounty on my head. Mrs. O'Grady immediately said, with her Irish brogue, 'Oh, Kenny, Kenny, Kenny, I can't believe my adopted son would do such a thing but I would do anything for you – of course you can stay with us!' This was the beginning of a strange phase in my life – a 14, or was I 15, year old boy living on my own. My first night on my own was sweet, it was a long tiring day but I ended it in style. I took Jordan to the Greek Diner on Broadway for dinner; we ordered a couple of greasy cheeseburgers, some fries, and two cokes. When our food and drinks came out I raised my glass and said, 'Here's to my beautiful girlfriend, our great friends, and to Mr. and Mrs. O'Grady.' Jordan raised her glass and tapped mine and said, 'Here's hoping your brother never finds you!'"

Kelsie asked my dad, "Did you really do that toast?"

"Well, not technically but I'm sure we were both thinking it. So where was I? Alright, even if we really didn't have a toast like this it was still a nice night. After dinner I walked Jordan to Robin's apartment, said goodnight, and walked up the street to my new bachelor pad."

"Thank you for not mentioning any lovey, dovey stuff!"

My dad smiled and said, "Opps, I forgot to, but don't worry there's more coming up. Okay, let's see, where was I? Oh yeah, on my way to my pad I stopped in the O'Grady's apartment to thank them again for allowing me to live in their basement and to use their bathroom. Mrs. O'Grady let me in and I stayed up for about an hour talking to her about the day's festivities; I then excused myself and went to my room. When I got to my room I unlocked the padlock, opened the door, walked in, and pulled the string to turn on the light. The only clothes I had to wear were on my back; I sat down on the bed, kicked off my shoes, pulled off my shirt and tossed it on the chair. Then I reached up to turn off the light, and I laid down on my back. I couldn't sleep so I decided to listen to a record to help me unwind. I leaned over and reached for the record player, turned it on low, and listened to my favorite Styx song as I slowly drifted off to sleep...

♪ Oh Mama, I'm in fear for my life from the long arm of the law
Law man has put an end to my running ♪
♪ And I'm so far from my home
The jig is up, the news is out ♪
♪ They finally found me... [16]

I woke up the next morning with the record still spinning and the needle scraping back and forth on the center of the album.

My sister Tricia, who was attending St. John's day camp at the time, was very upset about me not coming home. Apparently she heard the angry conversations between my parents and Richie about some terrible thing I did and how I wasn't coming home. On Monday, after day camp ended, she went to the O'Grady's stoop where several of the girls were hanging out. When she walked over to the girls she began crying when she asked, 'Have you seen my brother Kenny? If you have please tell him to come home! I miss him and I don't want anything to happen to him!' The girls got up and one of them sat Patricia on her lap to comfort her. She continued on, 'I made him this peanut butter and jelly sandwich for him to eat; I don't want him to starve to death. Can you tell him, if he comes home, I promise never again to tell anyone he makes muscles when he looks at himself in the mirror! He's the best brother a girl could ever have!'

After comforting Tricia, the girls told her, 'Wait here, we'll be right back.' They walked into my Love Shack, I mean Bachelor Pad, I mean Mary's clubhouse, I mean the storage room, and told me, 'You need to come out and talk to your sister! She's outside crying because she's so worried about you! She's so worried and loves you so much she even brought you a sandwich – she is so cute.' I was hesitant at first because I wasn't sure what to say to her but I walked out and I saw her sitting on a window sill of a basement level apartment. I walked over, sat next to her, smiled, and said, 'Hi Trish, how you doing?' She said, 'Kenny won't you come home? I miss you and I don't want anything to happen to you!' I said, 'Relax, take it easy. You don't need to cry, I'm doing fine.' She asked me, 'Why won't you come home?' I told her, 'Well, I did something very bad. I stole Richie's car and I took it to Connecticut with some friends of mine and to make it worse I tore up the left door of the car. Richie is very, very mad at me and I just want to wait until Richie is no longer mad at me before I come home. I'm sure he'll get over it and I'll be able to come home soon.' She said, 'You can come home now, Richie won't be mad, I promise!' 'Patricia, Patricia, Patricia, you know how Richie loves his cars and how mad he gets when someone hurts them. You should have seen how mad he was when someone threw snowballs at his van – he was about to fight fifty guys on his own. Also, don't you remember when Karen keyed his car?' Tricia said, 'I'll talk to him to make sure he doesn't do anything to you – I promise he won't hurt you!' I said, 'I know, I know, but I want to give him a little more time before I come home. Don't worry, I'll be home soon and I'll be fine.'"

"Dad, Aunt Tricia was so cute."

"She was Kelsie, she really was. Anyway, then I said to Tricia, 'What do you have in the bag?' She reached for the bag and offered it to me. 'Kenny, I made you a peanut butter and jelly sandwich because I know you don't have any food to eat. Here, you can have it, it's for you.' I smiled, reached for the bag, opened it up, pulled out the sandwich, and took two bites and said, 'Mmm, Mmm, Mmm, this is the best peanut butter and jelly sandwich I've ever eaten. Did you make it yourself?' She nodded her head 'yes'. I continued on, 'Can you do two things for me? Since you make the best peanut butter and jelly sandwiches – can you keep bringing them to me every day? Also, can you go home and bring me some clean clothes?' She wiped the tears out of her eyes and said, 'Yes, sniff, sniff, sure.' I then told her, 'You better get home before mommy starts wondering where you are and gets worried.'

True to her word, she visited me every day with a sandwich in her hand until I returned home.

Over the next three weeks I lived in my basement apartment and went to work at Walbaums when I was scheduled and I made some extra money when the situation presented itself..."

"What do you mean you made some extra money when the situation presented itself?"

"Well there was the 'Walbaums Meat Market Scam', the 'Raffle Ticket Scam', and 'Pizza with the Fireworks Scam' – all of which will need to wait until you're older or I'm on my deathbed before you hear them but I can tell you about 'The Love Shack'...

The Love Shack...

"We can't hear about meat, raffle tickets, or pizza but we can hear about the love shack – you seem to have a warped sense of what's appropriate for young children to hear."

"Good one Kels. Well, for better or worse, I'm going to tell you this story. My new bachelor pad became the hangout for me and some of the guys and like any good bachelor pad I tried to take advantage of it. I attempted to turn it into my own little LOVE SHACK! This is what I called it when I was talking to my guy friends; I never mentioned it in front of the girls.

♪ Love Shack, Love Shack Baby (Love Shack Baby)
Love Shack, Love Shack Baby (Love Shack Baby) ♪
♪ The Love Shack is a little old place
Where we can get together...♪ [28]

John and I were hanging out in the 'Love Shack' one afternoon and I said, 'You know this is a great place to live but what's the fun of living on my own if I don't take advantage of it.' 'What do you mean?' 'I mean, this is like my first bachelor pad and I haven't even had Jordan over by herself yet. I don't know if she would come over by herself but wouldn't it be perfect if we invited Susan and Jordan over? We could pickup some beer, we could play some music, we could dim the lights a little, and who knows what might happen; remember I have a bed and a recliner! What do you think John? Isn't it perfect for a nice small, intimate party?' John said, 'I agree it's perfect but do you think they'll come?' 'I think it's worth a try. What's the worst thing they can do, say no.' 'Or slap us in the face and break up with us.' 'True, but that's a chance I'm willing to take.' John smiled and said, 'Okay Kenny let's give it a shot. When do you want to do it?'"

"Dad I told you I don't want to hear any lovey, dovey stuff and this is more than lovey, dovey! This is gross!"

"Don't you see Kelsie? This is what guys do. Guys only have one thing on their minds – doing kissy face with girls!"

"Not all of them Dad!"

"Okay, maybe not all of them – only the ones who like girls. I'm sure the guys you watch on 'Say Yes to the Dress' don't think this way."

"Dad!"

My dad continued, "So I said to John, 'Let's invite them over tonight? Jordan and Susan are usually out by about 6:30 or 7:00. We can call them and ask them to meet us here. We have enough time to pickup the beer and clean this place up a little.' Then John said, 'Make sure you kick those roaches near you under the bed. Also, those little black bugs – what are they?' 'I don't know. I just noticed them yesterday when Mr. O'Grady woke me up when he was hosing down the alley way with steaming hot water.' Then I said, 'Okay John, do you want the recliner or the bed?' 'I'll take the bed. I'm more experienced than you.' I said, 'Yeah right, in your dreams? But how are we going to make sure Susan sits next to you on the bed and Jordan sits next to me?' 'I think we need to tell them where to sit. We'll just have to say, 'Jordan you sit next to Kenny on the recliner and Susan you sit next to me on the bed." 'What?? We can't say that!' 'Why not?' 'What do you mean 'why not' – I don't know. I just know if we say 'sit next to me on the bed' we'll sound like we only have one thing on our mind.' He said, 'Yeah, so, isn't that all we do have on our minds?' 'Yeah but we can't make it that obvious because Jordan will flip out especially if you and Susan are here. We have to be more subtle.

We need to keep it simple. What if we do this – let's put something on the bed so there's only room for one person to sit on it and then we won't have to worry about them sitting together. I just don't really have anything to put on the bed. All I have is the pair of pants standing in the corner, two pairs of underwear I wore last week and a few smelly shirts. Hmmm, wait, I got it. We can put the stereo on the bed, no, no, how about we put a bunch of records on the bed. Yeah, let's put the records on the bed – we'll spread them out.' 'Yeah, that's perfect Kenny. Then when they come in we both stand up and ask them to sit down. Only one of them will be able to sit on the bed and the other will have to sit on the chair. We'll let them pick where they want to sit and then we'll sit down next to them!' We both nodded our heads feeling pretty good about ourselves. Next we went to work getting the beer and cleaning the room – especially the little bugs we didn't recognize.

Later on that night the 'Love Shack' was ready. The beer was chilling on ice, the room was as spotless as a basement bachelor pad could be, the records were strategically placed on the bed (leaving just enough room for one girl to sit down), John replaced the light bulb with a dim 20 watt bulb, and we waited patiently for our lady friends. When the ladies got to my room they knocked on the door and I said, 'I'll be right there.' I took a half step to the door and opened it to greet them. I said, 'Hi Jordan. Hi Susan. How are you? I'm glad you two could make it – come in.' They both stood there in the doorway but before they walked in they looked around the room; they looked at the beer, the bed, the recliner, and then they looked at John and me. They squinted their eyes partly because the lighting was so dim but also because they were suspicious about being invited to my 'Love Shack'. As they stood there looking over the situation they listened to the song on the record player, a Rod Steward song, 'Tonight's the Night'.

♪ Stay away from my window,
stay away from my backdoor too ♪
♪ Disconnect the telephone line
Relax baby and enjoy this time ♪
♪ Tonight's the night [29]

The girls looked at each other, slowly shook their heads, pursed their lips, and said, almost in unison, 'Kenny, John what are you two trying to do?' I said, 'We thought you both would like to spend time with just the two of us for a while.' Susan said, 'John, why is it so dark in here? Did you change the light bulb to make it darker?' 'Uh, um, no, ish. Not really.' He got himself together and said, 'I'll tell you what, instead of standing there, why don't you sit down and make yourself at home?' Jordan stepped into the room and looked at the album playing on the record player, 'Hmmm, 'Tonight's the Night'. Kenny, I'm curious – do you know what this song is about? Do you have any idea?' I quietly responded, 'Hmm. I'm not really sure. I think it's about having a good time. Like, 'Tonight's the Night' to have a good time.' She smiled as if she didn't quite believe me and said, 'Oh really, is that what you really think? I think it means a little more than that – don't you? What is going on in your mind? What do you think you're going to be doing tonight with us in here? My guess is 'Tonight's NOT THE Night' for what you think it is. I don't mind hanging out here with you but if you think 'Tonight's the Night' here in this basement room, with spiders and roaches, and some small black bugs over there, sorry, I think you're going to be a little disappointed. Don't get me wrong, this is a great 'bachelor pad' or what do you call it – oh yeah – I've heard you call it the 'Love Shack' – but tonight is NOT the night.'

She continued, 'Yes, Kenny, this place is great but, NO, tonight's not the night – not here, not now, and not with John and Susan three feet away from us. Sorry to disappoint you.' She said this with a little smile on her face with her eyebrows raised. I tried to defend myself, 'What are you talking about – we just wanted to spend time with you two…' She now had a smirk on her face, 'Oh, I'm sorry. I must be letting my mind and common sense run wild on me.' I said, 'I guess there's no getting through to you. We were just trying to show you how much we care for you. What's wrong with that?' 'Kenny there's nothing wrong with THAT. Where are we supposed to sit down? Was the PLAN for me to sit on the bed or the chair?' 'The chair.' She said, 'You guys are too funny.' I was starting to get upset, 'You're making it sound like we had this all planned out.' 'Oh, I'm sorry, you didn't have it planned out? Now that is really funny!' She chuckled to herself and said, 'Are you saying ALL you want to do is show us how much you care about us? Susan, what do you think?' Susan said, 'I'm sure they want to show us how much they care about us. I'm just wondering how they were planning on showing us.' They both laughed but we weren't as amused. Susan said, 'I think they want to show us 'how much they care' while I'm on the bed and you're on the recliner.' Jordan said, 'Susan, funny, that's exactly what I was thinking too.' Then they both walked out."

"Dad, they really put you in your place!"

"Kelsie, yes they did. So you see? Doing kissy face with chicks is the only thing boys have on their minds."

"No Dad, not all boys, only you and your weird, desperate friends."

My dad ignored her and got back to his story, 'John and I stood there for a second perplexed by what had just happened; we were partly mad but mostly disappointed. When we eventually walked outside we saw Jordan and Susan with the rest of our friends. When I got close I looked at Jordan as if to say, 'Can you come here so we can talk?' She raised her eyebrows, turned her head a bit as if to say, 'Okay, if you have those ideas out of your mind we can talk but only if they're out of your mind.' She walked over to me and leaned up again the car I was standing by. I said, 'I'm sorry I just really wanted to show you how much I care about you.' She said, 'It's okay, I think, but I'm not going sit down and make out with you, or whatever you wanted to do, while John and Susan are doing the same thing five feet away. I thought you knew me better than that.' 'Okay, I know it was a bad idea but wait – are you saying you would have liked it if it was just you and me?' Now I had a big smile on my face. She smiled back and said, 'I guess you'll never know.' 'Wait, the night is still young. Is it too late to try it again but this time with just the two of us?' She just laughed and shook her head.'"

"Dad, you got denied!"

"Yup Cam – denied! But I picked myself up and brushed off the dirt. I'm sure I tried and tried again because Kels, THAT'S WHAT BOYS DO!' My dad smiled as he said this.

He continued, 'Okay, so over the next few weeks my life continued on; living in my bachelor pad, working at Walbaums, and hanging out with my friends. My life really wasn't too bad for a 14 or 15 year old living on my own...until a very unfortunate incident occurred causing the life I had made for myself to come crashing down around me. Keep in mind my bachelor pad was near the alleyway where the tenants in the building placed their trash and so there were occasionally rodent and bug problems, in fact, Mr. O'Grady frequently had to hose down the alleyway with hot water in an attempt to kill the fleas that tended to collect near the trash. One morning, after weeks of wondering what those small, black bugs in the room were – I finally found out.

About three weeks into my stay I woke up in the morning scratching myself on my arms, legs, and then all over my body. I rolled out of bed, turned on the light and looked at my body and I was covered from head to toe with little black bugs – fleas! If ever I screamed like a girl it was then."

"You screamed like a girl?"

"No, not really but I wanted to. It freaked me out! I ran out of my room to the alleyway and into the O'Grady's house wearing nothing but my Fruit of the Looms. I raced into the O'Grady's bathroom, tore off my underwear (again, it sounded like Velcro), jumped in the shower, and began scrubbing and scrubbing and scrubbing. Because of the fleas I decided it was time to go home and face up to my responsibilities. Later on that day I called my mother and asked her if I could come home. She said, 'Yes, come home now!' With my flea experience I wasn't as worried about my brother's temper – after all, how much could a few blows to the head with a bat hurt? When I returned home I didn't see Richie for the next few days; when I knew he was home I did my best to avoid him.

YOU SEE KELSIE! YOU START DATING, THEN YOU STEAL CARS, YOU WIPE POOP ALL OVER YOURSELF, YOU DRIVE INTO GAS TANK PILLARS, THEN YOU END UP LIVING IN A BASEMENT, EATING PEANUT BUTTER AND JELLY SANDWICHES, WHILE YOUR DIRTY UNDERWEAR IS STANDING IN THE CORNER, AND YOU HAVE FLEAS ALL OVER YOUR BODY! IS THIS WHAT YOU WANT?!"

"You're so weird Dad!

So when will you tell us the meat, raffle tickets, and pizza stories?"

"I really shouldn't tell you these stories because they took place during a time in my life when I was totally lost and searching for meaning. I didn't know where to turn to and how to find it; I just started drinking more and more and I engaged in more and more destructive behavior. I think I did these things while I was looking for meaning but maybe I was just trying to be cool – who really knows.

I'll tell you a few stories about this destructive behavior. The funny thing, not 'ha ha' funny, but funny, is that I still thought I was a good kid while I did these things.

You know, come to think of it, I'll need to leave out the pizza story – I'll go to my grave with this one."

"Why?"

"Because I'm ashamed of it."

"Why?"

Kelsie, "I just am. I did a lot of bad things during this time in my life. Things which could have put me in jail if I got caught; it took me a long time to forgive myself for doing some of these things. I hope the people who knew me at this time have forgiven me. I'll tell you a couple of these stories because maybe it's good for you to hear some of the bad decisions I made and some of the bad things I did. Hopefully, it will show you how important it is to forgive people and to never give up on them because there's hope for everyone – even when it looks like there's no hope. In the end I turned out alright..."

Kelsie smiled and said, "That's debatable Dad but go ahead – I want to hear these stories."

SECTION VII
Crime and Punishment

♪ There I was completely wasted, out of work and down
All inside it's so frustrating as I drift from town to town ♪
♪ Feel as though nobody cares if I live or die
So I might as well begin to put some action in my life ♪
♪ Breaking the law, breaking the law [44]

The Sting – In the Bronx

"…I received a call a few days later from someone who worked at Waldbaums asking me if I could come in for an interview. The interview went well and they needed cashiers so I was hired on the spot.

Waldbaums was one of the two big grocery stores in the neighborhood. It was right down the street from my apartment building across Broadway in a little strip mall along with Peppinos, a Chinese restaurant, and Chase Manhattan bank.

I was hired as a cashier but not the type of cashier they have nowadays; I was a cashier when a CASHIER was a CASHIER. We didn't have these fancy schmancy scanners like they have now – NO – we had to key everything by hand – AND WE LIKED IT! Back then to be a cashier you had to smart and fast! It was a skilled job; kind of like a surgeon or a nuclear physicist…"

"Really Dad?"

"Don't believe him Cam. He's making this up."

My dad looked at me and said, “Yes, really Cam, ignore little Miss Curmudgeon over there. You see Cam, we had to do everything manually – we did everything the scanners now do automatically. We picked up the item, read the price tag, key entered the department code, and then we key entered the price of the item.”

“Sounds tough DOCTOR…”

My dad reached over and gave Kelsie a punch on the shoulder and continued, “Okay where was I? Oh yeah. Waldbaums was always jam packed with shoppers and so we had to be fast to move people through the long lines quickly. Accuracy was also very important, however, since we key entered items so quickly – errors were common. Because of this the women kept a sharp eye on the amount the cashier ‘wrung up’ to make sure they weren’t over charged. When a cashier inadvertently over-charged an item the customer very quickly pointed out the error, ‘Oh, excuse me young man – you overcharged me for that item. It says $1.09 and you charged me $1.19!’ Some errors were made in the customer’s favor, however, human nature being what it is; these errors were not pointed out with the same frequency and fervor.

I was about 15 when I worked at Waldbaums. I already stopped going to school and so keep this in mind – it was one of the low points of my life.”

Kelsie laughed and said, “Awe, poor Daddy. We feel so bad for you. I bet you’re going to tell us you were feeling so low you robbed the store?”

My dad looked surprised. “Oh. I didn’t realize I told you this story already?”

“No! No way! You’re not going to tell us you robbed the store – are you?”

“Well, not exactly but…kind of. This is where I worked when I stole my brother’s car and drove to Connecticut to meet my girlfriend; I needed extra money to survive.

An idea how to make some extra money came to me one day when I accidentally key entered $4.99 for a $34.99 package of meat.

I realized I made the mistake when I was putting the meat in the brown paper bag. I turned to the lady and asked her if I could see the receipt and before she handed it to me she said, 'You know I think you might have under charged me.' She gave me her receipt and there it was $4.99 next to the meat category. The woman seemed a little embarrassed, which surprised me, she paid the additional $30 and left. It took a little while before I realized the woman knew I made a mistake but she didn't say anything because she wanted to save $30!

Then it struck me – most people would do the same as this woman! Most people would pretend not to notice being undercharged even though they watched it happen. And just like this woman, once it was pointed out to them they would quickly pay because they were embarrassed by what they were doing.

So from my honest mistake I came up with an idea to dishonestly raise extra money to help me survive living on my own. I only did it a few times but this is how my money raising scheme worked. When I noticed a woman put an expensive piece of meat on the conveyer belt I put the scam into action. Now keep in mind, people watched the prices they were charged with a sharp eye – especially the expensive cuts of meat! I rang up the inexpensive items first; ching, ching, cha-ching, and then I pushed the items behind me into the bagging area. When I grabbed the expensive piece of meat there was no ching, ching, cha-ching – it went ding, da-ding. I always made sure I missed just one number; if the meat cost $24.99 I rang up $4.99 or $2.49 and I pushed it behind me into the bagging area. I always noticed the woman watching the register as I key entered each item. When I missed one of the numbers the woman's reaction was interesting. Out of the corner of my left eye I could see her look at the piece of meat, then at the price on the cash register, then back at the piece of meat, and then back to the cash register. I could almost read the woman's mind, 'Did he just forget to charge me for the meat? Am I about to save myself $30? Is he going to realize he didn't charge me? Should I tell him?' Without exception the woman NEVER pointed out my 'mistake' even though it was obvious the bill was $30 less than she knew it should be!

Although it was a despicable thing for me to do and I'm ashamed of it I did find the people's reaction to be very interesting. I'm not sure what it says about people but I'm sure it's not good.

Anyway, where was I? Oh yeah. After I rang up 'all' the items I turned to the woman and said 'that will be $1.39 Miss' or some other amount which was significantly less than it should have been. Interestingly, she pulled out $2.00 and paid me, I opened up the cash register and gave her $.61 in change – and I left the drawer open. Now, at this point I could hear her mind screaming, 'Yes, I am going to save $30! I know I should say something but it's not my fault he didn't charge me for all my groceries! I bet I've been overcharged before and so now we're even! Plus if he realizes his error I can say I didn't realize it.'

The last part of the scam was when I turned around to bag the groceries. I put everything in the bag except the meat. When I grabbed the $30 piece of meat I held it up, looked at it, I put a quizzical look on my face, and said to the woman, 'Hmmm, I don't remember charging you for anything that cost $30.' Invariably she said, 'Really? I was wondering why it was so inexpensive.' Again, this was my low life scam but it was amazing to me how these people lied about not noticing.

I said to the woman, 'I'm sorry. That will be $30.' She handed me the money and since my cash drawer was still open I put it in my drawer without ringing it up and she left without asking for a receipt because she was embarrassed. I put the $30 in my pocket when I counted out my drawer at the end of my shift."

Kelsie said, "That is just terrible. Terrible! You teach Cameron and me to never lie, cheat, or steal but when you were our age you were a thief, a thug, a punk, – a common criminal! I'm afraid to ask but was this the only time you ever stole anything?"

"Yes, I know – I was a punk but I needed money to survive."

"So, did you ever do anything else like this?"

My dad had a look on his face like he was caught picking at the Turkey before Thanksgiving dinner. He said, "Yeah, a few other things like this."

"Like what?"

Crazy Eddie's Raffle Tickets

"Okay, so have I ever told you how Pat and I were sports fanatics when we were growing up?"

"Yeah Dad, you told me you two played basketball, stickball, and road skateboards all over Kingsbridge everyday from early in the morning until dinner time."

"Okay, I just wanted to make sure. Well, this next story started when Pat and I were both about 16 years old. I think Pat was a junior at Sacred Heart High School and I was…I was…um…I was in between jobs."

♪ Yeah, I'm sitting on this bar stool
Talking like a [darn] fool ♪
♪ Got the twelve o'clock news blues
I've got too much time on my hands ♪
♪ Too much time on my hands [45]

"Nice song Dad but are you sure you were in between jobs or could it have been you were in between temporary furloughs from – PRISON?!!!!"

"Cam, I don't know where I went wrong with Kelsie. She used to be so cute, so nice, so sweet, so loving but she's become so judgmental! So where was I before I was so rudely interrupted by 'Miss Holier Than Thou'?!!! Oh yeah, I was starting to tell you how Pat and I were playing basketball behind St. Johns when a couple of Tricia's friends came up to us and told us they weren't going to have a basketball team because they didn't have a coach.

When we heard this we discussed possibly coaching the team ourselves. We knew it would be very unusual for teenagers as young as Pat and me to be allowed to coach the team but there was a chance because we came with impressive credentials. Pat played for St. John's in grade school, Sacred Heart in high school, and later on he played college ball for Mount Saint Vincent. I also played for St. John's, I made the Catholic All Star team which was scheduled to travel across Canada – did I mention that before..."

"Yes, you mentioned it before but you didn't tell us the whole story."

My dad gave a little smirk and he said, "I'll save that story for another time. Okay, where was I? Oh yeah, credentials. Yeah, I also played for the St. John's CYO Team.

Even though we had impressive credentials it was still unlikely we would be allowed to coach young, impressionable boys but we decided to ask. We scheduled a meeting with Father McCarthy, who was responsible for school sports at the time for St. Johns. During our meeting with him we made our case; we discussed our credentials, our approach to coaching, and the fact we were ready, willing, and able to handle this responsibility. It wasn't an easy decision for Father Mac because of our age. Young boys need positive roll models and it wasn't clear two 16 year old boys were right for the job. After a few days of consideration, Father Mac agreed to take a chance on us. By allowing us to coach the team he put a tremendous amount of trust in us. Pat and I took this trust very seriously and we did our best to coach the team and positively influence the boys on the team – at least initially. Wait, I take that back. I started out strong initially but lost interest later on; Pat, on the other hand, did an excellent job from the time we started until the end of the season.

After we were given the reigns of the team there was a lot of work to be done. First of all, there was administrative work, such as making sure all the students knew there would be a basketball team, scheduling tryouts and practices, working with the league leaders on the game schedule, distributing uniforms, and figuring out the logistics of getting the team to away games. In addition to the administrative aspects of coaching there were long nights reviewing game film, reading scouting reports, and developing game plans."

"Cam, don't believe this. You know Dad didn't review game films. They didn't even have cameras when he was 16."

My dad ignored Kelsie and continued, "So after a lot of administrative work we had tryouts and once we selected our team we had some of the toughest practices known to St. John's basketball to prepare for the upcoming season. Since Pat played high school basketball he usually came up with the practice schedule and ran most of the practices.

The early practices went well and the first few games of the season our team was very competitive but winless. As the season continued our losses mounted and my original optimism started to wane. Instead of learning from our mistakes and working on the team's weaknesses to improve our chances of winning future games I lost interest. I let the kids scrimmage most of the time during practices. Sometimes I split the teams up by race during practice which at the time I thought would make for a more interesting practice – BAD IDEA! When I look back on it I don't know what I was thinking. Even though all the kids on the team were really nice – when I did this the games got heated and I had to break up several fights!"

Kelsie jumped up and said, "WHAT? I CAN'T BELIEVE YOU WOULD DO THAT!"

"I know, I can't believe I did it either. By the way, I don't think Pat was at these practices – I doubt he would have supported this approach. Okay, I need to get back to the point of the story. About 2 months into the season Christmas was approaching and like I said earlier, 'I was between jobs' and so I didn't have any money for Christmas presents. I had to come up with a way to raise money for the noble purpose of buying Christmas presents for the needy…"

I said, "You had to buy presents for the needy? Like who?"

"Well, maybe I shouldn't say I had to buy presents for the needy. Maybe I should say I had to buy a Christmas present for my girlfriend, who just happened to be needy. She needed me!"

"Good one Dad."

"Yeah that was pretty good wasn't it? So I had to buy presents for all the needy people around me but I didn't have any money. And since all the money I borrowed from my parents was spent on... um...on...um...on nightly refreshments I couldn't ask them for more money. So, since I didn't have any money coming in I needed to come up with a creative way to raise some money

It took me a few days to come up with the perfect fund raising idea. I have to admit, it was a creative money making scheme but just like my Waldbaums idea it wasn't exactly the most moral or ethical scheme I ever came up with. In fact, I'm pretty sure my fund raising scheme violated several federal and state statutes – but that didn't discourage me from implementing it.

The idea involved my basketball team; so I called a team meeting to make a few announcements. First, I announced to all the kids I was going to purchase new uniforms for the team and we'd have a team party at the end of the year. In order to raise the money necessary for the uniforms and the party, I told them they had to sell some raffles tickets. I said, 'You only have to sell fifteen raffle tickets each – which should be easy. All you have to do is knock on a few doors in your apartment building or go down to the local bar and you'll sell them all in a matter of minutes.'

Prior to the meeting I met with a local printer, who printed raffle tickets for Kingsbridge Little League, and I ordered 15 books of raffle tickets with 15 raffle tickets in each book. The raffle tickets read, 'St. John's Basketball Team Raffle, Fund Raiser for New Team Uniforms, 1st Place – 12 Inch Color TV, 2nd Place – Panasonic Radio, 3rd Place – Spalding Basketball, $1.00 Each, Raffle Drawing – January 15th.' The actual raffle tickets cost fifteen dollars to print but they were donated by the printer, well...sort of, and therefore if all the tickets were sold we would have raised more than $200.

There were three differences between this fund raiser and typical fund raisers; first, the prizes were not donated by local businesses, secondly, the winning tickets would never be selected, and finally, there was no intention of using the proceeds from the sale of the raffles for uniforms or a team party – they would go to a different worthy cause – the Kenny Hand Christmas Fund.

When Pat heard about my plan he said, 'Let me get this right Kenny, you are planning on having these kids sell fake raffle tickets for you and you're going to keep all the money! You can't be serious! Kenny, you do what you want – but keep me out of this – I don't want any part of it!' I said to Pat, 'I'll split the money with you' but he turned and walked away with his arms up in the air and said, 'No thanks, keep me out of it.'

A week after I passed out the raffle tickets trouble began. A couple of the players began questioning me about the raffle. One boy asked, 'Kenny, who donated the TV, radio, and basketball for the raffle?' Another boy asked, 'Where and when is the party going to be and what are we going to do at the party?' When I answered their questions they stared straight into my eyes and didn't say anything other than, 'Hmmm, interesting. So your Uncle, who works at Crazy Eddies, donated the TV and radio. Hmmm, very interesting. And you're saying we are going to have a party at Gaelic Park and there will be food, drinks, and music. Ok. Hmmm. Interesting.' It was clear to me my answers weren't quelling their skepticism. Some of the boys insinuated, BEHIND MY BACK, the raffle tickets were a money making scam – CAN YOU BELIEVE THE NERVE OF THESE KIDS – AFTER ALL I DID FOR THEM!"

"But wasn't it a way for you to make money?"

My dad smiled, "Yes, but they didn't know that! I couldn't believe how ungrateful these rotten kids were after all I had done for them!

Well, the kids were the least of my problems because a few days later, before practice, as I was waiting in the gym for the kids to show up to practice one of the boys from the 230th Street Projects walked in with his mother. When she got close to me I noticed her lips were pursed together, her left eyebrow was raised, and she had an annoyed look on her face as she said, 'Mr. Hand?'

I said, 'Yes mam, I'm Kenny Hand.'

She looked at me and said, 'My son indicated this raffle might not be on the up and up and so before I give you money I want to talk with you face to face to ask you if it's legit. In case you don't know, I'm a single mother and where I live I can't have my son walk door to door selling raffle tickets because it's too dangerous and I AM

NOT going to send him into a bar – and so this money came right out of MY pocket and so this better not be a scam! I will be a very angry woman if it is! So tell me, why are you raising the money?'

I explained to her we are trying to raise money to buy the kids the newest state of the art uniforms and if there's money left over we'll have a party.

She then continued, 'When will the drawing take place? I would like to be there.'

'Oh, well, I am planning on having the drawing up stairs in the school auditorium.'

She continued to dig further and further; I responded by laying it on thicker and thicker.

'Where did you get the TV, radio, and basketball to raffle off?'

'I have a relative who works at Crazy Eddies and he donated the TV and radio, and I was given a basketball for my birthday which I'm donating to the cause.' I thought to myself – BAM take that lady!

'When is the drawing?'

'It says it right on the raffle tickets, January 15th.'

I thought to myself – Keep bringing it lady – I aint afraid of you!

She gave me a skeptical look as if to say, 'You know, that I know, that you know, that I know, you are running a scam and if I catch you – you'll regret it!'

I then assured her that this was a legitimate fund raising activity, which it was – sort of. Then I told her, 'I will call you when we get closer so you can be a part of it.' I thought to myself, and by the way – you don't want a piece of this lady!

Even with all the concerns from the players and parents the money began to trickle in – I even found it in my heart to extend the deadline for handing in the raffle money for several kids without it adversely impacting their playing status – I was very compassionate.

I think we raised a total of $150 for the Kenny Hand Christmas Fund. When January 15th came and went the kids on the team asked, 'What happened to the raffle? I thought you were going to select the winning tickets on January 15th.' I said, 'I'm glad you brought that up, I was actually planning on telling everyone about it after practice is over.'

After practice ended, I brought the kids together and announced, 'The new uniforms were ordered and will be available in time for next year's season and unfortunately because all the raffle tickets weren't sold there isn't enough money for a team party. Also, the winner of the TV was an old lady from Bailey Avenue – she loves it. The radio was won by some old man from 238th. And some Irish guy from The Liffy won the basketball – you wouldn't know them... ok, practice is over, see you on Tuesday."

"Dad, there is no way this story is true. No way! Cam, don't believe him."

My dad shrugged his shoulders and said, "Well Kels, maybe it's a good thing you don't believe me. I know it doesn't sound like a very nice thing to do and it wasn't. That's why I started to search for a legitimate job where I could earn money the honest way – OFF THE BOOKS."

I then asked my dad, "Do you have anymore stories about stuff like this?"

The Bumble Bee

My dad stared up toward the ceiling for a second and said, "Yes, but before I get to it I need to tell you something else.

Did I ever tell you about the first woman I fell in love with?

"No Dad! I don't want to hear it – it's not right that you loved anyone other than mommy!"

"Oh Kelsie get over it. Okay, here it comes."

"I'm not listening Dad!"

"Alright, the first time I laid eyes on her it was love at first site. When I was given permission to take her out for the first time I didn't want to take her home – no – I wanted to stay out with her all night long. That first night – I took her everywhere with me – we went to Sam's Pizzeria for dinner, we went to Cold Cut City to purchase a six pack of Molson, I took her to Godwin Terrace to show her off and to meet my friends. She was so beautiful all the guys were jealous of me – they wanted to take her for a ride!"

"DAD!"

"Oh Kelsie – get over it! I was in love. I took her to my favorite bar –Off Broadway. To me, everything about her was perfect – sure, she had been around the block a few times and I wasn't her first and I wasn't her last but for me, an inexperienced sixteen year old, she was perfect!

For a young teenager the first time you do it can be very awkward and scary. I thought I knew what I was doing; I dreamt about this for a long time but until your first time you never really know what it's going to be like. I was worried I'd put my hand in the wrong position, maybe I'd turn my head right when I should have turned it left, or maybe I'd stop when I should have gone forward, or maybe I'd go when I should have stopped. Of course I knew things would get better with experience but the first few times can be embarrassing especially if someone else is looking while you're having problems. Another problem is that back in the 1970's nobody used protection…"

"DAD!! I'm leaving!!"

"Kelsie, you and Cam need to hear this. I could have used protection but it was a pain to put it on – especially after I got in and got going. I mean after you get going who wants to stop to put on protection.

"Mom!!!! Do you hear what Daddy is telling us??"

"My first love was born in 1972 and in her younger days she had an awesome body – her body was smooth and shapely – but by the time I became intimate with her she was starting to show signs of aging; this didn't matter to me because looks didn't mean everything to me, I just wanted to be able to depend on her through all kinds of weather and all kinds of situations.

I was very thankful she was dependable – but she had her needs – first of all she had an insatiable appetite. Her appetite cost me a tremendous amount of money on any given night – and the longer we stayed out together – the more she wanted me to spend on her. Then there were the pet names – now, most people don't like admitting they have pet names for the love of their life – but I'm proud of the pet name I called her. I didn't come up with the name, actually one of my best friends, Billy, came up with it when we took her on an afternoon trip to Rockaway beach. We were riding her across the Tri-Boro Bridge on our way to Shawn's Aunt's Bungalow and Billy said, 'I got it, she's yellow, she makes kinds of a buzzing sound when she goes over fifty miles per hour – let's call her 'The Bumble Bee'!

'The Bumble Bee' was my first love – a 1972 Ford Maverick – my first car. The Bumble Bee was the greatest $160 investment I ever made; it was the most dependable car I ever had, it wasn't much to look at but its overgrown lawnmower engine never failed to start. Unlike the fancy cars of today, it had character – its yellow paint was faded to a dull off-white, rust covered the front and back ends, the two front doors were corroded all the way through, and the floor in the back seat was rusted out. In other words, your feet could touch the pavement on the street like Fred Flintstone.

The only problem with The Bumble Bee was that she required gas to run and tires to drive on – and they both cost money which was a problem when I was between jobs.

I remember one particular Friday night my friends and I had plans to go to Rockaway the following day but the Bumble Bee needed new tires. It had not one, not two, but three flat tires – and if my gum gave out it would have needed another one. Since I was between jobs I didn't have enough money to buy them so my friends and I had to come up with a solution to this problem.

I think it was Shawn who came up with a solution. He said, 'I just came back from Gaelic Park where I watched one of Tommy's Irish Football games. There's a service station right across the street and there is a yellow Ford Maverick which looks exactly like The Bumble Bee. We all looked at each other without saying a word; then one by one we began to smile.

I said, 'Sounds good to me but how can we do it?' Shawn said, 'We can use my father's jack and the milk crates in the back of St. John's. We'll jack up the front, right side of the car, take off the tire, and put a milk crate under it to keep it up. We'll do the same thing to all four tires and The Bumble Bee will have a lifetime supply of tires.' I said, 'Well, I know the street outside of Gaelic Park is deserted at night and so I don't think anyone will see us do it.' Shawn said, 'Exactly, if four of us go we can have the tires off in about five minutes and then we can roll them back here where we'll put them on The Bumble.

Mark stopped us and said, 'Let me get this straight – you're going to steal the tires for the Bumble Bee from a car that is parked in a service station across the street from Gaelic Park?! Are you guys $#%^& crazy? I'm not doing that!' I said, 'That's the only way we'll be going to Rockaway tomorrow – without the tires we'll be hanging around here in the school yard.' Mark shook his head and said, 'You guys are crazy.'

By 9:00 p.m. it was dark and so we walked down Godwin Terrace, made a left on 231st Street, a right on Erwin Avenue and walked the eight blocks to Gaelic Park. When we arrived at the corner of Ervin Avenue and 239th Street we stopped and regrouped.

The service station was only about twenty-five yards down the street and so we looked to see if there was anyone in the area or if there were any cars driving around – there were neither.

Mark had agreed to go with us but he decided to wait on the corner to keep watch in case anyone walked or drove by. All of us other guys walked to the service station; Shawn jacked up the car, John unscrewed the lug nuts, and I pulled the tires off and put the crates under the wheel drums. We decided three tires would be enough. The whole operation was amazingly quick and easy; Jeff Gordon's pit crew couldn't have done a better job. Within five minutes the four of us were bouncing three tires down Ervin Avenue, up 231st Street, back to Godwin Terrace where The Bumble Bee was fitted with three new tires – 'Mission Accomplished!'

♪ The machine of a dream
Such a clean machine ♪
♪ With the pistons a pumpin
And the hubcaps all gleam ♪
♪ When I'm holding your wheel
All I hear is your gear ♪
♪ When my hand's on your grease gun
Oh it's like a disease son ♪
♪ I'm in love with my car
Gotta feel for my automobile ♪ [35]

"That's terrible Dad!"

"I'm not done yet."

"You have more? You did more bad stuff?"

Rockaway

"The next day we went drove to Rockaway but I was still short on cash; I had to come up with a way to raise money for gas, food, and beer. I occasionally borrowed money from my friends but I didn't like to so I generally tried to raise money on my own – remember 'The Sting' and 'Crazy Eddie's Raffle Tickets.' But this day I needed some seed money so I asked Scott for $2.00. I told him I'd pay him back later on in the day. He asked me, 'How are you going to pay me back today?' I smiled, nodded, and said, 'Just trust me, I'll pay you back!'

Rockaway was a run down beach about an hour away from Kingsbridge; it was the lower-middle class version of the Hamptons. Although it wasn't a very popular place to go at the time it was still difficult to find legal parking spaces near the beach. When you found a space it usually required you to put coins in the meter several times a day – a real pain in the neck if you wanted to relax on the beach.

There was an empty private lot across the street from the beach; it was covered in tall weeds and garbage. When we got to the beach I dropped my friends off near the boardwalk and I drove to the local Woolworths. I bought a magic marker and a poster board; then I drove back to the empty lot. I drove my car into the empty lot and wrote on the poster board, 'ALL DAY PARKING – $5.00.' I then stood at the curb for about an hour and I waved cars into my parking lot and about forty-five minutes and ten cars later I had $50 in my pocket."

"You didn't really do this did you dad?"

My dad smiled and said, "Would your daddy lie to you?

After forty-five minutes I walked across the street to the beach, I paid Pat his $2.00 back, and I had enough spending money for the weekend."

Kelsie was sitting there shaking her head, "I can't believe my father is a criminal!

SECTION VII!
Is This The Real Life?

♪ Is this the real life
Is this just fantasy ♪
♪ Caught in a landslide
No escape from reality ♪
♪ Open your eyes
Look up to the skies and see ♪
♪ I'm just a poor boy
I need no sympathy ♪
♪ Because I'm easy come – easy go
Little high – little low ♪ [30]

Ron's Party

"My dad continued on the subject of dating for a while since Kelsie was still interested in dating Dylan. He was convinced she should postpone dating until she was older and so around this time he told us a story...wait...I have to be honest...he didn't actually tell us this story in the exact format you'll read below. I took a little artistic license in retelling it. The story you'll read is a combination of the story my dad actually told Kelsie combined with a story I vaguely overheard him and his friend Tommy discussing when we visited New York a couple of year ago.

"Okay, I know you still need to be convinced not to date boys at such a young age. Do you want to hear what boys really, and I do mean really, have on their minds?"

"No, not really, but I don't think I have a choice. Go ahead."

"Okay Kels, I've told you about Ron before right?"

"Is he the coach who let you workout over his house and put a gun to your head because you mixed up his socks?"

"Well it was actually because he thought we stole his money, but that's the guy. Okay, when I was a little older Ron moved from Sedgwick Avenue in the Bronx to a small house on an eighth of an acre of land in Yonkers. It was a very nice house with a one car garage located in the backyard about twenty feet behind the house. It had five rooms; a living room, dining room, kitchen, bedroom, and one room set-up for lifting weights – it also had a basement and an attic he 'finished' after he lived there for several years.

Ron, Tommy, and I remained friends over the years, even after the 'Ron's Hole Affair' and all the pranks we played on him. Although we remained friends, Ron decided it was better not to allow us to use his house for weight lifting and working out. This edict lasted for a couple of years until one day when Tommy, Mark, and I were hanging out on the corner of 231st and Godwin Terrace.

Ron drove by in his El Camino; when he saw us standing there he stopped his car to say hello. Since we didn't have much to do that day, except to stand around drinking beer, we decided to be especially nice to him, because we planned on asking him if we could workout at his house. At first Ron said, 'Absolutely not, what do you take me for, Hand? I've learned my lesson with you and your friends.' But after a while of talking he let his guard down and made a decision he surely regretted later. He said, 'I'm going on a three day tour at the Fire House, and it starts at 6:00 tonight so you guys are welcome to work out for a couple hours until I leave. Come on, hop in.'

Tommy and Mark opened the passenger door of the El Camino and jumped in. Since there wasn't enough room for me in the front I jumped into the back bed of the El Camino and lay down. When we got to Ron's house we went straight to the weight room and started lifting. Ron offered us some Lipton Iced Tea to drink while we were working out, but he also said, 'That's all I can offer you because I haven't been to the grocery store and what's in the refrigerator is for my dinner when I get back on Monday.' We worked out focusing mainly on the bench press, and we had a competition to see who could lift the most. Mark was the biggest and strongest of the three of us; he was able to bench press 275 pounds, Tommy maxed out at 255, and I 'benched' 205 pounds – which I was proud of since I only weighed 150 pounds at the time.

While we were lifting weights Ron was outside most of the time taking care of his yard and washing his car, but later he came in to wash his dishes and to vacuum the carpet in the living and dining room. As you might remember – Ron was a very particular person – some would say neurotic when it came to cleanliness; everything had its' place and everything had to be in its place – if something was even slightly out of position he could tell. He was so particular he vacuumed his carpet in a certain direction so all the carpet fibers laid north to south. He was strange in this way, but he wasn't a bad guy, actually he was very nice. Ron was always good to us kids even though he shouldn't have been.

After a few hours of lifting weights, drinking iced tea, and watching TV – Ron came into the weight room and said, 'Alright guys, I need to leave, and you know what that means – you gotta leave too.' Probably as a result of him getting along with us that day, he made a friendly gesture and said, 'But I'll tell you what; you guys can stick around a while longer if you clean up and lock up the doors when you finish – it's up to you. Of course you'll need to walk to the City Line and take the 20 Bus back to the Bronx.'

When Ron told us he was 'going on a three day tour and we could finish lifting weights as long as we locked up when we were done' my mind started going wild! I thought to myself, 'We have the keys to a house that will be empty for three days – three whole days – YES!!! It's Saturday night and you know there will be a million people who would love to come over for a party!!' Even though this is what was going through my mind I stood there calm, cool, and collected and acted like a responsible young man. I looked over at Tommy and Mark and wondered what was going through their minds. When I looked at Tommy – he lifted his left eyebrow, and I thought I noticed a slight nod of his head – as if to say, 'Yes, Kenny…I know…but keep calm until Ron leaves'.

We tried to act as calmly as possible in front of Ron; I told him, 'Thank you. Yes, we'll workout for a little while longer, clean up, and then we'll lock up, and walk to the bus stop. Thanks Ron, we really appreciate it – and we won't let you down – I promise. When we leave the house it will be spotless – just like you left it.

Ron said, 'You're welcome Hand – you little prick. Hey Tommy, I'm taking my pickup truck to work, but the El Camino is blocking me from getting out. Can you pull out the El Camino into the street so I can pull out?

Tommy said, 'Sure, where are the keys?'

He said, 'They're hanging on the wall next to the refrigerator.' Tommy grabbed the keys and walked outside to the driveway and as Ron walked out he said to me, 'Hey Hand, remember, no funny stuff! I'm trusting you.'

I said, 'Ron, have I ever given you a reason not to trust me?'

Ron looked at me, squinted his eyes, and said, 'You don't really want me to answer that do you Hand?' Then he turned and walked out the door.

After Ron pulled out of the driveway Tommy pulled the El Camino back in, walked back in the house, and said to me, 'So are you guys thinking what I'm thinking?'

Mark said, 'What?'

'I'm thinking we have an empty house, it's Saturday Night, and none of us are going out with anyone. I think we need to invite some girls over for a party!'

Tommy and Mark looked at me, smiled, and Mark said, 'Sounds good to me but are you sure? Isn't Ron the man who took you guys to Ron's Hole and put a gun to your heads?'

I said, "Yeah but he wasn't serious – at least I don't think he was. He wouldn't kill us…right Tommy…he wouldn't kill us…would he?'

Tommy said, 'I don't think so, but if we have a party here and he finds out he might kill us. I wouldn't put it past him, and I wouldn't blame him. But I think it's worth the risk. I say we do it.'

Since none of us were going out with anyone we had to decide which girls to invite. Once we figured out who the 'lucky girls' would be we had to figure out how to get them to Ron's house. We also needed to buy beer and some food; luckily we had some money, and there was a grocery store and a pizza shop right down the street.

We came up with a short list of girls to invite, Tommy and Mark wanted to invite two girls from the neighborhood, and I wanted to invite this one girl I had dated before, but I wasn't even sure if she would talk to me."

"What was her name dad?"

"Cam, I don't know. I dated so many chicks; how could I ever remember all of their names?

"Really?"

"Not really. So where was I? Oh yeah, so we finally decided who the 'lucky girls' would be; Robin, Jennifer, and Natalie. We also decided to invite John and Susan because we needed a way to get the girls from the neighborhood to Ron's house – and we knew John would make it happen.

It was around 5:30 when I called John at his apartment and told him our plan. I asked John if he could call the girls and meet them on 231st Street to take a cab to Ron's house. John said, 'I don't need you to tell me how to do it – just tell me where and when and I'll have the girls there. You just worry about having cold beer and something to eat – I'll take care of the rest.'

I said, 'John this can't be a big party – we want it to be a small intimate party – if you know what I mean. We'll have four girls and four guys; make sure no one else comes. You know what we're hoping to do at this party – don't you?'

'What do you think I am – an idiot? Don't worry – I've got it covered.'

I then said, 'Call the girls and then call me back – Ron's number is (914) 867-5309. It's 5:35 what time do you think you'll call me back?'

John said, 'I don't know. I'll call you when I call you. It won't be long; I'm going to call Susan right now.'

While John and I were trying to get the girls to the party – Tommy and Mark walked down the street to pickup beer, chips, and pizza. While they were gone I put away the weights, straightened up the place, and put on the stereo. Ron had some records but mostly Perry Cuomo and Bing Crosby so I turned on WPLJ.

Then the phone rang; it was John, he said, 'Kenny, I got with Susan and she called Robin and Jennifer. They both said they'd come, and Natalie is sleeping over Robin's tonight so she'll be there too. We're going to meet at 6:15 outside Cold Cut City, and we'll take a Miles Cab to Ron's.

I said, 'YES!! That's perfect!! So you'll be up here by about 6:35. Tommy and Mark are getting the beer and some food. This is going to be great! I can't believe you got it done so quickly.

Did the girls say anything about the kind of party we're having? You know the fact that it's only four girls and four guys?'

John said, 'No, I don't think so, but I didn't ask Susan about that.' 'Well as long as they are willing to come to this kind of party – that's a good sign. Call me if you don't leave by 6:15'

John said, 'Alright Mommy, if we don't leave by 6:15 I'll call you.'

'I'll see you and the girls around 6:30 p.m.'

The plan was in place and everything was set. The music was playing, the beer and food was on the way, and most importantly – THE CHICKS WERE COMING!"

"Chicks, Dad?"

"Yes, CHICKS, Kels. You see, the only thing teenage boys have on their minds are CHICKS! Now, let me get back to my story.

Okay, about fifteen minutes later Tommy and Mark walked in with the beer and food. They brought in four cases of beer; two cases of Budweiser, one case of Heineken, one case of Molson, three large cheese pizza's, and several bags of chips and some dip.

We put the beer in the refrigerator; there wasn't enough room for all the beer so we had to take a few items out to make room. We took out the container of Iced Tea, a gallon of milk, some butter, and some left over spaghetti, which was Ron's dinner for Monday, and placed it in a cabinet next to the sink (to keep it out of eye sight). We took out two large bowls from the cabinet above the sink and filled them with chips. Then we opened up the dip and put it on the coffee table in the living room. We placed the pizza boxes on the dining room table with some plates and napkins next to them. When we finished 'setting up' for the party we cracked open a few cold beers, sat down, put our feet on the coffee table, and waited for the girls and the party to begin."

"Don't you mean chicks, Dad?

"Good point Kels. Hopefully now you're realizing that teenage boys only have one thing on their minds – ONE THING!"

"What's the one thing Dad?"

My dad smiled, "They want to play tonsil hockey with chicks and they're looking to score a goal!"

"That's just weird, Dad!"

"Okay, let me continue with the story. So there we were sitting down in the living room feeling pretty good about ourselves and our party; our hearts were pounding with nervous anticipation. After what seemed an eternity, we heard a car pull up outside the house. I jumped up and looked out the window. I saw four beautiful girls step out of a white Miles Cab. It seemed to happen in slow motion – like in the movie *10* or was it *Fast Times at Ridgemont High* – I watched as beautiful legs step out of the car, I saw hair flipped back, and I saw luscious lips being smacked together. I thought to myself,

'Oh my gosh, what babes! This is going to be a perfect night, exactly how we planned it!'

I ran to the front door, I hit my shin on the coffee table on the way, and I screamed, 'Ahhh shoot!!!' But by the time I hopped to the door I had a smile on my face which stretched from ear to ear. I opened the door and said hello to all the girls – using the deepest, most manly voice I had. The first one through the door was Jennifer, then Susan, next was Robin, and finally Natalie walked in. Behind the girls, also with a smile from ear to ear was John – as he walked by me we gave each other a quiet 'thumbs up' and a 'high five'. I turned to close the door, but before it closed another car caught my eye.

This car was also white and had the words 'Miles Cab Company' on the side door…and it also stopped right outside of Ron's house. As I watched, it reminded me of the night my family went to the circus, you remember, when a million of us climbed out of our Volkswagen. I watched a million people climb out of that Miles Cab – it seemed like a never ending stream of people. My eyes were wide open, my jaw was lying on the floor and I thought, 'What's going on? How many people are getting out of this cab and who are they – they're not the girls we invited – those girls are inside the house – these are guys and other girls – but not the four guys and four girls in the house – OH NO!!!'

Then another cab pulled up, and another, and another; and every cab that pulled in front of Ron's house was – PACKED FULL WITH PEOPLE! They were all friends of mine – they were my best friends – but this was not a 'Best Friend' party – this was a 'If You Want My Body and You Think I'm Sexy' party'!!! I turned my head and yelled, 'Hey John – come here!' As John walked over, my other friends streamed past me with their bags of beer and food, each one of them said, as they walked in the house, 'Hey Kenny, thanks for inviting me to the party! Where should I put my beer?' I just shook my head and said, 'Ahhh…just put it in the kitchen…'

When John walked over – I said, as quietly, but as forcefully as I could, 'John, WHAT DID YOU DO? You were only supposed to bring Natalie, Robin, Jennifer, and Susan – it looks like you invited the WHOLE neighborhood – WHAT DID YOU DO?!'

John said, 'What did you want me to do? Did you want me to line up our friends and call out the names of the people who were lucky enough to be invited and tell everyone else, 'Sorry, you didn't make the cut."

I said, "Yeah, what's so bad about that – at least then we would be here with just the four girls we invited! John, if I knew you were going to invite everyone in Kingsbridge, Marble Hill, Riverdale, Bailey Avenue, and 238th Street I would have stood at the door and had a cover charge – I'd have $1,000 in my pocket by now if I did that! And what if Ron comes home – I could have explained to him why I invited 4 girls over – that would have been easy! But how can I explain this to him!'

I looked around and the house was packed with our friends and they were already drinking beer, smoking cigarettes, dancing, and singing. I said, 'John, if he saw this – I can guarantee he would finish the job he started when he took Tommy and me to 'Ron's Hole'!'

John said, 'Well what are you going to do? Do you want me to help you tell everyone they have to leave?'

'No, you know we can't do that but crap – Ron is going to kill me!' I shook my head and thought to myself, 'Okay, I better make the best of this. Maybe it will go okay. My friends like having a good time, but no one is going to trash the place, it will be fine…just keep telling myself this…maybe I'll start believing it.'

I took a deep breath, looked in the house and tried to decide where I'd go first. As I turned to close the door I was almost run over by another wave of friends, Johnny said, 'Hey, we almost missed the party – lucky John told Sam at the Pizza shop where the party was!'

I loved my friends and loved hanging out with them, but it wasn't my house, and I had already trashed Ron's apartment before – now I was destined to trash his house."

"You never told us you trashed his apartment."

"Oh, that's a whole other story. I don't think I can tell you that one.

Anyway, before the night was over, two other cabs showed up at the house, and instead of having a small, intimate party of eight by 8:00 p.m. Ron's house was like Animal House – only without the Togas. There was beer everywhere, girls and guys dancing in the living room, people playing quarters in the dining room, people smoking cigarettes in the living room, girls hanging out in the bathroom, and guys taking leaks in the back yard – it was total chaos."

My dad continued, "Throughout the night I walked around and talked with everyone and made sure they were having a good time – and I also made sure no one was trashing the place. Around 9:30 I checked out the kitchen; I opened the refrigerator and it was still packed with brown bags full of six packs of Budweiser, Heineken, Molson, and Michelob. The overflow of beer was in the sink covered with ice from Ron's freezer. I shook my head and thought to myself, 'Ron is going to notice his ice cubes were 'disturbed'. I reached into the refrigerator and pulled out a Molson. I took out my keys and popped off the cap. Then I put the cap between my right middle finger and thumb, lifted my right arm, put my right hand beside my head and snapped my fingers. The cap shot out from between my fingers and it spun like a miniature Frisbee headed for Billy's forehead – but Billy leaned to the side and the projectile missed him and hit the dining room window. I then took a big swig of beer and walked around checking out the party."

"You were drinking beer?"

"Yes, of course! That's the kind of parties boys have when they invite girls!"

Kelsie said, "No, they don't Daddy!"

My dad ignored her and got back to the story. "In the dining room there were about fifteen people around the table, some on chairs, some on their knees, and some standing up. They were playing 'Quarters'; a game where you put a glass of beer or a shot of liquor in the middle of the table, and you take turns trying to 'bounce' a quarter into the glass. If you're lucky or skillful enough to bounce the quarter into the glass you chose who had to drink the glass or shot – which had to be 'downed' in one gulp. If you were good at bouncing the quarter into the glass you could select the same person to down the glass over and over again, and in a short period of time the person got drunk, puked their brains out, or both. Billy was an expert at Quarters, and when he saw me walk into the dining room he bounced another quarter in the glass and pointed to me.

I said, 'Billy, you know I don't play Quarters…I'll puke my brains out if I start guzzling.'

Then everyone at the table started chanting, 'Kenny, Kenny, Kenny, Kenny, Kenny!' So I stepped over to the table and grabbed the beer and drank it down – hoping it wouldn't come up as fast as it went down. As I guzzled the beer they chanted, 'Chug, chug, chug…!' When I finished I slammed the glass down on the table and said, 'That's it! Billy, if I start to puke I'm coming back here, and I'm puking all over you!' I smiled and walked away to the next room."

"Did you puke?"

"No but I was about to. After I almost puked I walked past the bathroom which was closed – I heard a flush and several girls talking and laughing – I thought to myself, 'They go to the bathroom in packs even in a 4'x4' bathroom – weird, very weird.'

Next, I walked over to the other bedroom, where Ron had his weights set-up – the room Mark, Tommy, and I lifted earlier in the day. Two of my friends, Teddy and Johnny were having a 'weight lifting competition' to see who could bench press the most weight – not a smart thing to do in their condition.

"What condition?"

"Um, out of shape. There was 150 pounds on the bar when Teddy lay down on the bench; he grabbed the bar with both hands and pushed. Neither one of them knew how to lift weights so they didn't put collars on the bar which was a bad idea. Since Teddy's right arm was stronger than his left, the bar was uneven when he pushed and ALL the weights slid off the left side of the bar, and they came crashing down on the floor. Once all the weights on the left side of the bar were off the right side came down and all those weight came crashing to the floor – luckily for both of them neither one got injured. Teddy sat up with the bar in his hands, looked at the weights on the floor, then at Johnny, and almost in unison they both screamed, 'That was AWESOME!' I stared at the situation, shook my head, and thought to myself, 'Ron is going to kill me.' Then I walked away on my way to the basement.

When I got to the basement door it was closed so I put my ear to the door and listened; I could hear a girl's voice say, 'Let's do the roller coaster.' I heard several girls scream, 'Yeah, let's do the roller coaster.' Next there was a lot of commotion; the sounds of feet stomping and shuffling up and down stairs, bodies banging into each other and against the walls. Then it quieted down and someone said, 'HERE WE GO UP THE HILL', then the same girl's voice screamed, 'HERE WE GO DOWN THE HILL – HOLD ON!' Then I heard all the girls scream, 'WHOA!'

I was curious and I opened the door a crack and peaked through it, and I saw the backs of about a dozen girls – each one of them sitting behind the other on a different step, holding onto each other – like they were riding on a toboggan or a 'roller coaster.' As the girl in the front screamed out the approaching curves and hills, all the other girls leaned into the 'turn' and screamed, 'Whoa!' It was quite a sight to see. I stood there for a minute watching until they road down the last hill. I quietly closed the door, smiled, shook my head, and thought, 'That was just plain weird!'

The next place I came to was the attic door. I quietly opened it and walked up to the first landing and looked in the main room; I didn't notice anyone so I turned around and started back down the stairs. Before I reached the door I thought I heard something so I stopped. I listened for a moment and heard a girl's voice say, 'Owe! I think I have a Fireman's Boot sticking in my back. I quietly finished walking down the stairs.

When I got downstairs I decided to look for, Natalie but it was so crowded I couldn't find her. On my way to the living room I ran into a couple of the guys coming in from the side door, which was off of the kitchen. I looked at them and said, 'Where were you guys? What were you doing?'

They said, 'Kenny, the bathroom has been filled with girls all night long and we had to take a leak.'

I looked at them and said, 'Where did you take a leak?'

'Outside'

'Yeah, I know you went outside – but where outside? Did the next door neighbors see you?'

They both said, 'I don't think so' and they walked past me back to the party. I had to see where they peed so I opened up the side door and went outside. When I got outside I looked around and right next to the back door I saw the giant initials KG and RS on the siding next to the back door written in urine – which was dripping down the side of the house into a small, little puddle. Then another three or four guys came out from behind the house zipping up their zippers with toilet paper stuck to their sneakers. I thought to myself, 'RON IS GOING TO KILL ME!'

When I got back inside I saw Natalie in the living room, along with about thirty other people, sitting on the couch – laughing with a few of her friends. It was a small living room and it was packed with people; some were sitting down, some were standing up, and some were on the floor leaning against the furniture. Almost everyone had a beer in their hand; some of the girls were smoking, and everyone had a smile on their face while they were talking, laughing, and singing to the music. When Scott arrived earlier in the night he came with his radio. He didn't usually let it out of his sight but this night he left it in the living room for everyone to enjoy.

There was almost no room for me to fit in, but I managed to squeeze into a place on the floor near the end of the couch. I thought, 'The party was my idea, and not only can't I sit next to the girl I invited – I can't even find a seat.'"

"It wasn't just your idea, Dad."

"Yeah, I know but you get the point. I wasn't able to get close to the chick I invited."

"Chick?"

"Yes, chick. I couldn't get close to my chick, but I was close enough to the fun, and so I decided to stop worrying about the house and not being with her and to instead start enjoying myself.

John got up from the couch and asked if anyone needed a beer. I sucked down the last few sips of my Molson and said, 'Yeah John, can you get me one Molson? I only want one – just one – please don't bring me back a case? I don't want a case, and I don't need a case. I just want one.' I smiled on the inside wondering if John understood my sarcasm."

"Dad, I don't understand your sarcasm? Why did you say that to him?"

"Cam, I wanted him to bring just one girl for each of us to the party – he brought the whole neighborhood. I asked him for one beer – I didn't want him to bring the whole case of beer. You get it?"

"Um, no. Not really."

"Don't worry about it Cam, it was probably a bad joke. Well, when John got back he handed the beer to me; again I popped off the cap with my key, put it between my fingers, snapped, and I clipped one of my friends in the dining room in the back of the head with the bottle cap. I took a big, long drink of beer, leaned back, and looked around.

Although I was at the party and had been watching everything throughout the night it was different as I sat there. Instead of just looking at everybody I was now sitting quietly observing them. It was kind of a surreal, almost an out of body type of observation; everything around me seemed to slow down and even the noise sounded muffled.

I looked around and thought about the party and my friends. I saw Tommy, Mark, Pat, Shawn, Tony, Billy, John, Jordan, Robin, Jennifer, Beth, Susan, Lorinda, Kelly, Marie, Maureen, and all my other friends and I thought, 'This really is a great party, everyone is having a great time – and the party was my and Tommy's idea.' Although we didn't plan it this way, it still made me feel pretty good.

We had intended to have a small, intimate party with just a few of the girls. I wanted to reconnect with my old girlfriend, but I thought, 'Maybe we'll reconnect another time. Maybe it didn't work out like I planned, but this isn't so bad and actually – it's pretty good. I really am lucky to have so many good friends; I've known most of them since fifth grade and they're all really nice people – maybe a little wild sometimes but always nice.'

Sometimes life gets so busy you don't have an opportunity to step back and evaluate your life, but this night I did a little. At this time in my life I needed to change a lot of things; I needed to go back to school, I needed a steady job, and I needed to stop drinking. But one thing I didn't need to change were my friends – they were great! They would do anything for me and I would do anything for them. We all came from the same background – working class Catholic families from the Bronx. We went to the same Catholic grade schools, we all lived in small apartments, we liked the same music, we drank the same beer, we loved to have fun together – but most importantly we all really liked each other.

It was a great party, and the night flew by, but like everything it had to come to an end; slowly people called cabs and left in small groups. By about 2:00 a.m. the house had only eight people in it – the eight people the party was intended for; Tommy, Robin, Mark, Jennifer, John, Susan, Natalie, and me – it's funny how it eventually worked out the way we intended. When we looked around the house it was a mess – it wasn't trashed, but we had a mess to clean up. There were beer bottles everywhere, bottle caps on the floor, brown paper bags in each room, empty six pack holders, empty boxes of cigarettes, pizza boxes, bags of half eaten potato chips, and a lot of other junk all around.

The eight of us were sitting in the living room, relaxing after the best party we had ever been to. Then Robin sat up and said, 'Natalie, I hate to say this, but we really need to leave. You're sleeping over my house, and I told my mother we'd be home by 1:00, and it's already after that.'

I sat up and said, 'We'll call you a cab and pay for it. We'd go with you but we have to stick around and clean up before we leave.'

Natalie said, 'We can help clean up before we go.'

I said, 'You don't have to do that – we invited you to the party – but thanks anyway.' Before I was finished with my sentence – all the girls got up and began cleaning. Since there were so many people in the house the rug was all matted down; it had a lot of little torn beer labels on the floor, so I went to Ron's bedroom and pulled out the vacuum.

I took it into the living room and Natalie said, 'Kenny, I can do that for you.'

I said, 'No, that's okay. I can vacuum.'

She looked at me, smiled, and said, 'Come on Kenny – you're a guy you can't vacuum; let me help you.' She walked over and reached for the vacuum; her hand touched mine and my heart started to go pitter patter."

"Dad, STOP!"

My dad smiled and secretly winked at me, "So where was I? Oh yeah, after her hand touched mine, we began to vacuum the living room together. FEELING HER HAND AND BODY BRUSH UP AGAINST MINE AS WE VACCUMED UP THE TORN BEER LABELS WAS INTOXICATING."

"Dad, is this true?"

"Cam, would your daddy lie to you?"

"It doesn't matter if it's true or not – I'm still telling Mom!"

My dad ignored her, but he still had a smile on his face when he continued, "After the steam in the living room settled down a song came on the stereo:

♪ I was a fool to ever leave your site
Me minus you is such a lonely rhyme ♪
♪ The breakup we had has made me lonesome and sad [31]

"Dad! I'm going to get sick if you don't stop!"

My dad was laughing, "Okay, okay Kels! I'll stop but remember this is what happens when you start dating when you're too young. YOU FALL FOR CHICKS AND YOU END UP VACCUMING LIVING ROOMS WHILE LISTENING TO PEACHES AND HERBS SONGS. IS THIS WHAT YOU WANT?"

"Hmmm?"

"Don't answer that! After we finished vacuuming we picked up all the garbage, straightened out the chairs and moved the couch back to where it was supposed to be and I said to Natalie, 'Do you realize this was supposed to be a quiet, intimate party with just a few of us?'

She said, 'Really? Was I one of the 'few of us'?'

I raised my eyebrows, smiled, and said, 'Yes, you were the first one on the list – my personal, special guest!'

'I guess I should feel honored to have been invited to the great Kenny Hand's party.'

'I didn't mean it in that way…'

She turned and said, 'In what way did you mean it?'

'I'm just saying that I wanted you to come – you know – I wanted to see you. Did you have a good time?'

'Kenny, I had a great time and I am flattered you invited me, but remember – we're not going out with each other.'

'Yeah, I know, but I thought maybe by asking you to this party – I might be able to change that.'

She stopped, raised her eyebrows again, looked around garbage bags filled with beer bottles, pizza boxes, and the vacuum which was now in her hand, and said, 'Well Kenny, you really know how to sweep a girl off her feet.'

"Is this story over yet?"

"Kelsie, you know you love lovey, dovey stories. And NO it's not over yet – I still need to tell you about the heartache that comes with dating at a young age.

Okay, after my passionate vacuuming love connection in the living room Jennifer walked in and said, 'I have bad news – all the cab company phones have been busy for the past thirty minutes. I bet we don't get a cab tonight. We might as well walk to the bus stop near the City Line.' The City Line was about a two mile walk from Ron's house – up and down some of the steepest hills in Yonkers. After the two mile walk to the City Line we would still have to catch the 20 Bus to get back to the neighborhood.

When I heard what Jennifer said I walked into the dining room to get Tommy; I motioned to him to meet in the kitchen. When we were in the kitchen I said, 'Tommy, the girls are talking about walking to the bus stop!'

'Yeah, so?'

'We can't let them walk home – we need to do something.'

'Like what? Do you want to drive them home in the El Camino?'

I raised my eyebrows and had a little evil smile on my face – 'No, not me – YOU! You've driven Ron's El Camino before. I think you should drive us home. Think about it, Tommy – you'll be a living legend if you do this!'

'A legend, hmmm, you are so full of crap, Kenny!'

'No, I'm not – I'm serious. Someday someone will write a book about us, and you'll be the main character! You'll be like Burt Reynolds in White Lighting! You need to do this Tommy – you have to!'

Tommy looked at me, shook his head, and said, 'I don't know. Who will go?'

'Everyone!'

'What are we going to do? Are we just going to drive them home, and then come back and park the car?'

I said, "Yeah, that's it. It's a piece of cake. We drive them to 231st Street, drop them off, drive back here, and then we'll take a cab home. You see – it's easy to become a legend!'

Tommy asked, 'What about Ron? What if he finds out? He probably keeps track of his odometer.'

'Don't worry about Ron – I'll talk to him if he finds out – I'll take the blame – it'll be fine – don't worry. So what do you think? Are you going to do it?'

Tommy shook his head and said, 'Get the keys for me.'

The keys were hanging on a hook in the kitchen next to the refrigerator; I grabbed them and flipped them to Tommy. We both walked outside. Tommy opened the driver side door and slid behind the steering wheel. I got in the passenger side and said, 'Looking good Tommy – you look like a natural. You are going to be a legend!'

Tommy said, 'Would you shut up – I already said I'd do it – you can cut the BS!' I guess he knew I was buttering him up.

"You haven't changed very much, Dad."

"Really Kelsie? Have I mentioned how beautiful you are, lately?

So where was I? Oh yeah, John, and Mark were oblivious to the conversation between Tommy and me, and so they had already decided to walk to the City Line. I walked back into the house and Robin said, 'Kenny, the house is all cleaned now; all we need to do is put the garbage outside, near the front curb, and then we can walk to the City Line.'

Tommy was still outside in the car when I said, 'We don't have to walk to the City Line – did you think we would invite you to a party and then make you walk home? The cab is here – it's waiting outside.'

Jennifer said, 'What do you mean 'the cab is here'? The cab company's phones are all busy.'

I said, 'Well let's lock up and walk outside and you'll see what I mean.' We all walked outside with a garbage bag in our hands. I was the last one out because I had to turn off all the lights and lock the front door. When everyone looked in front of the house there wasn't a cab there and, when they looked in the dark driveway all they saw was Ron's El Camino. A second later I locked the door and walked down the front steps. Then as the girls were about to ask, 'Kenny, there's no cab here!' Tommy turned the ignition key, revved the engine several times, and turned on the headlights. I jumped off the last step and said, 'Girls, your cab is here!'

They looked at each other with their eyes wide open – and Jennifer laughed – 'No way – no %@#$ing way! Who is driving the car?' John and Mark walked to the car to see who was in the driver's seat, and they saw Tommy.

I walked over to the girls, but before I could say anything – Natalie, who looked very nervous, said, 'Do you seriously think we're going to let Tommy drive us home? He doesn't even know how to drive.'

'Sure he does – Ron always lets him drive his car – he's driven it a million times. Come on let's hop in.' Right after I said that it started drizzling and the girls ran to the car to keep dry, but then they realized an El Camino has an open back area – not the perfect car to drive in the rain.

Robin said, 'You mean we have to ride in the open back – we're going to get soaked?'

I looked up at the sky and said, 'It looks to me like the rain will pass. Come on – hop in!' Jennifer, Susan, and John squeezed in the front cab next to Tommy. Robin and Mark stepped up on the back bumper and jumped in the back – Natalie stood back hesitating to get in. I walked over and said, 'What's wrong?'

She said, 'This is crazy – we shouldn't do this – it's dangerous.'

I put my right arm around her waist and said, 'Don't worry it will be fine – it's a short drive home – come on.'"

"You're so smooth, Dad."

Kelsie said, "Cam, don't encourage him!"

My dad said, "You got that right, Bud. I'm a chick magnet! Okay, let me get back to the story.

I jumped onto the bumper, put my hand out, and she reached for it. She grabbed my hand pulled herself up and into the back of the car. As we both stood in the back of the car she whispered in my ear, 'Kenny, do you promise me it will be okay?'"

"Dad, I don't want to hear about this!"

"Kelsie, don't worry – you're resilient. You'll get over it – I promise."

"I doubt it."

"Alright, so I grabbed her other hand, and said, 'I promise everything will be fine, my love.'"

"You're killing me dad!"

My dad was still smiling as he said, "Kelsie, just sit back and listen. I don't need any comments from the peanut gallery. So, she stepped in and sat in the corner furthest away from the cab, facing forward. I sat close to her, and since it was still drizzling and a little cool it gave me a perfect excuse to put my arm around her – I told her I would keep her warm, dry, and safe."

My dad smiled and said, "I was so smooth, so charming. You see Kelsie, this is what boys do; they're always looking for an opportunity to make their move!"

I asked, "Did it work, Dad?"

He slowly nodded his head, "Like a charm, Cam – she was putty in my hands." He continued, "John stuck his head out of the window and said, 'Are you guys ready to go?' I gave him the 'thumbs up'.

Tommy took the car out of park, put his foot on the gas too hard and some of the gravel from the driveway shot up and sprayed against the garage behind us. He lightened his touch and we pulled out of the driveway onto Tibbett Road; we were on our way back to the Bronx.

Ron usually took the Saw Mill Parkway to the Major Deegan to get home and so that's the way Tommy went. He made a left on McLean Avenue, and just past the bridge he made a right at the Getty Gas Station where there was a small sign which read, 'Saw Mill Parkway South – New York'. He made a right turn down, what appeared to be, a residential street to the entrance to the parkway. The Saw Mill was dimly lit, extremely narrow, and it had a guardrail separating the northbound from the southbound traffic. On the shoulder there was a grassy area which led up to trees which buffered the houses from the noise of the cars driving by. To get on the parkway from the entrance there was a short, sharp turn. Drivers had to quickly make a decision when to get on, and once they made the decision they had to 'floor it' to keep from getting run over by the on coming traffic.

As Tommy approached the parkway he slowed the car down; I could see Tommy looking to his left at the oncoming traffic. I could see the oncoming traffic as clearly as Tommy and with each small gap in the traffic I thought to myself, 'No Tommy…you can't make it. Wait for the next one…be patient…don't go yet.' And with each gap which quickly closed it was clear Tommy was getting impatient; maybe he wanted to get the girls home sooner, maybe he felt pressure that we'd think he was being too cautious, maybe he didn't know how to judge distance, I'm not sure. All I know was I was getting nervous Tommy wasn't going to pick the right time to 'floor it'.

I looked over at Natalie, and she looked nervous. I still had my arm around her, and I could feel her shaking; I squeezed her even tighter to comfort her because this is what guys do. She turned to me and said, 'Kenny, do you promise everything will be alright?' I was trying not to show I was having second thoughts myself so I smiled and said, 'Yes, I promise. Tommy's fine. Don't worry.'"

"Yeah Dad, you're so charming."

"Cam, these are the things guys say to pickup chicks. See Kelsie, Cameron knows. Okay, so when I turned to look back at the oncoming traffic there was a small opening after the next car but there wasn't enough room. I thought to myself, 'Tommy, don't go! You really shouldn't go. Don't go. Wait. Wait, Tommy!' But inside I knew Tommy wasn't going to wait again. A split second later Tommy 'floored it' with a car quickly approaching! It was hard to tell how far away the car was, but I could see it's lights barreling down the highway toward us, and if Ron's car didn't have great acceleration – we were about to be in a horrible accident! As Tommy floored it and turned the steering wheel sharply onto the parkway he made a mistake. He turned the wheel too sharply causing the right back tire to ride up on a high curb. All of us in the back felt a hard jolt and then, for a fraction of a second, it felt like the car was about to turn over. Tommy corrected his mistake and turned quickly to his left; this took the car off the curb and onto the entrance again. When the back right tire came off the high curb the car bottomed out and bounced in the air; I grabbed Natalie's shoulder to make sure she didn't fall out. Finally, the car's four tires were back on the road, and Tommy floored it again.

When we turned back onto the parkway, the car I saw just a few seconds earlier was still barreling down on us about to hit us, I screamed, "Get down!", and we all laid down waiting for the worst! A split second later we heard the sound of screeching tires and the blaring of a car horn. When we looked up we saw they car behind us swerving out of control. A second later he regained control of his car and he sped past us. We gave him the one finger salute and yelled, '%@#$ you. You #@#$ing jerk!!' Jennifer watched from the safety of the cab and thought it was hilarious; she couldn't stop laughing at our terrorized faces.

About a mile up the Saw Mill, past the entrance, there is a fork in the road; to the right is the Henry Hudson Parkway which takes you to Riverdale and eventually into Manhattan and to the left is the Mosholu Parkway which takes you to the Major Deegan. As Jennifer sat laughing at us Tommy turned his head around to see what was so funny – I guess he was oblivious to us almost losing our lives. A quick look would have been fine, but the car was quickly approaching the fork, and Tommy was in the middle of the road headed straight for the guardrail. I motioned to Tommy to turn around; when he didn't turn around quick enough I screamed, 'Tommy!! Turn your head around; we're going to crash!!!' Tommy turned around and quickly jerked the car to the left narrowly avoiding the guardrail.

This road was the most dangerous part of the trip; there were several curves and a lot of bumps and pot holes in the road. This section of the road was surrounded by the Van Cortland golf course. On the left were holes three through seven and on the right was holes two and twelve. This area was known to be dangerous; several young people died while drinking and driving on this road – exactly what we were doing. In the daylight you could see the hand made crosses with the flowers laid next to them in memory of some loved one who lost his life while driving on this road.

At this point in the trip I looked deep into Natalie's eyes, and I could see she was frightened!"

"Dad, you are so making this up!"

"Kelsie, would I ever lie to you – this is what guys do to try and butter girls up?"

"Uh yeah, Dad. Sure."

"Well, anyway. Where was I? Oh yes. Although I would never show it; I was nervous too. I could never forgive myself if something happened to Natalie because I wanted to impress her."

"Dad, I'm about to puke!"

My dad raised his voice and looked at Kelsie. "I SQUEEZED HER TIGHTER AND TIGHTER WITH MY RIGHT ARM, AND THEN I REACHED AROUND HER AND HELD HER WAIST. THE PASSION I FELT…"

"Dad, if you don't stop I'm leaving."

My dad smiled and quieted down as he continued, "I was nervous Tommy would want to see how fast he could drive the El Camino. When Tommy and I were twelve years old we went with

Ron to Williamsport, Pennsylvania to watch the Little League World Series. On that trip Ron got into a race with another car on one of the back roads – Ron 'floored' the El Camino and by the time the race was over we were racing down the highway at 130 miles per hour with the other car left in the dust. So I knew Tommy knew how fast it could go; I just hoped Tommy wouldn't try it. When we went 130 it was on a wide open empty road; not a narrow parkway where kids were known to drive off the road.

When Ron wanted to go fast he put the car in L2 for about 10 seconds – L2 revved the engine but held it back. At the right time Ron shifted out of L2 and into 'drive' – when he did this it was like the car had a turbo rocket behind it! As I was holding Natalie I was watching Tommy, and I saw him reach to the shift lever on the steering column. I leaned forward and yelled, 'Tommy! Don't put it in L2!' But Tommy couldn't hear me and everyone else in the cab was watching Tommy. When he put it in L2 the car slowed down abruptly, jerking everyone forward, then Tommy floored it. The car was probably going 60 miles per hour for most of the trip but now it started going faster. Jennifer turned to face us; she put seven fingers up in the air – 70 miles per hour! She then looked back at the speedometer and when she turned her head back around her eyes were wide open – she put eight fingers up in the air – 80 miles per hour! She then looked back at the speedometer and when she turned her head back around her mouth was wide open – she put nine fingers up in the air – 90 miles per hour!

At this point Natalie said to me, 'Please make him stop, Kenny. You promised me! Please make him stop!' Just then we hit a pot hole in the road, and we were almost thrown from the car again. The car bottomed out and scrapped the ground – spraying sparks behind us. When I looked up, I saw the off ramp which led to the entrance to the Major Deegan, and so I knew Tommy had to slow down. Thankfully, I was right. He made a quick turn which threw us across the bed of the truck like we were riding the Scrambler at an amusement park, and he got on the entrance to the Major Deegan. Once we got on the Deegan it was a short distance to the Van Cortland, 240th Street exit.

Tommy knew he had to be careful in the neighborhood; he didn't want to be stopped by the cops. He made a right on 240th Street and drove across Broadway to Erwin Avenue because it was a quiet street, and we were unlikely to come across cops on it. We drove down Erwin Avenue past Mark's house and Billy's building all the way to 232nd Street where we made a left. We drove up the hill between PS 7 and St. John's Middle School; then we made a right onto Kingsbridge Avenue. We then made a left on 231st Street and finally a quick right up Godwin Terrace where Tommy parked the car outside of Robin's apartment building.

Before getting out of the car I gave Natalie another tight hug and whispered in her ear, 'You okay?' She still looked terrified. I was so thankful nothing had happened to her."

Kelsie said, "Would you please stop!"

My dad smiled and raised his voice, "SHE SAID, 'KENNY, I WAS SO SCARED! I WILL NEVER DO THAT AGAIN – NEVER AGAIN IN MY LIFE!' I JUMPED OUT OF THE BACK AND SAID, 'HERE, LET ME HELP YOU OUT.' SHE GRABBED MY HAND AND STEPPED OUT. WHEN SHE GOT OUT HER LEGS WERE STILL SHAKING AND I STILL HELD HER HAND. I ASKED HER IF I COULD WALK HER TO KATHY'S."

He started talking in his normal voice again, "Robin was already out of the car walking toward her alleyway, and she said, 'Natalie, I'll leave the door open. Don't let Brownie out and make sure he doesn't bark and wake everyone up.'

She turned to me and said, 'I really need to go in with Robin. I don't want her to get in trouble.'

I said, 'That's fine, but can I still walk you to her door?' She squeezed my hand and pulled me towards Robin's alleyway, and we both began to walk."

"Dad!!!"

"Kelsie, I'll stop right here. All I'll say is when we made it to the alleyway it was the most amazing 23 seconds of my life! I never felt so violated!"

My dad was smiling, "You see Kelsie – this is part of every guy's master plan! They pretend to be nice, but when it's all said and done all they want is 23 seconds of hanky panky in a urine infested alleyway!"

"23 seconds of hanky panky? You are so weird!"

"Okay Kelsie, I'm done with the lovey dovey part. Alright, so after I walked Natalie to Robin's door the guys got in the El Camino and headed back. The trip back was uneventful until we got to Ron's street. By this time it was about 3:00 a.m. but to our surprise the street was full of Ron's neighbors. Of course our party wasn't an intimate affair, but apparently the party got the attention of everyone in the neighborhood especially after we took the car.

Ron's neighbors reminded me of a peasant mob from a Frankenstein movie; they were carrying pitch forks and torches and chanting, 'Kill the monsters, kill the monsters!' When we reached the mob, Tommy got nervous and drove past Ron's house. Unfortunately, Tibbett Road was a dead end street and so we had nowhere else to go – we had to turn around and face the mob."

"What could they do to you?"

"I don't know, Cam. I guess nothing but we didn't know that at the time. Okay, so Tommy stopped at the end of the street, and we talked about what to do; we decided we'd just turn the car around and act like nothing happened – a plan, a bad plan, but a plan nonetheless. We all hopped back in the car and Tommy proceeded to back up but he wasn't an experienced backer upper. He got closer and closer to the hedges of one of Ron's neighbor.

I was turned around looking at the back of the car and I said, 'Tommy you're getting close, Tommy you're getting closer, Tommy slow down…Tommy STOP!' But instead of pressing on the brake he pressed on the gas – something I realized isn't all that unusual. By the time I finished yelling 'Tommy, STOP' the car was resting on the neighbor's hedge, and the car stalled.

I said, 'Tommy, just pull straight ahead.'

He said, 'The car won't start.'

'What do you mean the car won't start?'

He said, 'It won't f@#$ing start – that's what I mean!' John, Mark, and I decided to push the car off the hedge and so we got out and started pushing. We looked down the street and the mob was still there; pitch forks, torches, and all. John said, 'Don't look at them – just push.' After about 15 minutes of rocking and pushing we finally got the car over the hedge and we began pushing the car down the street towards Ron's house. When we were halfway up the street Tommy tried starting the car again, and it worked this time. We drove the car quietly past the mob while they continued to chant 'kill the monsters, kill the months', but we ignored them and drove back into the driveway."

"So Dad, what happened next? Did Ron ever find out about the party or about you guys stealing his car?"

"I don't remember all the details, but I do remember Ron having to pay his neighbor about $100 to replace his ruined hedges. By the way, I still owe him about $50 for my share. Also, I think that was the last time I ever went inside Ron's house."

"What happened to the girl at the party?"

"Hmmmm, I don't remember, but I do remember the point of this story.

YOU SEE KELSIE! YOU START DATING, THEN YOU END UP STEALING CARS, DRINKING BEER, PEEING YOUR INITIALS AGAINST THE SIDE OF A HOUSE, AND YOU START HALLUCINATING YOU'RE RIDING ON ROLLER COASTERS! IS THAT WHAT YOU WANT? DO YOU WANT TO BE A CAR STEALING, BEER DRINKING, INITIAL PEEING, ROLLER COASTER RIDING, DRUG ADDICT – IS THAT WHAT YOU WANT, KELSIE?"

"Maybe, Dad – you make it sound pretty appealing."

Then I asked, "Dad, do you have any non-girl stories you can tell us?"

He said, "Sure Cam. Do you want to hear a story about skiing?"

Of course I said, "Yes."

Snowball Express

"The best place for a boy from the Bronx to go skiing was in New Jersey. The most popular ski resort in New Jersey was Vernon Valley/Great Gorge, but a short distance away there was smaller, less well known resort called Hidden Valley. Hidden Valley was only about an hour and a half away from the Bronx. This was the place I learned how to ski and where I took a girlfriend on a date.

At the time my sister Chris was dating a guy named Rick Maddox. Rick was a wild man who was a lot of fun to be around, and he loved skiing. While Chris was dating Rick I got to know him pretty well because he'd occasionally come up to our apartment, and he went to all our family get-togethers. So when Rick asked me if I wanted to go skiing with him I jumped at the chance. I had always wanted to go skiing and when Rick told me he was going with Eddie, Angel, and their girlfriends it sounded like a lot of fun. Rick told me I could bring my girlfriend with me – I told him, 'Uh, yeah…that will be great…I think she'll like it.'

At the time I was dating Michelle, a ravishingly beautiful girl from 238th Street."

"Ravishingly beautiful, Dad?"

"Sure. Ravishingly."

"What does that mean?"

"I don't know, but it sounds good. Okay where was I? Oh yeah. Michelle had a great sense of humor and an infectious laugh. I met her when Amy, who knew her from Tolentine, invited her to one of our parties at Ewen Park or maybe it was St. John's School yard – I'm not sure. She was ravishingly beautiful and a lot of fun to be around, but I wasn't sure if she could ski.

When I asked her if she wanted to go skiing, she said, 'Sure, it sounds like fun!' Later when I mentioned my sister and a couple of her friends were going she said, 'Whoa, hold on!' Michelle wasn't sure if she wanted to go with them because she was the same age as my sister and her friends and Michelle was dating me – my sisters 'little brother'. She didn't want these girls to make fun of her for dating a younger boy – even if the younger boy was as good looking as me."

"As good looking as you? Nice Dad."

"Yes, as good looking as me! But anyway, another reason she was hesitant was because Chris and her friends were considered to be part of an older, cooler crowd and this intimidated Michelle.

She said, 'What if they don't think I'm cool? I don't want them to think I'm a schmuck! We need to come up with a plan!' She said, 'I got it! We need to act like we're arrogant and obnoxious instead of young, immature kids. Let's not talk to them. Let's pretend like we're too cool to talk to them. When they try talking to us we need to pretend like they're annoying us. We'll make them think, we think, they're the jerks!'

I looked at her and said, 'Um, okay, sure.'

When the day to go skiing came Michelle and I waited outside her building to be picked-up by Chris and her friends. We stood there wearing our leather jackets, smoking cigarettes, our hair was greased back, and we put the meanest, most carefree look on our face we could come up with."

"Now I know you're being silly."

"Okay, maybe we weren't dressed like that, but we were trying to act cool. When we were picked up in Angel's van we got in the back seat and slumped down, with an attitude I might add. We complained about having a hangover from the night before so it would seem like we didn't want to be bothered. Michelle's plan didn't last for long because Chris and her friends were actually very nice to us. They offered each of us a beer, and then Angel asked us if we ever skied before; one conversation led to another, and before we knew it we arrived at the ski resort. When we got to Hidden Valley we rented skis, poles, and boots; then we carried them to the slope.

Now, I always considered myself to be athletic and coordinated; but I have to admit skiing, at first, was difficult. The boots hurt my feet, I kept falling down, and I couldn't figure out how to move forward, but luckily there was a ski class being conducted within hearing distance and so I listened to the instructor for about 15 minutes. From these instructions I learned everything I needed to know to become an expert skier."

"You became an expert skier from listening to an instructor for 15 minutes?"

"Well, maybe not an expert, but I did learn enough to get on the Bunny Hill. The Bunny Hill at Hidden Valley was a long run that wasn't very steep but if you didn't slalom back and forth you could build up a lot of speed going down the hill. It was such a long run to get to the top of the hill we had to ride a chair lift instead of using a tow rope like they have on most Bunny Hills. Michelle didn't do much better than me getting used to the skis, but she eventually made it over to the Bunny Hill chair lift and got in line with me.

You guys have both seen chairlifts; you know how the chair swings around the corner and it smashes against the backs of your legs and then you're forced to sit down and the chair scoops you up and takes you up the hill."

Kelsie said, "Yeah, I remember when we went to Vail, Colorado to go skiing. When the chair hit me in the back of my legs it really hurt."

"Exactly. It hurts if you don't turn around to slow the chair down before it hits you. Anyway, when Michelle and I were getting on the chair lift it slammed against the back of our legs, and it carried us up the hill. The ride up the hill was fine, we watched two and three year old kids and eighty and ninety year old adults swishing and swooshing down the hill and so we thought, 'How hard can it be if little kids and old people can ski?' We thought it was going to be a lot of fun going down the hill, but then we remembered – we had to get off the chair lift! To get off the chair lift we had to lift up the 'sissy bar' which kept people from falling off. Then we had to put our poles in one hand and when our skis hit the ground we had to push ourselves off the chair and ski off to the left so that the chair wouldn't hit us.

This maneuver seemed simple enough, but for some reason Michelle struggled with it. When we reached the exit point at the top of the hill I skied off to the left and when I turned around I saw Michelle's legs buckle and she fell to the ground – then the chair hit her in the side of the head. At this point the chair lift attendant turned off the chair lift. When the lift was abruptly stopped the chairs swung backwards, and since Michelle was still lying on the ground she got hit by the chair again but this time on the other side of her head.

Once the attendant pulled Michelle to 'safety' she didn't give up. Like a trooper she was ready to go down the hill. Now, as you know to ski safely you need to slalom back and forth from one side of the slope to the other – this keeps you from picking up too much speed and skiing out of control. Without skiing back and forth you can easily pickup so much speed that if you run into a pole, a tree, or someone else you could seriously injure them, yourself, or both.

Michelle either didn't understand this concept, or she just couldn't master the slalom move; I'm really not sure which it was – all I know for sure was she skied STRAIGHT down the hill! When she picked up too much speed and got scared she just fell to the ground and wiped out – she did this several times down the hill, and I knew she must have been in serious pain but, like I said, she was a real trooper, and she got back on the chair lift again and again with me. Every time – yes, I said EVERY TIME, she rode the chair lift up the hill, she fell off, got hit in the head by the chair, the chair lift attendant turned off the chair lift, the chair swung back, and Michelle got hit in the head a second time."

"No way, Dad. She didn't continue to let it happen, did she?"

My dad was laughing, and he said, "I'm not kidding Cam. EVERY TIME she got off the chair lift it hit her in the head – once on the left side and then on the right. But that wasn't the worst part of her skiing. After we went down the hill several times she was determined not to wipe out; she said, 'I think I'm getting the hang of this, and there is no way I'm going to wipe out and end up lying on the ground again while these kids and old people ski past me and around me!'

I looked at her and said, 'You're getting the hang of this – are you sure?'

She said, 'Yeah – it's not that tough.'

When she went down the hill the next time, she started out fine, she didn't fall, but again she didn't ski back and forth. Her skis were lined up parallel to the hill and because of this she was flying – she flew by all the kids and old people like they were standing still. She was going so fast I couldn't keep up with her. I looked down the hill and saw several trees and she was heading straight for them; luckily she narrowly avoided them. I breathed a sigh of relief because I thought she was home free, but then I saw something that meant certain disaster!

At the bottom of the hill was the long line of skiers waiting to get on the chair lift, it had dozens of kids from the ski school and old people from the local retirement home lined up with their backs to the hill – AND MICHELLE WAS HEADING STRAIGHT FOR THEM! She was like the Iceberg to the Titanic – nobody saw it coming, but it was about to wreak havoc, and their lives would never be the same again. I yelled as loud as I could, 'RUN AWAY, RUN AWAY', but the unsuspecting victims couldn't hear me until it was too late. When they finally heard me they all turned around in unison, and they saw Michelle barreling straight for them with her arms flailing and waiving at them to move out of her way. Michelle ran into them at 'ramming speed'! It was unbelievable! It was like watching a giant set of dominos being run over by a Mack Truck.

From where I was all I could see were skis, ski poles, hats, gloves, arms, legs, canes, walkers, and false teeth flying all over the place! When I made it down the hill the victims turned on Michelle, and she was being pummeled by the people she just ran over; the old ladies and men were hitting Michelle with their canes and walkers, and the kids were kicking her with their ski boots. After Michelle was beat to a pulp, she apologized vehemently but no one accepted her apology.

All they did was mumble under their breath, 'What's she doing on the ski slope?', 'Schmuck!', 'Jerk!', 'Whipper Snapper!', 'Should be illegal for someone so uncoordinated to be on the slope!'

At this point Michelle decided she was a better 'Snow Bunny' in the ski lodge rather than a 'Skier on the Bunny Hill' and so she called it a day and sat in the lodge with Angel and Eddie. This worked out perfectly for both Michelle and me; she was able to sit and flirt with a couple of guys, and I was able to go on the black diamond slopes with Chris and Rick..."

Kelsie said, "Didn't you mind your girlfriend was hanging out with a couple of older guys? You didn't get jealous?"

"No, not at all. Michelle and I were more friends than boyfriend and girlfriend. Just like most of my relationships it was a more platonic – she loved me for my bod."

YOU SEE KELSIE! YOU START DATING, YOU PUT GREASE IN YOUR HAIR, YOU BUY LEATHER COATS, YOU FALL OFF CHAIR LIFTS, YOU GET HIT IN THE HEAD MULTIPLE TIMES, AND YOU GET BEAT UP BY THE AARP! IS THAT WHAT YOU WANT?

Kelsie shook her head and said, "No Dad, I want to hang out with the guys in the ski lodge."

Okay, I'm going to change the subject for a second. Have I told you about the Fingerling Affair?"

"Uh, yes Dad, about a million times!"

Overcoming the Fingerling Affair

"Okay, good, then you'll appreciate this story.

Although I didn't consciously realize it The Fingerling Affair left me with deep emotional scars; just thinking about gift giving caused me to break out in a cold sweat! How did I handle my neurotic, phobic fear of gift giving? Did I face it head on? No! I ran away from it. When I was a preteen I ran away from my fear by conveniently being sick on the day Secret Santa or Kris Kringle gifts were exchanged at school, however, during my teenage dating years I had a more notorious way of running away from my fear.

When I was dating a girl and a holiday like Christmas, Valentine's Day, or when her birthday was approaching I conveniently found a reason to break up with her. I had a long list of reasons to choose from; 'I still care for you but our dating is interfering with my academic career and so unfortunately we need to break up.' Actually, I don't think I ever used this one. Or I might say, 'I'm sorry, I really care about you, but I'm just not ready for such a deep emotional commitment at this time in my life.' Hmmm, come to think of it I don't think I ever used this one either. Another I might use is, 'I like you, but I just don't want to go out with anyone right now.' Yeah, I'm pretty sure this is the one I used most often.

Now keep in mind, the girl I dated didn't know anything about the deep, emotional scars I carried around with me as a result of the Fingerling Affair and so when I broke it off with her she had no idea of the true reason why. And, at the time, I don't even think I consciously knew it either. The girl might have assumed I was a free spirit, not wanting to be tied down, like James Dean in, 'Rebel Without a Cause' or maybe they just thought I was a CHEAP SKATE!

Of course when I broke the news to my girlfriend, there was a lot of 'weeping and gnashing of teeth'! If I heard it once I heard it a thousand times, 'No, don't break up with me – you're the greatest thing that ever happened to me! You're cool, funny, handsome, and smart and if you leave me I couldn't go on anymore – I LOVE YOU!!'"

"Yeah, right Dad!"

My dad ignored Kelsie and continued, "After I broke up with my girlfriend and walked away she always lunged for me, her nails digging into my skin as she slid down my back. While on her knees she broke out in a song to try to win back my love…

♪ I remember times my love when we really had it all
You were always there to make me smile, help me when I fall ♪
♪ Ooh, I can't believe you're leaving
When there's so much more to say – I can't let you go ♪
♪ Ooh, every time I look at you I still can feel the flow
Let it be, let it grow ♪ [32]

♪ Love me, please, just a little bit longer
Together we can make it ♪
♪ Our love is much too young to break it
Love me, please, just a little bit harder ♪ [33]

Kelsie said, "Dad, you are so weird!"

I asked my dad if he seriously broke up with girls before their birthdays and Christmas. He told me, "Yes, I'm serious and eventually it got embarrassing because I got a reputation for it. For example, when I first dated this girl named Michelle it was September and at the time I didn't know when her birthday was. When I learned her birthday was coming up soon on October 13th I broke out in a cold sweat, my heart began palpitating, and so I had to do what I had to do. I told her, 'I like you, and I want to continue being friends, but I think it would be better if we stopped going out with each other.' When I said this to her she tilted her head, furrowed her brow, and with a confused look on her face said, 'What? You're breaking up with me? Why?'

I was very nice about it, I just told her, 'I would just rather be friends'.

A day or two later when she told the other girls in the neighborhood about me breaking up with her another one of the girls, who shall remain nameless, told her, 'Don't worry, he'll ask you out again – right after your birthday. Just wait, you'll see. He always does this – I should have warned you about this before.'

At the time I didn't know Michelle was told this and so about three days after her birthday, I asked her out again, and she said, 'I was told you would do this. Is it true you always break up with your girlfriend right before her birthday, Christmas, and Valentine's Day?'

I said, 'What? Huh? Who? I have no idea what you're talking about.' I stumbled around looking for the right words, but I never found them.

Eventually she said, 'Ok. Sure. I'll go out with you again'. Although she said yes she was very skeptical about my commitment to the relationship – Christmas was right around the corner.

After this episode, I did some deep soul searching. I resolved to overcome the Fingerling Affair's grip on my life, but I wasn't sure how? I wondered if there were psychiatrists who specialize in gift giving phobias. I wondered if this fear was so deep seated it would require Shock Therapy. Could I overcome this fear on my own with some guidance from Self Help Books? I decided Self Help Books were the way to go; I asked my mother to drive me to the book store at Cross County. I spent hours in the store, pouring over book after book, trying to find the perfect one to help me break the chains of the gift giving phobia. After four hours I finally narrowed it down to five books:

- "101 Ways to Transform Your Life – After Giving Your Best Friend a Doll for Christmas"
- "I'm OK, You're OK – Even If You Give a Guy a Doll for Christmas"
- "Change Your Thoughts, Change Your Life; After Giving a Guy a Doll for Christmas"

- "The Power of Self Coaching; Overcoming the Emotional Shackles of the Fingerling Affair"
- "Self Hypnosis; Conquering the Fear of Gift Giving"

I opted for 'Self Hypnosis; Conquering the Fear of Gift Giving', and when I got home I read it from cover to cover at one sitting; amazingly enough it worked. Like Ebenezer Scrooge I had a new lease on life, and I wanted to run through the streets showering family, friends, and especially ex-girlfriends with gifts to make up for my years of gift giving neglect.

With my new positive attitude towards gift giving I not only bought a wonderful gift for my girlfriend – a beautiful set of rhinestone embroidered oven mitts – I also bought a gift for her parents."

Kelsie said, "Why did you buy a gift for her parents?"

"I don't know. I think it was John's idea or at least I heard he was getting something for his girlfriend's parents. But when I think back to it, I think it made sense for John because he used to go over to Susan's house all the time – he had a great relationship with her family. On the other hand, I barely knew Michelle's mother, and I don't think I ever met her father. So in retrospect, it was a pretty bad idea to buy them a gift, but after reading 'Self Hypnosis; Conquering the Fear of Gift Giving' I guess I was blinded by my enthusiasm for gift giving.

But again, it seemed like a good idea when my friends and I discussed doing it. The gift everyone planned on bringing to the parents was liquor. It still seemed like a good idea when I was trying to decide which liquor I would purchase. I wondered, 'Should I go with a Bordeaux or Burgundy wine?' Then I decided to go with the Burgundy – I think they'll like that, plus it's less expensive. It's cheap, but it's not Ripple so I think it's a good choice.' It still seemed like a good idea when I asked the Liquor Store Clerk, 'Can you please gift wrap it, in that festive Christmas cellophane with the snowman and snowflakes on it. Oh, and can you tie a red ribbon around it please?' It still seemed like a good idea while I walked from 231st Street to Michelle's apartment building on 240th Street.

When I walked into her apartment building lobby whistling Bruce Springsteen's 'Santa Claus is Coming to Town', I rang her buzzer and Michelle's dad answered over the intercom, 'Yeah, what do you want?' After hearing his gruff voice I thought to myself, 'Hmmm, maybe this isn't such a good idea after all.' When I took the elevator to the third floor, pushed open the elevator door, and walked down the long hallway to her apartment, I thought to myself, 'What am I doing? I'm 15 years old, I bought liquor – which is illegal – and I'm giving it to a couple of adults who I barely know.' I then said to myself, 'I'm not going to do this – they'll think I'm nuts. I'm going to drop the wine down her trash shoot.' But then I remembered what Chapter 4 in 'Self Hypnosis; Conquering the Fear of Gift Giving' taught me; it said, 'Repeat over and over to yourself, 'I give great, exciting gifts; people like my gifts! I give great, exciting gifts; people like my gifts…!' So I found the nerve to continue.

When I got to the door, her dad opened it. He was a big, powerful, intimidating man with a deep voice – in a moment of weakness I put the gift behind my back before he noticed it. He sneered as he looked me up and down. After what seemed to be an hour he nodded his head, made a monosyllabic grunt, turned and walked in the apartment, leaving the door open behind me – which I assumed meant 'Won't you please come in?' I followed him into the living room and sat down on the couch.

Michelle yelled out of her room, 'I'll be right there.'

I said, 'Take your time.' In my mind I thought, 'Michelle, get out here now – I think your father is going to eat me!' When she finally came out I breathed a sigh of relief. And I also decided to follow through on giving the gift to her father.

I tried to sound as upbeat as possible. I said, 'Mr. K…'

He looked at me and said, 'Mr. Who?'

I said, 'Uh, Mr. Flarity.'

He said, 'Who?'

I said, 'Uh. Bob?' He looked at me but didn't say anything this time. I said, 'I brought you a gift to wish you and your wife a Merry Christmas.' From behind my back I pulled out the bottle of Burgundy Wine wrapped beautifully in cellophane and a red Christmas ribbon.

Her father had a confused or maybe it was a suspicious look on his face; it was as if he was saying, 'Why the hell is this fifteen year old punk, who is dating my daughter, handing me a bottle of booze?' He didn't reach out for the gift, he didn't say anything; he just sat back and looked at me and my arm with the bottle of Burgundy Wine dangling at the end of it.

My mind was screaming, 'It's happening again – IT'S THE FINGERLING AFFAIR ALL OVER AGAIN!' I whispered to myself as quietly as possible, 'I give great, exciting gifts; people like my gifts! I give great, exciting gifts; people like my gifts…!' Her dad eventually grabbed the wine out of my hand and placed it on the floor next to his shoes."

Kelsie said, "That was kind of rude of him. Why didn't he even say thank you?"

"I'm not sure, Kelsie. Maybe he actually did and I didn't hear him because I was so nervous. I guess I should be thankful he didn't stand up and scream, 'Somebody bought me a doll!'

SO YOU SEE KELSIE! YOU START DATING, YOU BREAK UP WITH PEOPLE BEFORE THEIR BIRTHDAYS, YOU BUY WINE FOR PEOPLE YOU DON'T EVEN KNOW, THEY STARE AT YOU AND MAKE MONOSYLABIC GRUNTS WHILE YOU'RE HOLDING CELLOPHANE WRAPPED BOTTLES OF WINE IN FRONT OF THEIR FACE! IS THAT WHAT YOU WANT? IS THAT WHAT YOU WANT LITTLE GIRL?!"

"You are so weird, Dad."

The Piper's Kilt...

This next story is about a big change in my dad's life; one that set the groundwork for bigger and better things in his future – not in his immediate future, he was still meandering down the wrong road, but at least he was walking in the right direction.

"Like I said, I was very irresponsible, but something positive happened to me when I was about 16 years old, and I have my Uncle Richie to thank for this. He set the stage for me to eventually turn my life around. I'm not saying my life turned around immediately but at least it got me on the right track."

"You see, my Uncle Richie was more than an uncle – he was family."

"Huh? Isn't an uncle family?"

"You get my point, Schmelsi. See, when my family moved to the Bronx from Suffern my Uncle Richie was still living at my grandmother's house. He moved out a few months later, probably because of all the noise, but I remember spending a lot of time with him while he lived there.

He helped turn the basement into a family room so we'd have a place to play and watch TV. Also, my father and uncle owned a Sabrett Hotdog stand for a while. Not only that, he was one of the R's in 'R&R Catering' – a catering business my mother, father, uncle, and my Aunt Marion were partners in. I remember working many days and nights in Grandma Doyle's kitchen rolling out their world famous Swedish meatballs. As I recall, everyone loved their food, and they made good money, but eventually it got to be too much work for everyone involved.

My uncle was a career college student at this time in his life; the type of person who thrives on learning something new everyday. When he lived with us he was attending Lehman College in the Bronx. I remember the long political discussions he had with my parents and my brother Richie after dinner. My favorite memories were when he shared information from his logic class with us. He gave us riddles or brain teasers and we sat down with him at the dining room table for hours trying to figure them out. The most memorable brain teaser was about a guy driving to Albuquerque – it stumped us for days."

"Yeah Dad, you told us that before, and you still haven't told us the answer!"

"Yeah come on – tell us!"

"Sorry little Miss 'My Dad Goes Into Too Much Detail' – I'm not telling you. You thought I'd forget about that didn't you?"

I spoke up and said, "You have to tell us the answer! You can't leave us hanging like that!"

"I'll tell you after you guys think about it for a little while. In the meantime, let me get back to my story. Okay, where was I? Oh yeah my Uncle Richie.

Well, after my Uncle moved out of the house he began tending bar at P&K's. P&K's is a bar and grill in the Bronx owned by a couple of guys – Buster Patrick and John Knowles. P&K's logo is a picture of an Irish guy in a kilt holding a beer and a burger. The name P&K's has a double meaning – it's short for 'The Piper's Kilt' but it also stands for 'Patrick & Knowles'.

Buster was the tough business minded side of the partnership; he was the idea guy and the tough guy when it was required, while John was more the silent partner. It's not that he was really silent it's just that he let Buster do what he was good at doing – running the business. I think P&K's opened up in October 1975. It's located on the corner of 231st Street and Albany Crescent. It started out as a bar with a small kitchen in back which was used to cook a few burgers for some of the regulars. Their ground beef came from Joe Duffy's Meat Market down the street. He had a 'secret recipe' for ground beef – a recipe which made P&K's hamburgers – 'The Best Burger in Town'! Eventually word of these great hamburgers spread around New York City, and before they knew it they had to expand. They knocked down the wall next door to create a dining room to hold the crowds of people clamoring for a P&K's burger.

For years Joe Duffy's recipe was kept a secret – nobody other than Joe Duffy knew the exact mixture of meats to create such a delicious burger – it was the Colonel Sander's Secret Recipe of hamburgers! Before long P&K's opened up a restaurant in Eastchester, New Rochelle, Inwood, and Sarasota, Florida. This recipe was given only to P&K's and as a matter of fact, it wasn't until Buster and John opened P&K's in Sarasota, Florida that Joe Duffy gave out the secret recipe – along with a confidentiality agreement signed in blood..."

"Signed in blood, Dad? I don't think so."

"Well, maybe that's a rumor I just started, but I'm sure they had to promise to never share the recipe with anyone else.

So where was I? Oh yeah. P&K's is a Kingsbridge landmark, and it's still a favorite stopping point for people who moved upstate, out of state, or across the country when they come back for a visit. When I go back home I still go there for lunch or dinner for a medium rare 'Kingsbridge'.

P&K's cliental were primarily working class people; cops, firemen, sanitation men, and construction workers – they're all characters who were fun to be around and very generous with their money!"

"What do you mean they were characters?"

"Well, for example there was this guy Gene, wait, before I tell you about him, let me finish telling you about P&K's.

Okay, during the day there was a large lunch crowd which also included bankers, teachers, and shoppers from 231st Street. At night it was a popular place to go for dinner and a few drinks – sometimes a lot of drinks. They didn't have a parking lot and so most of the people double parked their cars outside and nearby. From behind the bar you frequently heard the bartender call out, 'There's a blue Chevy double parked outside! You're blocking a car in! Can you please move your car?!' The culprit quickly jumped up with a bite of hamburger still in his mouth and ran outside to move their car.

The lunch rush served about 200 to 300 lunches and on busy nights they served 400 to 500 dinners..."

Kelsie interrupted my dad again and said, "Dad, you're doing it again. You're getting into too much detail."

"Kelsie, I can't help it – I have fond memories of P&K's, but for my whiney little girl I'll cut back on the details."

"Promise, Dad?"

"Promise Dookie Dookie Padookie Doo. So where was I? Oh yeah. They served a lot of people with a small crew of employees. In the early morning there was a porter to clean the place; the day shift had one bartender, one cook, one 'side person', and one or two waitresses. The bartender started at 8:00 a.m. and prepared for the day by ordering and stocking all the beer and liquor and serving any of the early birds, which was unusual – except for a few people who came in to drink coffee, read the newspaper, and talk. At 9:30 the kitchen staff and waitresses began; they prepared all the food and set-up the dining room for the lunch crowd.

At 10:00 every morning Joe Duffy carried over two or three hundred pounds of ground beef and dropped it off in the kitchen. The cook, side person, and one of the waitresses shifted to hamburger patty mode; each of them grabbed a hand full of meat (after sanitizing their hands), placed it on the scale, made sure it weighed .50 pounds, and put the balls of meat in a pile. Once the meat was weighed and placed in the piles it was time to 'patty them out'

It was a smooth operation and one way or another by 11:30 the bar, kitchen, and dining room were ready for business. By 11:35 the bar was usually packed with cops, firemen, and construction workers. The dining room was packed with teachers, bankers, doctors, and women taking a break from shopping. The orders came in fast, went out fast, and the food was eaten fast! There was a lot of yelling, screaming, and cooperation – the workers were all in it together, and they knew it. On busy days the bartender got help from the cook and vice versa. When the bartender needed help he yelled, 'Can you go down stairs and tap a keg of Bud for me?'

The more efficient they were, the happier their customers were, which translated into bigger tips! Like I mentioned earlier P&K's customers were very generous; except for the teachers – they were notoriously CHEAP! On one occasion one of the more eccentric waitresses, Flo, received a $1.25 tip from a group of teachers, and she followed them outside and threw their tip back at them, 'Excuse me ladies, I think you need this more than I do!' Although there were some episodes like this, it was unusual; P&K's was a place to get away from the struggles of everyday life. It was like *Cheers* – a place 'where everybody knows your name' and you were always with friends!

♪ Making your way in the world today
Takes everything you've got ♪
♪ Taking a break from all your worries
Sure would help a lot ♪ [34]

After the lunch rush, P&K's slowed down for about 2 hours which allowed the team to regroup and restock the beer, liquor, and soda. It gave them time to make more hamburgers and prepare the restaurant for the night shift. The night shift at P&K's was busier than the day shift, there was more yelling and screaming, but there was also more laughing and singing. The night bartenders like Doug McSweeny and Keith O'Hare were the right combination of fun loving and tough – if any problem arose they took care of it. When they arrived at 4:49 p.m. they walked into the kitchen to put on their ties and to make sure every hair was in place before it was show time.

To be a bartender at P&K's you had to be a well rounded individual; you had to be a ladies man, a family man, a sports encyclopedia, a movie and TV critic, and a politician. But mostly you had to be likeable! P&K's not only had the 'Best Burgers in Town' they also had the 'Best Bartenders, Cooks, and Waitresses in Town' and that's why it was so popular.

So this is where my Uncle Richie worked. He started out bartending and working in the kitchen, but when Joe and Randy bought a couple more places they needed a manager, and my uncle was offered the job – he accepted.

It was a few years after he became manager when I was given an opportunity to be a part of P&K's. William Hanrahan, an older Irish gentleman worked as the porter in the morning. He worked Monday through Friday from 5:00 a.m. until about 9:00 Like I said, he was an older gentleman, and he had some medical problems which caused him to miss work occasionally..."

"What kind of medical problems?"

"Well, at the time I heard a few people refer to him having the 'Irish Flu'. Anyway, my uncle asked me if I could do the porter work Monday through Friday early in the morning before school; he wasn't aware I was on a two year hiatus from formal education. I jumped at the opportunity to do the job even though I didn't know what it entailed because it paid $30 per day which was $150 per week – a lot of money to me at the time. The best part about it was it didn't conflict with sports or my social life!

My job was cleaning the bathrooms. By the way Kelsie, the girl's bathrooms were nasty and disgusting after a night of heavy drinking and partying!"

"Why are you looking at me like that – I didn't make the mess!"

My dad ignored her and continued, "I also had to rake the floor every day…"

"Did you say you had to rake the floor?"

He raised his eyebrows and said, "That's right, Cam, I said I raked the floor. At this time P&K's floors were covered with sawdust. Yes sawdust, Cam, I guess it gave the restaurant character and ambiance. I raked the floor on Monday and Tuesday, and on Wednesday I swept it up and laid down new saw dust which came in once a week from the 'Sawdust Man' – that's true too. The best thing about sawdust was the customers lost coins, dollar bills, and occasionally five, ten, and twenty dollar bills under the saw dust! Every day was a virtual treasure hunt for me, and many days I gathered some extra pocket change which I used to play the jukebox or Donkey Kong. After I cleaned the bathrooms, bar, and dining room I cleaned the kitchen. I cleaned the deep fryer, the oven, the grill, and hot trays, etc. I also cleaned anything else that needed cleaning like the grease trap – a nasty trap which caught all the grease and slime that went down the drains. All in all I loved the job and was very grateful to my Uncle Richie for giving me an opportunity to work at P&K's. I genuinely tried to work hard to show my appreciation to him."

"So the opportunity your uncle gave you was to clean dirty bathrooms and rake up sawdust?"

"No, the opportunity my uncle gave me was not just to clean dirty bathrooms and rake up saw dust – Miss Smarty Pants!

Sometimes the best things in life happen because you're in the right place at the right time; that's what happened with me. After I finished cleaning P&K's in the morning I usually made myself a hamburger for breakfast. Then I sat down at the bar and had a few pilsner glasses of Budweiser before I went home…"

Kelsie sat up and said, "What? You drank beer for breakfast?! That's terrible, Dad!"

My dad said, "Yeah, I know it wasn't exactly the breakfast of champions but...but...but...it's what I did at that time in my life. I can remember one particular day I was sitting down eating breakfast and drinking my beer when I overheard my uncle say someone quit and 'they won't be in today'. He looked over at me and asked if I could hang around and help the cook in the kitchen. Since I didn't have any other pressing business – LIKE SCHOOL – I said, 'Yeah sure, what do you need me to do?'

My uncle trained me, and eventually I started getting good so he asked me if I wanted to do this everyday. I said, 'Sure' because I didn't have any other pressing business – LIKE SCHOOL!"

"Uh Dad, you already said that. You need to update your material."

"I did this job for a while, and since I did a good job eventually I was trained to be the main cook. After being a cook for a year I got another fortunate break.

Great Expectations...

My break involved my Uncle Richie again. He wanted to open a restaurant of his own for a long time. He saved up a lot of money for a restaurant and an opportunity presented itself to him in New Rochelle. He went in as a partner with Joe and Randy in a new P&K's restaurant in New Rochelle. Since my uncle was opening up his own restaurant his manager position opened up and Cheryl Donnelly, a long time worker and good friend of Buster and John was offered the job. Cheryl was one of the day waitresses who also worked in the kitchen as a cook on a rotational basis with the other waitresses. She was smart, fast, tough, and a really nice person – I had a tremendous amount of respect for her as a manager and as a person.

When Cheryl was promoted it opened up a position on the day shift. Buster decided he wanted to stop the rotations between cooks and waitresses; instead he wanted a person who would just cook during the day so the cook and waitresses could focus on what they did best. The day cook was responsible for ordering supplies, food, and everything the kitchen needed; it was kind of an assistant manager position although that's not what they called it. It paid more money and came with more responsibility. When people found out she was leaving her day position there was a question of who would take over for her. Several of the waitresses and bartenders wondered out loud who would be offered her job – a few even requested it themselves, but they were turned down because the job was offered to – me.

I was young and inexperienced, but Cheryl offered it to me. I never even considered I would be offered the job; it never entered my mind because I was very young and hadn't been cooking for long compared to some of the others. At first I didn't understand why I was offered the job, but a few days later I found out.

Joe called me and asked me to meet him at P&K's early in the morning. When I met him we sat down in the back dining room underneath the big picture window – the one which looks out over 231st Street. Joe was a big bulky man who intimidated a lot of people – including me. When I sat down he said, 'Kenny, do you know why you were selected for this job?'

I said, 'No, not really, there are a lot of other people with more experience.'

Joe said, 'That's true but I can see something in you that you probably don't see in yourself. I see a sharp, hardworking young man. How old are you?'

'Seventeen.'

'When I was seventeen I was probably like you, a little too much into partying, not enough school work, and on my way to nowhere. It took me a while to get my life on the right track, and when I did I became very successful. I now own four restaurants; I drive a Cadillac; I have a home in Florida and Eastchester, and I'm financially set for life because I was given some opportunities when I was your age that I took advantage of.'

I nodded my head to show him I was listening and paying attention. He said, 'George Steinbrenner has hired and fired Billy Martin dozens of times. He can buy and sell Billy Martin like a whore; that's because George has money, and Billy doesn't. I would rather be George than Billy, and that's why I will continue to buy more and more businesses. I don't have an education – I had to learn the hard way; from hard work and from taking advantage of opportunities I've been given. I want to give you an opportunity to make something of your own life.'

I was fixated on him as he said, 'I know you're thinking that it's just a restaurant or just P&K's, but I expect you to use this opportunity to improve yourself – you will earn about $500 per week. I'm sure that's more than you have ever made before, the question is – will you use this money to make something of yourself or not? Will you use it to start your own business? Will you use it for college? Or, he paused, or will you blow it and be a bum for the rest of your life?

I'm betting you'll make the most of this opportunity and make something of yourself. I expect some day I'll be laying on the beach in Sarasota and I'll find out you made it big and I'll be able to smile to myself and think, 'I was the one who gave that kid a kick in the ass to get him started.'

I was choked up but I didn't want Joe to know. I had never heard someone say they were helping me because I had potential or at least I never heard this when it wasn't related to sports. I was being told I had potential in life – I HAD POTENTIAL TO BE SOMEBODY!

I am very grateful for the opportunity both he and my Uncle Richie gave me. I hope someday Joe and my uncle will know the opportunity and the kick in my rear paid off."

I asked, "So I guess this is when you turned your life around?"

"Well, this helped me to become more responsible related to work; but I still was a dropout and I drank too much – and like I said – this came with other consequences."

Kelsie said, "Cool Dad. Now will you tell us about that guy you mentioned? I think you said his name was Gene."

The Color of Money

"Gene was an older gentleman, probably in his upper 60's but he looked a lot older. He was about 5'9", 200 pounds, he wore a heavy coat most of the time, and he looked like he lived a long, tough life. Every morning when I was working I let Gene in around 7:00 a.m. I opened the door for him and said, 'Good morning Gene – how ya doing?' Gene's typical response was, 'Ah, a little rough getting out of bed but I'm doing fine now – how ya doen kid?' I assumed he called me kid because he couldn't remember my name but maybe this was just how he referred to any young guy. He always came in with the New York Daily Newspaper and a cup of coffee from the corner donut shop. When he walked in he always sat in the booth next to the picture window which looked out over Albany Crescent.

We always had superficial conversations about the weather or sports; I never got to know him too well. On several occasions I noticed him having animated conversations with a couple of big burly men outside the bar. The guys stood staring into his eyes, nodding their heads in obedience. This raised my curiosity and so I asked one of the bartenders, 'Hey Joe, Gene comes in every morning, he's seems real nice, but he also hangs around with some nasty looking guys who look like they would break your neck if you looked at them wrong – what does he do? Is he in the Mafia?' Joe told me 'Kenny, he's a loan shark. The people you see him talking to help him collect money if someone is behind on payments.'"

"What do you mean they help him collect money?"

"Cam, I'm saying he loaned people money and if they didn't pay him back these two guys broke their knuckles, arms, legs, or beat them up until they paid Gene his money."

"Really?"

"Yes, I'm serious. When Joe told me this I thought it was interesting; he looked like a tough guy but he didn't act like one –

at least not around me. Gene didn't drive; he always had someone pick him up outside the bar to take him places. One Thursday morning his ride didn't show up and so he asked me if I could drive him to Johnny Mac's on 238th Street.

I told him, 'Gene, I would but I don't have a car.'

He said, 'Cough, cough, can you borrow Joe's car to drive me?'

I shrugged my shoulders and said, 'Sure, if he'll let me drive it.'

Gene yelled across the bar, 'Hey Joe I need your keys so the kid can drive me to Johnny Mac's.'

Joe said, 'Yeah, just remember not to roll down the driver side window because the power windows go down but they don't go up.' I drove him the eight blocks to Johnny Macs. The whole ride I was dying to roll down the window to let out the smoke to get away from the smell of a hacking cougher.

During the short drive I made some small talk with him. I mentioned to him, 'I can't buy a car because I can't afford the down payment. Until I establish my credit I can't get a loan and my parents won't co-sign for me.' After our short conversation I dropped him off at Johnny Macs and drove back to P&K's.

A few days later I was working and Gene knocked to come in; he sat down at his regular table and I went back to raking the saw dust. A little while later Gene called me over in his gruff voice, 'Hey kid, ya gotta a minute?'

I said, 'Yeah, I have a couple of minutes – what's up?'

I sat down across from Gene and on the table was a thick envelope which Gene pushed over to me and said, 'Here's some money for your new car.'

Inside I was jumping for joy – I felt like I just won the lottery because the envelope was filled with forty $100 bills. I thought to myself, 'Wow, I must be like a son to this man for him to give me $4,000…' but before I finished my thought Gene spoke up and said, 'Kid, I like you and when I heard you needed some money for a car I thought I'd give you a break and help you out…cough…cough.'

I was exploding inside as I said, 'I can't tell you how much I appreciate this, this is the nicest thing anyone has ever done for me...'

He looked at me and said, 'Hold on kid. You do realize you have to pay me back – don't you? Do you know what I do?'

I said, 'I think so but I'm not sure. Are you a Loan Shark?'

Gene stared at me in a disapproving way, he coughed several times and cleared his throat as if I had insulted him and he said, 'Not a Loan Shark – I'm a Money Lender. I provide people with business and personal loans and I'm going to give you the best rate you could ever get from a Money Lender. I'll loan you $4,000 and you pay me $100 per week for the next 50 weeks.'

I really didn't care about the details all I knew was I had money to buy a new car! But when I look back at it now he loaned me $4,000 and I had to pay back $5,000 – $1,000 in interest in one year! This was an incredibly high interest rate to pay a legitimate banker but apparently it was a great rate for a Loan Shark or Money Lender.

Okay, that's my story about one of the characters at P&K's. There were a lot more interesting people I'll tell you about some other time..."

Action Park with Alice Cooper

The next story my dad told us was about an awesome place he says will never exist again. He told us about it around the same time he was discussing dating with Kelsie.

"Do you guys want to hear about Action Park?"

"What's Action Park?"

"What's Action Park? What is Action Park? It's only the GREATEST action park there ever was. Okay, I need to tell you about this place. It really was an amazing place."

"What does this have to do with me dating Dylan?"

"You just sit back and relax little girl – you'll see. Okay, as I was starting to say, Action Park was a combination amusement/water park that was built sometime in the mid 70's; my friends and I went there several times in the early 1980's. The park was located in Vernon Valley, New Jersey on the side of a mountain which was used during the winter time as a ski resort.

My words will never be able to do this park justice; it was something you had to be experience to truly appreciate. Action Park had so many unbelievably exciting and dangerous rides it must have been developed by a bunch of crack heads at the height of the drug craze."

"Crack heads, Dad?"

"Cam, I'm not kidding. It was so dangerous some people called it 'Traction Park'."

"Traction Park?"

"Yes, Traction Park. I'm serious. People called it this because all over the park there were kids limping around with blood spouting out from their knees, elbows, and heads. Let me tell you a little about it so you'll understand what I'm talking about.

Earlier I said it was part amusement park, but I don't think that's totally accurate because it wasn't like going to Great Adventure or Disney World – it was different, it was better.

Keep in mind water parks, during the 70's and early 80's, were rare; I think the only water park on the East Coast of the U.S. was Wet n' Wild in Florida, and so a water park was new and exciting to us. The only things close to water parks to us were pool hoping, swimming in the Jerome Avenue Reservoir, or diving off of Columbia Rock into the East River. Action Park had great water rides! It had the Canon Ball; which was a tube that ran underground and it shot you out into the ice cold mountain water 20 feet below. There was the Jungle Jim rope where you swung out over the same ice cold mountain water and dove into the water 20 feet below. They had a bunch of water slides, surf hill, a wave pool, and the most incredible manmade mountain pool I've ever seen before or since.

This pool was built on the side of the mountain under a canopy of hundreds of trees. It wasn't a typical pool; it had cliff diving, slides, swings, tunnels, rafts, and mats. The one thing it didn't have much of was lifeguards."

"There is no way they didn't have lifeguards, Dad."

"Kelsie, I'm not saying they didn't have any lifeguards; I'm just saying there weren't many of them. There definitely weren't as many lifeguards as they have at places like Blizzard Beach or Typhoon Lagoon. You know what it's like when we go to a water park or an amusement park now? They all have bars, ropes, and lines you have to stand in. Everyone has to go one at a time and you have to wait until the person in front of you is SAFELY out of the way."

"Of course, Dad, that's just to make sure nobody gets hurt."

"I know, Cam. It's all done to keep people from getting hurt. But I think we've gone way overboard as a society trying to keep people from getting hurt. We are so obsessed with keeping people safe that we'll never have another place like Action Park.

When I was growing up danger was part of life; it wasn't something to be avoided at all costs. If you did something stupid and got hurt it was your fault. You didn't try to blame someone else, and you certainly didn't try to sue someone else. Well, maybe some people did but most people took responsibility for their actions. But, I think, it began to change in the 80's. At least that's when I started to notice it. I think the mid 80's is when people started hiring blood thirsty personal injury lawyers whenever something bad happened to them. And because of this I think we've lost something as a country. I think we have become obsessed with safety."

"But Dad, don't you think it's important to be safe?"

"Of course it's important to be safe, but even with safety you can go too far. In life we have to accept some danger otherwise what's the fun of living?"

Kelsie said, "I don't agree with you on this. I think it's important to be safe."

"Kelsie, again it is important to be safe, but it can't be the most important thing. For example, it's safer to run than it is to drive a car. So I guess we shouldn't drive a car. It's safer to walk than to run so I guess we should never run. You see, we make decisions everyday to do things which are more dangerous because we're willing to take the additional risk. But now it seems like people look for a reason to sue someone else when something bad happens.

Let me give you some examples of how ridiculous this has become. The cardboard windshield shade I have in my car says, 'Do Not Drive with Sun Shade in Place.' I was in a public toilet near the Grand Canyon and on the tank it said, 'Do Not Drink Water.' The Pepper Spray I have for protection says, 'May Irritate Eyes.' The Silly Putty I bought for you when you were 5 years old said, 'Do Not Use as Ear Plugs.' The stroller we bought for you when you were a toddler, Kelsie said, 'Caution: Remove Infant before Folding.'

You see? WE HAVE LOST OUR FREAKING MINDS IN THIS COUNTRY.

Like I said, when I was growing up we didn't need all these silly warnings – everyone knew life was inherently dangerous, and if you hurt yourself when you did something stupid or dangerous – IT WAS YOUR OWN FAULT.

If society was so overprotective when I was a kid then Action Park would have been required to have warning signs all over the park, 'Warning: If you need a warning sign you shouldn't be here!' or 'Warning: If you don't like pain you've come to the wrong place – Great Adventure is in Southern New Jersey!' or 'Warning: If you need medical care find a dime and call someone who cares.' But the one sign they really needed to post was, 'Warning: Six people have died at Action Park – Don't say I didn't warn you!'

"Did people really die at Action Park?"

"Yes. I read somewhere that 6 people died there. They never died while I was there as far as I know but I saw a lot of people get hurt."

"Wow, Dad, that's amazing but what does this have to do with me dating?"

"Kelsie, I'll get to it just be patient. Wait, I started telling you about the cliff diving pool before I went off on one of my tangents. Okay, so I was starting to say there were areas where you were supposed to dive in, but there weren't enough lifeguards, and so you could do as you pleased. You could dive off the cliffs or slide down the slides anywhere you wanted. You could do flips. You could jump or dive off the cliffs together with your friends at the same time. You could get on top of someone else's shoulders and jump in together. Like I said, it was a free for all. It was so much fun, but it could also be dangerous because people occasionally landed on top of each other or ended up doing belly flops from the 40 foot cliffs. I never saw anyone get seriously hurt at the pool, but there were a lot of bumps and bruises. But of course the pool wasn't the dangerous part of the park.

The dangerous part of the park was the dry part. It had motor speed boats which you could ride around in a snake infested moat. They had Formula 1 racing cars which could hit speeds up to 100 miles per hour and all you had to show was your Drivers License. Oh let me tell you a quick story about the Formula 1 cars.

There was one time I went to Action Park with Christopher James and Alice Kilkenney. I worked with them at P&K's, and we decided to go there for a fun afternoon. I drove my car, but I didn't have my drivers license because it had been revoked for some reason. Of course I wanted to drive the Formula cars, but since I didn't have a license I couldn't. But then I came up with an idea. Back then drivers licenses didn't have pictures on them because computers and digital cameras didn't exist or at least they weren't wide spread.

Alice did have her license with her, and so I said, 'Alice, let me borrow your license.'

She said, 'They won't let you on with a girl's license.'

I said, 'Just let me borrow it.' After she gave it to me I walked over to the desk where you have to sign all these waiver forms so I wouldn't be able to sue them if I got hurt. The guy behind the desk asked me for my license, and I handed him Alice's license.

When he looked and read 'Alice Kilkenney' he had a skeptical look on his face as he said, 'Your name is Alice?'

I confidently said, 'Yup. Just like Alice Cooper.'

He responded, 'It has an 'F' for sex.'

I nodded my head and said, 'Yup, it stands for frequently'. No, I'm kidding, I didn't say that. I said, 'Yup, the person who made my license thought the same as you. He assumed Alice was only a girl's name. When I got my license in the mail I didn't have time to get it corrected.' I don't know if he really believed me or not. He probably wasn't sure, but he let me drive the Formula cars.

Alright, let me get to the most dangerous part of the park – it was the Alpine Slide. Let me see – how can I explain this to you? Oh yeah. Do you remember watching the Winter Olympics?"

"Yeah."

"Do you remember watching the bob sledding? You know when 3 or 4 guys pushed the sled down a track or maybe it's more like an icy slide that's like a half tunnel?"

"Yeah."

"Well, the Alpine Slide was sort of like that track. There was also the alpine sled, about the size of a plastic snow sled with four small wheels on the bottom which extended or retracted by pulling up or pushing down on a large lever located in the front, middle of the sled. If you pushed down you went fast, if you pulled back it slowed you down. Like I said the track was similar to a Bob Sled track in that it went down a step hill; it had a lot of twists and turns to it and the sides swept up, especially around turns, to keeps the sled from going off the track.

To get to the start of the track up the mountain you rode the chair lift. The worker placed the sled on the back of the lift, you sat down as the lift smacked into the back of your legs, and the park attendant pulled down the sissy bar to keep you from falling off. The ride on the way up was fun because you got to yell at the people below, but the best part was seeing people 'wipe out' going around the steep turns.

Once you got to the top of the hill you jumped off, and the park attendants pulled off the sleds. You then carried your sled to the tracks; there were three tracks which started out side by side at the top of the hill, then separated during the middle portion of the ride, and then came back together at the end of the ride. This set-up was perfect for Alpine Slide Racing – which was very dangerous but very fun. You sat on the sled with your legs out in front of you with your hands on the lever; by pushing the lever forward this extended the wheels and allowed you to start; to pickup speed you kept the lever pushed as far forward are you could – but the longer you pushed it forward the more dangerous the ride became. On the ride down the hill it was safest to pull the lever back prior to going around a turn or one of the many steep banks. But many people didn't slow down while they went around the steep banks and so it was normal for people to fly off the sled and for their bodies to be ripped apart by the concrete track."

"Dad, this is interesting, but what does the Alpine Slide have to do with dating?"

"Oh yeah, Kelsie, I forgot. Okay, when I was 16 years old all my friends and I decided to go to Action Park together. Somebody organized the whole thing; I'm not sure who. We rented a bus; we brought sandwiches, beer, soda, chips, and snacks. We planned on leaving at 8:00 a.m. in the morning so we would get there by about 9:30. I was looking forward to going because it would be like a party on the bus, and I didn't have to worry about drinking and driving."

"You worried about drinking and driving?"

"No, not really, but I thought that would make me sound more responsible."

"You said you were 16 years old, and so if you were drinking at all you weren't being very responsible."

"Thank you, Miss Goodie Two Shoes! So where was I before I was interrupted by my little Miss Perfect? Oh yeah. I was looking forward to going on the bus with all my other friends, but then a day or two before the trip my girlfriend was told she had to work that day until noon.

Now, I could have told her, 'Sorry, I guess you'll have to miss it.' But I didn't. I waited for her to get off work and we both drove together to Action Park in the Bumble Bee. Anyhow, I'll never forget when my girlfriend and I made it to the park. We met our friends as they were eating lunch on a bunch of picnic tables near Surf Hill. It was obvious most of them had already been on the Alpine Slide because when we got to the picnic tables and saw the guys it looked like a triage center. My friends had long strips of skin torn away from their elbows, knees, forearms, calves, and the backs of their thighs. It looked as if they were dragged behind a pickup truck along the highway with only their shorts on."

"What happened to them?"

"I asked them, and they told me they were racing each other on the Alpine Slide, and when they went around the turns they didn't slow down and so they flew off their sleds. They said they were going so fast they slid along the track, and it just tore their skin off. Not only did they lose a lot of skin, they also had a lot of bumps and bruises because when they fell off the sleds they hit their heads, knees, and elbows. Also, some of them got hit by the sled behind them. They told me they were lucky because 'some guy broke his arm when he fell off his sled'.

Oh, one more thing about Action Park. Like I said they had some dangerous rides there, and they were always getting more and more dangerous. The last time I was at the park I saw this new ride they were building. It was like the Canon Ball where you hopped into a tube with running water in it but it was much, much bigger. To get to the opening of the tube you had to walk up steps which were about 50 feet high. At the top you jumped feet first into the tube, and the tube dropped at a sharp angle towards the ground. When the tube reached the ground it did a loop-de-loop, and then it shot you out from the tube into pool about 10 feet below. It looked like an awesome ride but as far as I know it never opened up – probably because Action Park would have been sued because people would have had a heart attack going on this ride."

"Did you say you drove your girlfriend home?"

"Yes, I did."

"Okay, so how does this relate to me dating Dylan?"

"I guess it really doesn't – I just wanted to tell you about Action Park."

Turnpikes & Tow Trucks

Another one of the stories my dad told us was about a trip him and his friends went on. My mom didn't want him to tell it to us because she thought it glorified bad behavior. Maybe it did, but Kelsie and I didn't care – we just like it.

"Alright, it happened during the summer. I think I was 16 because I already had my driver's license revoked for some reason I can't recall ..."

"What?! You had your driver's license revoked?!"

"Um, yes, but that's a whole other nefarious story; let me finish this one first. Okay, so I was 16, I didn't have a driver's license, and did I mention The Bumble Bee didn't have insurance..."

"What's The Bumble Bee?"

"What's The Bumble Bee? What's The Bumble Bee? It was only my first car! A rusted out, faded yellow, 1973 Ford Maverick. The best car I ever had; I'll tell you a few stories about it someday when you're both older."

♪ The machine of a dream
Such a clean machine ♪
♪ With the pistons a pumping [35]

"Dad, please stop singing! What did you say about not having insurance?"

"Okay, I didn't have a license, no insurance, it was 90 degrees outside, and John, Tommy and I were sitting on the Ewen Park steps with a few of the girls – with nothing to do.

"I thought there's always something to do in New York."

"There is, but it took a little while for us to think of something; then it hit us – road trip! I don't remember who it was, but someone said, 'Let's do something!' John spoke up, 'My family's in Belmar. Do you want to go there?' I looked at Tommy and we both said, 'Sure, I'll go.' The girls asked, 'Can we go too?' Of course we said, 'Yes.'"

Kelsie looked at my dad and said, "No way! No girls would go with you if you didn't have a license or insurance."

"Kelsie, I guess you don't know Bronx girls are different – they're nice, but they're tough. The girls I grew up with were a throw back to a time when women were women – tough as nails!"

"You used that line in a different story."

My dad ignored Kelsie and continued, "We grabbed our beer and the six of us loaded into the Bumble Bee. John, Robin, Jennifer, and Beth got in the back, and Tommy was my co-pilot. After we got in we drove up Riverdale Avenue near the Century and then we got on the Henry Hudson Parkway near Kappock Street. To get to the Jersey Shore we crossed the George Washington Bridge going toward the Jersey Turnpike. The drive to the Jersey shore takes about an hour and a half so we rolled down the windows, cracked open some Molson's and..."

"Dad!!!! You were drinking and driving???"

"Yeah, it wasn't a smart thing to do. I had no license, no insurance, the car was packed with kids, and I was drinking and driving. At the time I wasn't concerned about it – the only problem I had with drinking and driving was – going to the bathroom."

"What? What do you mean?"

"Well, Cam, when you drink it goes through you like, like, like...it goes through you like, like, like beer. By the time we were on the turnpike I had to go to the bathroom – BAD!!"

"Do we really need to hear about this?"

"Well it explains why mom and I tell you to make sure you go to the bathroom before we go on a long trip. Anyway, I should have gone to the bathroom behind a tree at Ewen Park before we left, but since I didn't I needed to find a rest stop as quickly as possible. I felt guilty about stopping; I didn't want to slow our trip down, but I was desperate, so I turned and asked, 'Anyone else need to take a leak?'

"Take a leak, what's that?"

"It's Bronx lingo for going to the bathroom. Alright, I wasn't the only one who had to go, so when we got on the turnpike I began looking for a rest area. We drove and drove and drove but no rest area. We kept drinking as we searched so by the time we reached the first turnpike toll plaza we couldn't take it anymore – I pulled over to the side of the road."

"You pulled to the side of the road to go to the bathroom?"

"Yes, I drove about a quarter mile past the toll booth and said, 'Sorry, but I'm dying – I'm pulling over right up here.' Everyone jumped out of the car. The girls went about 15 feet off the road behind the nearest bushes. John, Tommy, and I stood by the side of the road with all the vehicles driving by. When the trucks drove past us the ground shook so hard we had to be careful not to pee on ourselves. As we stood there watering the grass I heard a very loud siren and saw bright flashing lights. When I turned my head I saw a New Jersey State Trooper Cruiser driving toward us with its siren blaring and lights flashing.

The State Trooper pulled up along side of us and before the last pee trickled out we heard over a loud speaker, 'Turn around and put your hands on your head.' We quickly zipped up, turned around, and put our hands on our heads.

John whispered, 'What are we going to do?'

I said, 'We have the beer in the back seat; we're all drunk, nobody has a license, and the car isn't insured – there's nothing we can do.'

The Trooper stepped out of his car. He was about 6'3" tall, he had a chiseled jaw, a crew cut under his hat, and as he walked toward us his hand was open ready to pull his gun from his holster if necessary. As he walked passed The Bumble Bee he glanced in the window then back at us. He then squinted his left eye, nodded his head slightly up in the air and asked, 'Who's the driver of this car?'

I stepped forward and nervously said, 'Sir. I am sir.'

He stepped toward me and asked me for my license and insurance card. When I told him I left them at home he said to me, 'Let me get this straight young man. You're drinking and driving; you don't have a license, you don't have insurance, and you stopped a half mile from a toll booth to relieve yourself. Not a smart move boys, not a smart move at all.' Then he looked over his shoulder and noticed Robin, Jennifer, and Beth, walking out from behind the bushes. He shook his head and said, 'Oh, and you brought some girls along for the ride.' He shook his head and mumbled, 'I thought I'd seen everything.'

He looked at me and said, 'Let me tell you what we're going to do. Since none of you can drive this vehicle I'm going to impound the car. A tow truck driver will come and tow your car off the highway, and you'll have to call someone to come and pick you up. Now – I need all of you to sit in your car until I get back.'

He walked to his car and talked to someone on his CB. After about 10 minutes he came back and said, 'A tow truck will be here in about 15 to 30 minutes. He'll take you and your car to an impound site about 10 miles away. You can be picked up from there. I have another, more important, call to take care of, and so I'm going to leave you here on your own. Wait here until he comes. Whatever you do – DO NOT do anything stupid. Uh, let me restate that, do not do anything stupider than you already have. In other words, don't leave before the tow truck gets here! Do you understand?'

I said, 'Yes sir. We'll wait here. Thank you for being nice and not putting us in jail.'

He said, 'You're welcome and I hope you've learned your lesson and don't ever do something like this again.' As quickly as he appeared he was gone.

We quietly walked back to The Bumble Bee and sat down – so thankful we didn't have to call our parents to be bailed out of jail.

We sat there in silence for several minutes. Finally one of us spoke up, 'Are there anymore Molson's left? This broke the silence, and we started talking. 'Holy crap! I thought we were going to jail!' 'Why did we stop so close to the toll booth?'

'Did you notice that trooper – he didn't have a hair out of place?'

'My father would kill me if he had to pick me up from jail!'

Then John reminded us, 'It's not over yet! We still need someone to pick us up when we get dropped off at the pound.'

We sat in the car for about 30 minutes until the tow truck pulled up in front of The Bumble Bee. John and I got out and met the driver. We talked to him for a few minutes about what had just happened. He looked to be in his thirties; he was wearing a baseball cap, overalls, and a pair of construction books. He had grease and dirt on his hands, face, and all over his clothes – he seemed to be a little rough around the edges.

When we told him about our problems I don't think he cared – he had problems of his own. I don't think he listened to us much at all. He was too busy cursing and complaining under his breath. He complained about long hours and not getting paid enough. He complained about being on the shoulder of the New Jersey Turnpike picking up a bunch of kids and having to drop them off, he said, 'I'm not a &%$^&(*& chauffer!

John pulled me aside, 'Kenny, how much money do you have?'

I said, 'About $15.'

He continued, 'Let's see how much money, everyone else has. We can offer this guy some money to drop us off? He keeps complaining about not making enough money. Let's give him some money and I bet he let's us go.'

I doubted he would take the money but I thought, 'It's worth a try.' We walked over to the Bumble Bee and stuck our heads in, past the rolled down window, and John asked, 'You guys have any money? We're going to offer this guy some money to drop us off?'

The girls looked shocked, but they reached into their purses and gave us all the money they had. When we added up all the money, we had about $50.

We walked back to the tow truck driver and John resumed talking to him, 'I know you're having a bad night. What if we give you $50 would you tow the car off the turnpike and let us drive home? You'd be doing us a favor and you'd have a few extra dollars in your pocket.'

The man looked at John and said, 'Fifty bucks?'

John calmly said, 'Yeah, fifty bucks. I wish we had more but we don't. What do you think? Can you help us out?' The man looked up in the air for a second, and then he said, 'I have a place I can drop you at the next exit. Tell your friends to stay in the car while I lift it up. You two can drive in my truck.'

John and I walked back to the car with smiles on our faces. I told Tommy, Robin, Jennifer, and Beth, 'Stay in the car. He's going to drop us off at the next exit. John and I will ride in the truck cab with him. We'll pay him when he lets us go.'

The driver raised the front of The Bumble Bee up in the air and chained it in place. John and I got in the cab and we drove off the shoulder onto the turnpike. A few miles up the road we exited and stopped at a Mobile Gas Station. The driver got out and lowered the Bumble Bee to the ground and unchained it. John shook his hand and handed him a twenty, a ten, a five, and fifteen wrinkled singles. The driver put the money in his pocket and said, 'Good luck guys. Take it slow.'

We got back in The Bumble Bee and I pulled on the road; I turned to Robin, and said, 'Any more Molson's left?'

♪ Believe it or not – I'm walking on air
I never thought I could feel so free ♪
♪ Flying away on a wing and a prayer
Who could it be? ♪ [36]

After escaping a night in jail we decided not to press our luck – it'd be safer to drive back to the Bronx. Instead of driving back the same way we came we decided to take the scenic route. We drove east through the Lincoln Tunnel into Manhattan. Once we entered the city we drove north through SoHo, Greenwich Village, Midtown, the Upper West Side, and into Harlem on our way back home.

The drive back was interesting; especially when the Bumble Bee overheated in Harlem. God sent a guardian angel to watch over us that night; a nice older black man saved us from a street gang at 2:00 a.m. but I'll save this story for another day."

Kelsie shook her head, "It sounds like your guardian angel worked a lot of overtime when you were a teenager."

My dad nodded his head, "You're right Kels, he did. Do you guys want to hear another time when he came to my rescue?"

We both said, "Yes."

The Great Adventures of Dating

This next story is about my dad going on a date with his girlfriend. It didn't sound like my dad was a very good boyfriend; at least not at this time in his life. He used his bad example as a boyfriend to try to convince Kelsie she shouldn't date until she was older.

"Kelsie, the next story is about dating and why you need to stay away from it until you are ready to receive Social Security."

"I thought you told me by the time I'm old Social Security will be bankrupt, and I won't receive it?"

"You're starting to catch on little girl."

He laughed, "I'm kidding, but if this story doesn't convince you you're too young for dating I don't think anything will. It's a story about going on a date to Great Adventure."

"Who was your girlfriend?"

"Cam, how many times do I have to tell you – I had so many girlfriends it's impossible for me to remember all their names?"

"Dad, your material needs to be updated. You used this one before."

"Okay, whatever. Alright, now keep in mind I was never much of a planner when I was a teenager; I liked doing things on the spur of the moment. So when I asked her to go on a date to Great Adventure I didn't put much thought into it.

I should have thought about how much money it would cost because a date to Great Adventure was expensive. There was the cost of breakfast, lunch, and dinner for the two of us. Then, of course, there were tolls, parking, admission to the park, beer, and or course gas."

"Dad, too bad Kelsie wasn't with you – she has a ton of gas!"

"Cam, I don't even think Kelsie has enough gas to fill up the car I was driving at the time. My father got rid of the Bumble Bee and the Red Barron, so I usually drove around in my father's green Fleetwood Cadillac which used so much gas I had to fill it up for a trip around the block."

"Really, Dad?"

"No, Cam, but it felt like it. My friends and I called it the Green Hornet, but we should have called it Audrey II from *Little Shop of Horrors*?"

♪ Feed me, Feed me [Kenny]
Feed me all night long ♪ [37]

"Dad, can you please do me a favor?"

"Sure, what?"

"Don't ever sing around my friends."

My dad ignored Kelsie, "If I was smart I would have written down all the expenses to determine if I had enough money, but of course I didn't. I just looked in my wallet and saw a couple of twenties, and a few singles so I assumed I had enough money."

"Why didn't you count your money?"

"I don't think I wanted to know how much I had. I already decided to go on this date and I didn't want facts and figures to get in the way.

Okay, when I got up in the morning I hopped in the shower, scrubbed some *Head-n-Shoulders* in my hair, rubbed *Irish Spring* on my body; I smelled sweet and clean for my lady friend.

"I'm not listening to this daddy?"

My dad raised his voice a little, "When I got out of the shower I put on my most stylish Terrycloth shirt, my cleanest cut off shorts, and I grabbed my leather Nikes. I poured some baby powder in them to absorb the sweat and smell of my feet. Then I grabbed my father's car keys off the coffee table and walked out the door, on my way to the Caddie. As always I had to maneuver the Caddie out of a tight parking space; then I drove to Johnson Avenue in Riverdale to pickup my woman from her apartment."

"She had her own apartment?"

"No, Cam. It wasn't her own; we were only 16 years old. Okay, so I pulled up outside her apartment, jumped out, and walked across the street to her lobby, where I rang her buzzer.

She answered, 'I'll be down in a second my sexy stud muffin man!', and then…"

"Yeah right, Dad – sexy stud muffin – I doubt it…"

My dad smiled, "I got back in my car and waited. When she walked out of her building her hair was still slightly damp; she was wearing a pair of well fitted Jordache jeans, a beige spaghetti strap top, a pair of brown leather open toed sandals, and she was carrying a small brown leather purse – she was a babe."

"Dad!"

"Sorry Kels, but this the only thing on boy's minds – it's all about the booty!"

"Dad, it's all about you BEING WEIRD!"

"Anyway, she walked across the street, around the front of the car and got in. She leaned over, gave me a kiss hello, folded her left leg under her right leg, put her left hand on my right shoulder, and said, 'Mmmm, Terri clothe, baby powder, ***Irish Spring***, and ***Head-n-Shoulders*** – you look and smell great!'"

"Oh yeah, Dad, I'm sure that's what she said."

"Well maybe that's what I said to her, but I could tell by the look in her eyes she was thinking it. I put the car in drive, turned up the radio, and we were off to Great Adventure.

The ride to Great Adventure was great; I wasn't much of a talker but even back then I could sing."

♪ You in the moonlight
With your sleepy eyes ♪
♪ Could you ever love a man like me? [38]

"Dad, you can't sing, you're a terrible singer."

"That really hurts little girl, but I think I'll get over it. Anyway, I had two cassette tapes in the car; Meatloaf's *A Bat Out of Hell* and the soundtrack to *Grease* – I loved those tapes. Although, we mostly listened to music and sang we also talked about a few things, like our plans for the future.

At this time in my life I had dreams of playing professional baseball; I excelled at this sport, and the team I played on, the Riverdale Graduates, occasionally had professional scouts at the games. In fact, one summer our team picked up a player, Stanley Jefferson, who was later drafted by the pros. He played in the major leagues for the Yankees, Mets, and Orioles. Becoming a professional baseball player was a long shot for me, probably impossible, but I didn't have any other realistic dreams to think about. Dreaming of becoming a doctor, lawyer, businessman, or teacher wasn't in the realm of possibilities since I was a high school dropout. My girlfriend, on the other hand, dreamt of being a world traveler.

The drive to Great Adventure took us across the Henry Hudson Bridge where I paid a toll; across the George Washington Bridge to the NJ Turnpike where I paid another toll! I didn't count the remaining money in my pockets as I paid each toll. I guess I hoped it would miraculously multiply in my pockets, like the loaves of bread and fishes the apostles used to feed the people when Jesus taught the 'Be Attitudes'.

When we finally made it to Great Adventure I paid for parking and I paid for both of us to enter the park. We had a great day at the park; we rode every ride, played all the games, and we ate hot dogs, hamburgers, and funnel cakes. With every penny I spent I thought to myself, 'I hope I have enough money to get home' but I never took the time to count my money. Again, I guess I didn't want reality to infringe on the fun we were having.

By the end of the day I knew it was possible I didn't have much money left; I could only feel one or two pieces of paper and some change. There was a chance the paper I felt included a twenty, a ten, or at least a five but it was unlikely. I opted to put off the moment of truth until we left the park and reached the car. This was when I decided to count my money; if I was short on money I would tell my girlfriend – if I wasn't…"

"What? Are you saying she didn't know you didn't have enough money before you left?"

"Kelsie, I didn't say I didn't have enough money left. I said I didn't know."

"Okay dad. That's a big difference."

"When we reached my car, I put my hands into my pockets; it wasn't good news – there were no more loaves and fishes. I pulled out some crumbs and a few fish eyes; two, one dollar bills, three quarters, a nickel, and six pennies. It was at this point I asked my girlfriend, 'Um, can I ask you a question?'

She said, 'Yeah, sure.'

'Um, do you have any money?'

'Well I might have a couple of dollars but not much.
Why do you ask?'

Now came the moment of truth. 'Um, because I think I did a poor job estimating how much money I needed for our date. The food, parking, tolls, and gas were a little more than I anticipated and I'm short on money. I don't think I have enough money to make it home.'

'Well, how much do you have?'

'If I include everything I have in my pocket and in the car – I have two dollars and eighty six cents. How much do you have?'

She checked in her purse and said, 'I'm sorry. I don't get paid until tomorrow and so I only have two singles and some change; I think fifty cents. How much do we need to get home?'

'Well, the three tolls on the turnpike will cost about a dollar fifty and the George Washington Bridge Toll will cost about two dollars. The problem is the gas; we're almost on empty and my car only gets about two miles to the gallon. By my calculations we need about twenty dollars in gas to get home.'

She turned her head slightly, squinted her eyes, and asked, 'When you did the calculations this morning what did they tell you? Did they say you had enough money to go on this date?'

I looked at her with the most pitiful face I could muster, and I batted my eyes hoping for some sympathy, 'I guess my calculations weren't accurate this morning because I was blinded by my excitement about being here with you.'

She rolled her eyes and said, 'Well what are you going to do now?'

I said, 'Let's go to a gas station first, then we'll get on the highway to go home. We'll try to get through some of the tolls without paying; if we do this we'll have more money for gas. I'll drive slowly to conserve gas; I've heard the slower you drive the more miles per gallon a car gets. When we go down hill I'll take my foot off the gas pedal; maybe that will save some gas too. If it looks like we'll run out of gas I'll pull off the road and call my parents to ask if they can meet us to bring us money. I'm sure they'll do that for me, um, I think they'll do it for me, hmm, I hope they'll do it for me, uh, alright, they probably won't but I'll ask anyway.

When we pulled out of Great Adventure's parking lot we had a total of five dollars and eighty-six cents. We stopped at a nearby gas station and I told the attendant, 'I'll take five dollars and eighty-six cents of regular.'

He stepped back, looked at my caddie, and said, 'Five dollars and eighty-six cents of gas? That's not enough for this boat to drive off this lot. Are you sure you don't want more?'

I said, 'Sure, if you give it to me for free.' He laughed but he didn't give me any free gas.

When we left the gas station the fuel gauge arrow was pointing just below the quarter tank marker.

My girlfriend turned to me and said, 'If I ever go on a date with you again we need to go somewhere that's within walking distance or maybe you need to sell raffle tickets before all of our dates.' She was referring to an innocent money making scheme I engaged in several months earlier."

"What was the money making scheme?"

"I'll tell you when you're older. Okay, in my attempt to conserve gas I tried every trick in the book; when I got on the Turnpike I gradually built up speed, when I was on the road I kept a consistent speed, when I was driving down hill I took my foot off the pedal, and I tried to drive behind eighteen wheelers as much as possible to reduce the wind resistance. Unfortunately, even with all these fuel conservation measures the fuel gauge arrow looked like the second hand on a Rolex watch – it swept closer and closer to the 'E'."

"What's the 'E' dad?"

"Cam, the 'E' stands for empty – no more gas.

♪ Running on, Running on empty…"♪ [39]

Kelsie gave my dad a look. He stopped singing and continued his story, "We drove down the Turnpike, past by Rahway Prison, which was well known at the time because of a program they had called 'Scared Straight'. Scared Straight was a program which encouraged troubled, delinquent boys and girls to turn away from their evil ways."

"It sounds like a perfect home away from home for you dad."

My dad sneered at Kelsie and said, "Anyway, about 10 minutes later we were near exit 32 a short distance from a rest area, the arrow on the fuel gauge was now far past the 'E' so I said, 'I'm going to pull into the rest area and call my parents or maybe I'll call my Aunt Dot to see if she can meet us.'

New Jersey rest areas were very nice; this one had a gas station, a nice restaurant, vending machines, phones, and large restrooms. We rolled into the rest area on fumes. I pulled into a parking space outside the front door of the restaurant near the public phones.

Since I didn't have any money I picked up the phone and dialed '0' for the operator and said, 'I'd like to place a collect call to area code (212) 549-5446. Tell them it's their favorite son Kenny calling.' When I was growing up I could hear everything the operator was saying to the person on the other end of the call. She dialed my number, the phone rang three times, and then I heard someone pickup the phone. My heart stopped when I heard the voice on the other end say, 'Yeah?' I panicked, 'Oh no – it's Philip!' I yelled, 'Phil, please say yes, please say yes, say yes, say yes, come on Phil, you can do it!' but he couldn't hear me. Then I heard the operator say, 'I have a collect call from Kenny will you accept the charges?'

Philip responded, 'No way!'

I yelled again, 'Operator, just tell my brother his brother Kenny wants him to say yes.'

She said, 'I'm sorry sir I can't do that. He turned down the charges. I can't put the call through.'

I could hear my mother in the background say, 'Who's on the phone?'

Philip responded, 'I don't know?' 'Then hang up the phone Phil, your father and I are going out to Doubledays, and you need to eat dinner.' I told the operator, 'Ohhhhh, never mind!' Then I said, 'Wait! Can you give me the phone number for Dorothy Benentendi in Ridgefield Park, New Jersey?'

'Sir, you need to deposit ten cents for directory assistance?'

I yelled, 'Ten cents!!!! I don't have ten cents – can't you do me a solid and look it up for me?' 'I'm sorry sir, I can't do that – directory assistance costs ten cents.'

I yelled even louder, 'Oh, forget it!' I hung up the phone, turned around to my girlfriend, tried to smile, and said, 'Well that didn't work out as well as I hoped but I still have a few ideas to get us home.' She just looked at me and shook her head.

I walked to the back of the Cadillac, opened up the trunk and rummaged through all the junk searching for something – my girlfriend watched me in the trunk tossing things around, but she had no idea what I was looking for. A few minutes later I slammed the trunk closed and mumbled under my breath, 'I can't believe there's not one in here! There are golf clubs, golf shoes, clothes – everything except what I need!'

My girlfriend said, 'What are you looking for?'

I said, 'I'm looking for a garden hose so I can siphon gas out of one of these cars.'

She looked at me in disbelief, 'Why would you expect to find a garden hose in the trunk of someone who lives in an apartment? Does your family siphon gas often?'

I said, 'No, we don't siphon gas and actually I've never done it but Ron Klaus taught me how to do it when he taught me how to hot wire cars.'

She said, 'Oh my gosh. What are you planning on doing?'

I said, 'All I need is a garden hose, a container, like a bucket or a plastic milk container, and a gas tank. I'll stick the hose in the gas tank, suck on it like a straw, and the gas will flow out of the tank and into the plastic container. It's really easy.'

Her eyes popped out of her eye sockets, 'Hold on, let me get this straight – I'm on a date with a guy who's going to 'siphon gas', also known as 'steal gas', to bring me home. I've never been on a date with someone who committed grand larceny while I was on a date with him."

I smiled, "Well, like I always say, you should try everything once."

She said, 'I don't think you should steal gas; it's illegal and you might get arrested!'

I raised my left eye brow, put a small little smirk on my face, and said, 'You make it sound so dirty, so wrong.'

She said, 'Yeah…well.'

I said, 'All I'm going to do is find a hose and a container and then I'll fill it up with gas. We just passed by a prison where there are murderers and rapists – they're bad people – I'm not – all I'm doing is borrowing some gas so my girlfriend can get home safely to her family – what I'm doing is a noble thing, a chivalrous thing...'

She interrupted me and said, 'That sounds very eloquent but I don't think the Police will agree with you?'

I smiled and said, 'Ok, sit back and relax, I'll be back in a few minutes to save you.'

"Dad, you were really bad!"

"You're right Kelsie – I was bad just like all teenage boys."

"Not all of them are bad!"

My dad ignored her and said, "I walked around to the back of the restaurant, and found exactly what I was looking for. There was a water spicket on the back of the building with a short hose connected to it; the kind restaurants use to hose down and clean their rubber floor mats. There was no one near by, and so I strolled over to the hose and unscrewed it and borrowed it."

"Stole"

"I BORROWED it, and then I walked to the dumpster and pulled out a large, empty plastic potato salad container. Behind the restaurant, off to the side, was a parking lot for the employees of the rest area. It was a dimly lit lot, and as far as I could see there were no cars coming or going, and I didn't see any people walking around. So I nonchalantly walked, with my hose and bucket in my hand, to the back of the lot and I picked out a 1978 Chrysler Lebaron. I looked around, and when I saw the coast was clear I quickly squatted down by the side of the car, I unscrewed the gas cap, put one end of the hose in the gas tank, and put the other end in my mouth. Then I sucked as hard as I could to siphon the gas out of the tank into the plastic container. But instead of sucking in the gas causing it to flow into the plastic container – I sucked in two lungs full of gasoline vapors! The vapors overtook me, and I was knocked down to the ground; a moment later when my head stopped spinning – my stomach started turning and guess what."

"What?"

"I filled up the container. Unfortunately it wasn't filled up with gas – it was filled up with everything I ate at Great Adventure.

At this point I wasn't about to try sucking out the gas again, and so I walked back to the car dizzy and defeated. When I got back to the car my girlfriend said, 'Ewe, what's that smell? It smells like a combination of gas, vomit, and I think I detect a hint of a Great Adventure hot dog with a touch of mustard and onions. What happened?'

I looked at her, wiped my mouth with the bottom of my shirt and said, 'Well, when I got to the car I thought about what you said, and I decided you were right – siphoning gas is immoral and wrong. Thank you for helping me to see the error of my ways – you are my moral beacon, my guiding light, my light house in the sea of darkness!'

She looked at me, smiled, and said, 'Yeah right – what happened? Did you swallow some gas and throw it up? By the way, do you think you'll be able to get me home, or should I call my mom to come and pick me up?' I started to answer, but before I did a police cruiser pulled into the parking lot and parked a few spaces away from the Cadillac.

My girlfriend said, 'Why don't you just walk up to the police and ask them if they can help us? Aren't they supposed to help people in distress?' This seemed reasonable, but unfortunately I had to inform her that not only didn't I have money for gas – I also didn't have a license because it had been revoked several months ago and the car didn't have insurance. So it probably wasn't a good idea to walk up to a police officer, however, considering we didn't have any other options left I decided to take her advice. I took my wallet out of my back pocket and handed it to her, 'Please hide this in your pocket book and no matter what happens don't pull it out.'

I walked over to the squad car and tapped on the window; there were two officers in the car and the one on the driver's side rolled down his window. I said, 'Hello officers, I have a problem, and I hope you can help me. My girlfriend and I drove to Great Adventure from the Bronx, but while we were at the park either I lost my wallet on one of the rides or someone stole it; unfortunately, I don't have any money to pay for gas, and I'm running on empty.

The officer said, 'What's that smell? It smells like gasoline, vomit, and hot dogs.'

I grimaced, 'Yeah, I know, I got sick earlier. Do you know anyone who can help us?'

He said, 'I don't know who can help you, but can I see your driver's license and your insurance card?'

I said, 'I would show it to you but, like I said, I somehow lost my wallet which had both of those in it along with my money.'

He said, 'Oh, right. Well I don't know what to tell you – we can't help you.'

I said, 'Thank you sir' and I walked away. I walked over to my girlfriend, put my arms around her and said, 'I need to make it look like I'm crying. Pat the back of my head like I'm crying. Please don't ask why right now, just do it.'

A minute later the squad car pulled up next to us where I was 'crying', and one of the officers lowered his window and said, 'Hey young man, come here. I can lend you ten dollars if you promise to pay me back. Here's my address, now let me have yours.' He handed me a pen and paper. I wrote down my name, address, and phone number on it and gave it back to him; I took the officers information and the ten dollars and put it in my pocket. I thanked him vociferously and had every intention of paying him back…"

"Did you?"

"No, but this time I really planned on paying him back. After he gave me the money I pulled my car up to the pump and put ten dollars worth of gas in the tank – enough to get me to my Nanny's house but that's a whole other story.

So you see Kelsie? This is what dating is like when you're young and immature. IS THIS WHAT YOU WANT? DO YOU WANT TO BE A JORDACHE JEAN WEARING, GREASE SINGING, HOT DOG EATING, COLLECT CALL CALLING, GAS PUKING, SCARED STRAIGHT DATING LITTLE GIRL??? IS THAT WHAT YOU WANT?"

"No Dad, I just want to date Dylan."

Heaven Can Wait – for My Dad

Most of the stories I've shared with you up to this point have had a humorous shade to them, however, if you've read between the lines I bet you noticed my dad's childhood wasn't always as much fun as I've presented. If you didn't pick up on this don't feel bad – neither did I until my dad told me his next story.

This story brought all his earlier stories together and it finally made sense why he left the Bronx. He explained to me that after many years of drinking, dropping out, and getting into trouble; it all caught up with him. Towards the end of his teenage years when he compared himself to the people around him – he didn't measure up very well. With this came low self esteem, depression, and despair. These feelings manifested themselves outwardly as anger toward the people he cared for the most. Did he have any objective reason for feeling this way, no, but that didn't change the way he felt. Instead of embracing the people who cared about him – he pushed them away. My dad told us this next story was the beginning of the end of his life in the Bronx.

"It started when I got into a nasty argument with my girlfriend after a long day of drinking with my friends at Off Broadway. I don't recall what it was about, but I'm sure it was related to my jealousy and insecurity.

♪ You cause me so much pain, I think I'm going insane
What does it take to make you see? ♪
♪ You just keep on pushing my love over the borderline [40]

Based on the intensity of the argument most people would have assumed our relationship was over, but it wasn't the first time it happened, and so in the back of my mind, I assumed we would eventually get back together.

A few days went by and neither one of us called the other, a few weeks went by and still neither one of us called the other, a month went by, and I couldn't hold out any longer – I needed to talk to her because I missed her. I called several times but was told she wasn't home. This probably wasn't true, but since she never returned my calls it became clear to me our relationship was over. Breaking up with her was difficult, but when I looked back on our relationship I didn't blame her for wanting to end it to find someone new. Like I said before, I hit rock bottom, and I wasn't exactly the nicest guy to be around – and that's putting it nicely.

The only way for me to deal with the breakup was to stay busy; I began riding my bicycle more, I played basketball at Manhattan College, I lifted weights, and I worked overtime at P&K's every chance I got. I worked doubles in the Bronx, I covered in Eastchester, and I worked Saturday and Sunday brunch in New Rochelle.

One Thursday night when I was covering the night shift for Tony I thought I noticed my girlfriend walk by the kitchen door on her way to the back room. A minute later I thought I noticed her walk past the door again on her way back towards the tables near the front door. I was pretty sure it was her, but to be positive I walked out to the bar to get a soda. I looked across the bar, through the bottles of liquor, and there she was; only she wasn't there with her friends – she was on a date with an older guy I knew. Seeing her sitting there was shocking and painful to me. It shouldn't have been, but it was. Yes, we had a rocky relationship, but even with all our problems I thought we'd always be together. The shock and pain I felt was something I had never experienced before, at least not to this extent, I turned and walked back into the kitchen and stood there in shock.

One of the waitresses, her name was Gay, walked in the kitchen, looked at me, and said, 'What's wrong? It looks like you've seen a ghost.'

I looked down, shook my head, and said, 'I just saw my old girlfriend.'

She said, 'I thought that was her, but I wasn't sure.' She walked over and rubbed my back and said, 'Can I do anything for you? Can I get you a drink?' I nodded my head. She came back a short time later and handed me a vodka and pineapple. This helped, but not enough; my heart was aching and my body was shaking.

When she came back in the kitchen to check on me she asked, 'Are you alright? Let me know if there is anything else I can do. I know how much you care for her, but you WILL get over her – I promise.'

I said, 'I need to say hello to her?'

'Well, if you want to say hello to her, she's standing next to the jukebox by herself – BUT KENNY – don't say anything you'll regret.'

I said, 'I won't, I just want to say hello.'

I decided to walk over to her; the last thing I wanted her to know was how I felt inside. I didn't want her to know I was crushed – now that I could see she had moved on with her life without me. When I walked up to her she appeared to be surprised to see me; she was polite, but I could sense she was uncomfortable with me being there. I didn't stay for long – just long enough to say, 'Hi, how are you – good to see you again.' But on the inside I wanted to scream, 'Why haven't you called me? Don't you know how much I miss you? Don't you know how much I care?' But I didn't, I just forced out a smile and said, 'Bye, I'll see you around.' I turned and walked back in the kitchen with my legs shaking and my stomach in knots.

♪ Take it easy on me, it should be easy to see
I'm getting lost in the crowd, hear me crying out loud ♪
♪ Just want you to know I know that you have to go
It's all up to you, but whatever you do ♪
♪ Take it easy on me [41]

In my mind my life hit a new low because now EVERYONE in my life had given up on me.

The next day, even though I was down and depressed, I was still able to put on a mask before I walked into work the following day. As I completed the prep work I talked with Debbie, Margaret, and Christopher about the situation the night before. As I told them what happened I tried to act like it wasn't a big deal, but as I thought more and more about it I became more and more upset. To drown out my sorrows I decided the best cure for my pain was 'Pickle Can Therapy'. This therapy temporarily deadened my pain, but instead of solving my problems it eventually made things worse – almost with devastating consequences."

"What's Pickle Can Therapy, Dad?"

"It was a stupid way to get my mind off my problems. It involved Absolute vodka, pineapple juice, and a cleaned out pickle can."

"Oh, drinking again?"

"Yes, drinking again. So, after our prep work was complete I opened the basement trap door and walked down the steps to the supply room for the ingredients. When I came back upstairs I cleaned out an empty pickle can and poured in the vodka. Throughout the day I filled a 9 ounce Hi-Ball glass with ice, vodka, and pineapple juice. My co-workers incorrectly assumed I was drinking pineapple juice the whole day.

The first therapeutic drink took place at 11:30 a.m. and the therapy continued throughout the day, and it worked like a charm – it took my mind off all my worries; I laughed and joked the whole day, but by 4:00 I was in no condition to continue working. Then something unusual happened; we got a late rush. Before I knew it I had hamburgers, steaks, and chicken on the grill and a dozen more orders coming out of the kitchen printer. Luckily Tony, the night cook, came in early and I asked him to take over. When he asked me where I was with the kitchen orders I slurred, 'I have no idea', and I took my apron off and walked out.

As I was walking out, the bartender stopped me and said, 'Kenny, you have a phone call.' I staggered to the pay phone holding onto the bar stools to keep from losing my balance. When I picked up the phone it was Wayne, a cook who worked at the Eastchester restaurant. Wayne said, 'I just want to remind you you're covering for me tonight.'

I said, 'Holy &#$%! I forgot I told you I'd cover for you! I have something else going on tonight but hey, Sharon is looking for some extra shifts, I'll ask her if she can do it. Don't worry I'll make sure you're covered.'

I called Sharon at home and she said, 'Yes I can work tonight, but I don't have a car. I need someone to drive me there and take me home after the shift is over – can you?'

'Uh, yeah, sure, just meet me here in a half hour, and I'll drive you.' By this time I could barely see straight, but when Sharon walked into the restaurant I slobbered, 'Are you ready? Let's go.' We got into my car, drove up the Major Deegan to the Cross County Parkway, exited on Eastchester Road, and drove north for about two miles.

When we got to the Eastchester P&K's I walked her in, and I sat down at the bar for a couple more drinks; by this time I couldn't see straight and I was extremely TIRED! I told Sharon I was going to rest in my car for awhile until she was ready to leave; I walked out the back door and went to P&K's parking lot for a nap. I couldn't get comfortable in the front seat so I folded down the back seat, laid down, and went to sleep.

A couple hours later I woke up to the sound of heavy rain hitting the car. I rubbed my eyes, stretched out my arms, and had a splitting headache! When I sat up I looked around; I had no idea why I was sleeping in my car in the back of P&K's parking lot.

My head was pounding, not only because of all the alcohol I drank that day, but also because of all the thoughts of my life running through my mind; drinking, dropping out, stealing, being dumb, being angry, having no future, family giving up on me, friends giving up on me, and my girlfriend giving up on me. I looked at myself in the rear view mirror; my eyes were bloodshot and my hair was a mess. I thought to myself, 'Nobody cares about me. Why should they? I don't blame them.' Earlier in the day the alcohol exaggerated my happiness, but now it was exaggerating my sadness – as it usually did. Instead of sitting in my car until my head cleared I rolled into the front seat and drove back to the neighborhood.

♪ You see the world through your cynical eyes
You're a troubled young man I can tell ♪
♪ You've got it all in the palm of your hand
But your hand's wet with sweat and your head needs a rest...♪
♪...How can you be such an angry young man [42]

As I drove through the pouring rain on Route 6 – terrible thoughts ran through my mind. 'I'm stupid; a dropout; I have no future!' I pressed my foot down on the gas pedal. 'Nobody cares about me – why should they?' I pressed my foot further down on the pedal. I drove faster and faster and more and more reckless as I thought about my life and the mess it had become. Every aspect of my life was a disaster; what made it worse was I didn't see anyway out of it. I didn't know who or what to turn to for help; all the people I cared for most seemed to have given up on me.

As I approached the Cross County Parkway I thought to myself, '&*%$ it', and I decided to drive around the cars stopped at the traffic lights, and 'whatever happens – happens.' I floored the gas pedal and raced through several intersections where the lights were red – narrowly missing the cross traffic. I turned onto the Cross County Parkway on-ramp with the pedal still on the floor; when I jerked the car onto the parkway I lost control of my car! The road was so wet my car spun around several times while it slid across the highway. When it finally stopped spinning I was facing toward the oncoming traffic. Through the rain covered windshield, all I could see were dozens of blurry lights racing toward me. Then I heard the loud sound of a horn and I saw the bright lights of an 18 wheeler swerving to avoid me. As it swerved, it clipped my front bumper, spinning the car around, and throwing me into the passenger side seat. I felt the wheels of the car hit a bump; my car was thrown across the highway onto the shoulder. Instead of being thankful for still being alive – I was disappointed. I don't know what the truck did after it hit me, all I know is I turned the car around and got back on the road – headed for the Bronx.

I should have gone home to sleep it off, but I didn't. Instead, I eventually found myself outside of Ehring's. Prior to walking in I put on my mask of happiness. I ordered a drink and laughed and joked with my friends. A short time later SHE walked in with a few other girls and I began making arrogant, obnoxious comments about her, but my friends covered my mouth to keep her from hearing me. I yelled '#$^&(% you guys, and I decided it was time to go. Pat, Billy, Shawn, and John knew I had too much to drink, and they said, 'Kenny, don't go! We'll all go out and have a great time to help you forget about her. They thought she was my only problem; they didn't realize she was one part of many problems I had. They said, 'Come on, Kenny, we'll go to Yonkers and meet some girls! We'll have a great time!' They tried everything to stop me from getting in my car, but I wouldn't let them.

When I got up to leave they tried to steal my car keys, but I ran outside before they could stop me. When I was inside my car Pat and Shawn tried to convince me to give them my keys and not to drive. I rolled down my window a crack and yelled more obnoxious things about her, but they closed the door to Ehrings so she couldn't hear me.

Then I drove my car up on the sidewalk almost driving through the front doors, but I changed my mind and yelled, 'I'm out of here!' I floored the gas pedal again and drove down the sidewalk of 231st Street. Several people jumped out of the way to keep from being run over. Outside the Fish Market there was an open parking space where I pulled off the sidewalk and onto the street. Once I was on the street I floored it again and drove through a red light on Broadway – narrowly missing a bus making the turn onto 231st Street.

At this time I wasn't sure where I wanted to go I just wanted to get away. I could barely keep my eyes open so I went home to get some sleep. I couldn't find a parking space on my street so I double parked at the top of the hill and stumbled upstairs to my apartment. I wanted nothing more than to lay in my bed and sleep, but before I could, I got into a nasty argument with my mother and father. I have no idea what it was about; all I remember is when I tried to make my point I kicked a wooden desk chair which was in the hallway. My father recently brought it home, and I didn't know how heavy it was. I thought it would fly across the hallway when

I kicked it, but unfortunately it was made of solid oak – it didn't budge! The pain was excruciating but I couldn't let my parent's know. I hobbled out the door and slammed it behind me, knocking the hallway pictures off the wall. I limped outside with my badly injured foot, and when I made it outside my car was gone.

I leaned against a parked car and assumed it was stolen until I saw it down the street near the crosswalk. Earlier, I must have forgotten to put the parking brake on, because somehow it rolled down the street. Amazingly enough it didn't roll into the middle of Kingsbridge Avenue; it didn't hit any parked cars, and most importantly it didn't hurt anyone. Apparently it rolled straight down the street and made a sharp left turn at the cross walk because when I found it the front left wheel was on top of the sidewalk.

I carefully got into the car and drove it to the Waldbaums parking lot where I fell asleep for a few hours with my throbbing foot. When I woke up, some time in the middle of the night, I assumed my mother and father were asleep, so I hobbled back up the street into my apartment building and eventually into my bed.

Early the next day I received a phone call from Denise. She called to find out if I was still alive, and at this time I didn't remember much of the previous night. She told me some of the things I did the night before, and they were so humiliating I couldn't listen anymore. I hung up the phone and thought I had done the impossible – I thought I made my life worse!

A short time later I called her back and apologized for hanging up. I sat and listened to her tell me the rest of what she knew. As she told me what she saw me do the night before it started to come back to me – and I didn't like what I remembered.

At this time my foot was a dark shade of black and blue, it was swollen, and the pain was agonizing. I asked her if she would go to the emergency room at Montefiore Hospital with me. She said she would if I picked her up. I ignored my family as I got dressed and walked out the door. Then I drove my car to her apartment, and we went to the Emergency Room together. When I finally saw a doctor he said, 'You didn't break your foot, it's just badly bruised.' He gave me crutches and said to keep my foot elevated for a few days.

These were the worst days of my life. While I lay in my car the night before I asked God, 'Please help me?'

♪ What about me?
It isn't fair ♪
♪ I've had enough
Now I want my share ♪
♪ Can't you see? I wanna live
What about me…♪ [43]

We were both quiet after he finished this story. It took my dad a few seconds before he said anything. Then he turned to us, eked out a smile, and said, "This is when I decided to leave the Bronx to start my new life. But remember, even though I left the Bronx when I was a boy – You Can't Take the Bronx out of the Boy!"

One of my dad's favorite movies is 'City Slickers' with Billy Crystal. His favorite part is when Danial Stern is going through some difficult times and Billy Crystal says, 'Your life is a do-over.' My dad has told us on several occasions his life was spinning out of control when he was a teenager and he asked God for a do-over and God answered his prayer.

SECTION IX
Revelation

♪ There are places I remember all my life
Though some have changed ♪
♪ Some forever, not for better
Some have gone and some remain. ♪
♪ All these places have their moments
Of lovers and friends I still can recall ♪
♪ Some are dead and some are living
In my life I've loved them all…♪
♪And I'll never lose affection
For people and things that went before ♪
♪ I know I'll often stop and think about them
In my life I love you more…♪ [1]

Redemption…

These are just a few of the stories my dad told my sister and me during our Saturday breakfasts at McDonalds and the other times we were together. I tried to share the stories which would give you a general understanding of my dad's world; the time, place, and people in his life. It wasn't easy – I had so many stories to choose from. Most of his stories are still sitting comfortably in my memory waiting for the sequel.

You might wonder why I didn't mention any of the stories about my mom and dad and how they met. Let me assure you it's not because they don't have stories because believe me – they do.

Instead, I left these stories out because they are being reserved for my next book – "Redemption". It's a book about how much my dad's life changed after he left The Bronx.

There's one more thing I need to share with you. My father and I worked on this book together; I wondered why he was so eager to put his stories in book format. I also wondered what he was referring to when he frequently repeated "[his] drinking came with consequences".

Several months before this book went to the printer he sat Kelsie and me down and told us, "Kelsie, Cameron, you might not know this but alcohol destroys your body which can eventually lead to death. The doctors have done everything they can for me. This is why I've told both of you these stories and why I wanted you to write them down. I don't want you two to ever forget your daddy..."

Through my tears I asked my dad, "What do you have?"

My dad bit his knuckle and said, "I have an acute case of pretendanitus, and, Cameron, there's no cure..."

Kelsie leaned over and held my dad. Her eyes were filled with tears; she looked into his eyes, and said, "The Office, Dad?"

"Yup...The Office, Kels..."

The End

Epilog

In case you're wondering, I still tell my kids an occasional story but as they get older they're more interested in sports, music, TV, friends, boys, and girls. So sometimes they don't have as much time for their daddy as they did in the past – I guess they're busy making their own stories to tell their kids.

Maybe this is a little selfish of me to say, but it does make me a little sad that we don't spend as many Saturday's together at McDonalds but I guess that's life. They're growing up and I am very proud of the young adults they have become – but like I said in my dedication – I will be forever grateful to Kelsie and Cameron, for allowing me to relive my childhood by telling them my stories. A daddy couldn't ask for better kids.

Kenneth M. Hand

Song References

1 "There Are Places I Remember"
The Beatles, Songwriters: Paul McCartney, John Lennon

2 "New York, New York"
Frank Sinatra; Songwriter; Fred Ebb

3 "The Way We Were"
Barbra Streisand, Songwriters: Alan Bergman, Marilyn Bergman, Marvin Hamlisch

4 "I Am Woman"
Helen Reddy; Songwriters: Ray Burton, Helen Reddy

5 "He Ain't Heavy…He's My Brother"
The Hollies; Songwriters: Bob Russell, Bobby Scott

6 "Breakfast in America"
Supertramp; Songwriters: Rick Davies, Roger Hodgson

7 "War"
War; Songwriters: Papa Dee Allen, Harold Brown, BB Dickerson, Lonnie Jordan, Charles Miller, Lee Oskar, Howard E Scott

8 "Free Bird"
Lynyrd Skynyrd; Songwriters: Allen Collins, Ronnie Van Zant

9 "The Way We Were"
Barbra Streisand, Songwriters: Alan Bergman, Marilyn Bergman, Marvin Hamlisch

10 "She Works Hard for the Money"
Donna Summer; Songwriters: Donna Summer, Michael Omartian

11 "Only the Good Die Young"
Billy Joel; Songwriter: Billy Joel

12 "Dancing Queen"
ABBA; Songwriters: Bjorn Ulvaeus, Benny Andersson, Stig Anderson

13 "Aqualung"
Jethro Tull; Songwriters: Ian Anderson, Jennie Anderson

14 "No-No Song"
Ringo Starr; Songwriters: Hoyt Axton, David Jackson

15 "Hitchin' A Ride"
Vanity Fare; Songwriters: Mitch Murray, Peter Callander

16 "Renegade"
Styx; Songwriters: Tommy Shaw

17 "You Took the Words Right Out of My Mouth"
Meat Loaf; Songwriters: Jim Steinman

18 "Paradise By the Dashboard Light"
Meat Loaf; Songwriters: Jim Steinman

19 "Super Freak"
Rick James; Songwriters: Rick James, Alonzo Miller

20 "Lonesome Loser"
Little River Band; Songwriters:

21 "Devil Woman"
Cliff Richards; Songwriters: Britten, Holmes

22 "Carry On Wayward Son"
Kansas; Songwriters: Kerry Livgren

23 "Taking Care of Business"
Bachman-Turner Overdrive (BTO); Songwriters: Randy Bachman

24 "Love Is In the Air"
John Paul Young; Songwriters: Harry Vanda, George Young

25 "Love Machine"
The Miracles; Songwriters: William Griffin, Warren Moore

26 "Can't Fight This Feeling"
REO Speedwagon; Songwriters: Kevin Cronin

27 "When I Need You"
Leo Sayer; Songwriters: Albert Hammond, Carole Bayer Sager

28 "Love Shack"
B-52's; Songwriters: Kate Pierson, Fred Schneider, Keith Strickland, Cindy Wilson

29 "Tonight's The Night"
Rod Stewart; Songwriters: Rod Stewart

30 "Bohemian Rhapsody"
Queen; Songwriters: Freddie Mercury

31 "Reunited"
Peaches and Herb; Songwriters:

32 "Take it Easy on Me"
Little River Band: Songwriter; Wayne Nelson

33 "If I Can't Have You"
Yvonne Elliman; Songwriters: Barry Gibb, Robin Gibb, Maurice Gibb

34 "Cheers Song"
Gary Portnoy; Songwriters: Gary Portnoy, Judy Hart

35 "I'm In Love With My Car"
Queen; Songwriter: Roger Taylor

36 "Greatest American Hero"
Joey Scarbury; Songwriters: Mike Post, Stephen Geyer

37 "Feed Me"
Little Shop of Horrors; Songwriters; Alan Menken, Howard Ashman

38 "Leather and Lace"
Stevie Nicks and Don Henley; Songwriter: Stevie Nicks

39 "Running On Empty"
Jackson Browne; Songwriter: Jackson Browne

40 "Borderline"
Madonna; Songwriter: Reggie Lucas

41 "Take It Easy On Me"
Little River Band: Songwriter; Wayne Nelson

42 "Fooling Yourself (The Angry Young Man)"
Styx: Songwriter: Tommy Shaw

43 "What About Me?"
Moving Pictures: Songwriters; Garry Frost, Frances Swan

44 "Breaking the Law"
Judas Priest: Songwriters; Robert Halford, Glenn Tipton, Kenneth Downing

45 "Too Much Time On My Hands"
Styx: Songwriters; Tommy Shaw